PAMPHLETS ON AMERICAN WRITERS • NUMBER 103

UNIVERSITY OF MINNESOTA

Randall Jarrell

BY M. L. ROSENTHAL

UNIVERSITY OF MINNESOTA PRESS • MINNEAPOLIS

Printed in the United States of America at
Jones Press, Minneapolis

Library of Congress Catalog Card Number: 72-619530
ISBN 0-8166-0646-3

Excerpts from the poetry of Randall Jarrell are reprinted by
permission of the publishers: From *The Complete Poems* by
Randall Jarrell, copyright © 1935, 1936, 1937, 1940, 1941, 1942,
1944, 1945, 1946, 1947, 1948, 1949, 1950, 1951, 1952, 1965, 1966,
1967, 1968, and 1969 by Mrs. Randall Jarrell, copyright renewed
1968, 1969 by Mrs. Randall Jarrell. Reprinted with the permission of Farrar, Straus & Giroux, Inc., and Faber and Faber Ltd.
From *The Lost World* by Randall Jarrell, copyright © Randall
Jarrell 1948, 1961, 1962, 1963, 1964, 1965. Reprinted by permission of The Macmillan Company and Eyre & Spottiswoode (Publishers) Ltd. From *The Woman at the Washington Zoo* by Randall Jarrell — "The Woman at the Washington Zoo" copyright ©
1960 by Randall Jarrell; "In Those Days" copyright 1952 by the
Curtis Publishing Company; "The Elementary Scene" copyright
© 1960 by Randall Jarrell; "Windows" copyright 1954 by Randall Jarrell. Permission to reprint granted by Atheneum Publishers. Lines from "To a Conscript of 1940" from *Collected
Poems* by Sir Herbert Read, copyright 1966. Reprinted by permission of the publishers, Horizon Press, New York, and Faber
and Faber Ltd., London. Robert Lowell and John Crowe Ransom
granted permission to use prose passages written by them. I am
grateful to Sally M. Gall for her editorial assistance.

PUBLISHED IN THE UNITED KINGDOM AND INDIA BY THE OXFORD
UNIVERSITY PRESS, LONDON AND DELHI, AND IN CANADA BY THE
COPP CLARK PUBLISHING CO. LIMITED, TORONTO

RANDALL JARRELL

M. L. ROSENTHAL, poet, critic, and professor of English at New York University, is the author or editor of many books, among them *Beyond Power: New Poems, The New Poets: American and British Poetry since World War II,* and *A Primer of Ezra Pound.*

⤴ Randall Jarrell

Although Randall Jarrell wrote a very witty novel and a good deal of lively criticism as well, his most enduring interest as a writer lies in his poems. Between the appearance of an early group in the New Directions anthology *Five Young American Poets* in 1940 and his death at fifty-one in 1965, he prepared seven books of verse. Their usually melancholy titles suggest the desolation with which he constantly contended and which seems to have won out in the breakdown he finally suffered.

To review very briefly the curve of this psychological struggle as it manifests itself in the succeeding volumes: The first book, *Blood for a Stranger* (1942), reveals amid its many echoes of Auden and others certain underlying motifs of loss and confused focus. The next volumes, *Little Friend, Little Friend* (1945) and *Losses* (1948), take their main strength from a number of elegiac war poems. In these poems Jarrell was often able, because of their concreteness and directness, to objectify the motifs that had knotted up so much of his previous work. Also, he learned a good deal about immediacy from such poets of World War I as Siegfried Sassoon and Wilfred Owen. A period of broadening perspectives followed, marked by the appearance in 1951 of *The Seven-League Crutches*, in 1954 of the novel *Pictures from an Institution*, and in 1955 of *Selected Poems*. This last-named volume, containing only two new pieces, was the result of careful reconsideration and, often, revision of past work.

It was not until 1960, actually, that Jarrell published his first book of new poems since *The Seven-League Crutches*. But in the decade and a half after the war he had had a varied experience.

5

He had been literary editor of the *Nation*, poetry consultant at the Library of Congress, visiting lecturer in American colleges and abroad, and, with occasional interruptions, a professor in the Woman's College of the University of North Carolina. He had established himself as one of a small, elite group of poets, protégés originally of Allen Tate and John Crowe Ransom. But Jarrell's outward successes did not anesthetize him against his painful need to gain inward clarification, which finally led him to write the autobiographical poems of *The Woman at the Washington Zoo* (1960) and *The Lost World* (1965).

In a sense, Jarrell tried to make a European of himself, to change over from a bright young American southerner to a sort of German-Austrian-Jewish refugee of the spirit. His interest in Rilke, in the German *Märchen*, and in the neglected European heritage of Americans seems in part an effort to repossess for himself a nourishment denied him in his childhood. Yet this effort, by a process analogous with that described in Keats's "Nightingale" ode, eventually "tolled him back to his sole self."

The word *fey*, meaning both *intensely excited or gay* and *doomed*, is perhaps too grim for Jarrell's poetic personality. Yet it is useful when we think of that side of him which is at once high-spiritedly brilliant and superciliously overinsistent, engaging yet irritating, and which assorts so ill with his capacity for gentleness and for an almost sentimental love of the quieter and more pedestrian virtues — and with the absorption of his imagination by bleakness and horror. The impact on others of this complex of qualities comes through strikingly in the collection of affectionate essays and reminiscences, *Randall Jarrell, 1914–1965*, that appeared in 1967 as a memorial volume. An unusually valuable piece in this excellent collection is "A Group of Two," written by his widow. It is a lovingly drawn portrait of a baffling man: his varied enthusiasms, his childlike ebullience and depressions, his sparkling if somewhat shrill spirit. Mrs. Jarrell is straightforward but protective. She never spells out the nature of his psychic disturbance or the exact circumstances of his death while walking on a highway. She does nevertheless suggest that he carried about with him throughout his life the burden of childhood insecurity, both psychological and financial. His parents were divorced, and for a while he lived happily with his paternal grandparents and great-grandmother, working-class people, in Hollywood, California, before his reluctant return to his mother in Nashville, Tennessee. The gifted, volatile child never "grew up" entirely. The intensity, the traumatic moments, and the accumulated guilt and resentment behind these experiences were never resolved.

He recurs to the Hollywood period a number of times in his poetry, most notably in the title sequence of *The Lost World*. The confusion and displacement of that period are crucial, though many of their implications are suppressed. "Mama" and "Pop" in Jarrell's poems are the *grandparents*, while his mother is "Anna." The sense of universal sadness, betrayed vulnerability, and emptiness at the center of the self in Jarrell's work is rooted in these childhood events and relationships, and doubtless helps account for his strong attraction to European literature of tragic consciousness.

In his poems there is at times a false current of sentimental condescension toward his subjects, especially when they are female. But more often another current carries us toward a realization of the ineradicable innocence and pity of the common life in all its alienating reality. This current did not really show itself, as a directive element in Jarrell's art, until the war poems of his second volume. In the first, *Blood for a Stranger*, some of his major themes were visible but neither voice nor tone was yet quite his own. One hears a sort of Auden-static everywhere, with other voices cutting in every so often. In the most accomplished

7

poem of the book, "The Skaters," the voice seems a duet of Hart
Crane and Edwin Muir:

> I stood among my sheep
> As silent as my staff;
> Up the sea's massy floor
> I saw the skaters pass.
>
> Long like the wind, as light
> I flowed upon their track
> Until at evening's edge
> I marked their breathless flocks.
>
> I sped among them then
> Like light along its lands —
> Love wreathed their lips, and speed
> Stiffened their tissue limbs. . . .

Half vision, half nightmare, the poem closes in on a note of
lost personal focus. The speaker discerns in the stars the image
of "one obsessing face," with which he comes into a precarious
sympathy or relationship while caught up in the swirling skaters'
movement that controls the curve of the poem. But finally,
abandoned and abandoning, he is whirled into "the abyss":

> But the iron's dazzling ring, the roar
> Of the starred ice black below
> Whirl our dazed and headlong strides
> Through the whirling night into
>
> The abyss where my dead limbs forget
> The cold mouth's dumb assent;
> The skaters like swallows flicker
> Around us in the long descent.

These motifs of coldness and distance, and of a fantasy realm
that is only a heightening of desolate reality, persist throughout
Jarrell's career. It is hard not to see "The Skaters" as a suicidal
projection of the symbolic search for the irretrievably lost mother:

> The million faces flecked
> Upon my flickering gaze

> Bent to me in the stars
> Of one obsessing face . . .

A hopeless distance, a bewildering cosmos. Another poem in the volume, "The Bad Music," is addressed to "Anna" and uses the same pattern of symbolic imagery as "The Skaters" without reaching the glitteringly impersonal final set of that poem. Here the speaker sits by a window watching students as they return home from caroling. They carry candles that "wink out and on and out, like mixed-up stars," and

> I sit here like a mixed-up star:
> Where can I shine? What use is it to shine?
> I say; and see, all the miles north inside my head,
> You looking down across the city, puzzling. . . .
> High over the millions who breathe and wait and sparkle . . .

"The Bad Music" makes almost embarrassingly explicit the buried reference, which is not the literal meaning, of "The Skaters." In its first stanza, the speaker blurts out his accusation of abandonment to Anna:

> The breast opening for me, the breaths gasped
> From the mouth pressed helplessly against my wrist
> Were lies you too believed; but what you wanted
> And possessed was, really, nothing but yourself:
> A joy private as a grave, the song of death. . . .

Poetically, what is interesting in the relation of the two poems is the similarity of their *process*. Each starts in a state of passive melancholy and moves into active despair. Under surface differences of tone and theme, they share a configuration of feeling and imagery. The "mixed-up star" symbolism in both poems projects the speaker's relation to the elusive object of his love. Faces appear as part of a subjective constellation in which confusion reigns, and it is all but impossible to sort out lover from beloved (son from mother) or either one from the shifting mass of other people or, indeed, from the whole objective universe.

The pattern of movement is characteristic of Jarrell: a static initial state of sadness; then a phase of confusion that lets deeper depression flood into the poem; and then a final bitter thrust. We see it working in the famous five-line war poem "The Death of the Ball Turret Gunner":

> From my mother's sleep I fell into the State,
> And I hunched in its belly till my wet fur froze.
> Six miles from earth, loosed from its dream of life,
> I woke to black flak and the nightmare fighters.
> When I died they washed me out of the turret with a hose.

This poem is "impersonal." The speaker is not the poet himself but a dramatic character, a soldier who has been killed in the war. Yet the ironic womb imagery recalls the earlier mother theme, as of course the word *mother* itself does. We begin with the abstract yet unhappy assertion in the first line, an assertion that the young man received into the military world from the dreaming family world of childhood has hardly had time to emerge from fetal unconsciousness before he is in a new womb, that of war. Attention shifts in the next line to the chill, metallic character of that new womb. Suddenly then, the next two lines transport us to the gunner's moment of "waking" into nightmarish vision, at the moment his plane is hit by flak in the sky. The image is fetal; a note by Jarrell in *Selected Poems* stresses the fact that, "hunched upside-down in his little sphere," the gunner "looked like the foetus in the womb." The scene itself here is close to the confused cosmos of the two poems already discussed. Life is seen as only a "dream," whereas death is the reality into which the protagonist is born. In the harshly distorted womb images of this poem, we have once again the motif of love betrayed.

What Jarrell forces on our imaginations through his grotesque symbolism is the obscenity of war, its total subversion of human values. In highly compressed form, he has summoned up his

subconscious preoccupations and the dynamics of poetic association they generate to make a poem that gets outside his own skin.
The conversion process was not simple, though the result is em-
phatically clear in its narrative movement and in its succession
of tones and intensities. Instead of the anapests that launch the
first two lines, a suddenly lurching hovering-accent gets the third
line off to a wobbling start that helps shake the poem open to
let in wider ranges of felt meaning. (Effects of confusion and
ambiguity, in rhythmic shifts as in the literal suggestions of
language, often have this function in poems.) The brutal nasti-
ness of the closing line refocuses the poem sharply, yet the final
effect is not abrupt. The line is in hexameter, longer by a foot
than any of the preceding lines. It has the impact of a final
"proof" of war's nature as a mockery of all that is life-giving.

It is easy to see how such a poem was prefigured in *Blood for a
Stranger*. If we think of that book as comprising a definite unit
of sensibility, we shall perceive it as, in large part, a complaint
against loss of the world of childhood. (Jarrell specialized in
psychology as an undergraduate at Vanderbilt University and
was, in his omnivorous way, a reader of Freud; he is very likely
to have "psychoanalyzed" himself to some degree at least.) The
unresolved discontents of childhood are certainly present, but
the real complaint is against separation, against initiation into
adulthood, against the loss of an insufficiently discovered and
savored life of innocence. "What we leave," mourns the opening
poem ("On the Railway Platform"), "we leave forever." Another
poem, "90 North," makes explicit the contrast between the secure childhood where

> At home, in my flannel gown, like a bear to its floe,
> I clambered to bed,

and the present, "meaningless" moment where

> all lines, all winds
> End in the whirlpool I at last discover.

True enough, a bear climbing onto its floe is not the most secure of beasts; but the nightmares of childhood, in Jarrell's poem, do end in "rest" and a "warm world" of dependable certainties where "I reached my North and it had meaning." Of the poems in *Blood for a Stranger* specifically about childhood and separation, the most poignant is "A Story," a monologue by a boy sent away to school. It has none of the portentous phrasing that mars "90 North" and other poems of this volume. Its thoughts are always appropriate to the speaker. "I liked home better, I don't like these boys" is more to the point than the generalizations in "90 North" about "wisdom" and "pain."

Not to linger overlong with this first book, it has other, though related, points of interest besides this central one of the child soul's vulnerability. In "Children Selecting Books in a Library," for instance, Jarrell meditates charmingly, if slightly pedantically, on the value of reading fairy tales. Another piece, "The Cow Wandering in the Bare Field," has been praised by Allen Tate, who remembers seeing it when Jarrell, then a freshman at Vanderbilt, was seventeen. Its beginning at least is slightly reminiscent of Hart Crane's "Black Tambourine," the details at once starkly literal and accusatory:

> The cow wandering in the bare field,
> Her chain dangling, aimless, —
> The Negro sitting in the ashes,
> Staring, humming to the cat. . . .

Jarrell rarely again tried this kind of distanced yet incisive presentation. Indeed, he loses track of it later on in this very poem; he was after a faint modulation toward a theme of social protest, perhaps, and he did think of himself as a "radical" in his youth. But that side of him is seen in poems strongly indebted to Auden and Spender, with such titles as "The Machine-Gun," "The Refugees," "A Poem for Someone Killed in Spain," and "For an Emigrant." Part I of the last-named poem, with its final stanza greatly altered, was salvaged for the *Selected Poems* and retitled there as "To the New World." It was interesting as showing special sympathy for the victims of the Nazis and for its insight into the life of exiles:

> Free — to be homeless, to be friendless, to be nameless,
> To stammer the hard words in the foreign night. . . .

"For an Emigrant" shows, also, Jarrell's early realization that, ultimately, the refugee condition is universal; the balm of America is only a salve:

> You escaped from nothing; the westering soul
> Finds Europe waiting for it over every sea. . . .

"For an Emigrant," despite its political clichés and its sermonizing, meant something for Jarrell's future development. Much of it has to do with the effect of anti-Semitism and fascism on a *child's* life in Europe, and it attempts to assimilate the political lessons of the thirties in such a way as to bring the poet's childhood-obsession into a wider, more adult context of awareness. The poem anticipates, as well, Jarrell's later tendency to assume a European consciousness and graft it onto his American personality — a tendency for which Pound and Eliot had doubtless provided models. Jarrell, however, differed from them by playing the role of an exile in his own land, if far more modestly than they and with a lesser genius though a real, and kindred, sense of cultural mission.

Jarrell served in the Army Air Force between 1942 and 1946. "In the first months of the War," Robert Lowell writes in an "appreciation" appended to the 1966 paperback edition of *The Lost World,* "Jarrell became a pilot. He was rather old for a beginner, and soon 'washed out,' and spent the remaining war years as an aviation instructor. Even earlier, he had an expert's knowledge. . . . Nine-tenths of his war poems are air force poems, and are about planes and their personnel, the flyers, crews, and mechanics who attended them. No other imaginative writer had his precise knowledge of aviation, or knew so well how to draw inspiration from this knowledge." His mind was similar to Hardy's and to Owen's in its fusion of informed objectivity with a compassion as close to sentimentality as intelligence and taste would allow. Of course, the world of which he wrote was very far from Hardy's, and he lacked Owen's combat experience. But in his war poetry he was like Hardy in bringing to bear on it his whole, extraordinarily literate intelligence — an intelligence of the kind that feels imaginative literature as the distillation of considered experience, the usable treasure of a contemplative mind. And he was like Owen in the way the pressure of his empathy with the pilots he knew made him envision their war experience in a vivid, accurate manner unmatched by most of his writing having to do with civilian life. The poetry of their condition lay for him, as for Owen, "in the Pity." For both poets this is a sort of passionately apprehended disproportion between the young soldiers' ultimate innocence and the terror they both suffer and inflict. It is realized not in sentiment but in action.

Jarrell's war poems are found mainly in his *Little Friend, Little Friend* and *Losses* volumes, which came directly out of the war years, and there are a few more in *The Seven-League Crutches*. His vision of the soldier as betrayed child is clearly epitomized in "The Death of the Ball Turret Gunner," a poem strategically placed at the end of *Little Friend, Little Friend*. As with most American and British poets of the second world war, the ultimate implied attitude is an ambiguous, or at any rate a tentative, one. The shock, horror, and questioning that mark the poetry of the first world war were the discovery of a generation, a discovery crystallized on the run, in the midst of death — the discovery that war *was* the trenches, the barbed wire, the humanly pointless slaughter while, in Owen's words, "God seems not to care." Jarrell and his contemporaries had been teethed on that earlier work; for them it was the definition of war experience. All later war poetry is in an important sense informed by the World War I "tradition." However, there are at least two significant differences for Jarrell's generation. First, they felt a far greater initial detachment from official rhetoric and from the assumptions of the social system. And second, though there was a good deal of old-fashioned combat in the later war, the over-all organization and the far greater importance of the air forces and long-range technology and communication made the involvement of most soldier-poets far less immediate than before.

These differences may be overstressed, but I am trying to suggest that the poetry of Jarrell's generation feels the impact of war with a double awareness. It is still in touch with the original shock of World War I, but is further away from the almost tribal sense of participation in a ritual gone wrong. Herbert Read's poem "To a Conscript of 1940" is a bridge between the two positions in time. The ghost of a soldier of 1914–18 speaks to the poet, a survivor who now faces the new war situation:

We think we gave in vain. The world was not renewed.
There was hope in the homestead and anger in the streets
But the old world was restored and we returned
To the dreary field and workshop, and the immemorial feud

Of rich and poor. Our victory was our defeat.
Power was retained where power had been misused
And youth was left to sweep away
The ashes that the fire had strewn beneath our feet.

But one thing we learned: there is no glory in the deed
Until the soldier wears a badge of tarnish'd braid;
There are heroes who have heard the rally and have seen
The glitter of a garland round their head.

Theirs is the hollow victory. They are deceived.
But you, my brother and my ghost, if you can go

Knowing that there is no reward, no certain use
In all your sacrifice, then honour is reprieved.

To fight without hope is to fight with grace,
The self reconstructed, the false heart repaired. . . .

Basically, this is the position — acceptance of the war (presumably because of the policies and aggression of the Nazi government) but without any chivalric or apocalyptic illusions. The history of the between-wars governments was too well known; certain Marxian and pacifist conceptions, admittedly contradictory, had irrevocably entered Western sensibility; and the fact that military victory would not solve the great social problems of the age was widely understood. Jarrell's way of encompassing all this was, on the whole, to adopt an existential approach. Here were men — *child*-men, really — in circumstances beyond their control or even their comprehension. It was not existential*ist* — neither a revolutionary perspective, nor a challenge to men to be as fully and heroically human as possible in the circumstances of limited choice open to them, is implied. Jarrell's emphasis is on the saving innocence of those whom these circumstances have after all made, as he says in "Eighth Air Force" (*Losses*), "murderers." That is a bitter word, yet Jarrell uses it a bit lightly and ironically. Because the young American airmen also run the risk of death, as he himself does not, he compares them with Christ. The comparison has some validity. Whitman, in "A Sight in Camp in the Daybreak Gray and Dim," had used it for the soldier as *victim*; and even when the soldier is constrained to kill he is in some sense still a victim. Pressed too hard, though, the argument is obviously forced and sentimental. Could one have put the case otherwise about young German soldiers in the same situation? Hardly. And if not, must not one say also that the most hardened killer is ultimately an innocent victim, a Christ crucified on the cross of his particular fate? But Jarrell did not follow the logic through:

The other murderers troop in yawning;
Three of them play Pitch, one sleeps, and one
Lies counting missions, lies there sweating
Till even his heart beats: One; One; One.
O murderers! . . . Still, this is how it's done:

This is a war. . . . But since these play, before they die,
Like puppies with their puppy; since, a man,
I did as these have done, but did not die —
I will content the people as I can
And give up these to them: Behold the man!

I have suffered, in a dream, because of him,
Many things; for this last saviour, man,
I have lied as I lie now. But what is lying?
Men wash their hands, in blood, as best they can:
I find no fault in this just man.

In these lines Jarrell makes explicit the prevailing social assumption about war: that men cannot be held responsible for what history compels them to do, especially when they are on the "just" side of the struggle. But he tries, too, to make a subtly paradoxical argument to get past the objections to this assumption, and his style turns to putty in the process because the thought is too contrived. The reality of the situation requires the most relentless intellectual toughness and unwillingness to be an apologist for war mentality. Otherwise, the paradoxical fact that one can, in a sense, be good and innocent while behaving murderously becomes merely another sophistical argument for further mass murder. Jarrell himself recognizes this problem by his play on the word *lie*, but self-irony does not always purge a speaker of the error he confesses by it. Indeed, Jarrell's note on this poem, given in his introduction to *Selected Poems*, has no self-irony at all: " 'Eighth Air Force' is a poem about the air force which bombed the Continent from England. The man who lies counting missions has one to go before being sent home. The phrases from the Gospels compare such criminals and scapegoats as these with that earlier criminal and scapegoat about whom the Gospels were written."

The limitation in Jarrell's war poetry is not, however, political or intellectual. It is a matter of energy. He focuses on the literal data of war — their irreversible actuality, and the pity of the human predicament implicit in that actuality. The poems stop short of anger, of programs, of anything that would constitute a challenge to soldiers or to their commanders or to the statesmen who make policy. Letting the facts of war experience speak for themselves, Jarrell sank all his real poetic imagination into primary acts of empathy; ordinarily he resisted any obvious political rhetoric. In "Eighth Air Force" we have a rare instance of his swinging out of his usual orbit to deal with the moral issues of mass bombing. His failure to handle the problem poetically lay in inadequate resources of emotional complexity and intellectual power.

But within the narrower limits of its engagement, Jarrell's war poetry is often superb. In poems like "A Front," "A Pilot from the Carrier," "Pilots, Man Your Planes," and "The Dead Wingman" — the last of these a dream poem, but one that presents the essence of a familiar situation: a pilot searching for a sign of a shot-down wingman — the poet's entire effort is to project the sense of men and machines in action, from the viewpoint of a participant. In all the poems just named, Jarrell has a double aim. First, he wishes to get the technical and atmospheric details in coherent order (a bombing plane whose radio has gone bad, so that the pilot cannot be diverted from a closed landing field to another still open and therefore crashes; a plane that has been hit and is burning, from which the pilot parachutes; a carrier under attack from a Japanese torpedo plane; the situation of the airman hunting for a lost comrade). And second, he desires to make the perspective that of a living, suffering man. "A Pilot from the Carrier" and "A Front" are in the same volume,

Little Friend, Little Friend, as "The Death of the Ball Turret Gunner." They carry a kindred birth-death motif, though less explicitly. The pilot in the plane from the carrier, "strapped at the center of his blazing wheel," tears himself loose from that womb of death and is reborn via parachute

> Into the sunlight of the upper sky —
> And falls, a quiet bundle in the sky,
> The miles to warmth, to air, to waking:
> To the great flowering of his life. . . .

The pilot in "A Front" cannot be wrenched free in time, and perishes. In *Losses,* the men on the carrier in "Pilots, Man Your Planes" are sleeping "hunched in the punk of Death" until awakened into their own literal deaths unless they escape in time. The pilot in "The Dead Wingman" searches in his dream over that same amniotic sea into which so many figures of "Pilots, Man Your Planes" have disappeared, but he never finds the dreadful evidence of the birth into death that he seems to need for deep inward confirmation of his own reality:

> The plane circles stubbornly: the eyes distending
> With hatred and misery and longing, stare
> Over the blackening Ocean for a corpse. . . .

I have not really meant to labor this womb referent, which appears and disappears, usually very fleetingly, in Jarrell's shifting float of associations. His creation of an ambience of confused details, a dream of total self-loss, before a final note of profound sadness is equally important in all the poems I have just mentioned. What gives them more authority than the poems of *Blood for a Stranger* is not only the precision within the confusion, but also the definiteness of the military setting within which the lost, childlike psyche of Jarrell's soldiers (with the poet's voice standing in for them, as it were) speaks its pain. Several times in the two "war" books the persons spoken for are women or children.

The title of *Little Friend, Little Friend,* which evokes just the childlike psyche to which I have referred, is taken from a phrase used in the book's opening poem, "2nd Air Force." Here, as Jarrell's note tells us, a "woman visiting her son remembers what she has read on the front page of her newspaper the week before, a conversation between a bomber, in flames over Germany, and one of the fighters protecting it: 'Then I heard the bomber call me in: "Little Friend, Little Friend, I got two engines on fire. Can you see me, Little Friend?" I said, "I'm crossing right over you. Let's go home." ' "

The woman of this poem might just as well have been the mother of the ball turret gunner in the closing poem. Her son — this is the whole burden of the poem — has indeed fallen from her womb into that of the state. The barren and dangerous world of the air base appears amid "buses and weariness and loss," with its "sand roads, tar-paper barracks," and "bubbling asphalt of the runways." A specific womb image dramatizes what has happened to her transplanted son: "The head withdraws into its hatch (a boy's)." This alien world — "The years meant *this?*" — is her and our bleak introduction to what the war means for the soldiers as Jarrell understands them. Between "2nd Air Force" and "The Death of the Ball Turret Gunner," then, the volume makes its journey through a wasteland of deadly machinery and pathetic soldiers who "pass like beasts, unquestioning," through their new life where "the bombers answer everything."

Both *Little Friend, Little Friend* and *Losses* contain many closeups and vignettes of soldiers: men being classified, a soldier whose leg has been amputated, prisoners, a soldier being visited in the hospital by his wife and baby, men being discharged from service, a field hospital. Politically and historically, the war may have been unavoidable, but for Jarrell this is more an existential than a moral reality. Despite his recognition of the monstrousness of the Nazis in "A Camp in the Prussian Forest" (*Losses*) —

> Here men were drunk like water, burnt like wood.
> The fat of good
> And evil, the breast's star of hope
> Were rendered into soap —

it is the pointlessness and cruelty of the war that emerges as the
poet's repeated insight. Each soldier, as the mother sees in "2nd
Air Force," is "heavy with someone else's death" and a "cold
carrier" of "someone else's victory." The poem "Losses," in the
earlier book but clearly the source of the later one's title, utters
a complaint on behalf of all the young *and* of their victims. Although its speaker does not explore the moral dilemma involved,
he does raise an ultimate question:

> In bombers named for girls, we burned
> The cities we had learned about in school —
> Till our lives wore out; our bodies lay among
> The people we had killed and never seen.
> When we lasted long enough they gave us medals;
> When we died they said, "Our casualties were low."
> They said, "Here are the maps"; we burned the cities.
>
> It was not dying — no, not ever dying;
> But the night I died I dreamed that I was dead,
> And the cities said to me: "Why are you dying?
> We are satisfied, if you are; but why did I die?"

It is interesting that World War II produced no great poem
at once absolutely ruthless in its fidelity to the realities of human
experience in the war and encompassing in its understanding of
all their complex contradictions: particularly, the crushing
choice seemingly thrust on the most advanced spirits between
pure pacifism and accepting the need to destroy the Nazi power.
The rhetorical questions at the end of "Losses" — slightly confused because of the ambiguous use of the word "I" in the closing
line — suggest the epic psychological exploration needed, but not
furnished, to give body to their meaning. At a pragmatic and
popular level the questions were certainly answerable by refer-

ence to recent history. The answers were both moral and practical, involving the fate of nations and of ethnic groups as well as of political and economic systems. The contradiction lay, as Malraux perceived in an only slightly different context, the Spanish Civil War, in the fact that the methods of war compel imitation of the enemy and indeed outstripping him in his own methods. It is indeed possible to present the voice of an innocent and ignorant soldier asking "Why?" Yet even the boys Jarrell wrote about had more of a sense, however inarticulately they might express themselves, of "why" than he quite gives them credit for. As for the poet himself, a number of the pieces show the usual intellectual's grasp of the economic and historical aspects of modern war. Of the American poets who emerged immediately after the war, only Robert Lowell was keyed to the demands of the materials, but on the other hand he had neither the literal experience nor the inclination to work on *the* war poem. Perhaps Pound and Eliot, by their keen location of the inner contradictions of Western culture, had rendered a large effort of this sort redundant for later poets.

That Jarrell wanted to suggest large historical and mythological considerations is clear from "The Wide Prospect," which comes just before "The Death of the Ball Turret Gunner" at the end of *Little Friend, Little Friend*, and from the two poems that close *Losses*: "In the Ward: The Sacred Wood" and "Orestes at Tauris." The influence of Marx via Auden is obvious in the opening stanza of "The Wide Prospect":

> Who could have figured, when the harnesses improved
> And men pumped kobolds from the coal's young seams
> There to the west, on Asia's unrewarding cape —
> The interest on that first raw capital?
> The hegemony only the corpses have escaped?

The poem ends, after a determinedly sustained exposition along these lines, with an imagery of ritual sacrifice that links Marxian, Freudian, and myth-and-ritual oriented motifs:

> the man-eaters die
> Under the cross of their long-eaten Kin.

> All die for all. And the planes rise from the years . . .
> When men see men once more the food of Man
> And their bare lives His last commodity.

The poems at the end of *Losses* are superior in being free of the long, expository sections, with a forced liveliness of imagery but without driving energy, of "The Wide Prospect." "Orestes at Tauris," the closing poem, was according to Jarrell an early composition written before any of the poems from *Blood for a Stranger* included in the *Selected Poems*. Very different in character from anything else in the war books, it shows Orestes arriving in Tauris after being pursued relentlessly by the Furies, under compulsion "in expiation for his crime, to bring back to Greece that image of Artemis to which the Tauri sacrificed the strangers cast up on their shores" (Jarrell's note in *Losses*). This long, partially surrealist narrative poem imagines the sacrificial beheading of Orestes by his sister Iphigenia, now a priestess, instead of their triumphant escape. Jarrell's recasting of the myth, in a well-sustained unrhymed pattern of four- and five-stress lines that focuses on the succession of impressions, states of feeling, and sensations that Orestes experiences, makes for an effect of terror amidst psychological confusion and barbaric splendors. The condition of Orestes and Iphigenia at the end then becomes a perfect mythic embodiment of Jarrell's vision of war as the sacrifice of driven innocents for the sake of a savage, mindless determinism inherent in our natures:

> The people, silent, watching with grave faces
> Their priestess, who stands there
> Holding out her hands, staring at her hands
> With her brother's blood drenching her hands.

"In the Ward: The Sacred Wood," which precedes "Orestes at
Tauris," is perhaps Jarrell's most determined effort to give mythic
dimensions to his theme of the sacrificed innocent in war. His
own description of the poem, in his introduction to *Selected
Poems*, goes: "The wounded man has cut trees from paper, and
made for himself a sacred wood; with these, the bed-clothes, the
nurse, the doctor, he works his own way through the Garden of
Eden, the dove and its olive-leaf, the years in the wilderness, the
burning bush, the wars of God and the rebel angels, the birth and
death and resurrection of Christ." This account, and the style of
the poem, somewhat recall the symbolic distortions of thought
and syntax of Lowell's early poems —

> Is the nurse damned who looked on my nakedness?
> The sheets stretch like the wilderness
> Up which my fingers wander, the sick tribes,
> To a match's flare, a rain or bush of fire. . . .

But Jarrell's movement does not rip free into Lowell's frenzied
piling up of associations and allusions. In this poem, however, he
surpasses Lowell in one important respect though he does not
achieve that state of passionate intensity of speech which makes
the whole language an electric field of highly charged, crackling
movements of realization. At each point along the way, as the
wounded soldier ponders the symbolic analogies with Christ
implicit in his condition, he nevertheless at the same time main-
tains a basic simplicity and a distance from the mental game he
is playing. Unlike "Eighth Air Force," this poem does not press
an identity between the dying soldier and Christ. The dominant
tone is one of a real man, without hope, letting go though aware
of a dream of divinity incarnate — a tone corresponding to the
progress of negative heroism in Read's "To a Conscript of 1940."
Negation is accepted quietly; this is one of Jarrell's most touching and thoughtful poems:

> And beneath the coverlet
> My limbs are swaddled in their sleep, and shade
> Flows from the cave beyond the olives, falls
> Into the garden where no messenger
> Comes to gesture, "Go" — to whisper, "He is gone."
>
> The trees rise to me from the world
> That made me, I call to the grove
> That stretches inch on inch without one God:
> "I have unmade you, now; but I must die."

Earlier, in discussing "The Death of the Ball Turret Gunner," I ventured a description of the characteristic structural dynamics of Jarrell's poems as involving a static initial state of sadness, then a phase of confusion that lets deeper depression flood into the poem, and then a final bitter thrust. Most lyric-contemplative poetry since the early Romantics has, in fact, a comparable structure. That is, an initial state of unease or depressed feeling is followed by the introduction of complicating matter for contemplation: any of a number of contexts of awareness that enlarge and, very likely, confuse the original perspective. The final "resolution" of the poem is a reorientation of the speaker's initial attitude in the light of the intervening complication. It may take the form of acceptance or reconciliation though at the same time what is being "affirmed" is defeat of a sort — what we might call "depressive transcendence." Needless to add that shifts of style, rhythm, intensity, and level of diction are as important as the literal statements.

Without forcing the point, we can say that Jarrell's whole poetic career follows a similar pattern of movement. After the early poems of childhood desolation, the speaking psyche confronts three bodies of material external to itself: war experience, the world of myth and folk legend (to which are added, often, the associations of music, painting, and literature), and individual human suffering. In the final phase of his career, the poet objectifies himself, in relation to his childhood life, as one of the sufferers over whom his attention has hovered with such empathy. That is, he has brought back his earliest preoccupations into the center of his work, but in a focus altered by the discipline through which he has passed and the knowledge he has accumulated. He has learned to isolate the pity of the irrecoverable and, therefore, of the irredeemable in existence and is free to present sharp, concrete memories and to play with them in a number of ways.

In *Losses*, we see the three bodies of "external" material (war, myth and legend, and suffering individual people) already present. War is of course the overwhelming major subject. But there are other myth-involved poems besides the two we have already examined, among them "The Märchen" and "The Child of Courts"; Jarrell's fascination with the German *Märchen* (folktales, in this case those of the brothers Grimm) is at this point related to the historical fatalism induced by his response to the war. The dreams and terrors of primitive life foreshadowed those of the modern age with its discovery of the limitations of man's hopes and prospects:

> Listening, listening; it is never still.
> This is the forest: long ago the lives
> Edged armed into its tides (the axes were its stone
> Lashed with the skins of dwellers to its boughs);
> We felled our islands there, at last, with iron.
> The sunlight fell to them, according to our wish,
> And we believed, till nightfall, in that wish;
> And we believed, till nightfall, in our lives.

These are the opening, and on the whole the best, lines of "The Märchen," a somewhat preciously proliferative poem which nevertheless shows Jarrell's characteristic wit, ingenuity, and sympathy with the common lot. He had learned, in his war poems, how to write with economy, but there is no economy in this poem of over a hundred lines of moderately roughened blank verse. Jarrell luxuriates in the way the *Märchen* bring folk motifs and folk wisdom, simple and often comic materials related to the life of peasants, together with the symbolic and archetypal motifs of religious or mythical tradition: Christ and the old gods, Hell, "the Scapegoat," "Paradise," and "the Cross, the Ark, the Tree." The perspective he introduces has to do with primitive man's desire, never fulfilled but never forgotten or relinquished either, even in our time, to make reality conform to his wish. Herein, for Jarrell, lies the inescapable pathos of the human condition, of which the vulnerable innocence of children is the most obvious embodiment. The *Märchen* show that it is not so much our inability to make wishes come true as the paltriness of the wishes themselves that is defeating. In Romantic tradition generally, it is the disparity between desire and reality, between subjective and objective "truths," with which the poet is obsessed — ultimately, the pity that we cannot stamp our own images on nature. In Jarrell there is a curious turn of emphasis: the inadequacy of imagination, driven as it is already by conditions imposed on it by nature, is the heart of the problem —

> Poor Hänsel, once too powerless
> To shelter your own children from the cold
> Or quiet their bellies with the thinnest gruel,
> It was not power that you lacked, but wishes.
> Had you not learned — have we not learned, from tales
> Neither of beasts nor kingdoms nor their Lord,
> But of our own hearts, the realm of death —
> Neither to rule nor die? to change! to change!

"The Child of Courts" (reprinted in *Selected Poems* as "The Prince") presents the ambivalent night-terror of a child who fears that the ghost of a buried man has come up out of the grave toward him but who then is disappointed: "I start to weep because — because there are no ghosts." The poem at first ambiguously suggests a prison atmosphere. But the child calls out "Mother?" — in an equally ambiguous context, however — and thus there is a suggestion not so much of a prison as of a castle or palace in which there is intrigue and insecurity. One thinks of young Prince Edward after Henry's death, a thought mildly encouraged by the two titles. The situation of this brief and simple poem suggests, at one and the same time, the well-known situations of Edward and other English princes, the grisly circumstances of certain folk legends, and the excited imagination of any sensitive child at certain times.

> After the door shuts, and the footsteps die,
> I call out, "Mother?" No one answers.
> I chafe my numb feet with my quaking hands
> And hunch beneath the covers, in my curled
> Red ball of darkness; but the floor creaks, someone stirs
> In the other darkness — and the hairs all rise
> Along my neck, I whisper: "It is he!"

Many years after *Losses*, in his 1965 volume *The Lost World*, Jarrell published "A Hunt in the Black Forest," which begins exactly as "The Child of Courts" does, except for a shift to the third person that heralds a new, or at least a redirected, point of view toward the same situation:

> After the door shuts and the footsteps die,
> He calls out: "Mother?"

The speaker now, however, is not the child but an omniscient narrator. The circumstances, like the title, suggest the world of the *Märchen*, projected in a Freudian nightmare fantasy. A king, out hunting, comes to a hut in the forest where a deaf-mute feeds him a stew that poisons him while a red dwarf watches through the window. At the end of this poem, whose every stage is brilliantly and dramatically clear and sinister, there is a blending of supernatural and psychologically pointed details that brings us all the way over from the climax of the king's death to the further, greater climax of the child sensibility underlying the entire story.

Then a bubbled, gobbling sound begins,
The sound of the pot laughing on the fire.
— The pot, overturned among the ashes,
Is cold as death.

Something is scratching, panting. A little voice
Says, "Let *me*! Let *me*!" The mute
Puts his arms around the dwarf and raises him.

The pane is clouded with their soft slow breaths,
The mute's arms tire; but they gaze on and on,
Like children watching something wrong.
Their blurred faces, caught up in one wish,
Are blurred into one face: a child's set face.

The mute, the dwarf, and the child thus share horrified, guilty
fascination; they are three facets of innocence, despite their involvement in a primal tragic scene. It would not be difficult to
"interpret" the story as one in which the child (into whose face
the other faces blend at the very end of the poem) is both the
victim — the stew that the king his father ate — and the killer
who destroys his father through the very act of being devoured
by him. If we put "The Child of Courts" and "A Hunt in the
Black Forest" side by side and consider each a gloss on the other,
it becomes clear that the addition of the third-person narrator
enabled Jarrell to fill out the symbolic context of the original
poem's conception. But he added to it the distanced understanding of an adult voice presenting the unresolved anguish of one
kind of disturbed childhood. "A Hunt in the Black Forest" brings
both its psychological and its archetypal motives directly to bear
on the tale it has been telling by a final refocusing of elements
present in the story from the start. It represents, as do the more
literally autobiographical poems of the final volume, an achieved
objectification of the speaking self and an achieved clarity as well.
Thought is presented experientially, with sharply sketched action
and description that leave room for shadows, depths, and implied
complexities.

One poem in *Losses*, "Lady Bates," especially foreshadows Jarrell's turn, after the war period, to poems centered on suffering individual persons, often women. The Lady Bates of the title is, says Jarrell in his notes to *Selected Poems*, "a little Negro girl whose Christian name is *Lady*." The child has died, and the poem is addressed to her as an epitome of everything helpless and betrayed in human existence. Viewed unsympathetically, the poem is an example of sophisticated sentimentality, a humanitarian southerner's attempt to speak to his knowledge of the hurt done to Negroes in a language appropriate to both. "Lady Bates," significantly, comes first in *Losses*, the only poem quite of its kind in this book, preceding all the war pieces. A certain oversimplification of the meaning of ordinary people's lives, comparable to that we have seen in the war poems, comes through in "Lady Bates" despite its genuinely touching aspects. The worst of Jarrell is concentrated into parts of this poem that mercilessly expose both his condescension and the presumptuousness of his spokesmanship for the girl:

> Poor black trash,
> The wind has blown you away forever
> By mistake; and they sent the wind to the chain-gang
> And it worked in the governor's kitchen, a trusty for life;
> And it was all written in the Book of Life;
> Day and Night met in the twilight by your tomb
> And shot craps for you; and Day said, pointing to your soul,
> "This *bad* young colored lady,"
> And Night said, "Poor little nigger girl."

"Lady Bates," with its weaknesses, continues Jarrell's development toward the objectification of the speaking self that I have suggested is the chief triumph of *The Lost World*. Like the many soldiers who are his subjects in the war volumes, the little black girl in this poem serves two functions in this development. First and most obviously, she is one of the many figures in his poems whose reality he seeks to repossess as persons outside himself. Secondly, though, she and the other figures are the beneficiaries (or victims) of an empathy that enables him to project onto them certain basic features of the child psyche familiar in his earlier poems — its confusion, innocence, and betrayal by life. It would be accurate to say that each of these figures is at once himself or herself *and* Randall Jarrell; not, of course, Jarrell the wit, translator of Rilke, and edgily competitive poet, but the essential Jarrell whose sensibility defines itself in his poems in the way we have been tracing.

This essential sensibility enters many of the speaking voices in Jarrell's next volume, *The Seven-League Crutches.* In fact, reading through this volume, one is pierced by the realization of how completely possessed by it his writing is and what a chilling desolateness he coped with. It is not only the specific *child* minds he presents that make the realization so forcible, though indeed this volume gives us several such characterizations to add to "Lady Bates." The one closest to "Lady Bates" in tone is "The Truth," in which, Jarrell explains in *Selected Poems,* "the little boy who speaks . . . has had his father, his sister, and his dog killed in one of the early fire-raids on London, and has been taken to the country, to a sort of mental institution for children." This poem has none of the cultural overlay of "Lady Bates," the treacherous sense of "understanding" the black child's world that cuts across Jarrell's finer sense of her as one abandoned by life in her own idiosyncratic way. "The Truth" is stripped down to the essential anguish and bewilderment:

> When I was four my father went to Scotland.
> They *said* he went to Scotland.
>
> When I woke up I think I thought that I was dreaming —
> I was so little then that I thought dreams
> Are in the room with you, like the cinema.
> That's why you don't dream when it's still light —

> They pull the shades down when it is, so you can sleep.
> I thought that then, but that's not right.
> Really it's in your head.
>
> And it was light then — light at *night*. . . .

And yet, as with the play of thought in "Lady Bates," one can well ask of this poem whether the anguish and bewilderment are really the little boy's or Jarrell's. All that charming talk about a child's notion of what dreams are is really in Jarrell's grown-up voice, reminiscing about his own memories. Naturally, these thoughts about dreams being like the cinema might occur to any child, and my only point is that Jarrell is using this kind of situation, so close to his own constant preoccupation, as a suitable instrument on which to play. He is a virtuoso of pity, and the form his virtuosity takes is to work his own voice into his materials so as to bring out their intrinsic pathos and his active insight simultaneously.

In "The Black Swan," a poem about another child, this fusion of sensibilities works superbly. The preface to *Selected Poems* tells us that this poem was "said, long ago, by a girl whose sister is buried under the white stones of the green churchyard." "The Black Swan" and a number of other poems in *The Seven-League Crutches* mark a considerable advance in the artistic isolation and redirection of Jarrell's deepest motifs. The loneliness, the sense of a chaotic universe, and the lost focus of identity (expressed as a shared or confused identity) of his best later work are all present at the very start of "The Black Swan":

> When the swans turned my sister into a swan
>   I would go to the lake, at night, from milking:
> The sun would look out through the reeds like a swan,
>   A swan's red beak; and the beak would open
> And inside there was darkness, the stars and the moon. . . .

This beginning, a decisive act of empathic imagination, opens up a world of associations to the end of recovering the stab of primal pathos. The swan images proliferate, and the mad or nightmare-ridden speaker becomes a swan herself as, out of the realm of heartless nature and death, her sister responds to her call. This poem alone would make it clear that Jarrell's poetic control had grown enormously by 1951. He could now deal purely and forcefully with psychological and mythic or archetypal materials and could write his own thoughts directly without over-intellectualizing and without superciliousness. "The Orient Express" opens *The Seven-League Crutches* on a note of unpretentious intimacy that combines his ever-present child-mindedness with his adult intelligence:

> One looks from the train
> Almost as one looked as a child. In the sunlight
> What I see still seems to me plain,
> I am safe; but at evening
> As the lands darken, a questioning
> Precariousness comes over everything. . . .

All of Jarrell is there, as simply apparent as possible. But the form itself has a new sort of interest when compared to much of Jarrell's earlier work. The ease and grace of movement, the sustained clarity of speech, and the engaging, concrete thoughtfulness keep the reader listening and moving along with the speaker. The lines of this passage, as in the poem as a whole, tend toward a three-stress unit but often — here in the two opening lines — depart from it. Rhyming effects (an exact rhyme in lines one and three, the echoing of -*ing* in lines four, five, and six, the repetitions of "look" and "one," and the sequence of the monosyllabic verbs "look" and "looked" and "see" and "seems" and "comes") are introduced lightly yet saturate the sound structure as in the even richer "The Black Swan." One finds a similar felicity and immediacy in the two poems that close the book, "The Venetian Blind" and "Seele im Raum" — poems which both recall, the former in its literal theme and the latter in its title, a poem of Rilke's. "The Venetian Blind" does indeed present its protagonist as a "Seele im Raum" or "soul in space."

> He is lost in himself forever.
>
> And the Angel he makes from the sunlight
> Says in mocking tenderness:
> "Poor stateless one, wert thou the world?" . . .
>
> The bars of the sunlight fall to his face.
>
> And yet something calls, as it has called:
> "But where am *I*? But where am *I*?"

Rilke's "Seele im Raum," written in 1917, has as its literal subject the condition of a soul torn from its body and suddenly become pure potentiality in a realm of pure being. The soul feels stripped of comforts, exposed, and tremulously fearful in its ignorance of its own destiny. Jarrell's "Seele im Raum" has in part the same theme, but the central situation of his poem is that of a woman who once had the grotesque illusion that an eland was present wherever she was. The woman's pathetic obsession would be hilariously absurd were it not, as her monologue shows, symptomatic of her sense of being a lost self despite the fact that she was a wife and mother. Her period of madness is now over; but in an important way she misses the eland, which was so tangibly and oppressively present to her and yet was the only thing that was hers alone: her soul's embodiment of its own misery —

> Today, in a German dictionary, I saw *elend*
> And the heart in my breast turned over, it was —
>
> It was a word one translates wretched. . . .
>
> — It was worse than impossible, it was a joke.
>
> And yet when it was, I *was* —
> Even to think that I once thought
> That I could see it is to feel the sweat
> Like needles at my hair-roots, I am blind

— It was not even a joke, not even a joke.

Yet how can I believe it? Or believe that I
Owned it, a husband, children? Is my voice the voice
Of that skin of being — of what owns, is owned
In honor or dishonor, that is borne and bears —
Or of that raw thing, the being inside it
That has neither a wife, a husband, nor a child
But goes at last as naked from this world
As it was born into it —

And the eland comes and grazes on its grave. . . .

The passage I have just quoted takes us from the punning proof that the eland had been for the speaker a projection of her soul's *elend* condition, its misery, to the bitter sense she has now of all that she has lost and then, finally, to that sense of being stripped of a human past and utterly out in space of which Rilke writes. Jarrell's absorption in Rilke was one his great passions; it must have been of tremendous importance to him in the progress of his art that I have described. He immersed himself in the greater poet, whose themes were so close to his own. The sensibilities of children and of women dominate the attention of both poets. Both are in search of points of directive contact with chaotic reality — both are "souls in space." Both, incidentally, had noncombatant military service involving a certain disillusionment, and there were temperamental affinities as well (as in their mixture of endearing traits with ruthless critical attitudes).

Rilke's essential influence on Jarrell seems to have been to encourage him to widen his poetic thought and to reach for a more concentrated and evocative imagery, a more personal and vital poetic speech and rhythmic movement, and a style both natural to him and in touch with European cultural tradition. It is interesting that *The Seven-League Crutches* begins with a section called "Europe" — poems with European settings to which Jarrell attaches his American awareness. The displacement of context enables him to convert old sets of thought into deepened historical and philosophical musings. Looking out from the Orient Express, he can see that the whole world (not just his own empirical life) is unassimilable to the soul in space and yet has its own aesthetic magnetism we cannot avoid:

> It is like any other work of art.
> It is and never can be changed.
> Behind everything there is always
> The unknown unwanted life.

One could conceivably make the same observation looking from an American train, but just that kind of consideration is involved in the implied comparison. It is just the sensed history behind the fields, people, houses, and villages that makes the feeling of an essential changelessness of existence such a powerful one. In "A Game at Salzburg," the same principle is at work. Jarrell's explanation in *Selected Poems* shows how much he relishes the knowledgeableness behind the poem, the kind of Europeanized wit its subject enables him to cultivate: "I put into 'A Game at Salzburg' a little game that Germans and Austrians play with very young children. The child says to the grown-up, *Here I am*, and the grown-up answers, *There you are*; the children use the same little rising tune, and the grown-ups the same resolving, conclusive one. It seemed to me that if there could be a conversation between the world and God, this would be it." And so, in the poem, the whole style is delightfully relaxed until the very end. The poet (during the year in which he was a participant in the Salzburg Seminar in American Civilization) is seen passing lazy, happy days amid the innumerable tokens not only of an old civilization but also of the recent war. One notices with some surprise and interest that his juxtapositions of a modern American intelligence like his own with all these surrounding signs and symbols, under circumstances at once so congenial and so poignantly and volatilely suggestive, have led him into a tone and rhythm that must have influenced Robert Lowell's style in *Life Studies*:

> A little ragged girl, our ball-boy;
> A partner — ex-Afrika-Korps —
> In khaki shorts, P. W. illegible.
> (He said: "To have been a prisoner of war
> In Colorado iss a *privilege*.")
> The evergreens, concessions, carrousels,
> And D. P. camp at Franz Joseph Park;
> A gray-green river, evergreen-dark hills.
> Last, a long way off in the sky,
> Snow-mountains.

These are the social and political and historical realities, all within the unchanged ancient landscape. When, later on, the poet finds himself playing the little game of *Hier bin i'* — *Da bist du*, with a three-year-old, there is an inevitably ironic echo from that opening scene. Reality is intractably itself, and the fact is softly underlined in the persistence of a language and a ritual even in a tiny girl "licking sherbet from a wooden spoon" as she engages the poet in the game. Later still, he moves "past Maria Theresa's sleigh" and the statues, mostly broken, in the garden where "the nymphs look down with the faces of Negroes." The two worlds suddenly related in this image are one world after all, as is the prewar world that became the one at war and then the postwar one. At the end, Jarrell's old, persistent insight is thrust into the foreground, but the voice adopted is a European one recalling the "dreamy" American to the imponderable:

> In anguish, in expectant acceptance
> The world whispers: *Hier bin i'*.

We cannot pursue all the examples of Jarrell's "Europeaniza-tion" in *The Seven-League Crutches*. One further instance is the translation of Corbière's "Le Poète Contumace." Corbière's tough-mindedness and scathing but funny self-characterizations show up the sentimental limits of Jarrell's own work. Nevertheless, Jarrell admired Corbière and aspired to his kind of mentality.

Jarrell's one novel, *Pictures from an Institution*, bears extended analysis because so much that was important to him is packed into it, and also because it is an extremely clever work of satire as well as a humanely intelligent book. It is set in a progressive women's college not altogether unlike Sarah Lawrence College, and its pictures of the academic and personal life of all concerned remain extremely amusing. I shall discuss it only very briefly, in relation to Jarrell's poetic development. It represents, I think, a completion of his attempt to assimilate his own frame of thought to that of cultivated and sensitive Europeans. The novel is written in the first person, from the viewpoint of a poet who has been teaching at Benton College for a number of years. The real hero, though, is an Austrian-Jewish composer named Gottfried Rosenbaum through whose eyes the provincialism, complacency, and emptiness of much of American education is made, somewhat lovingly, clear, while certain genuine American strengths and potentialities are seen as goods after all. Dr. Rosenbaum's mind is razor-keen, though he does not ordinarily use it to slash people. That role is taken by a visiting novelist, Gertrude Johnson, whose analytical savagery has no kindness in it and who is often malignantly inventive in her sizing up of people, all grist for her novels. She is going to do a novel about the college, and it will be merciless — presumably far more so than *Pictures from an Institution* itself. Yet this necessary comparison gives one to think. Gertrude, as it were, discharges the hostile and supercilious side of Jarrell's critical intelligence, while Gottfried represents a more genial ideal. John Crowe Ransom, in his contribution to *Randall Jarrell, 1914–1965*, notes the indications that Gertrude undergoes something like a "conversion" to a more humane attitude in the course of the novel, and I would suggest that the improvement of Gertrude is something in the nature of a purgation for Jarrell himself. The "I" of the novel, the poet who is ready to leave the limited campus scene at the end of the year, has been close to both Gertrude and Gottfried. Gottfried, with his elderly Russian wife who shares his cultivation and his sense of tragic history, will remain after the writers have left. With them will stay the talented and loyal Constance Morgan, who in her life embodies the best of American openness and possibility as Gottfried and Irene embody the living tradition of European art with which we must remain in vital touch. Constance, an orphan, is thus one of four figures who represent ideals or characteristics of Jarrell himself. The book reaches a certain serenity and insight into the best qualities of each of the characters, despite the fun at the expense of most of them along the way.

What an injustice I have done to this novel, with its marvelously amusing passages that Jarrell wrote in an ecstasy of acerbic release. It is his most balanced work, done not long after his marriage to Mary von Schrader in 1952, and it helped him gain a precarious personal balance. It was also a self-deceptive balance, a standoff between barely repressed total revulsion and sentimental voting for the triumph, in any one person, of decency over stupidity and mean-spirited worldliness. A variety of sexual repression is involved as well. In the novel, as in Jarrell's poetry, sexuality in itself seems hardly present as a factor in his own thought and emotions or in those of his characters. His attitude toward women is a little like his attitude toward unhappy children and a little like Sophocles' toward "the Mothers": awe, mystification, and, sometimes, a cozy sympathy with a bitter edge nevertheless. The sense of a life ridden by despair that comes through in his last two books of poems is linked with that bitter sympathy. The balanced feeling of control of the mid-1950's dissolves into something harsher, more convincing finally, and at its best more brilliant.

The three poems that open the 1960 volume, *The Woman at*

the Washington Zoo, are rather precise examples of Jarrell's feeling for women. He thinks about them a great deal, and passionately, but in the ways I have suggested. The title poem is one of a number written from the point of view of a woman, usually aging, who feels that, as she says, "The world goes by my cage and never sees me." (Jarrell discusses the composition of this poem brilliantly in one of his essays in *A Sad Day at the Supermarket*, 1962.) The poem begins with a tone of quiet desperation and in a sometimes banal cadence of a sort occasionally cultivated by Eliot, but rises to a hysterical pitch at the end — an accusation against fate and an appeal to be transformed. The woman's outcry is directed toward a vulture, both real and symbolic. She wants to be devoured and transformed, and her language suggests that the bird of prey to which her protest and prayer are addressed embodies the male principle:

> Vulture,
> When you come for the white rat that the foxes left,
> Take off the red helmet of your head, the black
> Wings that have shadowed me, and step to me as man:
> The wild brother at whose feet the white wolves fawn,
> To whose hand of power the great lioness
> Stalks, purring. . . .
> You know what I was,
> You see what I am: change me, change me!

It is the first time in his poems that Jarrell speaks so fiercely through a woman's voice. In the next poem, "Cinderella," he does so again, but here, for once, female toughness — and even hardness — of spirit comes through. Both Cinderella and her fairy godmother are presented as coolly anti-male. Cinderella, on her very wedding day, under the "pulsing marble" of her wedding lace, "wished it all a widow's coal-black weeds." Later she became "a sullen wife and a reluctant mother." The godmother is sophisticated into an archetypal "God's Mother" who comes into her own whenever her son is away. At these times she invites

Cinderella into the "gold-gauzed door" of her Heaven that exists only in the flames of the male-created Hell, and they gossip comfortably apart from male ideas, ideals, and laws. This poem is far more effective than the long, rather involved, and precious one that follows: "The End of the Rainbow." In this latter poem, about a woman "old enough to be invisible," Jarrell's proliferating details carry a certain pathos but, even more, suggest the poet's extraordinary identification with his protagonist.

After these opening poems of human sensibility gratingly out of phase come the four most striking pieces of the book — poems that, together with those in the title sequence of *The Lost World,* complete Jarrell's work by closing in on intimate realities of his own actual life and memory. Again we have an interesting parallel to Lowell, for both poets were moving into their confessional period at the same time. Lowell's *Life Studies* had appeared the year before, an enormous gathering of concentrated neurotic energy centered on his childhood and the personalities of his parents as somehow symptomatic of America's and the world's malaise. Although Jarrell's confessional poems are less ambitious formally and symbolically than Lowell's, they are in many ways closer to the anomie and the disturbances that mark the common life in our day.

Jarrell is in his own way as much an exotic as Lowell. The strains of his boyhood are as atypical as those of the privileged Bostonian, and the adult lives of both men have been atypical too. But often in these poems he summons up the world of plain-living, laboring souls and of the hardships and pleasures of ordinary life. The confusing images of his beloved grandmother wringing a chicken's neck, and of the already dead bird still running about in circles, recur, for instance, in a number of the poems. Each is an image of the brutal nature of existence and cannot be separated out from the meaning of love. Millions of ordinary folk know the experience described in "A Street off Sunset" (in *The Lost World*):

> Mama comes out and takes in the clothes
> From the clothesline. She looks with righteous love
> At all of us, her spare face half a girl's.
> She enters a chicken coop, and the hens shove
> And flap and squawk, in fear; the whole flock whirls
> Into the farthest corner. She chooses one,
> Comes out, and wrings its neck. The body hurls
> Itself out — lunging, reeling, it begins to run
> Away from Something, to fly away from Something
> In great flopping circles. Mama stands like a nun
> In the center of each awful, anguished ring.
> The thudding and scrambling go on, go on — then they fade,
> I open my eyes, it's over . . . Could such a thing
> Happen to anything? It could to a rabbit, I'm afraid;
> It could to . . .

The details here are as plain, and as hideous, as, say, those in John Clare's "Badger." Where Jarrell differs from a true *naïf*, though, is in his superimposed notes of observation, themselves simple in tone but implying meditative and informed intelligence: "righteous love" (a note of psychological insight, for the woman's look is a gesture both of self-encouragement and of apology and self-justification); "away from Something" (a note to underline the presence of universal terror); "like a nun" (again, the note of reaffirmed innocence, which is yet "the center of each awful, anguished ring"); and at last the deliberate pointing up of the child's reactions. The easily colloquial iambic pentameter lines run on quite naturally; one hardly notices the alternating rhymes that help rock the movement into hysteria — that is, into the child's momentarily traumatized hypnosis by the impossible thing that is happening. Jarrell uses this pattern throughout the "Lost World" sequence. It makes for a slightly relaxed, anecdotal tone that drags boringly at times but provides a frame at others for effects such as this one. This weakness, in itself, is a reflection of Jarrell's desire to keep his form open to common speech and common psychology — something he much admired in Robert Frost's work.

Returning to *The Woman in the Washington Zoo* and the four poems there that I have noted, we can see that "In Those Days" and "The Elementary Scene" are both exceedingly simple in form. "In Those Days" consists of four quatrains with the simplest of rhyme schemes, *abcb*, and is in a basic iambic tetrameter with much variation for naturalness and dramatic immediacy. It reads, except for the deliberate avoidance of smoothness of meter, like an afterbeat from Heine, particularly in the last stanza:

> How poor and miserable we were,
> How seldom together!
> And yet after so long one thinks:
> In those days everything was better.

Almost doggerel — but this ending shrugs off a painful nostalgia for a past love, the whole adolescent atmosphere of which has been evoked, with all its bittersweet frustration and sense of wintry isolation of the two young people, in the preceding stanzas. The poem strikes a new personal key for Jarrell, and serves as an overture to the further exploration of the speaker's lost past. Then come "The Elementary Scene" and "Windows," still quite simple in their diction and the scenes they envision: the first a rural elementary school at Hallowe'en, the second the home of dead elders who once loved and cherished the speaker. Jarrell's ability to suggest, with utmost economy, a milieu at once provincial and inarticulate and yet full of unmet challenge — the reality of an irretrievable folk past that might have led to a far different life for the speaker, less to be regretted, perhaps — is his greatest strength.

> The thin grass by the girls' door,
> Trodden on, straggling, yellow and rotten,
> And the gaunt field with its one tied cow . . .

— the lines recall his very early "The Cow Wandering in the Bare Field" and the curious persistence of images demanding clarification again and again during a poet's lifetime. The self-reproach at the end of "The Elementary Scene" — "I, I, the future that mends everything" — is the final evidence that this is one of his purest poems, a poem of unearned but heavily felt depression, in which the speaker takes upon himself the guilt of time's passing. So also in "Windows," it is the unbearable irrevocability of the past that the speaker lives with and endures (in this respect a true heir to Frost and E. A. Robinson). The beloved dead, imagined alive in their time, are compared in their vivid presence to "dead actors, on a rainy afternoon," who "move in a darkened living-room" on a television screen.

> *These* actors, surely, have known nothing of today,
> That time of troubles and of me. . . .
> They move along in peace. . . . If only I were they!
> Could act out, in longing, the impossibility
> That haunts me like happiness!

Sentimentality is held at a distance in this poem by the sheer force of illusion: the construction of a moment of the recaptured past so keenly present to the speaker's desire that it goes beyond imagination —

> It blurs, and there is drawn across my face
> As my eyes close, a hand's slow fire-warmed flesh.
>
> It moves so slowly that it does not move.

The poem "Aging," which follows, does not have the fine sensuous conviction of "Windows" and does lapse into sentimentality. When, in the "Lost World" sequence and in "Remembering the Lost World," literal memory again picks up these motifs, the intensity and concentration are sacrificed for the anecdotal colloquialism we have seen. These are poems banking on total rather than on selected recall and striving to hold their recovered, or reimagined, reality intact against the poisonous fact of elapsed time. Theirs is an opposite method, allowing room for something like a novelistic play of mind over bizarre contradictions of a child's life in Hollywood, a life at once disciplined by good gray work and indulged by an almost sensually remembered aunt and her friends, one of whom owned the MGM lion. It is a bath of charming, touching, and heartbreaking memory in the new open mode that Jarrell had discovered. The new mode seems to have freed him from a vision too sharp to be endured, and to have taken him over the line of belief in the present reality of the past. "Thinking of the Lost World" ends:

LOST — NOTHING. STRAYED FROM NOWHERE. NO REWARD.
I hold in my own hands, in happiness,
Nothing: the nothing for which there's no reward.

"I felt at first," writes John Crowe Ransom in the essay I quoted from earlier, "that this was a tragic ending. But I have studied it till I give up that notion. The NOTHING is the fiction, the transformation; to which both boy and man are given. That World is not Lost because it never existed; but it is as precious now as ever. I have come to think that Randall was announcing the beginning of his 'second childhood.' There is nothing wrong about that, to the best of my knowledge." Perhaps, but what Mr. Ransom is describing is the letdown, or failure of nerve, in the face of the issues (which Jarrell nevertheless did to a certain important extent face) that often takes the form of a paradoxically melancholy complacency in writers just below the energy level of genius. Jarrell himself approaches the issue wryly in the quoted lines, and also in the self-ironically named poem "Hope," which takes us into the poet's grown-up life with all its gaiety, fears, and gallant playing of roles. It is almost as though he had given the tragic its due in "The Elementary Scene," "Windows,"

45

and the very dark-spirited Rilke translations of *The Woman at the Washington Zoo* and then turned his back on the discipline of greatness.

But this would be too harsh a judgment. At fifty-one, Jarrell was still expanding his range of technique and of personal sympathies. He might well have reversed his direction once more and made another fresh start as he had done in the war poems and again in *The Seven-League Crutches* and the last books. With all the intelligence and openness to varied literary influences reflected in his criticism and his translations during the two postwar decades, he was surely capable of a great deal of further development despite a deep formal conservatism. Our poetry — and it is Jarrell's *poetry* almost exclusively that we have been concerned with — is today struggling in a new way with the question of the role of an active, many-sided intellectuality in essential poetic structure. Jarrell might conceivably have contributed something of interest to this exploration. Meanwhile, he remains a force among us as a poet of defeat and loneliness who nevertheless does not allow himself to become less spirited. He is like that ex-P.W. in his poem "A Game at Salzburg" who says, "To have been a prisoner of war in Colorado iss a *privilege*."

⅃ Selected Bibliography

NOTE: The quotations in the foregoing text are all taken from the original volumes rather than from the revised versions in *Selected Poems* and in *The Complete Poems.*

Works of Randall Jarrell

POETRY

The Rage for the Lost Penny. In *Five Young American Poets.* Norfolk, Conn.: New Directions, 1940.
Blood for a Stranger. New York: Harcourt, Brace, 1942.
Little Friend, Little Friend. New York: Dial, 1945.
Losses. New York: Harcourt, Brace, 1948.
The Seven-League Crutches. New York: Harcourt, Brace, 1951.
Selected Poems. 1st edition, New York: Knopf, 1955. 2nd edition, including *The Woman at the Washington Zoo,* New York: Atheneum, 1964.
The Woman at the Washington Zoo. New York: Atheneum, 1960.
The Lost World. New York: Macmillan, 1965. (Paperback reprint with Robert Lowell's essay "Randall Jarrell, 1914–1965: An Appreciation" appended. New York: Collier, 1966.)
The Complete Poems. New York: Farrar, Straus and Giroux, 1969. Includes *Selected Poems,* poems omitted from *Selected Poems,* and sections of "Uncollected Poems (1934–1965)" and "Unpublished Poems (1935–1965)."

FICTION

Pictures from an Institution, a Comedy. New York: Knopf, 1954.

CRITICISM

Poetry and the Age. New York: Knopf, 1953.
A Sad Heart at the Supermarket. New York: Atheneum, 1962.
The Third Book of Criticism. New York: Farrar, Straus and Giroux, 1965.

CURRENT AMERICAN REPRINTS

Complete Poems. New York: Sunburst (Farrar, Straus and Giroux). $3.95.

Pictures from an Institution. New York: Noonday (Farrar, Straus and Giroux).
$2.25.
Poetry and the Age. New York: Vintage (Random House). $1.65.
Selected Poems. New York: Atheneum. $2.75.
The Third Book of Criticism. New York: Noonday. $3.45.

Bibliographies

Adams, Charles M. *Randall Jarrell: A Bibliography.* Chapel Hill: University of North Carolina Press, 1958. (A supplement to this bibliography appears in *Analects*, 1:49–56 (Spring 1961).)

Gillikin, Dure J. "A Check-List of Criticism on Randall Jarrell, 1941–1970, with an Introduction and a List of His Major Works," *Bulletin of the New York Public Library*, 74:176–94 (April 1971).

Kisslinger, Margaret V. "A Bibliography of Randall Jarrell," *Bulletin of Bibliography*, 24:243–47 (May–August 1966).

Shapiro, Karl. *Randall Jarrell.* Washington, D.C.: Library of Congress, 1967. (Includes a bibliography of primary works and a list of Jarrell materials in the collections of the Library of Congress: manuscripts, phonodiscs, magnetic tapes, and motion pictures as well as books and uncollected poems and prose.)

Critical and Biographical Studies

Fein, Richard. "Major American Poetry of World War II." Doctoral dissertation, New York University, 1960.

Lowell, Robert, Peter Taylor, and Robert Penn Warren, eds. *Randall Jarrell, 1914–1965.* New York: Farrar, Straus and Giroux, 1967. (Essays by Hannah Arendt, John Berryman, Elizabeth Bishop, Philip Booth, Cleanth Brooks, James Dickey, Denis Donoghue, Leslie A. Fiedler, Robert Fitzgerald, R. W. Flint, Alfred Kazin, Stanley Kunitz, Robert Lowell, William Meredith, Marianne Moore, Robert Phelps, Sister M. Bernetta Quinn, John Crowe Ransom, Adrienne Rich, Delmore Schwartz, Maurice Sendak, Karl Shapiro, Allen Tate, Eleanor Ross Taylor, Peter Taylor, P. L. Travers, Robert Watson, and Mrs. Randall Jarrell. Pages xi–xii list all of Jarrell's books, including editions in preparation, as of the volume's date of publication.)

Mazzaro, Jerome. "Between Two Worlds: The Post-Modernism of Randall Jarrell," *Salmagundi*, Fall 1971, pp. 93–113.

Rideout, Walter B. " 'To Change! to Change!' " in Edward Hungerford, ed., *Poets in Progress.* Evanston, Ill.: Northwestern University Press, 1967.

Rosenthal, M. L. *The Modern Poets: A Critical Introduction.* New York: Oxford University Press, 1960.

FOOTNOTES

Pg 14

FOOTNOTES

Sidewalk Sermonettes

for

Saints and Sinners

by

Gaston Foote

Fleming H. Revell Company

Printed in the United States of America

Library of Congress Catalog Card Number 56–7439

Westwood, N.J.—316 Third Avenue
London E.C. 4—29 Ludgate Hill
Glasgow C. 2—229 Bothwell Street

Contents

FOOTNOTES

BEEFSTEAK AND NO TEETH

Some years ago while traveling with my father in west Texas I suggested that we stop at the next good hotel and have a nice beefsteak dinner. My father said, "I could use a nice juicy steak but have no teeth to chew it." That sentence packs a powerful punch. We live with such atomic fury from day to day that when we arrive at the opportunity to enjoy life we find we have lost the capacity to do so.

I have known parents who would have greatly enjoyed the fellowship of their own children, but they were so busy trying to improve their financial and social status that when the opportunity came to enjoy them, the children had already reached maturity. So they spoiled their grandchildren! It's a case of beefsteak and no teeth.

I know people who tremendously enjoy the companionship of great books, but their days are so crammed with lesser things that when the opportunity for reading does come they find they have lost the capacity to enjoy it. Many a man has yielded to the pressure of lesser things and put off reading the books he wanted to read, and studying the things he wanted to study, until, when the opportunity did come, he found that he had lost the desire to learn.

As a youth, Charles Darwin was greatly interested in music, in which he had considerable talent. After spending his life in the pursuit of the natural sciences, he retired to his English cottage to enjoy his hobby. With considerable nostalgia he said, "My capacity to enjoy great music has gone from me." Another case of beefsteak and no teeth.

A friend of mine confessed that his secret ambition was to "do a little painting for the fun of it." For forty years he pursued his occupation with relentless zeal, made a success of it. But when the opportunity to paint came his hands were so shaky and his nerves so shattered that all his efforts to pursue his hobby were futile, and his desire to do so died. It would have been infinitely better had he taken a little time out during his busy life to mess up a few canvasses every week or two. Then, when he had more time, he could have enjoyed his hobby.

No man ought to retire unless he has two or three good hobbies on which to depend to keep his mind alive. To retire from a life of great activity into a vacuum is tantamount to calling the undertaker. I have no doubt the undertaker needs the business, but let him wait a few years. He'll be better prepared to take care of you after the additional experience.

The conclusion of the matter is this: don't let the day-to-day rush crowd out your determination to do the things you have wanted to do just for the joy of doing them. The only day you have is today! Live it to the full! Don't be caught short with a juicy beefsteak and no teeth to enjoy it.

PARKING ON THE OTHER
FELLOW'S NICKEL

The other day I had to pick up my wife at a downtown store. The traffic was heavy, but I was fortunate enough to slip into a parking space with twenty minutes of unused time on the meter. Obviously there is nothing wrong in parking on space paid for by someone else. I've left a few minutes on meters myself and anyone fast enough to get in the space was certainly welcome to it.

But it set me to thinking. There are a lot of people who just cruise around looking for free parking space— space paid for by the other fellow.

What of the hosts of people who are directly or indirectly benefited by the church in the community but make no contribution to its building or its program? They would not want to live in a community without a church, would verbally "slay" anyone who suggested that the church be torn down. But they assume the church can live on their good wishes and are quite willing to let others furnish the cash. They park on the other man's nickel.

11

Hosts of parents send their children to Sunday school for years, expecting them to be taught the principles of Christian living by capable teachers without once considering their own responsibility in the teaching program. It's a case of using the other man's nickel.

Cities in America are greatly benefited by the many Red Feather agencies of the Community Chest or United Fund. Yet there are hosts of good people who receive the benefits of these humanitarian agencies without making any contribution whatever. They are willing to let the other fellow carry the load.

The responsibility of putting over civic enterprises benefiting the entire community is usually shouldered by a comparatively small number of men.

There are entirely too many people who are content to say, "Let George do it." They forget that George is tired from overwork, since he has his personal responsibilities too.

A boy in college or in the armed forces usually manages to provide for himself cheap transportation by hitchhiking. But the adult who thumbs his way through life letting the other fellow furnish the car, the gas, and the oil, is the one who makes a habit of parking on the other fellow's nickel.

The question is, are we hooking a ride through life, deadheading our way, getting by on a pass? Or are we carrying our fair share of the load, shouldering our share of the responsibility, paying our way?

BE NATURAL

I guess I slept through my share of college chapels and student assemblies when I was in school. It was a good place to catch up on your studies or your sleep, or just catch up. But after many years I still remember the introduction to one speech a fellow made. After he was introduced he walked over to a piano on the stage and struck one note. Then he began to speak.

"Do you know what note that was I struck on the keyboard? That was B natural, and that is the subject of my talk." Unfortunately, I went back to sleep and don't remember anything else he said, but it must have been a good talk.

Be natural. Be yourself.

It may be naïve, but I think God must have had a purpose in mind when He made us as individuals. No one of us is like another. They say no two blades of grass are alike, no two snowflakes are alike, no two leaves on a tree are exactly alike. And we all know that the lines on our finger tips are different from those of every other man's.

You remember the ancient quip about the school teacher who asked, "What is in our world today that wasn't here fifty years ago?" Imagine her surprise when the irrepressible Johnny piped, "Me." Well, Johnny had something. And the world had something too—Johnny! A Johnny that was different from all the millions of Johnnies ever born. If God made us different it's foolish to try to be someone or something other than one's natural self.

Of all the pains in the neck the person who is most irritating is he who tries to be someone else. In some instances it is bad enough to be one's self but to try to be someone else is worse.

Here is a fellow who inherited a hundred thousand from his Scotch father. He imagines himself to be Cornelius Vanderbilt, John D. Rockefeller and Ali Khan, all in one wad. One would like to say to him what the little boy said when he read the inscription on the tombstone, "He is not dead, but sleepeth." The boy mumbled, "He ain't foolin' nobody but hisself."

Nothing can hurt a man worse than to believe a near-sighted sentimental sister who sighs and says, "He's handsome." Henceforth, he struts as though he were an incarnation of Apollo. (Add a cluster of sour grapes.)

It's said a little knowledge is a dangerous thing. Well, a lot of knowledge is dangerous too—especially if a man is aware of it. A deluded soul's belief that he is brilliant doesn't necessarily mean that he really is. When a man assumes that he has all the answers, and is willing at the drop of a hat (his own) to divulge them, he usually turns out to be the biggest bore in the orchard.

Robert Louis Stevenson said, "To be what we are and to become what we are capable of becoming is the only end of life." John Stuart Mill put it another way when he said, "All good things which exist are the fruits of originality."

Be yourself. Quit posing as someone other than yourself. "Stir up the gift that is within you." Be natural. Only thus can you make your greatest contribution.

CHRISTIANITY, A LAYMAN'S RELIGION

Why is it that so many people get the idea that Christianity is primarily a religion for priests and clergymen? Is it because we have made too sharp a distinction between the clergy and the laity? Or because, in some instances, the voice of the Church has been identical with the voice of the clergy?

Christianity is primarily and basically a religion for laymen.

In the first place, Jesus Christ, founder of Christianity, was a layman. Jesus did not belong to the Temple priesthood or to the synagogue ministry. He was a carpenter by trade.

Furthermore, all of the disciples were laymen. There was not a professional priest in the group: all were drawn from various types of lay employment. They were Christianity's first witnesses, its first apostles, and were largely responsible for the firm foothold of Christianity in the first century.

15

The Christian layman has a tremendous advantage over the minister in propagating the faith. There are ordained clergymen who, by great influence and power, and by use of radio and television, influence hosts of people for the Christian faith. But, in the final analysis, religion is a spirit, and it is propagated, not by a creed that is taught, but by a spirit that is caught. This spirit is communicated through countless nameless Christians who, in daily life, incarnate the spirit of the Christ.

The minister is often regarded as a professional "salesman" for Christianity. But the layman who engages in Christian evangelism is regarded as a satisfied customer who has found religion so enriching and transforming in personal experience that he simply cannot keep it to himself. His living testimony before his fellow men is more compelling than the finished sermon of the eloquent preacher.

Laymen have rendered magnificent service through the centuries to Christian faith. The lay speakers, directed by John Wesley, were largely responsible for the revival of eighteenth-century England. In the nineteenth century, perhaps the two most influential servants of the Church were Charles Spurgeon of England and Dwight L. Moody of the United States. Both of these men were brought to Christ by lay workers.

On the foreign mission field the record of the laymen is even more impressive. Without the work of the lay teachers, doctors, nurses, agriculturists, and social workers, the foreign missionary enterprise could never succeed.

If the world of human relationships is Christianized it will be because laymen have taken the major responsibility.

In the nineteenth century William Wilberforce, a layman, succeeded in getting a law passed abolishing the slave traffic in the British Empire. The Christian layman, Lord Shaftesbury, sparked the social legislation which provided decent conditions for the British laborer.

As in the past, so it will be in the future. If the United States ever becomes a Christian nation it will be because laymen have taken their Christian convictions out of the sanctuary and applied them in the street. Christianity is a layman's movement.

CHRISTIANITY AND HEALTH

A prominent surgeon once said, "I have discovered the Kingdom of God at the point of my scalpel. It is written in the tissues. The right thing is always the healthy thing." *The British Medical Journal* said, "There is not a tissue of the human body wholly removed from the influence of the spirit of man."

What is the meaning of this? Psychologists and physicians are saying that there is a definite connection between healthy minds and healthy bodies. Illnesses caused by wrong mental attitudes can ultimately develop into organic disorders. Real dangers to personal health are resentment, fear, self-centeredness, and a sense of guilt.

Jesus, who never used the term "psychiatry," was Himself a psychiatrist. His beatitudes, meaning beautiful attitudes, are an appeal for healthy mindedness. "Blessed are the pure in heart." This is an appeal to be clean on the inside. Men can't cover up their past sins without suffering from an inner sense of guilt. This sense of guilt produces fear of exposure, which is unhealthy.

"Blessed are the merciful." The spirit of mercy is an attitude toward life. Mercy is love in action, a combination of righteousness and forgiveness. People who harbor grudges, who are victims of deep resentment, actually bring mental and physical suffering on themselves.

"Blessed are the peacemakers." To practice aggressive good will in all of one's relationships is health-producing. On the other hand, the husband who is nagged to death or the bullied wife whose spirit is broken, has a psychological hangover as real as that of one who had taken too much alcohol the night before.

"Blessed are the poor in spirit." These are the humble people who have freed themselves from the inner conflicts and tensions caused by jealousy and false pride. Abraham Lincoln was a tolerant and humble man. His wife, according to some historians, was intolerant, proud, high-tempered. Lincoln's mind was clear to the end, but his wife spent her last days in a room alone, her mind almost gone.

18

Do wrong mental attitudes affect physical health? The evidence indicates that they do. Dr. Stanley Cobb of Boston made a thorough study of mental attitudes and the abdominal disorder, mucous colitis. In 70 percent of the cases there was evidence of resentment, anxiety, and a sense of fear. The tensity of the abdominal nerves had, in some measure, produced the physical disorder.

A doctor friend of mine told me of a woman who thoroughly hated her son-in-law. To appear respectable, she visited him once a year. On each visit she became ill with arthritis; but upon her return home the arthritis disappeared. Obviously all arthritics don't hate their in-laws! But if we can believe our doctors there is a definite connection between mental attitudes and neurotic disorders.

When I was in Africa some years ago reliable medical missionaries said that a "curse of evil" pronounced against a person actually would cause him to die. I protested that a curse on him could not possibly cause a man's death. But the missionaries simply said, "We have buried men who were cursed." They made autopsies, and filed the report, "died from fear." Fear is public enemy Number One. Undoubtedly it aggravates such difficulties as high blood pressure and heart ailments.

The conclusion of the matter is this: more people are sick because they are unhappy than unhappy because they are sick. The preachers, the psychiatrists, and the physicians are now saying the same thing: phys-

19

ical health is, in some measure, determined by healthy attitudes. The family doctor used to ask, "How's your appetite?" Now he often asks, "How's your attitude?"

CHURCH BABIES

I hope I'm not going to far back into the dark ages, but I remember a song with the words, "Everybody loves a baby, that's why I'm in love with you." It was a fetching little ditty and was a top tune for all of a couple of weeks back in the "Roaring Twenties."

Everybody does love a baby! Baby monkeys, baby alligators, baby bullfrogs, baby elephants, human babies of all colors—with one exception. Most of us quite early lose our fondness for baby adults. When a person grows to maturity by clock and calendar, yet retains the disposition of babyhood—that's a real problem.

Paul had something to say about church babies nineteen centuries ago. "I could not address you as spiritual men . . . but as babes in Christ. I fed you with milk, not solid food, for you were not ready for it." It seems church babies have been around quite a spell, at least long enough to grow up.

Church babies are always crying for attention. They must be in the center of the stage. No supporting roles for them; they must be the star performers—or else! If they missed the public meeting when a decision was reached by a democratic process they grumbled, "They didn't consult me in the matter." If they were out of town when the committee met they were hurt because action was not postponed to suit their convenience. They will push a dozen people out of the way to get to the preacher and say, "You must have known my little grandson has the mumps. Why haven't you been to see him?" The preacher ought to just come out and tell the truth, no matter if he is a preacher, and say, "I haven't had 'em, I don't want 'em and I am not going." But he is usually more diplomatic.

A male church baby says to the preacher, "You haven't been around lately. What's the idea of neglecting me?" Under his breath he adds, "Wonder if he knows who I am." (The preacher does, which probably is the reason he hasn't been around.)

Church babies need a special diet. A big chunk of sirloin steak would do them good, but they must stick to milk, with a dash or two of pabulum. If the preacher doesn't want to hurt the feelings of these tender-skinned folk, he must water the Gospel down so as not to upset their digestive tracts. If he mentions gambling or drunkenness he had better have reference to Florida or California. If he talks about stingy people he should, for safety's sake, mention someone in Kalamazoo or Timbuctoo. Such great issues as the race problem, war and peace, Christianizing the social order, etc., are too much for them. Don't they go to church to be pacified?

Church babies keep the preacher awake at night.

21

A couple of quarreling church babies can do more to give a preacher insomnia than three cups of French coffee at dinner, conscience or no conscience.

Once I heard a preacher say, "Next time I change parishes I think I'll preach a farewell sermon on 'church babies.' That will probably help me ship my household goods F. O. B. instead of C. O. D."

CROSS-EYED RELIGION

It was the Apostle Peter who, in his moments of weakness, gave us a perfect example of cross-eyed religion. A man with a case of cross-eyed religion looks at one thing and sees something else. I once heard of a cross-eyed judge examining three cross-eyed witnesses. He turned to the first one and asked, "What's your name?" The second one replied, "Tom Smith." The judge turned to the second and said, "Shut up, I wasn't talking to you." The third replied, "I didn't say anything."

Peter seems to have been built on this order. He was on the mount of transfiguration with James and John when the Lord was transfigured and "his garments became white as light." Peter said to Jesus, "Lord, it is well that we are here; let's build three tabernacles." But Jesus led them down into the valley where there was human need, where He healed an epileptic with the

22

touch of His hand. Peter wanted to stay on the mountain top, where they could have a religious good time, but Jesus led them to a field of service. He saw a religious good time only in treating human need.

Too often the local church remains local. It concerns itself only with its own four walls, forgetting the world of need in which it is situated. It is easy for the church to become a fellowship club, a pink tea affair, a closed organization of like-minded persons in a common economic bracket. The preacher becomes a chaplain to a few families expressing "good views" rather than a herald of Christ proclaiming "good news." The church should not be simply a haven of rest for the saints; it should be a headquarters of redemption for sinners. More than a well-lighted banquet hall with tables laden with delicious food, the church should be a community center where the table of the Lord provides the bread of life. Too often we look at human need about us and see only a religious good time for ourselves.

In another instance Jesus told the disciples that He was to go to Jerusalem and be crucified. Peter took Jesus to one side and said, "This shall never happen to you." Peter could see only the tragedies of the crucifixion, not the redemption through the Cross. Many have been asked to teach a Sunday-school class, but all they saw was the irksome task of constant preparation, not the process of redemption in the life of a child. Many official boards have looked at the problem of juvenile delinquency in their community but all they could see was the cost of a program to do something about it. We forget that the church that will not bleed cannot bless, that the church that will not suffer cannot redeem, that the church that will not serve cannot save.

In another instance Peter asked the Lord which one of the disciples was going to betray Him. Jesus said, "What is that to thee? Follow thou me." Peter, looking at Jesus, actually saw, or sought to see, the betraying disciple. I have known many men who apparently were looking at Christ, but actually were looking at the hypocrites in the church. With their eyes on the hypocrites (and there are some), they refuse to become a part of Christ's Church. Many men have looked squarely at their Christian duty, but about that time they saw George and said, "Let George do it." Many have looked at their sins for a moment, but seeing the sins of other people, they did nothing about their own.

The truth is, a man with a case of cross-eyed religion gets nowhere. Only the man who looks with steady eyes into the face of the Master becomes a transformed person.

DON'T BE A QUITTER

Having been reared on a farm in Central Texas, I remember an incident of my childhood that taught me a most valuable lesson.

It was the summer of my eighth year. School was

out in May, and I was anxious to work by the side of my two older brothers, who were thirteen and fifteen years of age, respectively. They were driving teams to cultivators in the cotton fields, and my father felt that I was too young to handle a team. I kept incessantly after him about it, however, and in a few days he rigged up a "Georgia stock" and an old mule so I could plow by the side of my brothers in the field.

I can remember how I swelled with pride on being able to work with the "grown" folk in the cotton patch. The faithful old mule was so gentle he could almost do the plowing by himself, but I held on to the plow handles and succeeded in getting him between the right cotton rows.

Things went along well during the morning. I didn't get started until after nine o'clock, and the dinner bell rang before I really had time to grow weary. After a hearty dinner we all took a few minutes to sleep in the open hallway that ran through the house. I had no more than gotten to sleep, however, when my father said we had better get to plowing. We returned to the field about 1:30 P.M. and the sand, by that time, was so hot my feet were almost blistered. But I wouldn't dare let my father know everything wasn't to my liking. The afternoon dragged on—and I mean dragged. It seemed to me that it was like the day that Joshua commanded the sun to stand still, because I felt that it had become hung on something halfway between meridian height and the horizon and just stayed there. I became so weary that I tied the lines around my waist and let the tough-mouthed mule drag me along.

I finally determined to meet my father face to face and suggest to him that enough was enough. I had had plenty of plowing for one day. I shall never forget what he said. He looked at the sun, saw that it was three hours high, then looked at the unplowed cotton rows. Then he came to me, put his hand on my shoulder, and said: "You will have to go back to the plow, son—it's not sundown yet."

That was many years ago, but I have not forgotten the lesson. I went back to the plow, gritted my teeth and stayed with it until near sundown. I did the hardest week's work that day I ever did in my life. But I learned a lesson that I shall never forget.

When I'm tempted to quit, give up, unfurl the white flag, scream for help, I can hear my father say, "Go back to the plow, son—it's not sundown yet."

When I'm tempted to surrender my ideals, do an inferior piece of work, rest in the shade, it seems like I can hear God say: "Go back to the plow, son—it's not sundown yet."

EVERY MAN BUILDS HIS
OWN MONUMENT

"Vanity of vanities. All is vanity. What does man gain by all the toils at which he toils under the sun?" So asks the pessimistic writer of the Book of Ecclesiastes.

Man is born in pain, struggles to survive, suffers and dies. Death, the great leveler, ultimately allows only six feet of earth. All things living have to struggle for existence. Every form of life is born to struggle and to die.

But there is a great difference. The ant lives and works, but its only monument is a tiny anthill that the rain soon washes away. Man lives and works, builds his monument, big or little, useful or harmful, and Father Time seems to wipe out all that man has done, save the monument that he has left behind him.

The ancient Pharaohs of Egypt vied with each other in building great monuments. Zoser built the first of the great pyramids, which covered thirteen acres at its base and required sixty million tons of stone. One historian says a hundred thousand slaves worked under the lash of the whip for twenty years to build this one pyramid. Beneath it is the dead Pharaoh whose body, in mineral content, is worth less than one dollar. Zoser died believing that great honor would be paid to him because of the huge monument he left behind.

Visitors to Paris make it a point to see the tomb of Napoleon, one of the world's greatest military geniuses. You read on the tomb Napoleon's expressed desire: "I wish that my ashes repose on the banks of the Seine, among the French people whom I have so much loved." It would have been more correct to say, "Among the French people whom I have so extensively butchered."

A great killer was Napoleon, the moody Corsican boy who made himself Emperor of France and used his power as a tool for the promotion of his own glory. But truly great monuments are never seen by the eyes of men.

Only one man in millions can build such monuments as Pharaoh and Napoleon. But every man can build a monument of good character and unselfish service to his fellow men. And these monuments are of infinitely more importance than all the monuments of stone ever built.

In discovering radium, Pierre and Madam Curie built a monument that recalls their name to thousands of cancer sufferers. Dr. Walter Reed discovered how yellow fever was transmitted and thus has saved the lives of hundreds of thousands of people born after his death.

Benjamin Franklin, Robert Fulton, and Thomas A. Edison left monuments to useful genius that will influence the lives of men as long as history is written.

We mortal men are daily chiseling the monuments we shall leave behind us. A widow labors against untold odds for the physical needs of her children. By her consecrated life, she leaves a monument of honor and integrity deeply carved in the lives of her children. A father forgets himself in his labors for his family, for friends, for God; his monument will last through the ages.

Enduring monuments are made, not of stone, but of kind deeds. They are cast, not in bronze or copper, but in molds of character.

When the monuments to the Pharaohs and the Napoleons are destroyed, we shall still remember Lincoln, Reed, Curie, and a host of kind friends and devoted parents whose only monuments were carved out of the most durable element of the ages—character.

FAMILY RELIGION

Some years ago I was a guest in the home of a well-to-do Catholic in Florence, Italy. My host was an antique merchant who had married a charming American woman. They had two children, a son and a daughter. Their home was a rich treasure house of rare paintings and beautiful tapestries.

On Sunday morning the father said, "I want to show you the heart of our home." He opened a door leading off from the living room, and I was astonished to see a small chapel with a half dozen seats and an altar with crucifix and candles. I remembered that Paul had said something in his letter to the Colossians about "the church that is in thy house," but I had never actually seen one before. Here, in "the heart of the home," the family came together for prayers and devotions.

Consider, for a moment, the church that is in your house. If the Christian religion ever permeates the life of America it must begin in the home. There has never been, nor will there ever be, a substitute for the Christian home.

This fact is self-evident: inevitably, religion of some sort is being taught in your home. From the standpoint of religion there are a few atheists among us. But from the standpoint of psychology there are no atheists at all. Sabatier, the French philosopher, said, "Man is incurably religious." He meant that every man has some kind of a god. Henry Van Dyke said, "A man's god is that which he loves most." Every man has some supreme devotion, something that ultimately claims him. The days of polytheism are still with us. We are worshipers of many gods. The Greek god Bacchus was the ancient god of drunkenness and revelry. Bacchus still has a host of devotees worshiping at his shrine. Venus was the goddess of beauty. She still has her worshipers, though I've seen many women coming from the beauty parlor who didn't look as if they had been waited on. Mars was the god of war. Can there be any doubt about the number of Mars' worshipers, when we are spending $60 billion a year or a million dollars every nine minutes for instruments of war?

In every home there is some dominating spirit. (I'm not talking about the husband.) This dominating spirit is materialism, selfishness, force, or the spirit of Christ. Inevitably, religion of some sort is being taught.

Here is another self-evident fact: true religion is a spirit that is caught rather than a creed that is taught. I am not making light of catechism or creed. But if the child in the home becomes a Christian, it is usually because the spirit of Christianity has been caught from the parents. How do you teach your child to appreciate great music? Not by a lecture on Bach or Wagner, but by exposing the child to the great music of the masters. How teach appreciation of great art? Not by a lecture on da Vinci, but by exposure to great paintings. If the child catches the spirit of Christianity the chances are it will be caught from the parents.

Here is a final self-evident fact: young people desperately need the strength that only the Christian faith can supply. In an incredibly short time the little boy in your home will be out on his own. How can he stand against temptations to drink, to gamble, to cheat, to live as a beast? Only by well-developed habits of moral living. Parents cannot escape the moral responsibility of inculcating good habits in their children. And the time is now. How about "the church that is in thy house"?

FOLLOW THROUGH

Men who play golf know the value of the "follow through" after the club contacts the ball. The full swing of the club is absolutely necessary if the player is to get proper distance.

The follow through is no less necessary in life.

It is the power of perseverance to the end. Our generation has stressed the value of a good start. We have dozens of organizations, such as Scouts, Sunday schools and youth groups that try to give children a good send-off. As the twig is bent so grows the tree. Children who are denied a good start, who are physically, mentally, or morally handicapped, may have warped personalities, and may become a menace to society. We cannot overstress the value of a good start.

Sometimes, however, we do fail to stress the value of a good ending. I grew up reading Horatio Alger stories with those never-to-be-forgotten titles, "Rags to Riches" and "Sink or Swim." The plot was invariably the same. It was the story of a boy who had a bad beginning but always made good in spite of it. It wasn't great literature, but these books thrilled the kids of my age. They emphasized the value of a good ending. The reason I get a thrill out of every new biography of Abraham Lincoln or George Washington Carver is because here were men who had poor starts but followed through to glorious triumphs.

Most of us had a fairly good start. The average American is born in a good home, has God-fearing parents, a good environment in which to grow up, and a good school to attend, and all of us live under a government which guarantees the rights of personal liberty and freedom. But the tragedy in the lives of so many is that having been given a good start, they made a poor ending.

A newspaper man in New York, seeking a human interest story, went down to the Skid Row section of the city. He struck up a conversation with one of the most disreputable-looking professional bums he could find. After gaining his confidence by the price of a meal, the reporter was invited to visit the dirty room where the old man lived. The professional bum showed the reporter his prize possession among his few personal belongings. It was a Phi Beta Kappa Key! Here was a man who had had a wonderful start—and a tragic ending.

It is said that Leonardo da Vinci used living models in painting Jesus and the disciples at "The Last Supper." The face that gave him the most trouble was that of Judas. He could not easily find a person with Judas' treachery written in his face. One day, however, he found just the man who looked the part. When he brought him into his studio the man kept staring at the face of Jesus.

"Beautiful face," said the artist.

"Yes," said the man, "it was once my own." A few years before he had posed as Jesus, with strength and beauty written in his youthful face. Now after betraying his ideals one by one he was posing as Jesus' betrayer. A good start—a terrible ending.

Every new year we make a few good resolutions. The man is spiritually dead who doesn't make them. However, it is not resolutions made, but resolutions kept that make the man. There is one thing more important than good starting power. It is good staying power. Follow through!

GNATS AND CAMELS

Artists have unintentionally done violence to the portrait of the Man of Galilee. They have depicted him as a man of sorrows and acquainted with grief. This is only half the picture. He was also a man of joy and acquainted with humor. Let's note some of the humorous incidents in his words.

Did you ever see a man over forty trying to thread a needle? He squints his eyes, twists the thread, tries to shove, push, coax and otherwise herd it into the needle's eye, but in vain. He holds the needle close to his eyes, then as far as his arms can reach, but the results are the same. In disgust he hands the unfinished job to his wife.

Jesus said it was easier for a camel to go through a needle's eye than for a man who trusted in riches to enter the kingdom of heaven. Only a mummy would have failed to get a laugh out of that.

Jesus talked about the folly of putting new patches on old garments. When I was a kid I had to wear a couple of patches on the seat of my trousers. Imagine the ribbing I would have taken if my mother had decided to put a new red velvet patch on an old pair of faded trousers.

Jesus talked about straining at gnats and swallow-

34

ing camels. The Pharisees in His day were very particular about what they ate. Imagine one of them drinking tea on a hot day at a sidewalk café. Gnats are buzzing around him, getting in his eyes, his ears, his nose. Finally, one loses his sense of direction and power-dives into the hot tea. The Pharisee meticulously fishes out the drowned gnat, and proceeds with his beverage. About that time up walks a lumbering two-humped camel, puts his nose into the man's mouth, kicks until the first hump is out of sight, then the second hump, until, finally, all you see of the camel is his hind feet slipping down the Pharisaical esophagus. It was Jesus' way of driving home the point that men often make mountains out of petty things and quietly consent to gross injustices.

Historically, we have strained gnats and swallowed camels. Constantine, the first so-called Christian emperor, saw the sign of a cross in the sky and adopted the sacred emblem for his ruthless armies. Asking God's blessing on his conquests, he brought back thousands of men, women, and children as captives and sold them as slaves on the auction block in Rome. Following Christ? I doubt it.

In Victorian England there was a law against playing the piano on Sunday, since it was supposed such an act was irreverent. Yet children were forced to labor in British mines as many as sixteen hours a day and half of them contracted tuberculosis before they were twenty-five years old. In Colonial New England it was against the law for a man to kiss his wife in public, yet all the time the people were consenting to the death penalty for those "found guilty of witchcraft." Straining gnats and swallowing camels!

Religiously we have been guilty of straining gnats and swallowing camels. In my childhood the evangelists used to preach against dancing, bridge playing, and theater attendance. I knew people who did none of these things, but whose acid tongues wagged to the devil's music as they slandered their neighbors by damning gossip, kicked "niggers" and "greasers" out of town, and gave as little as five dollars a year for home and foreign missions.

At the last count there were some 259 religious sects or denominations in America. What separates them? Some believe in musical instruments, some don't. Some believe in celebrating the Lord's Supper one way; some another. Some believe in one type of baptism; some in another. We had just as well face it. Too often minor matters have occupied the major role. Micah the prophet had it right when he said, "What doth the Lord require of thee, but to do justly, and to love mercy, and to walk humbly with thy God?" It's about time we quit straining gnats of pettiness and swallowing camels of godlessness.

HANG UP YOUR WALKING CANE

Perhaps it's modesty which has prevented my making this confession long ago. But once I sang in a college quartet. It wasn't difficult, since the three other men could really sing and I, at least, had the ability to lean up to them sympathetically. One of the songs we sang was "Hand Me Down My Walking Cane." It was quite a long time ago.

If I had the ability to compose a song, I think I would write an answer to that one. The title would be "Hang Up Your Walking Cane." Jerome Kern could have done a good job with that. Too many people are running around with walking canes when they should be traveling under their own steam.

A minister friend of mine was telling me about his janitor finding a walking cane that had been left in the church. It stayed there for months, and the owner didn't even come back after it. That must have been a whale of a good sermon the preacher preached that day.

You remember, in the fifth chapter of John, Jesus told about a cripple who sat for thirty-eight years beside the pool of Bethesda waiting for the "troubling of the waters" so that he could get himself healed. But before he could get into the water some more agile fellow would always get in ahead of him and exhaust the healing properties of the mineral springs. Jesus said, "Wilt thou be made whole?" The cripple must have answered, "Sure, I want to be made whole!" Then the Master said, "Rise, take up thy bed and walk." And he did!

A lot of people I know have a whole rack of gold- and silver-tipped walking canes on which they depend to support their sagging frames. Let's interview some of them.

"You see, I didn't have a chance to go to college when I was young and I don't have an adequate education to succeed." I am tempted to feel sorry for this person, since, undoubtedly, a formal education is important. But I have met so many brilliant people who never set foot in college and so many dumb people who are college graduates that I know this is not the whole story. Books are cheap and the man who is willing to use a little brain sweat can dig out the facts. Ignorance is a walking cane on which we have been relying, and the sooner we throw it away, the better.

Another man says, "I guess I'm a victim of bad luck. I was born under an unlucky star." True, some people are lucky and some seem to get nothing but bad breaks. But hard knocks are the experiences which make us strong. A man can be "down" but never "out," unless he counts himself out. And as for being born under an unlucky star, the circumstances of birth have little to do with it. Remember the Master of men was born in a manger.

Still another man says, "You see, it's heredity. My physical, mental, and moral weaknesses are due to the sins of my grandparents." This is a convenient crutch when you don't want to take the responsibility for walking upright, moving forward under your own steam. But the argument simply won't hold up. The trouble with most of us is not in our grandparents but in our grandparent's grandsons.

It's a grand time to hang up the walking cane and do a little sprinting all by ourselves.

HEART TROUBLE

Some time ago I saw a documentary film produced by the American Heart Association entitled, "Guard Thy Heart." It portrayed the functions and characteristics of the heart; pointed out the causes of heart disease, and suggested methods of taking care of the most important organ of the body.

I was impressed by the definite connection between a healthy heart and a healthy mental attitude toward life.

Many people suffer from heart trouble because of hardened arteries. When our arteries lose their elasticity it puts an unusual strain on the heart. Psychologists point out that when we develop a cynical, surly, and sour attitude toward life, we are in danger of developing hardened arteries. In the presence of human need we must always "have a heart" of sympathy and willingness to help. Hardened arteries are frequently caused by hardened dispositions.

Many people suffer from tired hearts, hearts that are overworked. Yet it is amazing the amount of work some people are able to do, while others tire at the least output of energy. Why? Tired hearts result, not from the amount of work done, but from the spirit in which the work is done. Stop taking sleeping pills and let God take over the night watch. Then, next morning, approach your work poised and relaxed.

Bob Hope once said: "Today my heart beat 103,-369 times, my blood traveled 168 million miles, I breathed 23,040 times, I inhaled 438 cubic feet of air, I ate 3 pounds of food, drank 2.9 pounds of liquid, I perspired 1.43 pints, I gave off 85.3 degrees of heat, I generated 450 tons of energy, I spoke 4,800 words, moved 750 major muscles, my nails grew .00056 inches, my hair grew .01714 inches and I exercised 7,000,000 brain cells. Gee, but I'm tired." No wonder! Keep before you all of life's complicated problems, fuss over every detail, count your pulse, check your respiratory system, cuss the maid, kick the dog, abuse the wife and slap the children, and you'll come up with a good case of heart trouble.

Many people suffer from broken hearts. A middle-aged man recently died from no apparent cause. "What was the trouble, doctor?" I asked. "He died from a broken heart. His home life was not harmonious, his son was a disappointment and he lost a fortune; then he licked his wounds—and died."

A lot of heart trouble could be cured if we would

keep our hearts warm, live thankfully, labor leisurely, and love lavishly.

I have lived through two world wars, existed through a depression, suffered through national elections, have been cursed and caressed, bemoaned and blessed. But I still have two million-dollar eyes, a pair of million-dollar ears, a three-million-dollar stomach, a five-million-dollar appetite and a wonderful God on whom I can rely.

By the way, how's your heart today?

HOW OLD ARE YOU?

The question of age is a touchy one. We all seem to want to appear younger than we actually are. There is a universal desire among us to stay young.

Who among us is old? The writer of the Book of Ecclesiastes vividly described old age when he said, "They shall be afraid of that which is high." Who among us is young? Jesus perfectly reflected the spirit of youth when he said, "All things are possible with God." Do you see the contrast? Old age sets in when we become fearful of that which is beyond us. Youth sees the distant horizon as unlimited.

The sign of advancing age is not so much the "accumulation of years as the acquisition of fears; not particularly the deepening of the lines of care but the deepening of the lines of prejudice; not so much a matter of gray locks as gray looks." Youth believes the unconquered can be conquered, the unattainable can be attained. Old age reverses the process. Youth marches up the hitherto unscaled peak, believing the summit can be reached; old age retreats down the mountainside, assured that the top will forever elude him. "They shall be afraid of that which is high."

If we really want to find out how old we are we can examine our attitudes toward life's unsolved problems and unanswered questions. If we are afraid of things which are high, fearful that a warless world is impossible, fearful that economic justice is unattainable, fearful that racial feeling can never become less bitter, then we are approaching old age. But if we still dare to hope, prepare ourselves for the steep climb, believing that all things are possible with God, then we can be numbered among the world's youth.

We frequently hear it said that such and such a person will never grow old. The reason is because life, to some people, is always prospect, never retrospect. Too busy to look back, they look forward for more worlds to conquer. George W. Carver, Negro scientist, made numerous new discoveries concerning the peanut and sweet potato after he was eighty years old. Benjamin Franklin went as ambassador to France to gain recognition of the struggling American colonies when he was seventy years of age. Titian, Italian painter, produced his immortal "Christ of Pity" at the age of ninety-nine years. These people were not afraid of that which is high. They believed in attaining the unattainable.

42

The spirit of youth should be the characteristic of all Christian living. Jesus made His appeal to those who sought to do the impossible. We need not be unmindful of the forces of evil. But we must believe that good men, marching under the banners of God, can overcome them. Christian people will not lose their faith in the achievement of the unachieved.

Death may come slowly or it may come with a pounce, but whether it's slow or spry, when it catches up with us we should still be pressing on toward the high calling of God. This spirit will keep us forever young. And the world needs more young people of all ages.

I AM AN AMERICAN

You don't have to circle the globe more than once to realize it's rather important to you that you were born in America. For this you can thank your lucky stars, because, since your parents got here first, you had nothing to do with your birthplace.

We Americans display two types of pride. One is the false, egotistical pride people have who strut around before others, making a show of their power, their money, and their contemptible superior attitudes. This pride gets us into trouble. A few of our citizens who travel abroad have such egotistical airs about them that everywhere they go they lose friends for the United States.

There is another type of pride, born of a humility that is highly commendable. We should be proud we live in a country in which there is freedom of speech, freedom of worship, and freedom of political expression. We must never take this great heritage for granted. We should thank God for it, use it, defend it, preserve it for our children. We should remember that every heritage of a free democracy carries with it a great responsibility.

What makes for good American citizenship? We are not good citizens simply because we were born here. Thousands of our lawbreakers, murderers, dope peddlers, rapists, and swindlers were born here but are certainly not good citizens. On the other hand, that great Justice of the Supreme Court, Benjamin Cardozo, who interpreted our Constitution to others, was a foreign-born Jew.

Nor are we good citizens because we belong to a particular race. Among the 164 million citizens of the United States there are innumerable blood strains which converge in the common stream of American life. We have here 80 million Anglo-Saxons, 20 million Teutons, 15 million Negroes, 12 million Irish, 11 million Slavs, 6 million Jews, 3 million Greeks, and a liberal sprinkling of Italians, French, Poles, Lithuanians, Orientals, and Indians. With our racial groups you can find some of our best, as well as some of our worst citizens. Racial heritage, it seems, has little to do with good citizenship.

By the same token, we are not good citizens because of a particular religious affiliation. In our system of free worship there are some 53 million Protestants, 26 million Roman Catholics, 6 million Jews, 2 million Greek Orthodox, 3 million Episcopalians, half a million Christian Scientists, half a million Mormons, and so forth. But Americanism is not simply a particular religious affiliation.

Americanism is not a process of mechanics, such as the accident of birth or religious affiliation. Americanism, in its true sense, is of the spirit. It means freedom for yourself—economic, social, political, religious. It means sharing the convictions of the writers of the Declaration of Independence when they said: "We hold these truths to be self-evident; that all men are created equal; that they are endowed by their creator with certain inalienable rights; that, among these, are life, liberty and the pursuit of happiness. That . . . governments derive their just powers from the consent of the governed." These sentences are among the greatest ever penned by men. Could you imagine the men in the Kremlin writing them? Americanism is not hamburgers or cokes or popcorn. Americanism is the spirit of Jefferson and Franklin and Hancock living in the hearts of men today.

This great heritage of American freedom, however, is neither ours to squander nor selfishly to enjoy. It is ours to propagate. If we seek freedom for ourselves, as good citizens we should seek freedom for all our fellow Americans, freedom for all freedom-loving people

45

everywhere. It is axiomatic, that if we deny freedom to others we will ultimately lose it for ourselves.

I am humbly proud that I am an American. The true spirit of America is a process—a process of maximum freedom of the individual within society. It is a procession of men who lived and died because they believed in it. I am proud to be a part of that procession.

INCUBATOR CHICKS

When I was a boy on the farm I was impressed by the solicitous care of the mother hen for her chicks. She would start out early in the morning and scratch her toenails down to the cuticle in order to provide food for them. When she found a juicy worm she would break it up into small bits and call all the chicks in for their share of the tender morsel. She kept both eyes open for possible danger and would issue a warning cry when she heard an unusual noise or when a chick strayed too far. If a hawk approached, she would call the biddies in, spread her wings to cover them, and frighten the hawk away. At noontime she insisted that the chicks take their afternoon nap. And at night she shared her body to keep them safe and warm. I could not help but feel that the maternal instinct went all the way down in the lowly Rhode Island Red.

In a machine age it's to be expected that the do-

mestic life of a fowl should experience quite an up-
heaval. The home-grown chick, like its cousin the dodo
bird, is as rare as pickled pigs' feet. Mother hen, reading
the "sign of progress," has given way to the mechanical
incubator. Above the cackle of the barnyard you can
hear the old refrain, "Times aren't what they used to
be." Millions of adolescent chicks never see their
mothers from the shell to the skillet. If there's an un-
broken family circle in heaven I can imagine the chaos
that reigns in the poultry corner.

From the increase in juvenile delinquency it looks
as if, so far as the human family is concerned, we have
entered the incubator age. There are far too many
"doorkey kids" who never see their parents in daylight.
Home is Flat No. 127J, where human chicks get bed and
breakfast only. Too often home is simply a paint shop
for women and a filling station for men. It is a place to
go when there's no place to go, a place for Girl Scouts
to pursue their hobbies pending mother's arrival from
the hobby lobby, while the Boy Scouts are tracking
down father. There are entirely too many incubator
adolescents, too few home-grown.

Young people are as good or as bad as is their parents' concern or lack of concern for them. They need
someone to teach them, by precept and example, how
to scratch for themselves, how to develop independence and resourcefulness. They need someone to warn
them of danger, someone to protect them, share the
warmth of life's experiences with them.

A father who takes time to talk to his son about
his school problems, his love life, his plans for the fu-

47

ture, is doing himself and his son a favor. If the father plays golf with his son, worships with him in family worship, goes fishing with him, he is spending the best years of his life where they count most. A mother who takes time to share her life sympathetically with her daughter will reap rich rewards.

Above all, young people need to be loved. A frail, maladjusted child at an orphanage was making no progress whatever. The psychiatrist said to a nurse, "Take this child as your very own and give her all the love that you have." The child showed immediate improvement.

Incubator chickens don't get sentimental over a piece of tin. Nor do adolescents fall in love with a roof and four walls. They respond only to the environment of a home where love abides.

IN SPITE OF ——

Among the four hundred Freshmen who enrolled in the university when I was a student was a blind boy. When he was five years old, he was cutting a rope from the neck of his dog when the knife slipped and the point struck him in an eye. He lost the other eye too, as a result, and was left in a world of total blindness. What did he do—get a monkey and a cup and start begging? Not that boy. He went to Austin, Texas, enrolled in the school for the blind and graduated with a high school diploma at the age of sixteen. Having a wonderfull ear for music, he learned to play with considerable skill, the piano, saxophone and clarinet.

At the university, his fellow students read the lessons aloud to him and, because of his remarkable memory, he never missed a word. He learned his way around the campus better than most men with sight. When he marched across the platform to receive his degree, he received a mighty ovation from the student body. He is now president of the Arkansas Lighthouse for the Blind, a $300,000 institution that gives employment to one hundred sightless persons. He has marvelously achieved, in spite of—.

Some men achieve because of favorable circumstances. Others achieve in spite of unfavorable circumstances. Real heroism is usually found in the latter category.

In a hospital for crippled children in Philadelphia was a woman physician who practiced from a wheelchair. As a child, Dr. Mary McCracken was badly crippled by infantile paralysis. She wanted to study medicine, but the colleges in America would not admit her. Undaunted, she went to China and took her degree in medicine at the University of Peking. She returned to her native city and for years was staff physician at a famous children's hospital. This was great achievement, in spite of—.

Robert Louis Stevenson, man of letters, once wrote, "For fourteen years I have not had a day's real health; I have awakened sick and gone to bed weary, and have done my work unflinchingly. I have written in bed and out of it—written when my head swam from weakness. I was made for a contest and the powers have so willed that my battlefield should be this dingy, inglorious one of the bed and the medicine bottle." Here is history's record of great achievement, in spite of—.

We Americans, in spite of our favored position, quite early develop a disposition to fret and complain. We point our accusing fingers at the government, unfavorable circumstances, bad luck, and betrayal by friends. We are sure these external situations are the cause of our difficulties. But when you point an accusing finger at another, remember that there are three fingers pointing back at you!

Our world is filled with plenty of difficulties. But what kind of life would you have if there were no difficulties to overcome, no mountains to climb? Tall mountains make sturdy legs. Heavy wind resistance lifts the heavy air cargo. Difficulties make heroes. They are the stones on which you can climb. I have a feeling that this is a great day for people who ask no favors and fear no roads—for people who will achieve, in spite of—!

JONAH AND THE WHALE

Some people think of the Old Testament story of Jonah and the whale as a joke. The fact is, the Book of Jonah is one of the great books of the Bible. It is a story of a man who ran away from God, suffered as a result, repented and returned to do God's will. "The word of the Lord came to Jonah . . . saying . . . arise, go to Nineveh . . . but Jonah rose to flee to Tarshish, from the presence of the Lord."

There are two cities on every man's highway. One is Nineveh, the city of duty, responsibility, God. The other is Tarshish, the city of selfish irresponsibility and godlessness. Since we all seem to be going somewhere, we are moving directly or indirectly toward one of these two cities.

Jonah, like a lot of his modern contemporaries, determined to flee from God and bought a boat ticket to Tarshish across the Mediterranean sea. His ticket, like all other tickets leading away from God, had some interesting notations on it. Let's look at some of them.

The first notation was: NONTRANSFERABLE. Men fleeing from the presence of the Lord pay their own fare. We seek to place responsibility for our moral failures on our heredity, our environment, our work— anywhere but on our own shoulders. But if we look at life objectively we realize that every man is responsible for his own conduct. Shakespeare had one of his characters say, "The fault, dear Brutus, is not in our stars, but in ourselves. . . ."

The second notation on Jonah's ticket was: GOOD ON THE FOLLOWING LINES. There are many roads that lead to Tarshish, away from God. The trunk lines labeled "lust of the flesh," "selfishness," "hate," and "indifference," all wind up in the popular resort city. Keep on these roads and you will ultimately land in Tarshish, city of godlessness.

A third notation was: DEDUCTIONS FOR THE WHOLE FAMILY. Even the airplane companies offer reduced rates for the family outing. Have you not seen fathers whose irreligious influence on the family has led mother, son, and daughter away from God? The saddest picture being painted in the modern drama of life is of a father who, by precept and example, leads his innocent children away from the good life.

A final notation on Jonah's ticket was: ONE WAY ONLY. Men can go to Tarshish by running from God, but they will never arrive at Nineveh by continuing in this direction. Jonah found this out. Men who flee the presence of God suffer. Thus Jonah landed on the inside of a whale. In such a position he thought his time had come. There were no light switches, the floor must have been extremely difficult to walk on, the air must have been stale, and Jonah could never be sure of the habits of a whale.

But the whale could not stomach such a culprit

52

as Jonah, so he delivered Jonah on land. Jonah was so frightened that he didn't even thank the whale for the free ride. He hit the land, running toward Nineveh. Tradition has it that Jonah was invited to lunch at the home of a friend on the road. "We have fish for dinner," the friend said. "No more fish for me as long as I live!" and Jonah kept on going to Nineveh. And in Nineveh, the city of God, he wrought a mighty work.

KEEP YOUR TEMPER

One of the things I admire about football, which is a rough-and-tumble affair, is the way most players have of keeping their tempers. It would be great if we could do half as well in the larger game of life. Of course, life is much more than a game, though our winning or losing is not much more important to us than is football to the boy who plays it. What is of supreme importance is the spirit in which we play, and the first lesson we should learn is not to lose our tempers.

When a man loses his temper he loses something else at the same time. For one thing, he loses his sense of balance. There is no poise, no sense of proportion, no mental equilibrium about us when, for the time being, we lose our tempers. We become both unfair in our judgments and reckless in our words. If a football player loses his temper, at that moment he begins to play poorly. How can he properly execute a play when he has lost his head? If a boxer loses his temper, he becomes an easy prey for his opponent; sometimes almost loses his head literally as well as figuratively. Loss of temper means loss of efficiency. And in an age when efficiency counts for so much we should be as careful to keep our tempers as we are careful to keep our car keys. The loss of either puts us at great disadvantage.

Loss of temper means loss of dignity. Loss of one's temper produces, for the moment, a sense of mental exhilaration, a feeling of superiority, an intoxicating idea that one is the sort who can't be pushed around. But this is pure illusion. One really looks and sounds like a little child who has a way of shouting and screaming until he gets what he wants. The sight of a man who is temporarily "beside himself" is a rather pitiful sight; but the sight of a man who is under great pressure, yet in quiet command of himself, is one we like to remember.

Loss of temper usually means loss of friends. Friendships are sometimes broken by silence or forgetfulness. They are more often broken by temper tantrums. In such situations one always says what he really does not mean and someone is deeply hurt. A man in a rage can destroy a friendship he has taken a quarter of a century to build. If apologies follow, it does not completely repair the damage. The open wound may heal, but the scar remains.

What shall we do about our tempers? Keep them under control. Every man has enough minor irritations to "blow his top" every morning before breakfast if he refuses to control himself. If irritating thoughts come to your mind seeking expression through sharp words and violent acts, steady yourself. You will be surprised how one victory can lead to another. Sooner than you think, you can develop the habit of meeting the most irritating situations with absolute calmness.

Keep your temper! Nobody else needs it!

LEFT-HANDED SOLDIERS

". . . there were 700 chosen men, left-handed; everyone could sling stones at an hair breadth, and not miss." This strange story, recorded in the Book of Judges, is of more than passing interest.

Who were these 700 left-handed soldiers? They were soldiers who, in the 14th century B.C., had fought with swords and shields, the swords on their right arms and the shields on their left. But they had been wounded on their right or fighting arms, had abandoned their swords and shields, and had mastered the art of the slingshot with their left arms. The result was that they were among the best fighting men in the army. Long before the enemies came near them they could lay them low with a well-aimed stone in the temple.

These men did what some of us never do. *They faced their handicaps.* They acknowledged that their right, or fighting, arms were useless. To have sought to

55

do battle with the sword and a wounded right arm would have been suicide. They recognized this, and recognition of one's handicap is the first step toward overcoming it.

Some of us are not so wise. We do not like to take a long, objective look at ourselves. We prefer to throw a smoke screen around our weaknesses, cover them up, refuse to acknowledge them. We can never handle handicaps well unless we admit we have them. A person who refuses to admit his ignorance will never learn. Charles Darwin had extremely delicate health. Had he sought to use his body as though he were perfectly healthy he would have killed himself. Facing his handicap, he chose science and changed the scientific thinking of his generation.

Not only did these soldiers face their handicaps; *they overcame them*. They changed their weapons from sword to sling. Think how awkward this must have been. The number of hours these men had to practice the art of precision with the left hand must have been almost incredible.

There are just two things any of us can do with our handicaps. We can supinely submit to them, or we can superbly surmount them! Teddy Roosevelt was handicapped from birth with a weak body. By surmounting his difficulty he became a Rough Rider. George W. Carver was born a Negro slave. But he died a great scientist. Between these two sentences is an almost incredible record of the heroic handling of handicaps.

These soldiers not only overcame their handicaps,

they made their handicaps contribute to their bless-ing. They turned their disadvantages into advantages, their stumbling-blocks into steppingstones. They could fell the enemy a hundred yards away and thus avoid the danger of hand-to-hand fighting. It could be that Bee-thoven was a great musician, not in spite of his deaf-ness, but because of it. It could be that Milton was a great poet, not in spite of his blindness, but because of it. At any rate, history records that life's greatest battles are won by left-handed soliders—soldiers who keep the fighting spirit in spite of handicaps.

MARGINS

Millions of dollars are spent by book publishers to provide the margins on the pages. Approximately one-third of the average book page has no printed matter on it whatever; that third constitutes the margin.

But the margins are by no means useless. Pub-lishers know that unless they devote a third of the page to good margins, there is a good chance that the re-maining two-thirds of the page will not be read. Try reading a book with the margins covered up and see how difficult it is.

Good margins are like good manners. As the page is made attractive by good margins, so is one made attractive by good manners. Margins and manners are the extras of life which make for more attractiveness.

One day I stepped into a crowded elevator. The attractive young lady operator said, "Ladies and gentlemen, floors please." An unpleasingly plump gentleman, whose left heel was on my little toe, grunted, "Seven." "Thank you, sir," the operator said. When Mr. Jumbo was safely delivered to the seventh level the operator said, "Good day, sir." As the door closed, I scanned the faces of my ascending fellow passengers. They were wreathed in smiles. The courteous manner of the operator was contagious.

On my lunch hour I went to a department store to buy a fifty-cent pocket handkerchief. After the gracious clerk had shown me some fifty-seven varieties, ranging in color from azure blue to bilious "burple," I grumbled something about wanting a certain shade of pink (to match my physical condition). Since this was the only shade she didn't have, my sales resistance mechanism being in perfect working order, I started away. She said, "Thank you, sir, it has been a pleasure to serve you." That did it! I turned around, and bought a dozen bilious "burple" hankies I suppose I'll never use. Her courtesy paid off. I'm not even a sir—according to the English tradition—but I appreciate being overrated. There's no harm in calling a sergeant a major general.

Good manners cost so little, but are worth so much, not simply in terms of money but in happy human relationships. Many a man is wondering why he didn't get a promotion, when his bearish treatment of his subordinates is telling a great deal about the kind of man he really is. The man who rushes ahead in city traffic, goes to the front of the line, steps around others to board the bus, interrupts when others are speaking, ought to know why he cannot get ahead in his business organization. Manners betray the man.

I have known a few men who were regular lions at a party among strangers, but were skunks at home. They would dive twenty feet to retrieve a falling hankie for a strange woman, but wouldn't help their wives put on their coats. To balance the scales I hasten to say that I have known women who turned on all their charms for strange men but acted like spoiled brats before their husbands.

Southern chivalry may not be dead, but it is becoming more anemic daily. Good manners, like good margins, are the extras which make for attractiveness. By the way, how are the margins in your book?

MAKING MARRIAGE MEANINGFUL

The question uppermost in the minds of young people contemplating matrimony is, "How can we make our marriage pre-eminently successful?" Practically without exception, all young people expect their marriage to succeed. Why are there so many failures? Perhaps it is because many people think of the marriage vow and the wedding day as the end rather than the beginning. This is self-evident: the vast majority of marriages can be made to succeed. A happy marital relation is the basis upon which all other happiness depends. No matter what it costs to make a marriage succeed, it is well worth the price.

Happy marital relations involve four distinct unions of personality.

Marriage involves physical union, the most intimate physical union known to man. Young people are at first physically attracted to each other. Romance plays its part, and should. Keep romance in your marital relationship. Never let it be said that the days of romance are over. Tell your wife she is beautiful; tell your husband he is handsome. (A white lie here won't hurt.) There is nothing that brightens the day and lightens the load like the words of flattery. Speak them! Too often husbands and wives are literally starved for words of affection that should come freely from their partners. Furthermore, husbands and wives have a responsibility to keep themselves physically attractive to each other. You want your marriage to succeed? Keep on courting, keep romance alive.

Marriage involves mental union. It is a union of two minds in the solution of the common problems of the home. Let all the issues of the day be openly discussed. Take each other into confidence. Read books together. Discuss world issues together. Develop dependence on each other's judgment. Discuss money matters together. Plan the family budget together. Interest yourselves in the problems of each other. The wife should know enough of the husband's affairs to discuss them with him intelligently. The husband should interest himself in the affairs of his wife. Let marriage be the place of the merging of two minds.

Marriage involves social union. It is a sad day when a husband seeks hours of social recreation apart from his wife. The more things couples can do socially together, the stronger the marriage becomes. If both are interested in golf, let them play together. If it's baseball, let them enjoy it together. "The family that plays together stays together." Some time ago an explosion occurred in an American home. Both husband and wife were blown several yards away. After the wife collected herself, she pulled herself over to her husband and said, "I'm glad it happened. This is the first time we have been out together in years." That goes for a lot of homes.

Marriage, finally, involves spiritual union, union of ideals, united goals in life. It has been proven by statistics that the marriage of religious persons who daily demonstrate their faith in God by prayer, who identify themselves with a church, has nine times as many chances to be a successful marriage as has the marriage of persons with no religious faith. There are very few marital difficulties today that cannot be solved at a family altar. You don't believe it? Just try it!

MARKS OF AN EDUCATED MAN

What are the marks of an educated man?

First, he keeps his mind open on all issues until all the evidence is in. He never jumps at conclusions, never makes premature judgments on a basis of partial evidence.

We can best observe this rule by asking ourselves the following questions: (a) Do I really want to know the truth or do I want to prove that my preconceived notions are right? (b) When I am confronted with new facts am I willing to lay aside my convictions long enough to find out if those facts should change my viewpoint? (c) Have I ever, without prejudice, surrendered my mind completely to examination of the reasons for my most cherished opinions?

It is a great day when a man surrenders his life to the truth. This was the miracle that happened to Columbus when he discovered America, to Galileo when he invented the telescope, to Edison when he invented the incandescent lamp, to the Wright brothers when they invented the airplane. There are some people who are open-minded, others whose minds are closed. Only the open-minded learn the truth.

Second, an educated man listens to the man who knows. Did you ever notice how well-informed people do a lot of listening and a minimum of talking? Smart people are humble in the presence of the unknown. Copernicus, humble in the presence of the heavenly bodies, discovered that the earth moves around the sun. Young Lincoln, devouring the simple books that came to his hand, soon became a master with words. Only those who listen, learn.

A charming young college sophomore was seated at a social function near a venerable astronomer. To make conversation she asked, "What are your interests?" The venerable gentleman replied, "I study astronomy." "Astronomy," cried the sophomore, "I finished astronomy last year." Imagine anyone finishing astronomy!

Third, an educated man knows the value of good habits and how to form them. He disciplines his body, mind and spirit in such a way that they automatically do his bidding. His habits of work, health, play, and study are so firmly set that they assist him in all he does. All the forces of his life, working together, give him the greatest habit of all, the habit of success.

Fourth, the educated man looks ahead. He plans well the course of his future. It is not hard times that wreck businesses; it is failure to call in expert advice at the proper time. "It is not surgery that kills people," said Dr. William Mayo, "but delayed surgery." Intelligent men plan wisely for the future.

Fifth, the educated man is aware of the Unseen. He sees the unseen qualities of life in those about him —courage, virtue, devotion. He is aware of the fact that the greatest values are not material but spiritual. He recognizes that the essence of all education is that which gives life its meaning and purpose. He seeks to relate himself harmoniously to the whole of his environment—including God.

METHUSELAH

All you have to do to get your name in the paper is to grab firm hold on life and stay with it for one hundred years. If you have never before had your name in the paper, not even in the "I will not be responsible for any debts other than my own" section, you will get a good write-up, possibly your picture, if you live to be one hundred.

An old man in the Arkansas Ozarks lived to be one hundred, and the newspapers sent a reporter and photographer around for an interview and a picture. The old man attributed his long life to the fact that he had never tasted coffee, never smoked, never played golf, never argued with his wife, and had always gone to bed at 7 o'clock. Why he wanted to live to be one hundred under these circumstances I don't know, but that's what the record said.

The man who has the record for longevity, so far as I know, was a man named Methuselah. The Book of Genesis says that he lived 969 years. I do not like to speak disparagingly of the dead, but I don't have too much respect for him. If in all that time he ever did anything worth while, no one got around to mentioning it. His whole biography is crowded into one sentence: "And the days of Methuselah were nine hundred and sixty-nine years, and he died." That's about all a man could do, isn't it? After 969 years he just hauled off and died. He didn't write any books, compose any songs or poetry, discover, or invent anything, help any worthy causes or persons. He just vegetated.

My mind wanders at times, and one day I got to wondering just how much food the old man ate during his lifetime. It must have been several trainloads. If he went to as many church suppers as I have gone to, I wonder how much meat loaf he consumed. Someone said if all the meat loaf he had ever eaten were laid end to end he would let it lie there! And I can understand that. I wonder how many pairs of pants Methuselah wore out. If he sat around for all that time I have a pretty good idea just where he wore them out. They didn't have social security in those days, or he would have bankrupted the government. Imagine carrying a man like that on the government payroll for 904 years!

No telling how long Methuselah would have lived had he died a natural death. You see, he was killed in an accident. He was living with his grandson, Noah, and when God told Noah to build the ark He didn't tell him to bring his grandfather in out of the rain. So Methuselah drowned.

In sharp contrast to this long life of apparent uselessness, consider the life of Jesus—only thirty-three years. I have never seen a biography of Methuselah, but the libraries of the world are filled with volumes of great literature concerning the matchless Man of Galilee. He split the calendar into B.C. and A.D., and put church spires in the skylines of most of the cities and hamlets of the world.

The poet had it right: We live in deeds, not days. It's not how long you live that matters. It's what you live for.

MODERN MIRACLES

One summer my wife and I spent several days in a picturesque French village at the foot of magnificent Mont Blanc in the Alps. It is called Mont Blanc because its lofty summit is heavily crowned with snow. Because of the low hanging clouds in this region, one seldom gets a glimpse of its peak.

One afternoon, while feasting my eyes on the lavish displays of nature, I saw a miracle being performed immediately before my eyes. The clouds were rather light that afternoon, and through a rift I saw a shaft of sunlight dropping down on a stagnant pool of water near a riding stable. This water was dirty and filthy, but the rays of the sun seemed to be lifting it toward the sky to form more clouds. These new clouds were driven by the wind to hover over Mont Blanc's summit and shroud it in darkness. Then a fresh wind drove the clouds away, and for the first time in days we could see the beautiful snow-capped summit of the majestic mountain. The new mantle of snow glistening in the sunlight was almost blinding to the eyes.

Here was a modern miracle that God was performing before my eyes. The stagnant, dirty, germ-filled water had been lifted from the earth, suspended in the air, transformed into beautiful pure white snowflakes and transported to the summit of the mountain.

Skeptics insist that the days of miracles are over. Well, they are over for the man who believes they are, for the man who is so blinded by his own prejudice that he refuses to see. But every blade of grass is a miracle fresh from God. No scientist has ever been able to take a little hydrogen, oxygen, and nitrogen, mix them together, and come out with a blade of grass. It takes the resources of God and a whole universe to grow a blade of grass.

The human body is a miracle. The more we know about it, the more we realize how little we know about it. As soon as we pull back one curtain of darkness we find two more even more baffling. How two infinitely small cells can unite to form this intricate thinking machine called the human body is more than we can understand.

Sometimes, however, we overlook the fact that the greatest miracles are not in the realm of nature or of human nature. They are in the realm of the spirit. I knew a young man who, two years ago, had confessed that he had committed almost every sin known to man. But something profoundly important happened to him which changed his thought patterns, his actions, his habits, his character. Today you would hardly recognize him as the same man. Something changed him. Or, more realistically, Someone changed him.

If God can transform germ-filled drops of water into pure snowflakes; if, through the moonlight, He can transform the wayside puddle into a silver mirror, can He not cleanse and transform the lives of men? It happens every day. It can happen to you!

OF WHAT USE IS RELIGION?

Years ago there was a sign on the walls around the Kremlin in Moscow reading, "Religion is the Opiate of the People." What is the use of religion? Many people seem to get along well without it. Many who profess to be very religious are narrow-minded and bigoted. Of what value is a real religious faith?

In the first place, religion gives meaning and value to life. Here is what some who have no religious faith say about life: "Life is a disease, and the only sure cure is death." "Life is the jail sentence you get for the crime of being born." Clarence Darrow, American jurist of the last generation, said, "The outstanding fact I have learned is the futility of all life. The sooner a young man jumps out a skyscraper window, the better." (Darrow himself lived to a ripe old age.)

The religious man thinks of life, not as futility but as opportunity. He holds a high opinion of himself and his fellow men. The chief contribution of Christianity has been on the side of child labor laws, human justice, the inalienable rights of men. For this reason missionaries have gone to the disenfranchised people of the world. For this reason the Church has built schools, established hospitals, fought evils that weaken, maim, and destroy life. To the religious man, all men are of the handiwork of God, all are of supreme value. Jesus said the cattle on a thousand hills were not as important as a nameless little child.

A second thing religion does: it gives courage to carry on. Of all the needs of man, the greatest need is for personal courage. Here is a man of middle age, with heavy family responsibilities, who loses the savings of a lifetime. But, with chin up and no bitterness of heart, he digs in and starts over again. Why? His religious faith enters in and gives him new courage to carry on. Here is a young widow with two small children, without financial resources. It looks as though life has played a huge joke on her. But she rolls up her sleeves and starts to work, makes a good living for her family, becomes a wonderful mother to her children. That which helped her most was her realistic religious faith.

Some time ago a young soldier who had been a prisoner of the Communists for three years spoke in our city. In substance, this is what he said, "Amid short rations and hard work, people were dying all about me every day. I noticed that those without a deep religious faith gave up first and thus died first. Most of those with a will to live because of real faith in God pulled through. I know the only thing that kept me alive was my faith in God."

A final thing religion does: it gives a man grounds for a new start. You feel the need of a fresh start? That's the heart of religion itself—seeking to get men to get hold of themselves and make a new start in life.

In one of his books, Dr. A. J. Cronin tells of an experience when he was in charge of a small hospital. He had performed a delicate operation on a small boy and gave orders to the nurse to care for him through the night. About midnight the doctor was called, found the boy worse. In spite of all he could do, the boy died. The nurse had become frightened and had neglected to do her duty. Dr. Cronin wrote the nurse a letter of dismissal, read it to her. Having heard the letter, the nurse remained silent.

"Have you nothing to say?" asked the doctor.

"Give me another chance," pleaded the nurse. That's just what God does!

ONE LONELY MAN

The most significant thing about Jesus was that He was born a normal baby, grew up a normal child and lived, until His crucifixion, a normal individual. He was different to be sure (sinless) but the striking thing about Him was that he was so much like us. When God wanted to influence the world He didn't appoint a committee, pass a few laws, shake the stars, or send an earthquake. He simply sent one lonely man to live among us.

James Francis said of Him:

He never wrote a book. He never held an office. He never owned a home. He never went to college. He never traveled two hundred miles from where he was born. He had no credentials but Himself. Yet all the armies that ever marched, all the navies that were ever built, all the parliaments that ever sat, all the kings that ever reigned, *put together*, have not affected the life of man as powerfully as that one solitary life.

In this day of mass movements and mass production we need to recover the sense of the value of the individual. Someone went to the trouble of finding out that it took 70,276 drops of water to fill a gallon bucket. But when the container was full he had a bucket full of water instead of a bucket full of drops. Each drop lost its individuality in the mass. Too often the individual loses himself in society, assumes that he doesn't count, that he is only a drop in the bucket. Auguste Comte said, "Humanity alone is real; the individual is an abstraction." But this is not so! The individual is important.

We express our influence as persons. That influence can be for either good or evil. Someone is either better or worse by the way we live. We are a hero or a heroine to someone somewhere. There are no blanks in the social order. We either lift the standards of life

71

or we lower them by the way we live. Every person is important.

We respond to human need as persons. We do not respond to world needs as masses. If it is to help polio victims, war orphans, or an unfortunate family whose home has burned, we make our response as individuals. Furthermore, all reform movements have started with individuals. Behind the prison reform of the eighteenth century was John Howard of Bedford, England. Behind the movement to establish hospitals for the insane was William Tuke, a Quaker. Behind the Boy Scout movement was Sir William Baden-Powell. Back of the 4-H Clubs which have spread throughout the United States was Jesse Shambaugh of Iowa. Every worthy cause is promoted by individual response. Every man is important because he can stand for a cause that is worthy of his best.

Furthermore, only as persons can we be transmitters of moral and cultural power. Jesus said to His disciples, "Ye are the light of the world." If we do not live as we should, there will be darkness where there should be light.

In Switzerland there is a church with no lighting facilities. It was given to the small community by a well-to-do benefactor on the understanding that no lighting fixtures would ever be installed. Every person who worshiped at this church was asked to bring his own candle for the service. In the evening you can see the full beauty of the stained-glass windows depicting the life of Christ. And if a segment of the church is dark it is because some of the worshipers failed to let their lights shine.

Every man among us counts!

ON TALKING TO YOURSELF

For a number of years I thought a person who talked to himself was a mental case, destined ultimately for a psychiatric ward. But I have changed my mind. It's a good idea to get yourself in the corner and have a serious talk with yourself.

The prodigal son (Luke 15) would never have gotten out of the hog pen had he not "come to himself" and said, "How many hired servants of my father's house have bread enough and to spare, and I perish with hunger. I will arise and go to my father, and will say unto him, Father, I have sinned . . . am no more worthy to be called thy son . . . make me a hired servant . . ."

To begin with, healthy self-criticism is the best safeguard against neurosis. Our deepest psychological difficulties come when we make excuses for our failures rather than manfully shoulder responsibility for them. In a marvelous passage in "King Lear," Shakespeare has this to say, "This is the excellent foppery of the world, that we make guilty of our disasters the sun, moon and stars as if we were *villains by necessity, fools*

73

by heavenly compulsion, drunkards and adulterers by an enforced obedience of planetary influence."

Laying the blame for our moral failures on outside circumstances is a most dangerous habit. It is about time we get ourselves in a corner and face the truth, say to ourselves: You are vain, hotheaded, self-centered, stingy, etc., etc. It won't be an enjoyable half hour, but it will be both rewarding and redemptive.

By learning to talk to ourselves we can find a deadly weapon against self-pity! Young people complain about the raw deal they are getting from their elders; business men complain about the encroachments of the government; luxury-loving ladies complain because they can't spend as much money as their neighbors; elderly people complain because they aren't as spry at seventy as they were at seventeen. Everything about them seems to say, "Come and cry on me." Have a good talk with yourself and you will be ashamed to complain when you are more fortunate than millions of others.

Talking to yourself gives you self-confidence. Why is it that, among young men of equal opportunity and ability, some succeed while others fail? Is not the determining factor found in self-confidence or lack of it? Lay a plank a foot wide on the ground, and anyone who is sober can walk on it. Put it across the roof of two twenty-foot buildings and note how few people can walk it. They have lost confidence in their ability.

When a man, confronted with a difficult situation, says to himself, "I can do it," he has gone a long way to making his dream a reality. The prodigal son would have died in the hog pen had he not said to himself, "I will arise and go to my father."

Time off talking to yourself is time well spent. Try it!

OPEN DOORS

At a United States Veterans' hospital a young soldier had just been brought back from the fighting front. Though he had miraculously escaped death, he seemed to be hopelessly discouraged, even bitter. "You see, it's this way," he said as he pulled his wounded right hand from under the covers, three fingers missing, "I wanted to be a pianist and now the door is forever shut."

There's no use denying the fact that for many of us there are doors that are permanently shut. There are many people who are frustrated, disappointed, even bitter because the doors they anticipated entering have been permanently shut in their faces. But why beat our brains out against closed doors? Look around and see a few doors that are permanently open. In the Book of Revelation, John gave us this great affirmation of faith: "Behold I have set before you an open door and no man can shut it."

There is the open door of high thinking. Many of us were brought up in the school of economic adversity and heard from the lips of our fathers the phrase, "plain living and high thinking." We seem to like "high living and plain thinking" better. We have developed all kinds of synthetics, but never have I heard of anyone manufacturing a set of synthetic brains. If ever this is done, a lot of us could use them. Some people I've met seem to have missed breakfast the day brains and eggs were served.

There is no excuse for ignorance. For a dollar a man can buy a set of sixty-six books, the greatest ever written—the Bible. For two dollars a man can buy every play Shakespeare ever wrote. Master this three dollars' worth of books and you are well on the road toward being a fairly intelligent person. Two hours of study a day for ten years will give you the equal of a Ph.D. degree. Every man with normal intelligence can enter the door of high thinking if he is willing to pay the price.

There is the open door of creative achievement. In a democracy I do not believe anybody is a nobody. Everybody counts for something. There is something that you can do and do well, if you try. I have visited hospitals and sat by the bedside of attempted suicides. All said, "I'm no good. I don't count." But every man counts for something. I know a retired business man who, after sixty-five, became a Scoutmaster. He did a marvelous job. Some time ago I received a hand-painted saucer from a woman eighty-three years of age. Somewhere I read of a paralytic woman who lived near the entrance of a large factory. She learned the names of the men, smiled and waved at them from her wheel chair. When she died, the entire factory shut down for her funeral. Every man can enter the door of creative achievement if he tries.

There is the door of fellowship with Christ. He has said, "Behold, I stand at the door and knock. If any man will open the door . . . I will come in."

Holman Hunt, the artist, was displaying for the first time the picture, "Christ at the Door." Here was the Master, with lantern in hand, knocking at the door of a cottage, representing the human heart. Among those present at the exhibit was a young man who complained to the artist that he had left something out of the picture. "What have I left out, young man?" asked the artist. "There is the Christ, the door, the uplifted hand, but where is the latch?" "That's just it," said the artist, "the latch is on the inside." Christ respects the privacy of your personality. He will knock at your door, but He won't knock it down. The door leading to Him is always open.

Why cry about closed doors? Use the ones that are open!

PAGE THE PESSIMISTS

Dr. Karl Menninger, distinguished physician and psychiatrist of Topeka, Kansas, invites us to stretch our imagination a bit and suppose that a man took a movie of all the happenings on earth for the last two million years. He suggests that it would take a solid year to show the entire picture. In case anyone wanted to sleep during the showing it would be well to do so during the first eleven months and twenty-nine days since nothing of great significance was happening at that time. Man does not appear on the scene until 11:00 P.M. on the last day of the year—just one hour before the finish of the movie. Jesus Christ comes to the earth just ten minutes before midnight. Two and a half minutes before the movie is over man invents the printing press; with half a minute to go, Edison gives us electric light; with six seconds to go, the radio is invented; within the last two seconds the United Nations was formed at San Francisco, and at the stroke of midnight the first atomic bomb was dropped on Hiroshima.

Obviously, things aren't going very well with our world. We are spending a billion dollars every seven days for defense weapons against our enemies. Communism has been gaining an average of one hundred million converts a year since the close of World War II. The hope of an easy world peace has long since vanished.

From Dr. Menninger's imaginary movie, however, we see that, comparatively speaking, man has not been working on his dream of world peace very long. Only a few seconds ago Woodrow Wilson conceived the idea of the League of Nations, in which the nations of the earth would submit their grievances to a court of arbitration. It was not very effective, primarily because the United States didn't enter it. Now we have the United Nations. It hasn't done all that we would wish, but are there any other instruments more effective in averting war? If so, let's use them now!

This business of building for world peace is a very involved business. We certainly haven't been at it long enough to become discouraged to the point of forsaking interest in the avenues to arbitration. To abandon all hope of peaceful settlement means ultimate reliance on military power alone. Hitler did it—and lost. So did Napoleon—so did Alexander.

I hope I'm not a sentimental optimist, but I believe I'd rather be that than a perennial pessimist. There are millions of people who are hungry, but the economic situation is generally better today than in the days of the Roman Empire. Gibbons indicated that fewer than twenty families controlled the wealth of the world in Nero's day. Social progress has been slow but we have some gains to our credit. Women, once considered little above common slaves, are given equal, or near-equal, rights in practically every enlightened nation on earth. We still have death-dealing diseases, but we have made remarkable strides in scientific medicine. We are far from the Kingdom of God on earth, but the influence of the church in the community is probably more significant today than in any other period of Christian history.

I guess the chief reason I am an optimist is because I do not believe that man can mock God. If Napoleon, Hitler, Mussolini, and Stalin could get away with it, then God would be mocked. I can't believe it. Immorality ultimately destroys itself.

World peace may be a long time in the future. But I believe it *is* in the future. It's in the future because God is stronger than His adversaries.

PRAYING HANDS

In a famous art gallery in Europe hangs a picture entitled "Praying Hands." Behind the picture is a wonderful story I want to share with you.

In the year 1517 two young men in Nuremberg, Germany, wanted to become artists. Their parents were very poor and both young men, who lived together, had to work long hours at back-breaking jobs in order to eke out a scant livelihood. Observing that they could not make satisfactory progress in studying art at night after a long, hard day, the older of the two said to the younger: "Neither of us can become an artist this way, since we have too little time for study. Let us try another plan. One of us could make a living for both of us while the other gives full time to study. Then, when the paintings begin to sell, the one who has worked may have his chance to study."

"True," answered the younger, Albrecht Dürer, "but let me be the one to work first."

80

"No," said the older man, "I have a place to work; you have more talent, and I will work first."

So the older man had his way. Young Dürer worked faithfully at his art, while his friend scrubbed floors, washed dishes, and collected the garbage to provide food and shelter for the two of them.

At last the day came when Dürer came home with the money he had received from the sale of his first painting.

"Now," he said, "the time has come for me to be the bread winner, and you may devote your full time to the study of art."

So his good friend left his menial labors and took up his brush. But something had happened in those days during which he had worked so hard. The work had stiffened his muscles, enlarged his joints, and twisted his fingers so that he could no longer hold the brush with mastery and skill. He knew that his ability to be an artist had gone forever. When young Dürer learned what had happened he was filled with great sorrow. Returning one day unexpectedly to their little room, he heard the voice of his friend in prayer. When he saw the work-worn hands of his friend folded reverently in prayer, a great thought came to him.

"I can never give back the lost skill of those hands which have sacrificed for me. But I can paint those hands as they are now, folded in prayer, and the world will know of my appreciation for such a noble, unselfish friend. And when men look at the picture they will remember the sacrificial hands of those who have blessed them."

Dürer painted the hands as he remembered them, with broken fingernails and stiff and enlarged joints; hands that had lost their usefulness because of devoted, sacrificial love. One cannot look on "Praying Hands" without a sense of thankfulness for the visible and the invisible hands of those who have gone before, those who have blessed us because of their sacrificial love.

I wonder if our children realize that their education is due to the devoted hands of the mother who labors while they learn, the father who provides the food and clothing and seeks to meet their daily needs. Are they aware of the sacrificial labors of their teachers who pour their lives into the vital program of character education?

We Americans ought to be a thankful people. We are the best fed, best clothed, best educated, freest people on earth. These blessings are ours because of the sacrificial hands of those who went before us. Isn't it about time we stopped bewailing our fate and began counting our blessings? We need just one more organization in this overorganized age. Let's start an Order of the Thankful Heart!

PRODIGAL PARENTS

The most familiar parable in the New Testament is the parable of the Prodigal Son. I have known at least a hundred prodigal sons who have departed from the religious training of their parents and sought the fleshpots of vice and crime. But I believe I have known a thousand parents who have failed to give their children the proper training for responsible citizenship. Where I have known one prodigal son I have known ten prodigal parents.

There has been a revolution in the American home. Two global wars have resulted in a great number of physical casualties, and a greater number of moral casualties, particularly among children. The entrance of women in industry, the constant shifting of twenty per cent of the population of the United States every year, and the absence of the father from the home because of military service have had a devastating effect on the home life of America. The growth of a generation of doorkey children, children who return home from school to find the house empty, is a major cause of the increase of juvenile delinquency.

I would like to place the blame for the increase in juvenile delinquency where I think it belongs. The increased number of prodigal sons is the direct result of the increase in the number of prodigal parents. A prodigal parent is one who refuses to accept his moral responsibility for the moral life of his children. Some time ago a judge sentenced a father for refusing to provide food and clothing for his family. It is about time someone passed out a few sentences against prodigal fathers and mothers who refuse to provide for the spiritual growth of their children. The normal child needs generous helpings of examples of sobriety as well as of soup, of faith as well as of fats, of honesty as well as of ham. The home is the place where these principles should be taught.

Honesty is a way of living. A child learns the lesson of common honesty, not by parental lectures, but by the spirit of honesty in the father and mother. Virtue is a way of living. The child learns the value of virtue by example. We teach our children the value of prayer, not by the lecture method, but by getting down on our knees ourselves. If the child is allowed to grow up without benefit of the spirit of religion in the home, the fault is with the parents. This is the moral law of life: Prodigal parents produce prodigal sons.

Juvenile delinquency can be curbed if and when parents incarnate within themselves the principles of religious faith. Our children will not be convinced of the value of Christianity by argument. The only convincing testimony is Christian demonstration. A few tears of repentance from prodigal parents now are better than tears of remorse after prodigal sons wreck their lives. It is just as simple as this: There is nothing the matter with most of us that a good case of common-sense religion will not cure.

PROPER PERSPECTIVE

When Gutzon Borglum, the American sculptor, was carving the likenesses of Washington, Jefferson, Lincoln, and Roosevelt on Mount Rushmore, S. D., his greatest difficulty was lack of perspective. He was standing too close to the statue he was carving. He would work for a period of time, then dash out half a mile away and look back to see what he had done. He finally solved the problem by setting up a powerful lantern slide a half mile from the mountain, projecting the likeness of the subject on the cliff and carving where the lights and shadows indicated.

Proper perspective is tremendously important. It is the ability to see life and life's situations in focus.

We need the proper perspective of time. There is an overarching providence which helps shape the affairs of men after the purpose of the Creator God. We give up too soon because we can't see far enough. We lack the perspective of time. We are worshipers of the cult of the now. We want the job done by tomorrow noon. But things of great value never come that way. It is true that human life is far too cheap today. But it was only five thousand years ago that men began to have a sensitive conscience concerning the value of an individual. Freedom of speech and freedom of the press in many areas of the world are having a bad time of it. But we must remember there was no such thing as freedom of speech and freedom of the press three hundred years ago. There have been centuries of international conflict and we now have more war machinery now than ever before. But only in the last thirty years have men been working for world peace through international co-operation.

The point is, men of faith do not give up because these are troubled times. We have had troubled times since history began. We have had downright emergencies ever since I was born. (I hope there's no connection.) Men of faith view life from God's perspective. "And God fainteth not."

We need a proper perspective of the continuing quality of human goodness. Oh, yes, I read the papers; I see results of crime in high places and low. But I cannot conclude that everyone in the world is rotten. It may be popular to lose faith in men, but it is neither factual nor Christian. Someone recently conducted a survey to ascertain the amount of dishonesty in the country. After talking to hundreds of shopkeepers, taxi drivers, credit managers, newsboys, bankers, and others who deal with the public, they concluded that well over ninety-five per cent of our fellow citizens were basically honest.

There is an underlying central core of human decency which rarely gets in the headlines but is a powerful force for good. History may be written in a vindictive trail of blood, but we must not overlook the sacrificial trail of blood which good men have given for great causes. Their hopes and prayers have not been in vain. We must keep the perspective of human goodness.

We need a proper perspective of the leadership of God. James Anthony Froude, historian, said, "In the long run it is ill with the wicked; in the long run it is well with the good." It is God, not Moscow or Washington, who is ultimately going to have the last word in this fretting, fighting, fearful world. If these words are true, "In the beginning, God," this is likewise true, "In the end, God." We must retain a proper perspective of His leadership.

SILENCE, PLEASE

I was sitting in a broadcasting studio waiting to go on the air. After preliminary instructions by the studio manager, a sign flashed, "Silence, please," and then the signal to proceed. That sign, it seems, has a significance far beyond the walls of the studio.

We live and move and have our being in the noisiest world men ever have known. It is to be expected in an atomic age, since bombs are rather noisy. With the roaring of the city traffic, the backfiring of the bus, the hawking of the newsboy, the blaring of the jazz

87

band, the staccato sounds of the radio, the shriek of the siren, and the thunder of the jets above, it's a wonder our eardrums stand it.

Volumes have been written on how to win friends and influence people, how to have peace of mind, how to retire in comfort, how to be the life of the party, how to bake a cake, and how to get along with one's mother-in-law. It is about time someone made some noise on how to be quiet. They say silence is golden, but it looks like our generation has gone off the gold standard for good.

When someone who reads a book about United States foreign policy in 1929 begins to tell you all about the mistakes of the President and Secretary of State in handling foreign affairs, it is time to flash the sign, "Silence, please."

When someone launches forth on the contents of a book about which he has heard but never read, you would do the listeners a great favor if you pronounced the solemn words, "Silence, please."

When some learned gentleman and scholar is discussing, with factual evidence, the problems before us, and a prejudiced ignoramus seeks the spotlight by an irrelevant interruption, it is time for someone to say, "Silence, please."

When someone who spent a week end in Paris in 1918 tries to tell you what makes the "sick man of Europe" sick, it would be a great thing if some courageous soul said, "Silence, please."

When the conversation is about classical music and someone who doesn't know the difference between

Te Deum and "Tea for Two" insists on getting in the act, to the rescue—"Silence, please."

When some brother who was last seen at church Easter, 1941, tells you about what's wrong with the church, isn't the next order of business, "Silence, please"?

When you stand on the hill of Calvary outside the city of Jerusalem at sunrise, as I once did, and the first voice you hear is someone asking, "Anybody got a cigarette?" wouldn't it be nice if everyone knew the significance of silence?

Paschal said, "All the evils of life have fallen upon us because men will not sit alone quietly in a room." When noisy vulgar men put Jesus on the cross He was master of Himself, His temper, and His tongue because, amid the lonely hills of Galilee, He had spent nights in silent prayer.

SLEEPING THROUGH THE STORM

Years ago, the people of a small English village seeking employment were in the habit of going to the town square on Monday morning to be interviewed by prospective employers. If someone wanted his house painted, his corn harvested, or his livestock cared for, he went to the town square and engaged the workman he wanted.

One morning a farmer came seeking someone to help him with the general farm work, caring for the stock, keeping up the fences, helping in the harvest. He approached a robust young man and asked him if he thought he could qualify for the job. The young man answered every question put to him in the same manner: "I can always sleep on a stormy night." This struck the farmer as being very strange, but the man appeared otherwise normal so he was employed and put to work.

After some weeks, a storm struck in the dead of night with powerful suddenness. The rain fell in torrents and the wind blew a gale. The roar of thunder awakened the farmer and, fearing for the safety of his stock, he rushed to the attic to arouse his helper. But to the heavy knocks on the door there was no response save the steady snoring of the sleeper.

Determined to see about things himself, he hastened to the barns, where to his surprise, he found everything in order. The horses and cows were safe in their stalls. The doors and gates which, in former storms he remembered had made considerable noise, were barred securely. The chickens in the chicken house were unruffled by the storm. The windows were securely fastened and the loose piece of tin on the roof, which had been flapping for years, was nailed down securely. The hay-ricks had been so perfectly weighted down that the powerful winds did not affect them. When he returned to bed he remembered what the young workman had said the day he was employed: "I can always sleep on a stormy night."

These are days of storm, external, internal, and eternal. In the words of Marc Connelly, it seems that "everything that ain't nailed down is coming up." Happy is the man who does his work so well that he can "always sleep on a stormy night." Since we cannot avert the storms, the only sensible thing to do is to prepare for them, to do our work so thoroughly today that we shall be ready when the storm breaks.

There is the storm of physical testing. Just when we think our bodies are made of steel we find ourselves facing an unexpected operation or are victims of some disease. Our ability to pass the physical crisis may be determined largely by the preparation we made *before* the crisis.

There is the storm of financial reverses. Someone has suggested that we ought to add a 20th-century beatitude to those in the Bible: "Blessed is the man who makes a dollar and spends only 90 cents." This is no argument for hoarding, but a program of intelligent spending and saving is good sense.

There is the storm of mental testing. No man has a legitimate excuse for ignorance. If the answers are available we can find them. We can put the storehouse of truth in order so when the time comes we can be ready with the right answer.

There is the inevitable storm of temptation. If the path of the Nazarene led through the wilderness of temptation we cannot hope to escape. The most realistic fact of life is the temptation to dishonesty, immorality, inebriety. He is best able to weather tomorrow's storm who lives today according to fixed habits of honesty, purity, sobriety.

This is a good motto for any man: "I can always sleep on a stormy night."

SLOT-MACHINE RELIGION

There seems to be no end to the crackpot schemes calculated to produce economic utopias. If it isn't a Townsend Plan for "$30 every Thursday," it's a "Tom, Dick and Harry" plan for "$50 every Friday." There is one slight difficulty with these cheap economic schemes. They won't work. And, of course, we have plenty of cheap political schemes whereby cheap politicians gain office or stay in office by the simple method of inflaming the prejudices of the people. Unfortunately, cheap politics often does work, but not for long.

It was to be expected that with cheap economic theories and cheap political ideas, there would be a considerable amount of cheap religion. It is a sort of slot-machine affair; put in a few pious platitudes, or do a couple of curtsies before the Throne, and expect miraculous blessings in return.

It is a cheap slot-machine religion that is used as a means to an end rather than an end in itself. Would you like to have peace of mind? Try religion. Would you like to get along better with members of your family, with those with whom you work at the office? Religion might help. Would you like to have a healthier body, a healthier mind? Try religion. Don't misunderstand me. Religion does give peace of mind; it does provide better relationships; it does mean healthy minds in healthy bodies. But religion is not a means to anything other than the presence of God. We should seek God, not for what we can get out of Him, but for what He can get into us. We should love our earthly fathers, not to increase our allowance or inheritance, but because of our appreciation and respect for them and because they are lovable. We should love God because of our love for the things God loves. We should seek to be used of God rather than seek to use God.

Religion reduced to a magical contact rather than a mystical experience is a slot-machine affair. Why do so many people expect a special blessing simply because they have stood in a particularly sacred place, touched a sacred object, repeated some sacred words? Is not this a resort to magic? True religion is a mystical experience in which God lives in the human heart. It is in the realm of the spirit that the greatest miracles of today are happening.

It is a cheap religion that thinks of God as doing something for us rather than in us. We do not need so much to feel good as to be good. We need to be saved, not so much from the consequences of sin as from sin itself. Cheap religion seeks to manipulate God into the position of delivering us from the consequences of sin. Vital religion is personal surrender to God that He may motivate us to live above the desire to sin. Salvation is not getting God on our side; it is getting on God's side. It is not something that happens about us, but deep within us.

As a nation, we often look for salvation by law rather than by the spirit of Christ. We pledge allegiance to the Constitution which upholds demoncracy, and assume that the battle for democracy is won. We write liquor laws and assume that they make people sober. We join the United Nations and expect automatic international peace. But these are all external factors. As nations and as individuals, we are redeemed, not by the law, but by the life of God through Christ in us.

We are growing in grace when we pray fewer "give me" prayers and more "make me" prayers. "Make me clean, brotherly, whole, Christlike."

STOP, LOOK AND LISTEN

We are all familiar with the warning sign at the railroad crossing, "Stop, Look and Listen." Few of us really have considered what the sign says to us. It gives us some good advice, not only at railroad crossings but in every crossroad of life.

We are living in too big a hurry. Someone described life as an "oblong blur," quite an accurate description for some of us. We are all out of sorts if we miss the 8:10 A.M. bus, and fuss because we didn't get the first section of the revolving door. We rush madly in our cars between traffic lights only to grind the brakes to a dead stop at the intersection. What's the hurry? Like a child on a merry-go-round, we travel at a fast rate of speed, but we usually get off about where we got on.

How important it is for us to heed the sign, "Stop." The best tonic for tired nerves is a twenty-minute period of quiet meditation and relaxation. John Wanamaker, merchant of New York and Philadelphia, used to spend the first thirty minutes of every day in meditation and prayer. He said it was the thing that kept him from becoming a nervous wreck.

Creative living comes only to unhurried lives. Moses in solitude brought the Ten Commandments from the mountain tops. Jesus in solitude overcame the tempter. Victor Hugo wrote *Les Miserables* while in banishment on the lonely isle of Guernsey.

The second word of the railroad sign is likewise good advice, "Look." There are thousands of blatant advertisements and raucous voices that cry out for our attention. We must be selective in giving our attention; we can't look at everything. That which gets your attention gets you! Why not look at something beautiful every day? It's so easy to read of corruption in places high and low and finally lose faith in everything. But the whole world is not crooked! The merchants with whom I do business are not out to cheat me. My neighbors on my street are absolutely trustworthy. I find it is lots of fun to look every day for some kind deed someone does for another; some kind word of praise someone speaks in behalf of another. It keeps my faith in humanity fresh and vigorous. And if I look for something beautiful I'll always find it.

Again, the railroad sign says, "Listen." We are long on the art of being good conversationalists. A more rewarding art is that of being a good listener. Those who talk most learn least. Only those who listen, learn. Listen as someone speaks to you through the printed page of a significant book. Listen to the voices of all men of all colors and creeds throughout the world as they seek to articulate the principles of democracy. Listen to the heart beat of humanity and lend a hand. Listen to the still small voice within you, the voice of conscience, the voice of the Eternal.

Sound advice this—"Stop, Look and Listen."

THANKFUL FOR WHAT YOU HAVE

Tolstoy once told the story of a large landowner who promised one of his servants all the land he could run around between sunup and sundown. The servant was delighted with the prospects of becoming a rich man.

He set out just as soon as the sun peeped above the horizon, maintaining a fast gait westward. He ran until about ten o'clock, then turned south at a ninety degree angle. He kept the southern route until about one P.M., then he turned east. He was tiring now, and his feet were sore. But he kept doggedly on the trail. About four P.M. he turned north, hoping to make it to where he had started by sundown. His feet dripped blood, his eyes were bloodshot, his heart beat like a machine gun. Then the sun went down as, too exhausted to walk, he crawled on hands and knees in a last desperate effort to finish in time. The next morning searchers found him several miles south of his destination—dead from exhaustion.

Had he been satisfied with less he would have lived to enjoy it.

This man, however, is no isolated instance. The tragedy of most of us is that we are never satisfied with, and never grateful for, what we have. Many young business men say to themselves, "After I make my first hundred thousand I'll ease up a bit, start enjoying life." Did you ever see one satisfied after the first hundred thousand?

Some years ago I made a firm resolve to be thankful for what I have and stop bothering about what's beyond my reach. It proves to be the best resolution I ever made.

I have about 360 days of good health out of every year. I am not as young as once I was. I cannot run a mile race as once I did, and I seem to be taking the elevator more often now. But I am going to thank God every day for the good health I have.

I don't have the influential friends some people have. So far, the Hollywood and Washington hostesses haven't put me on their invitation list. I can't begin my speeches with the catchy introduction, "When I was a guest at the White House . . ." (I have offered a few prayers before the U. S. Senate, but I don't think anyone but God was listening.) I haven't walked many miles with the great or near-great, though I did "blow a couple of cups of coffee" with the late Will Rogers, and have had tea with the King of England (three thousand other Americans also were present). But I do have friends, wonderful salt-of-the-earth people, who believe in me, appreciate me in spite of my many imperfections. I am going to spend a few minutes every day thanking God for them.

I don't have a very up-to-date home, and my family isn't famous for anything I ever heard of. But I am grateful for a roof over my head, a warm fire, a devoted wife, and a worthy son. Never again will I enviously peek into my rich neighbor's house. I'll just thank God for what I have. Every day I hope to pray this little thanksgiving prayer:

> God, thou hast given much to me,
> Give me one thing more—a grateful heart.

THE CHRIST OF THE ANDES

The most beautiful plane ride I ever took was from Santiago, Chile, to Buenos Aires, Argentina. The plane rises from the 1,700 foot coastal plateau at Santi-

98

ago and in thirty minutes you are crossing the Andean hump at an elevation 23,000 feet. There are nineteen peaks in this area over 20,000 feet high, the highest being Aconcagua, 23,380 feet high. I crossed in August (South American winter) and the dazzling snow, sparkling glaciers, and frozen lakes made the view unforgettable.

Amid these high mountains runs the Chilean-Argentine border, and astride it stands the Christ of the Andes, erected by the two countries at the close of one of the many wars between them as a guarantee of eternal peace. At first the Chileans were angry because the Christ faced the Argentines. But they consoled themselves by saying that the Argentinians need watching more than the Chileans. At least, there have been no major wars since the statue was placed there.

It is at life's borderlands that we need the spirit of Christ. Consider the economic borderlands that run between the rich and the poor. On these borders class struggle, hatred and wars have their beginning. If capital and labor were willing to apply the simple principles of Christ here, the community, the nation, the world would be a much safer place in which to live. If labor sought to do an honest day's work and capital sought to give an honest day's pay, in the spirit of the Christian brotherhood, it would ease the economic tensions throughout the world.

Consider the color boundaries that separate segments of the family of mankind. Think of the bloody wars throughout human history which have been fought on this line. Where did we ever get the idea that certain people, because of certain pigmentation, are congenitally superior? Anthropologists tell us that pigmentation is determined by the relationship of our ancestors, through many generations, to the sun. In this topsy-turvy world a man whose skin is white has more doors opened to him than if his skin were black. But it's no cause for false pride. What have we done to deserve it? We didn't select our parents. If we are going to have peace on the color boundaries of the world, we must begin treating all men as men. This is what Christianity has been saying for two thousand years. Be brotherly or be bombed.

Consider the boundaries that separate us as nations. I don't know whether the United Nations will ever work or not. I see no use in arguing the point. But I do feel that if and when world peace becomes a reality, there will be some sort of international organization to which independent nations will give their support. Sixty-five quarreling men can never live at peace with each other until they mutually agree to some sort of system or law for the settlement of personal problems. If it is true of men, it is true of nations. But no agreement will work unless the spirit of the Christ operates on the national borders that separate us.

THE DEVIL'S CASH REGISTER

G. K. Chesterton, brilliant British writer, once said, "Show me the stubs in a man's checkbook and I will tell you the kind of man he is." The determining factor in character analysis is in the way a man spends his money. Acquisition determines wealth; distribution determines character.

Though Jesus lived in a day when psychiatry was unknown, He was a master psychiatrist. He was well aware of mental reactions. He put it this way: "Where your treasure is, there will your heart be also." A man's interest always follows his investment. Put your principle savings in a business venture and you may be sure your interest will be there too.

We frequently hear the phrase, "Money talks." The only thing it says to me is, "good-bye," but the way we spend our money tells a great deal about us. Money in itself is amoral, but money invested reveals the morals of the investor.

There are two cash registers in the business of life. One is the devil's cash register: it's a busy little machine these days. Investments in the devil's cash register exact a heavy toll. The interest compounds swiftly. Ten dollars for drunkenness, debauchery and degradation sets a pattern for future demands. Sin is a habit-forming disease. A ten-dollar bill can buy a wedding ring, symbol of purity, or it can buy a night of shame which destroys one's ideals forever. The most destructive force on earth is the force of money in the hands of men without character. The pages of history are crowded with the stories of men who have invested their money in the devil's cash register and thus have gone into bankruptcy of the spirit.

But in the business of life God, too, has a cash register. There is a future for men who invest in God's gilt-edge securities. J. J. Perkins, Wichita Falls, Texas, invests in the Perkins School of Theology of Dallas, and lifts the quality of ministerial effectiveness in our churches for generations. Leland Stanford invests in a great university in California and provides higher education for poor but ambitious young people on the West Coast. A. A. Hyde, mentholatum manufacturer, gives his major profits to foreign missions and gets interest on the investment decades after his death. Dr. Charles Mayo invests heavily in training promising young surgeons, and his work of healing becomes a merciful chain reaction.

Two thousand years ago a great Teacher summed it up in one sentence: "Lay not up for yourselves treasures on earth, where moth and rust consume and where thieves break in and steal, but lay up for yourselves treasures in heaven . . ." You don't have to validate your goodness by recitation of your creed or reference to your habits of piety. Just look at your checkbook.

THE GODS THAT FAIL

From the beginning of civilization there has been a conflict between the God who made us and the gods we make. Man is a worshiping animal and must have a god of some sort, either the true God or a false god of his own making. Nature abhors a vacuum, will not permit one to exist; neither can you have a vacuum in the human heart. Men don't live long without some sort of a god. Dr. Fosdick said, "A man's god is what he worships and which draws man's life together and gives it centrality and singleness of aim."

What are these false gods? When I studied comparative religions twenty-five years ago, I studied Buddhism, Hinduism, and Mohammedanism. Do any of these faiths pull men from the Christian faith today? In the twentieth century we have a new family of gods. Let's examine some of these gods men have made.

The first one is Nazism. Does anyone assume that the Nazis under Hitler were irreligious? On the surface it would seem so. They renounced the entire Christian ethic. Ludendorff said, "We renounce Christianity because it is Jewish, because it is international, because it preaches peace on earth." Hitler said, "Our task will have been accomplished when Christianity has been exterminated from the earth." But the Germans did not become godless. They scrapped Christianity and created a substitute. They put Hitler in the place of Christ, *Mein Kampf* in the place of the Bible, and love for the Fatherland in place of Christian devotion. Does anyone suppose that Fascism is dead? Is not rabid anti-Judaism, anti-Catholicism, anti-foreigner, anti-Negro, anti-capital, anti-labor, etc., but a survival of the Fascist faith?

A second contemporary idolatry is Communism. On the surface, Communism seems stupidly irreligious. Karl Marx said, "Religion is the opiate of the people." "Communism begins the moment atheism begins." But in denying God they created a false god to fill the vacuum. Communism rejects religion and proceeds to make itself a religion. Its Bible is Marx's Communist *Manifesto*. Its ruling hierarchy is the Kremlin. Its saints and martyrs are the tombs of dead communist slaughterers. Its missionaries are a dedicated priesthood trying to make converts for the Communist cause. It even has its paradise, a classless society. Communists are zealous believers in a spurious, almost inconceivably terrible, faith.

Let's go a step further. For man nationalism has become a false god. It is a survival of pre-Christian times, when every nation had its own religion. In Rome it was called Cæsar worship, and many early Christians lost their heads because they refused to worship the Roman State. Let it be said in six-foot letters: NO REAL CHRISTIAN CAN BE DISLOYAL TO HIS NATION. He will love his country best as he loves his family best. He will respect its flag and be loyal to it. But because every Christian believes in one God of all nations and all races he will never give to Cæsar that which belongs to God.

Is not materialism a god? Millions of Americans, having lost God, are trying to find secular substitutes. When we worship material success with the same zeal a saint longs for salvation, then materialism is our god.

These are false gods and betray the men who worship them. Augustine had it right. "Thou hast made us for Thyself, O God, and restless will be our hearts until they rest in Thee."

THE HEALTHY MIND

Ever so often my doctor tells me to drop by the clinic for a physical check-up. This is important; the health of the nation would be much better if periodic physical check-ups were a must on every man's calendar.

However, I would like to point out the value of a mental check-up. Surely the mind is as important as the body, since the body is largely regulated by the mind. A thought, properly employed, produces a healing effect on the body. We have only recently been hearing the term psychosomatic medicine. "Psycho" refers to the mind and "soma" refers to the body. The science of psychosomatics deals with the effect of thoughts or emotions on the physical body. Every physician knows how difficult it is to restore health to the body if the mind is motivated by unhealthy thoughts. One physician said that he would have little trouble in restoring health to most of his patients if only he could cut off their heads during convalescence.

What is healthy-mindedness? It is the development of the power of positive thinking. It is the control of the mind so that only those thoughts which are good will linger and evil thoughts be dismissed. Thousands of thoughts enter the normal mind in the course of the day. The healthy-minded person will magnify the thoughts of positive good, lift them into his consciousness, dwell on them; he will shut out the evil thoughts of fear, failure, mistrust, hate, envy, and jealousy.

The healthy-minded person will accentuate the positive good in his own life. He will underscore his blessings and leave no room for petty annoyances. I once heard of a sales manager who made a speech before his salesmen, seeking to stimulate greater production. He held up before them a large white cardboard in the center of which was a tiny black spot. Then he asked the salesmen what they saw. With one voice they said they saw a black spot. "That's just it," said the sales manager, "amid the acres and acres, comparatively speaking, of white cardboard, all you can see is a tiny black spot." That is a parable for some of us. Amid the innumerable blessings which we sometimes overlook we focus our attentions on the difficulties and imperfections about us. Someone said a poor man without shoes on his feet never thought of his blessings until he met a man without feet.

Muriel Lester, founder of Kingsley Hall, London, tells of a friend whom she regularly met on her way to work. He was stooped in shoulders and far advanced in years, but he had a radiant face and sparkling eyes. Knowing that he must be at peace with the world, she asked him the secret of his happiness. He replied, "I have had a habit of spending the first thirty minutes of each day thanking God for my blessings."

A healthy-minded person will accentuate the positive good in his world. Our world is a strange combination of dust and divinity. There is plenty of evil, to be sure, but you never see the world of reality until you see the good also. Two little girls, it is said, went out into the rose garden. One came to her mother and said, "I've been out in the rose garden, and there's a thorn for every rose." The other girl, returning from the same garden, said, "I've been out in the rose garden, and there's a rose for every thorn." They looked at the same garden. But the girl who saw roses amid thorns was more healthy-minded.

The healthy-minded person relies on the reality of the unseen. I know a man of great spiritual power who wakens every morning and says over and over to himself, "And underneath are the everlasting arms." And at night, when he surrenders himself to sleep, he says, "The Lord is my shepherd; I shall not want."

How is your mental health?

THE MEASURE OF A MAN

There are many jokes about men who die and go to heaven only to be stopped at the pearly gates by some pointed question of Saint Peter. Have you ever wondered what those questions would be like? Surely they would be profound rather than superficial. Saint Peter wouldn't be interested in our ancestry, education, size of our bank account or the organizations to which we belong. I can imagine the questions running something like this:

First, how fearless were you in the fact of manifest destiny? How well did you stick to your moral convictions? Once, in the Illinois State Legislature, a member gave a stirring address on the subject, "Put Down Lincoln." When he had finished, Lincoln arose to say, "I would rather die than change my views and, by that change, obtain office." On another occasion he cried, "You may burn my body, you may drag my soul down into the pit; but you will never get me to support what I believe to be wrong." No wonder Lincoln lost a lot of political battles; no wonder he won the most important one. In our day of cheap politics, we need statesmen who would rather die than compromise with truth.

Second, what kind of a steward of time, talent,

108

and substance were you? I can imagine that even Saint Peter is startled by the number of good people who keep 99 per cent of their substance for themselves and grudgingly give away the one per cent. The great majority of the parables of Jesus dealt with material prosperity. He said to the man who filled his barns to overflowing that he might eat, drink and be merry, "Thou fool!"

Third, how much did you really love? Jesus said the first commandment was to love God and the second was to "love thy neighbor as thyself." Let's not bother with our testimony at the prayer meeting. Let's have the record. Dr. Richard Storrs, minister of the Church of the Pilgrims in Brooklyn, was asked by a small boy to come and see his sister, who was gravely ill. Entering the wretched tenement, the minister found a sad situation indeed. A frail fifteen-year-old girl whose parents had died had sought to be bread-winner and mother to her ten-year-old brother. She had worked her fingers to the bone and now lay dying of tuberculosis as a result of malnutrition and fatigue. As the minister sought to comfort her she kept asking him, "How will God know that I belong to Him when I get to heaven?" Seeing her emaciated work-worn fingers, he replied, "Just show Him your hands."

Fourth, how did you take heartbreak and suffering? Did it break you, make a whining coward of you? Did you cry or pout because you had been mistreated? Or did you let the stones in your path become steps to higher living?

Eleven years ago, Captain Don Brown, son of

comedian Joe E. Brown, was killed when his army plane failed. What could be more tragic to a comedian than the loss of a wonderful son? At first Joe E. Brown rebelled, said there wasn't any God. Then, one day at an airport, he saw several boys in uniform with shoulder patches that indicated they belonged to Don's battalion. When Joe began to talk to them he felt that they, too, were his boys. "When you've lost your own son all the other boys become your sons." So Joe set out to amuse and entertain the whole army, both during and after the war. Joe lost his son, but opened his heart to all other sons, became a bigger man as a result.

Do not these pointed questions take a fair measure of a man?

THE POSSIBLE YOU

Once a lumberman found a nest of robin's eggs in the heart of a tree, perfectly perserved. The mother bird had made her nest in a slot of a tree trunk, but resin, on a warm day, had closed her nest and, as months passed by, the bark of the tree completely hid it. But for the closing of the nest, robins would have blessed the world with their songs. Imprisoned possibilities.

Our lives are literally filled with imprisoned possibilities, frozen Niagaras that lie dormant within the human breast. In every canvas there is a Madonna, in

110

every stone a statue, in every running brook a song, if we but have the patience to release them. Locked doors that lead to greater and more worthy achievements are ready to be thrown open—if we will knock.

Jesus was the world's greatest optimist. He saw the potentialities behind the walls of imprisoned personality. "To them gave he power to become . . ."

In the Apostle Peter he saw, not simply an impetuous, illiterate fisherman, but a flaming evangel who could preach with such power that three thousand people would be moved in one day to proclaim Christ as Lord. He saw in Mary of Magdala, not simply a beautiful face and a blackened soul, but a woman of such devotion as to be the last from the Cross and the first at the open tomb. To her he gave power to become her noblest self. He saw in Matthew much more than a tax collector for a hated foreign government. He saw a faithful disciple who would give his life rather than deny his Lord.

God has been in the business of releasing the imprisoned potentialities of men throughout history. No one on the streets of ancient Carthage would have expected much from the profligate young libertine named Francis of Assisi. But God released him from his dark prison of dissipation and he shook the world with his piety. And what of the diminutive monk with the terrible temper, Martin Luther? Yet, through Luther, God purified the Church and struck a mighty blow for religious liberty. David Livingstone was only a red-headed Scotch lad working in a cotton mill in Liverpool, England. But God saw in him a great missionary who would open a dark continent to the light of the Christian gospel. "To them gave he power to become . . ."

It is written, "The kingdom of God is within you." God is still seeking to get men to break from their prisons and become their selves—their noblest possible selves.

Couldst thou in vision see the perfect man God meant,
Thou never more wouldst be the man thou art, content.

While climbing a great cliff one day two boys found a nest of eagle eggs. They put the eggs under a hen in the barnyard, and in due time the young eagles hatched with the chicks and the mother hen cared for them as though they were her own. One day a great eagle swooped down over the barnyard and saw the young eagles on the ground. The young eagles, feeling kinship to the great eagle, tried their wings, found that they, too, could fly. Day after day the great eagle came. Day after day the young eagles tried their wings. Then one day the young eagles flew high in the air and followed the great eagle into the limitless sky, their native atmosphere.

Our native atmosphere is beyond anything we have yet attained. We have imprisoned potentialities that need to be released. Our native atmosphere is with God. We can well let go of ourselves and let God . . . "To us gave he power to become . . ."

112

THE TWO-YARD LINE

The most dangerous place on the football field is the two-yard line. It is here that most of the victories are won or lost. It is here that the strength or weakness of the team is revealed.

I have seen many teams receive the ball on their own twenty-yard line, march up the field with one first down after another, only to lose it on the two-yard line, six short feet from pay dirt.

The most dangerous place in life is on the two-yard line. It is where we almost win but actually lose.

Mark Twain and a friend were prospecting for silver high up on the side of a mountain. Water to wash the ore had to be carried from a stream down in the valley, and Mark Twain, as water carrier, had toiled for days at the dreary, discouraging task. After making many trips with the heavy pails of water without finding any silver, he rebelled, refused to carry another load. His partner's pleas were in vain.

The two tired men turned their backs on the mining claim and returned to a near-by settlement. That night a heavy rain washed the ore. A few days later other prospectors found the pan of ore washed by the rain, and in the bottom of the pan the prized grains of silver. When the law permitted them to take possession of the abandoned claim they worked for a few months and became rich as a result of their find. One more bucket of water would have washed the ore for Mark Twain. He lost a fortune on the two-yard line.

Consider the importance of the two-yard line in another area. A cub reporter on a New York daily paper, seeking a human interest story, became acquainted with a disreputable old man selling shoe strings on Skid Row in the Bowery. To his amazement, he found that the man had come from a fine home, had had every opportunity, had graduated from one of our greatest universities, and for twenty-five years had met with considerable success in his chosen profession. But he fumbled the ball on the two-yard line.

One of the finest men I ever knew was a prosperous and respected business man in a midwestern city. He was well educated, had a lovely family, was a community leader. After his children had married and established homes of their own, he diverted funds of other people to his own use, was convicted of embezzlement, and spent his sunset days in prison. He had fumbled the ball on the two-yard line.

Forty years ago, while chopping wood for the kitchen stove, my father expressed the idea when he said, "Son, it's the last lick that splits the log." The Book says, "Be thou faithful unto death . . ." Don't fumble on the two-yard line.

THE OLD VIOLIN

Some years ago I visited a lovely old couple who lived on a farm. Among the many things of interest in the living room was an old violin hanging on the wall behind the upright piano. I asked the old gentleman if he played it, and he said, "No, I haven't touched it for years. My fingers are too stiff; besides, the violin is cracked and badly out of tune.

I guess there are a lot of people whose lives are like the old violin—people who have capacity but are not using it, people with unreleased music in their souls.

That old violin was useless primarily because it was not being put to use. In his younger days, my genial host would take the violin and play all the familiar tunes of his childhood. But as the years passed, his hands became calloused, his fingers stiffened, and he was unable to play because of neglect.

Life is like that. When some of us were young we had ambitions that drove us day and night. Then we began to neglect the use of our talents and they left us. Did you once pride yourself on having a good memory? How is it now? There is practically no diminishing of the powers of memory until a person is sixty or more years of age. Why is our memory not as good at forty-five as it was at fifteen? The answer is we do not use it enough. We must keep cultivating the power of memory or suffer the loss of it. Here is one of the unwritten laws of life, "Use it or lose it."

The old violin was useless because it was damaged. It had probably fallen to the floor a few times during the years and its owner had not taken the time or trouble to fix it. What of the lives that have been damaged by corrosive, sinful habits? One day I heard of a promising young man who had lost a good job with a wonderful company. The president of the company said he had given the young man a half-dozen chances to make good, but he had muffed every one of them. His evil habits had become his master.

The old violin was useless because it was out of tune. What of the lives of men who are out of tune? The Christian faith puts a man's life in tune with his noblest self, with those about him, with his Master. Good architecture means harmonious lines. Good art includes harmony of colors. Good music involves harmonious sounds. Good religion means a life of interior and exterior harmony. When we are out of tune with ourselves, life is a cacophony rather than a symphony. When we are out of tune with other people, life is a battlefield. When we are out of tune with God, life loses its zest, its loveliness, its beauty, its purpose.

A story is told of a lonely shepherd far away from other men on the plains of Montana. He had a small radio and an old violin to keep him company. The violin slipped out of tune and the shepherd could not trust his own ear to put it in tune again. He wrote the National Broadcasting Company and asked one of the musicians to "sound A" on the radio for him. Because of the unusual request, a company official wrote him that on a certain date a musician would "sound A." The shepherd in Montana thus tuned his violin to a note in New York.

There is a far-away musician who can restore the music in our souls if we but invite Him. His name is God.

TOO MANY GODS

In a national poll some years ago 91 per cent of the people interrogated said that they believed in God. This is to be expected; we are living in a day of monotheism, belief in one God. We commonly suppose the day of polytheism, the worship of many gods, is over. I do not think so.

What is really a man's god? From the standpoint of theology, we have theists and atheists, those who believe in God and those who don't. But from the standpoint of psychology every man has a god. There are no real atheists. For a man's god is that factor in his life which he worships and serves, belongs to and cares most about, the unifying loyalty which gives a personality singleness of aim. A man's god is what he loves most. Since every man has an ultimate loyalty, every man has a god. It may be the real God or it may be a lesser god of his own design.

The Greeks and the Romans had many gods. Tacitus, Roman historian of the first century, said there were more gods in Rome than men. They had Bacchus, god of wine and revelry; Mars, god of war; Minerva, goddess of wisdom; Mercury, crafty and cunning god of commerce; Apollo and Venus, god and goddess of physical beauty; the Penates, gods of home and hearth. Even the heavenly bodies were worshiped as gods. The people had a sun god from whence we get the name Sunday. Saturn was the god of the harvest and from it we get the name Saturday. Thor was the god of thunder, from which we have Thursday.

If, from the standpoint of the psychologist, a man's god is that which he loves most, does anyone believe that polytheism is dead? Think of the multiplied thousands of people whose real god is Bacchus, god of wine and revelry. To be sure, there are no temples erected in his name. But three million hopeless alcoholics in the United States have given themselves to the worship of Bacchus with such reckless abandon as to lose body, mind, and soul. This year the American public will spend nine and one-half billion dollars for intoxicants. This means an expenditure of 26 million dollars a day, $253 for every family. Bacchus dead?

Does anyone suppose that the worship of Apollo and Venus died with the Roman empire? Look at our sensational pulp magazines, with their lavish display of feminine pulchritude. We spend more at the beauty parlors than we do for the religious education of all our American youth. Don't misunderstand me; obviously a certain amount of physical improvement is quite in order. I'm sure I look as though I could use a beauty treatment or two myself. But I've seen a lot of people coming from beauty parlors who looked as if they had not been waited on. And when we make physical adornment our primary purpose in life we worship at Apollo's ancient shrine.

What of the worship of Mars, god of war? Obviously, the deceit of our potential enemies is the chief cause of our annual expenditure of 50 billion dollars a year for weapons. But to rely on force is but to worship Mars rather than the God whose Son is the Prince of Peace.

Is not Minerva, goddess of wisdom, being worshiped by the man who feels he has no need of God or the Church? Are not the Penates, gods of home and hearth, being worshiped by the man whose religion is "just being a good father"?

This is a day of many gods. We are not actually suffering from too little religion. We are suffering from too much false religion, the worship of false gods; too little real religion, (the worship of the real God and Father of all men.)

Life is a choice between gods. Choose well the god you wish to serve because you always become like the god you worship. The choice is still between God and the gods.

119

WHAT'S RIGHT WITH
YOUNG PEOPLE?

Almost every day you will hear some oldster say, "The trouble with young people is . . ." and then he or she proceeds to give modern youth a scorching tongue lashing (*in absentia*, of course). To use a hackneyed phrase, there are two schools of thought about young people. One is that this generation of youth is about the sweetest, finest group the world ever produced, that the young people of today are ready to sprout wings from their shoulder blades. The other is that this younger generation, horns or no horns, is catapulting the world toward hell. I don't want to be contentious, but I agree with neither school. Young people today are about the same as they were when grandpap wore rompers.

While they haven't asked for it, I'd like to put in my two-cents' worth and tell you what I think is right with youth.

Modern young people are in love with life. You seldom find a surly cynic among them. They look on life as a glorious adventure and are determined to make the most of it. Feeling that they are foreordained to happiness, they throw themselves into life's experiences with boundless energy and reckless abandon.

120

While life may be filled with shadows they, like the sunflower, naturally gravitate toward the light. By and large, young people are congenital optimists, madly in love with life.

Modern young people are endowed with the wonderful quality of enthusiasm. This is a virtue which, in every generation, has removed mountains of difficulty, promoted worthy reforms, widened horizons, substituted new worlds for old. Jesus of Nazareth began His world-shaking ministry when scarcely thirty years of age. Francis of Assisi was but twenty-eight when he established the Franciscan Order and its ministries to the poor. Copernicus was thirty years old when he became convinced that the sun, not the earth, was the center of the solar system. The problems which baffle us, the cure of cancer, racial animosities, world peace, atomic control, are being enthusiastically tackled by young people. New worlds cannot be built without the fires of youthful enthusiasm.

Young people are remarkably free from hypocrisy. They are quite candid and frank about everything. Their wacky ways are often simply the open expression of the follies their fathers practiced in secret. If they rebel against our conventional systems they do it with candor. If they have doubts, they express them. They register their disgust at poor sportsmanship, but stand by their heroes with genuine loyalty. There is an openness about their lives which is quite admirable.

Young people, as a whole, are fundamentally good. They believe in fair play, are relatively free from prejudice, believe in our democratic rules, believe in themselves, in their world, in God. This is probably more than can be said for the average adult. If young people are leading the world to hell you may be sure that adults are showing them the way. Who brought back the tavern and made it popular to drink? Not youth, but adults. Who filled the magazine racks with salacious sex and crime stories? Not youth, but adults. Who promoted the gambling rackets? You know the answer.

Young people did not make the world in which they live—they inherited it from us. It appears that we gave them a rather sorry mess. If they are to correct the world's woes, they must be praised rather than persecuted, understood rather than undermined, believed in rather than berated.

Don't tell my son, but I believe this generation of youth is a wee bit better than the last.

ROAD SIGNS

Someone wrote a book about "Sermons in Stones." I've never been able to get one out of a rock, but I have gotten some sermon ideas in unexpected places. One day I had to make a speech in a town a hundred miles from home. Having no speech when I got in my car, I had to make it up on the way. I determined to use the road signs as points in the sermon. Of course, I couldn't use them all. The beer and liquor ads didn't give me much help, and I passed the shaving soap ads so fast that I missed the point, as well as a curve or two.

But here is what I came up with:

1. SPEED LIMIT, SIXTY MILES AN HOUR. These signs have always bothered me, since traffic cops never seem to agree with me concerning the speed I'm traveling. But I've found that life has its limits, and I get into trouble when I go beyond the limit. I've found I can't do everything, that I make a mess of everything if I try. Good living is a process of good selectivity. If I spread myself too thin, I will break under the strain.

2. DANGEROUS DIP. Why they don't build culverts over these paved ravines I don't know. If the mother-in-law is in the back seat she will swear you did it maliciously. Yet life inevitably has its dips, its depressions, periods of despondency. It is not because God is angry or because fate is against you—it is because life is like that. "Some days must be dark and dreary."

3. SHARP CURVE. This is a good sign to observe lest you go sailing off "into the wild blue yonder." It suggests that living often involves a change of direction. If we become slaves to bad habits, we must change our ways or suffer the consequences. If you expect to arrive in one piece, watch the curve signs.

4. CROSSROADS. Life has its choices from the cradle to the grave. Every decision you make is important. The crossroad signs warn you to be careful to take the right road.

5. HILL. This is a warning sign to put the car in second gear or take it slowly, lest you wind up at the

123

foot of the hill ready for the undertaker. It's easy to drift from high ideals into second-rate living. A shady deal here, a white lie there, and soon you're in the soup. Keep the right foot not too far from the brake pedal and your brake in good working order.

6. PEDESTRIAN CROSSWALK. In spite of several million cars on the highway and several billion on the used-car lots, a few people still walk. A poor fellow on foot is no match for a two-hundred horse-power chunk of steel. You can hurt people, you know. Anger, hate, slanderous tongues, are powerful instruments of destruction. Sin is a social evil. No man goes to hell by himself; he usually takes an innocent by-stander with him.

By this time I had arrived at my destination. All excursions must have an ending, including the journey of life. If you expect to arrive at your anticipated destination, it's best to keep your eye on the road.

P.S. They took up a collection and gave me $5.79 for my speech and, after the government took its part, I still had seventy-nine cents left. With a three-cent stamp I informed the Highway Department of my gratitude.

DANCING BEAR

Also by Chaim Bermant

The House of Women
The Patriarch
Now Newman Was Old
The Squire of Bor Shachor
The Last Supper
The Second Mrs. Whitberg

DANCING BEAR

Chaim Bermant

St. Martin's Press
New York

Library of Congress Cataloging in Publication Data

Bermant, Chaim, 1929-
  Dancing bear.

  I. Title.
PR6052.E63D3   1985   823'.914   84-18368
ISBN 0-312-18211-2

First published in Great Britain by George Weidenfeld & Nicolson Ltd.

First U.S. Edition

10 9 8 7 6 5 4 3 2 1

— Part One —

— Chapter One —

Why do some events linger in the memory while others fade? Are they etched by fear?

My earliest memory is of a bear. It seemed gigantic and towered over everybody standing round. It must have been tame, and was probably muzzled, a dancing bear of the sort one frequently saw at village fairs in Eastern Europe, but I must have been at least three by then, when the Russians were already in the country, and village fairs were a thing of the past. Yet I still remember my terror at the sight of the beast, its size, and the deep growling noise it made.

My next memory is of a fire, of people running, men shouting, women screaming, children crying, of flames leaping to the sky and lighting up the night, and the acrid smell of smoke.

Yet not all my early memories were fearful. I recall the friendly face of a young woman, red hair, green eyes, large, gleaming teeth, and more vivid than her appearance was the bar of chocolate she gave me. I still remember the wrapper with red cows on a green meadow.

And most vividly of all: a large, black dog moving slowly, and awkwardly, across a snow-covered field.

Thereafter people, places and events fall into a more ordered succession. A large house with spacious rooms, heavy furniture, and walls lined with books, and long corridors with doors on either side which always seemed to be locked. The sound of my footsteps in those corridors still echoes in my ears, for I was the only child of an only child, and in my early years I didn't even think of myself as a child, but as a shorter, smaller, more vulnerable version of the adults about me.

At first there weren't all that many adults about, and I later came to wonder why so few people needed so large a house.

There was grandfather, pink-faced, white-haired, with blue eyes behind rimless glasses, whose face lit up when I was around, but who otherwise rarely spoke and never smiled. There was grandma, large, fat and blonde, who never smiled even when I was around, and who was nearly always in bed. And there was Anna, old and grey-haired, who cooked and cleaned and looked after grandma, and sometimes played with me, and who spoke Russian, while the rest of us spoke German. There were other, shadowy figures, who came and went, and who left no mark on my memory. Overall, my early impressions are of space, emptiness, silence, as if all life was muffled in snow.

And then suddenly there was colour and commotion: soldiers on motor-cycles, soldiers in lorries, soldiers on foot, and the thump of boots on concrete. The place filled with young men with loud voices, but for some reason I was discouraged from having anything to do with them. And there were young women in crisp aprons, and laughter and music.

And it was then that I realized that grandfather was a doctor, and that home was a private sanatorium which had been turned into a convalescent home for German soldiers.

Grandfather was busy and I spent most of my time with old Anna, who lived by herself in a log cabin among the outhouses of the sanatorium. Her husband was dead and her sons were in the army, though I wasn't sure which army, and neither, it would seem, was she, for while we were German she was Russian and I took it they must have been in the Russian army. I learnt Russian from her and began to speak it, so that as I grew up I wasn't too sure who or what I was myself.

I remember two long hot summers in which I searched for wild strawberries in the woods, and can still recall the smell of the timber and resins, and swimming in a nearby lake and the distant sounds which came echoing over the waters on the warm evenings.

Then the sounds grew louder and more menacing, like sustained thunder. The earth began to tremble and the horizons filled with smoke. And suddenly there were soldiers everywhere, not in the orderly columns I had seen before, but a muddy torrent of tired, bedraggled figures.

One night I was wakened by the sound of voices outside, and the crunch of wheels on gravel. Someone came into my room and told me to dress and when I came outside I saw whole forests blazing in the distance and warm winds came wafting over us,

4

although it was nearly winter. There was a lorry outside piled high with books and pictures and one or two pieces of furniture. Grandma sat next to the driver while grandfather and I were helped on to the back. There were two other men with us I had never seen before, and a soldier with a rifle in his hand. I asked about Anna, but no one knew where she was.

It didn't occur to me then that people who were central to one's existence could disappear without reappearing. I assumed when I woke the next morning I would find her – as I so often did – standing over my bed, her eyes smiling. And if not by my bed she would be at the breakfast table, or in the kitchen, or the garden. But when I woke the next morning, there was no bed, no breakfast, no kitchen, no garden, and no Anna, and I was still swaying back and forward on the lorry.

Again I asked about Anna, and one of the men said gruffly: 'Forget Anna.'

I must have had complete faith in the restorative power of sleep, not merely in the sense that I would wake refreshed, but in the literal sense that it would restore the *status quo ante,* but when I opened my eyes the following morning and I was still on the lorry, I must have suffered a crisis of faith, and broke down. But my distress was short-lived, for there was too much happening.

I don't know how long or how far we travelled. Again there were soldiers everywhere. There were other lorries on the road, and horse-drawn waggons, all piled with shapeless figures huddled against the cold. And there were people on foot bent under the weight of their possessions. The crush of the traffic almost choked all movement and every few hours we had to get off the road to let an army convoy through.

At one point we had to wait at the side of the road for two days and two nights while a whole army passed, cars, motor-cycles, lorries, men on foot, gun-carriages, tanks and other tracked vehicles crunching up the road as they moved. Occasionally planes flew low overhead and people dived for cover, but grandfather said not to worry, they were ours. Otherwise he hardly uttered a word throughout the journey. The soldier with the gun, who seemed to be too old to be in uniform, wept silently to himself. The other two men talked in subdued voices in what I took to be Latvian.

After about a week on the road we came to what I was told was

5

a City. My whole world had hitherto been encompassed by the village in which we lived, or more particularly by grandfather's sanatorium, its spacious grounds and the surrounding forests, but I had often heard the word 'City' mentioned in conversation, usually in the context of such names as Riga, Koenigsberg, Hamburg, Berlin, and it featured in my imagination as a sort of more exalted universe with wide, paved thoroughfares, magnificent buildings, bright lights, many cars and tram-cars and buses, teeming crowds and grand people with fur collars. But this City was nothing like it, for it reminded me of a story Anna once told me of a cruel giant who ran amok and trampled down everything in his path, homes, churches and even castles, for there was hardly anything to be seen along the route we took except mounds of rubble. There were few people about and they moved slowly, with hunched shoulders, and they did not look round as we passed.

'Bombs,' said grandfather, which seemed too slight a word for devastation so great.

We passed through several such cities, moving at hardly more than walking pace, for we had by then caught up with other convoys, and each clogged the movement of the other till the traffic seemed to be in one direction, like the flotsam on a sluggish river. I saw women and children on other lorries. We looked at them and they looked at us, and never a word passed between us, and I felt as if I was moving slowly through some sort of endless dream; and the only time I experienced actual distress was when I woke from my sleep and found that the dream was not over.

After about two weeks – or maybe even a month – on the road, for I lost all sense of time, the traffic began to thin out and we stopped at a large building full of women and children and a few elderly men, where we were given a bed for the night and bread and soup. I remember the taste of the soup to this day. It was a thick barley soup with bits of onion and carrot and I thought that I had never tasted, and would never taste, anything so delicious in my life. And for the first time I discovered the company and friendship of other children.

I would have been quite content to remain there, but after a few days we moved on, and after a further week or two on the road we came to a small town which was to be my home for the next eight or nine years. We lived in a large house about half a mile from the town. It began to snow as we arrived, which made the setting look curiously like the one we had left. The house was almost as large as the one we had left, and full of people, and it was owned by a distant relative, a gaunt, white-haired woman, who seemed to have no time for anyone, especially children. There were about a dozen children there, but we were not allowed to run or play games, or raise our voices.

The nearest thing we had to recreation was a daily walk to the forest, where we gathered twigs for fuel. Half of the town seemed to be doing the same, and when all the twigs were cleared, people began to break branches from the trees, which was forbidden. Some came with axes and saws during the night and by the time the winter was over, the forest was a jagged mass of stumps.

Nobody had told me directly what was happening or what had happened, but I was by now old enough to piece the stray bits of information which came my way into a coherent picture.

My grandfather was a member of a German family which had lived in Latvia for generations, and sometime after he qualified as a doctor he opened a small sanatorium in a place called Resznitz, near the Polish border. In 1940 the Russians occupied the country and his sanatorium was closed down, but as German citizens he and his wife were otherwise allowed to remain unmolested. In 1941 the Germans invaded Latvia and took over the sanatorium. In 1944, when German troops began to fall back, we fell back with them. I was too young to have enjoyed the triumph of German arms and, so to speak, attained awareness only in the hour of defeat.

The word defeat, especially as uttered in German, carried grave intimations of calamity and misfortune, but it didn't seem such a bad thing to me. I remember when the British arrived in a long line of vehicles, cheerful, boisterous young men who shouted and waved to us as they passed. We did not wave back. Grandmother was in hysterics when she heard that I had been out in the street, and her huge bulk quivered with apprehension.

'Calm yourself, Herta,' grandfather said, 'they're British, what can they do to us?'

The enemy were the Russians, and everyone spoke in hushed voices about what they had done in Berlin; next came the French. The British came third, and finally the Americans, who do not

7

appear to have been taken seriously, at least not as enemies, and people drew reassurance, and perhaps even pride, from the thought that Eisenhower was of German origin. In fact I was at first given to believe that he actually was a German, which made me wonder who had been fighting whom.

One day a tall, thin man, accompanied by a short, squat one, both in uniform, the latter with a clip-board under his arm, came to look round the house. They moved from room to room, measuring a floor here, a window there, but never uttering a word to any of us, as if we weren't there, and for the first time in my life I felt something like resentment. I had been used to people patting my head, or pinching my cheek, or shouting at me to be quiet, but being totally ignored was new to my experience and I did not like it.

A few days later we were told that we would have to move. Grandma was indignant.

'There are eight families in this place. Where do they expect us to go?'

'We did worse things,' said grandfather.

'We were at war. You've always been like that, haven't you? In your eyes the British can do no wrong.'

This time at least my sympathies were with my grandmother, for the new place we eventually found was even more crowded than the old. I didn't mind crowding as such. In a way I enjoyed it, but where I had been able to share a room with two other boys, I now shared a room with my grandparents, and my grandmother seemed to fill the place, not so much with her physical presence, which was substantial enough, but with her aura of displeasure and grief. The walls seemed to be moist with it.

Although I was quick in some respects I was slow in coming alive to the fact that while some of my friends had young and attractive mothers, I had only an old, ailing and unattractive grandmother, and I taxed grandfather about the fate of my parents. I don't actually recall being told they were dead, but I surmised they were because so many other people were dead. Dead and death were about the most common words in use at the time and most of the boys I knew had a dead father, but I seemed to be singular in that I had a dead father *and* a dead mother. The fact that I had a living grandfather and grandmother was no compensation, especially as I would have been quite happy to see

8

my grandmother dead.

The first time I raised the matter with grandfather he said he would tell me later. When I raised it again he was, for the first time in his life, rather sharp with me and said:

'Really, Heinschein, you should be old enough to understand that when people don't want to talk about a subject you shouldn't press them.' I was six by then.

The British organized food supplies and our meals became more substantial and regular. Housing also improved and we moved into a small house on the edge of town where, for the first time since we returned to Germany, I had a room of my own, until we were joined by Aunt Carla.

Carla was grandfather's younger sister and I thought I had seen her before. I particularly remembered her eyes and her teeth, though her hair seemed to have changed colour.

'You couldn't possibly remember,' she said, 'you were only a baby.'

'I remember,' I insisted, 'I even remember the chocolate you brought me.'

She had lost her husband in the war and had come to keep house for grandfather because grandmother was no longer capable of doing so. Carla brightened my existence, partly because there was something bright and glowing about her very presence, and it was reassuring to have a close relative who was not elderly, dour or decrepit. I had begun to feel aggrieved against fate; now I began to feel almost privileged. I was sorry we had moved out of the crowded quarters we had occupied hitherto, for I would have liked to show her off to the other boys. They nearly all had collections of war trophies, spent bullets, shell-casings, medals, bits of shrapnel, even helmets, and war stories of fathers and brothers who had been at the front. I had nothing like that but they, on the other hand, had nothing like my aunt. She also talked to me. I was often addressed by my grandparents, admonished, instructed, and I sometimes elicited information in response to a question. Anna used to tell me stories, and I was a mere listener, but with Carla, for the first time, I discovered the pleasures of actual conversation. I had a great many observations to make on a great many things which I had never felt able to air in the presence either of my grandparents or even of my contemporaries, but I found an audience in

9

Carla.

Although we no longer went hungry, fuel was still scarce and we were often cold, and on wintry nights Carla would take me into her bed to keep me warm. It was so pleasant an experience that I tried to continue the habit even when winter gave way to summer.

I began school when I was about seven. Until I left Latvia I didn't know what the company of children was. Then I gradually made the passing acquaintance of this or that boy. In school, for the first time, I was among children *en masse* and it was an unpleasant experience, for I found the mass ganged up against me. They made fun of my accent though I never thought I had one, and said I was a Russian, or called me bastard (presumably because I was without a father or a mother). I found some compensation for this in the fact that I consistently came top of my class in every subject, which made me more unpopular still. And then one day somebody called me a Jew, which was meant to be, and which I certainly took to be, a term of reproach, though I was not too sure what it implied.

Now the subject of Jews was one on which not even Carla cared to be drawn. 'There aren't many about,' was all she would tell me, but why weren't there many about? And in any case there were many things which were virtually non-existent which were the constant topic of conversation, and I began to think of Jews as a sort of mythological animal, half man half beast, like mermen or satyrs, except that satyrs and mermen were jocund and playful whereas the very reticence about Jews suggested someone dark and sombre, even sinister.

When I was about ten, the local synagogue, a pile of rubble in the centre of the town, was rebuilt. There were pictures in all the papers of the consecration and shortly after it was opened the whole school was taken on a tour of the building. I approached the experience with morbid curiosity, not unmixed with dread, but it proved to be something of an anti-climax.

It was very modern and didn't look all that different from a new church which had been opened a few streets from us. One Friday evening our teacher took some of her prize pupils to an actual service, but the building was almost empty, with a few old men scattered about the pews.

The first Jew I actually met was something of a come-down, for he was a heavily-built man with a bushy moustache and I took an instant dislike to him, not because he was Jewish but because Aunt Carla liked him, and I only discovered he was Jewish because grandma mentioned the fact in a subdued voice, as if such things shouldn't be mentioned in the presence of children.

I became increasingly aware that the relationship between grandma and Carla was not all it should be, and there was a time when, to my distress, Carla moved out altogether and a large woman, with the same build as grandma but in infinitely better health, came in every day to look after her, and to keep house. I wasn't sure where she came from, but she wasn't German and grandfather spoke to her in Russian.

Grandfather, who worked in a hospital some miles away, had to leave early in the morning and I had to bring grandma a cup of coffee in bed and wait until the housekeeper came.

One morning I brought in the coffee and grandma was still asleep, snoring with her mouth open. She had always been very pale, but she used to have colour in her hair and her eyes. Now her hair was white and her eyes were shut. There was hardly any colour even to her lips, and she seemed to blend in with the pillow. I felt tempted to pick up a pillow and to stifle her there and then, and I might have done it had I not heard the front door open and the heavy tread of the housekeeper on the stairs.

The arrangement with the housekeeper didn't work because she would raid grandfather's drinks cupboard, and when he locked up the cupboard she tried to force it open, and when she couldn't do that she drank a bottle of spirits we used for the primus stove, and when I came back from school one day, I found her prostrate on the floor with grandma in hysterics beside her.

And so Carla came back, but as I was thirteen by then we could no longer share a room, and I slept on a couch in the lounge. I also did, or tried to do, my homework in the lounge, which wasn't easy because whenever Carla was about she always had the radio on, listening to the American Forces Network, and from time to time she would try to get me to dance with her, but I was long and lanky, with huge feet, which tended to get in the way of each other.

'You are going to be handsome, my little Heinschein,' she said, 'but looks aren't everything, you must learn to dance. You'll never get anywhere with girls if you can't dance.'

The thought didn't worry me, but the sensation of being pressed closely against my aunt was very pleasant, and I eventually learnt to fox-trot and to waltz and even the rumba and the samba.

Grandma had a bell by her bed which she would press when she needed help and I was afraid we mightn't hear her above the music.

'All the better,' said Carla. 'Let her drop dead. She's hanging on for spite.'

Then one afternoon as we were dancing a tango there was a noise like a roll of thunder from upstairs. We rushed from the room and found grandma jammed between the wall and the balustrades. She must have crawled from her bed, out on to the landing and then toppled down the stairs. She was incontinent and had left a thick, murky trail all the way.

I thought we should have called grandfather, but Carla called in a neighbour and between the three of us we managed to haul the old woman back up the stairs and into bed.

'Not a word to my brother about this,' said Carla, 'or he'll kill us both.'

She managed to clear up the mess by the time he got back, but grandmother died in the night.

I suppose I should have felt guilty, but didn't. Carla certainly didn't and the fact that we now shared a secret somehow consummated our relationship, and I felt emboldened to ask her questions I had hitherto kept to myself. In particular I wanted to know everything she could tell me about my mother. She had, she often told me, been very fond of my mother.

'I'm much, much younger than your grandfather, you must understand, so that I was almost like a sister to her. She was very pretty, very lively, very gay, everybody loved her.'

'Then why doesn't grandfather like to talk about her?'

'He's not an easy man, as you'll find out, and your mother, well, she could be difficult in her own way. She was an only child, and very spoilt. Your grandfather was "the little officer", as we always called him in the family – he was used to giving orders, and she never got used to taking them. I called her a sprite, she wasn't quite human.'

'Did she die in the war?'

'That's what I've been told, but don't ask me how, where or

when, because I don't know. It's the same with my husband. I last saw him ten years ago – almost to the day. I presume he's dead, but I was never officially informed that he died, or how or where or when – '

'Yes, but he was a soldier.'

'You didn't have to be a soldier to disappear in those days, and you didn't ask how people died – or, for that matter, what they had done to stay alive. Children growing up in Germany are not encouraged to ask questions.'

She couldn't tell me anything about my father.

'I never met him, I·never knew him, I know nothing about him.'

'Am I a bastard then?'

She looked at me with something like reproof, as if a boy of my age had no right to use such words or think in such terms.

'I've been called that in school, you know.'

'Boys always call each other nasty names, you should have more sense than to pay attention to them.'

'If you and mother were like sisters, wouldn't she have told you something about him?'

'That was all before the war.'

'Didn't you see her after she married?'

'Yes, but there was so much happening then, armies everywhere, frontiers closing, chaos, I can't remember.'

Apart from the gaps in her story, there were also contradictions, but a few facts became clear.

Mother, who was then eighteen or nineteen, had left Latvia a few years before the war to stay with a relative in Germany, but had instead gone on to London, where she had married and had a child. I was the child. Her action had caused outrage and distress in the family, and my grandparents refused to have anything more to do with her. No great precocity was required on my part to conclude from all that – and the complete silence about my father's identity – that my mother had not in fact married and that I was therefore, indeed, a bastard.

Was it possible then that I was also a Jew, for I had been called that too?

'How could you be?' said Clara.

'If my father was Jewish – '

At which point she became exasperated.

13

'Why should he be Jewish? I don't know anything about him. You don't know anything about him.'

Although I could by now regard Clara as a confidante, there were some matters which I couldn't discuss even with her, and one of them was the fact that I was circumcised. I had noticed early in life that I was in this respect different from other boys and grandfather had told me that I had injured myself as an infant by trying to climb over a barbed wire fence and I had had to have a small operation in the course of which my foreskin was removed; in fact I also had small scars both on my lower abdomen and on my groin, which seemed to confirm this story. I myself, however, had no memory of the incident or the operation, and my conversations with my aunt left me with the unhappy suspicion that I was probably not only a bastard but a Jewish bastard at that. The thought brought me little comfort.

Nor was there consolation to be had from my general circumstances. The death of grandma had, for a week or two, removed a cloud from my existence and even grandfather had brightened up a bit, but then I had the feeling that there were momentous changes in the offing. There were phone calls at all times of the day and night and telegrams, and distinguished-looking visitors in dark suits and dark glasses, who came and went in large cars, all of which led Carla to believe that we were about to move, to South America probably. I was extremely conservative as a child, for although I was not particularly happy at school I was, with grandma out of the way, happy at home. Things had become easier altogether. We ate well and were no longer cold. The house had been refurbished and refurnished, and we had a car in which Carla used to take me on long drives in the country on Sunday afternoons, and I found the thought of any change unwelcome. What made it worse was the uncertainty. Carla also complained about it.

'I don't know where I am or what I am,' she kept saying.

'Why don't you take it up with your brother?' I asked.

'Do you think I haven't? There's nothing to tell me, he says.'

Then, one evening over dinner, he announced his plans.

The fact that he was deigning to dine with us at all made us feel that something portentous was in the offing, for he rarely ate at home and, in fact, I saw him so rarely at table that I sometimes wondered if he ate at all, as if so mundane an activity was

14

somehow beneath him. Occasionally, when he came home from hospital, he might ask Carla to prepare something for him – usually a meal of herbs – which he would have by himself on the dining-room table with a decanter of water. He was as austere as his sister was indulgent. Carla and I ate together in the kitchen, a large, comfortable, brightly lit room, and had soups and meat and puddings, which she often served with wine.

'Even as a child he ate little,' she said. 'He lives on work and for work.'

The dining-room, which was narrow, dimly lit and dominated by a dark, refectory-style table, with hard, uncomfortable seats, somehow went with his personality, and his spirit cast a dampener over it even when he wasn't there.

That particular evening Carla prepared a festive meal, including roast duck, and lit candles on the table.

'Tonight we shall know the best or the worst,' she said, 'and I can tell you what it is now. We shall be going to South America.'

'Why South America?'

'He has friends there, people he worked with before. There are huge German colonies all over South America. I shall go with him if it's some big city in Argentina or Brazil, but not to some place in the backwoods.'

He was a little taken aback by the sight of the candles on the table.

'Are you celebrating something?' he asked.

'Yes,' said Carla, 'the end of uncertainty.'

He smiled at that and said, 'I am sorry. I have been dealing with people who do not always know their own mind and who are unable to make decisions without referring everything back to their superiors, and I didn't want to say anything until everything was signed, settled and sealed.'

'So what's it going to be?' asked Carla.

'Egypt.'

She was about to serve out some soup and dropped her ladle back into the tureen.

'Egypt? Why Egypt?'

'Because in Germany young men are taking over everywhere and I can get nowhere. Egypt is a country where they still appreciate experience. I also happen to speak Arabic.'

'Well, you can go without me,' she said.

15

He did not seem unduly put out by her announcement and I suspect he had not planned to take her in the first place.

'Will I have to come as well?' I asked.

'What an extraordinary question. Did you think I would leave you behind?'

'He could stay on with me,' said Carla. That was not something she had suggested before and I greeted the idea with enthusiasm.

'The matter of the boy's schooling was one of the things I was at pains to settle before I accepted the offer,' he said, 'but I have found an excellent school in which I believe he will do very well and be very happy.'

I don't know on what he based his belief. I was not an emotional boy but my whole world collapsed at the news and I wanted to run from the room. I was, as I said, unhappy at the idea of moving at all, but to move without Carla was unthinkable. Possibly because I was different, felt different and, to an extent, looked different, I had made few friends at school and had never been part of any inner or even marginal group, but I was never bothered by the exclusion as long as I had Carla around, and I couldn't imagine life without her. I managed to finish my soup, but could not touch the rest of the meal.

'You will like Egypt,' said grandfather, 'the people are friendly, we shall have a splendid home – '

'I don't want to go,' I said. It was the nearest I had come to rebellion.

'We shall discuss that tomorrow,' he said; 'now eat your supper.'

'You can't force the boy to go against his will,' said Carla.

'We shall discuss the matter tomorrow,' he repeated, and it occurred to me that I was not perhaps worried so much at the thought of being without Carla as of being alone with him.

I had detested grandmother, but with a sort of blunt aversion one feels for anything disagreeable. What I felt for grandfather now was a biting hatred. He had new rimless glasses with lenses so thick that one could barely see his eyes through them. They made him look at once vulnerable and malign and they seemed to radiate displeasure even when one thought he might be smiling.

That night I toyed with the idea of running away, and I might have done so but for the fact that the next day was a public holiday and Carla and I had planned to go out on a picnic.

16

Grandfather must have woken with the thought that he must make an effort to seem human, for he came downstairs in a Tyrolean hat and jacket, knickerbockers, long woollen socks and heavy boots. Both Carla and I stared at the apparition, half expecting him to yodel.

'May I come on your picnic?' he asked.

'Only if you bring your alpenstock,' she said.

He tried to be jocular as we drove out to the country, and got on Carla's nerves. I could see her knuckles whitening, and if she could have wrenched off the steering wheel she might have crowned him with it, but I began to warm to him, not because anything he said was amusing but because there was something funny and endearing about his very attempts to be funny. He was human, after all, and I began to ask myself how I could have hated him, if only for a minute. I ate with gusto the huge meal Carla had prepared, and when it was over and the debris had been cleared Carla lay down in the grass to sleep while grandfather and I went for a walk.

We strolled along in silence for a time, then he said:

'You're very attached to Carla, aren't you? I quite understand it for she is lively and colourful, which I'm afraid I'm not and which your poor grandmother certainly wasn't, and of course she is very fond of you, but you mustn't get too attached to her for she is still attractive and could remarry. In fact – and you mustn't breathe a word of this to her – one of the reasons why I accepted the Egyptian post is that she has adapted herself too readily to the role of housekeeper. She could do much better for herself and I feel that I have been standing in the way of her doing so. You mustn't think our present arrangement can continue forever, because she has her own life to lead and you have yours.'

I was nearly fifteen, but if precocious in some ways I was backward in others, for I still had the childish belief that what was must always be, and the thought that time must bring its own disruptions had never occurred to me.

'What will Carla do?' I asked.

'I wouldn't worry about Carla. She has many friends in many places. She speaks English perfectly and has more than a smattering of French, and it isn't difficult to find work in Germany these days. I discussed the matter with her last night after you went to bed, and, frankly, the idea of your moving with her to Hamburg or Frankfurt or wherever is not very practical. You would not be very happy and, although she didn't say so, I think you would be in her way. You understand that, don't you?'

I was beginning to, albeit reluctantly.

He then unveiled his grand plan.

'I'm going to Egypt to begin again, or rather to give you a new beginning, and, for a start, you will have a new name: no longer Heinz or Heinschein, but Harry. Will you remember, because you'll have to get used to it – Harry. And your second name is no longer Rhiner, but Newman. Remember, Harry Newman. A plain, ordinary name.'

'But why?'

'For your own good, and you'll understand why as you get older. You're a bright boy. You did well in Germany, you'll do better in Egypt, and when you've finished in Egypt I hope you'll go on to university in England. I nearly went to England to study – a pity I didn't. Things might have been very different, *very* different if I had, but there it is. There's no point in looking into the past. I hope it's something you'll avoid. I suppose as you get older you won't be able to stop yourself, but it's a bad habit and, believe me, it can cause a lot of unhappiness.'

I had never known him to be so expansive before and felt tempted to ask him something about my parents, but I took his advice against looking into the past as a warning not to. I was already taller than him, but still had the habit of regarding everything he said as the ultimate wisdom.

A few months later we left for Egypt. I could not have reconciled myself to the thought of parting from Carla completely, for when she came with us to the airport I somehow felt she would continue with us on the plane, or that she would make her way to Cairo ahead of us, for when we landed at the international airport I found myself searching for her face in the crowd. It seemed as if I was eternally doomed to be cut off from anyone who ever meant anything to me.

Grandfather had not gone into details about his work beyond telling me that he was to be the director of a new mental hospital. He had never in his life touched on the subject of money, but it must have been a highly paid job, for he came and went in a chauffeur-driven Mercedes, and we lived in a splendid villa on the outskirts of Cairo. The floors were of marble and one only had to lift an eyebrow and a dark-skinned servant would appear from nowhere. The house was built round an open courtyard, part of which was shaded with vines, and there was a fountain in the centre which spluttered sporadically and sent up a rusty liquid. The house was ringed with palm trees and the outside walls were bright with bougainvillaea. It was all a little like the setting for a Hollywood oriental extravaganza, and when I sat out in the courtyard towards the evening I half expected to see a line of scantily clad dancing girls emerge from the shadows. It was not at all the sort of home I would have associated with my grandfather, and in fact he hardly used it. He had an apartment at the hospital and usually slept there, but he would always phone me when he was away to see how I was, and to ask me to make sure that everything was locked. 'You can't rely on the servants,' he would remind me, and every night I would make a tour of the building with the housekeeper, a large man with a heavy moustache called Ahmed, to make sure that all the keys had been turned. There was, to be sure, no snow in sight, yet the silence, the long, empty corridors, the locked doors, the isolation, made me feel as if I was back in Latvia.

I went to an English school some miles from our home and was taken there and back by car.

I had learned some English at school in Germany, but I still found it difficult to follow the lessons and my grandfather engaged an English tutor called Mr Markham, a pale, skeletal figure in a white suit who looked like a ghost and moved like one.

The servants prepared tea for him when he arrived, but he often remained longer than the hour for which he was engaged and he sometimes stayed to dinner.

The school prepared pupils for Oxford and Cambridge and he asked me if I planned to go on to England when I was finished.

'Yes,' I said, 'grandfather wants me to go to Oxford.'

'A great mistake, dear boy. I was in India during the war and for a bit after, and when I returned to England I didn't recognize the place. I don't mean what Hitler did to the country, but what the socialists have done. Destroyed cities can be rebuilt after a fashion, but not a way of life. If you really want to savour the flavour of old England, Rhodesia's the place. I mean to settle there myself.'

Most of the boys at the school were Egyptian, and they kept to themselves. Some were British, and they kept to themselves too, and I had no place among either. After a time I noticed that the Egyptians were sub-divided between Moslems and Copts, but there was one boy who didn't seem to be fully accepted by either and who eventually befriended me. He was Jewish. Pariahs of the world unite! He was tall, dark, precious-looking, with jet-black hair, and had the improbable name of Gerald.

We both had bicycles, and I once invited him to join me for a bike ride, and he arrived, accompanied by a very tall, very lean, very black negro servant, who was also on a bike.

'We're rather well off,' he said apologetically, 'and mother's afraid I might be kidnapped, so she insisted Nero come with us.'

It was in the course of one such excursion that he asked me, à propos of nothing, if it was true that I was Jewish.

I was so surprised by the question that I nearly toppled off my bike.

'I'm sorry,' he said, 'I shouldn't have asked.'

'No, it's not that at all. I'm only wondering what could possibly have made you ask.'

'Something one of the boys said.'

'I'd have told you by now if I was.'

'So one would have thought, but there were Jewish boys in the school before who took immense pains to hide the fact. That's something rather western, I find. I wouldn't say that eastern Jews take a particular pride in their Jewishness, but I've never known them to be ashamed of it.'

'But isn't it awkward to be a Jew in an Arab country?'

'Egypt isn't really Arab, you know. The Arabs are parvenus. The Copts have been around for much longer, and so, as a matter of fact, have the Jews. My own family's been here since Roman times.'

I asked him how he came to have a name like Gerald.

'Father works for an English bank, and adores everything English – that's why he sent me to an English school. My sisters attend a French Lycée, but then he's never felt a girl's education to be that important.'

After about a year in Egypt I had sufficient command of English to dispense with the services of Mr Markham, but he would still invite himself over for tea from time to time.

One Christmas he called on me with a little package in hand. I opened it and found a pair of solid gold cuff-links. I felt intensely embarrassed, for I hadn't even sent him a card.

Some months later I found him waiting for me as I was coming out of school.

'I was passing,' he said, 'and wondered if I could give you a lift home.'

'I have a car waiting for me.'

'I know, but I thought you might prefer to go with me for a change. I have a new Austin-Healey. They're very brisk little things.'

We didn't drive all that fast because it was difficult to move through Cairo's traffic even then.

He was silent for a time as if trying to formulate his thoughts, then he said:

'I hope you don't think I'm suffering from paranoia, but I do have the impression that you've been trying to avoid me.'

What he said was true, but I felt bound to deny it.

'I wish I could believe you,' he said. 'You never seem to be in when I call, you never return my phone calls, you – '

'I've been away a lot, you know. I'll be finishing school in another few months and I've been trying to see something of Egypt.'

'With your friend, no doubt. He's Jewish, you know.'

'What difference does that make?'

'Well, if it makes no difference to a German – '

I cut him short, asked him to stop the car, and got out.

A few days later I received a letter:

'My dear, my dearest Harry:
     Mea culpa, mea maxima culpa.
     That thoughtless remark I made was unforgivable, but I still hope you will forgive it, because one of the many things which have drawn me to you is your generous, understanding nature. I, of course, have no claim on your affections, your time, or even your understanding, but I did let myself believe that our relationship had advanced to the point where I could think of you as a friend. If I can't I hope you'll forgive my presumption.
          Yours with apologies and regrets,
               Neville'

I felt persecuted. The very thought of him clouded my last

months in Egypt, and at the end of school I would make a wild dash for the car in case he should be lying in wait for me, but I saw nothing more of him, at least for the time being.

My headmaster had encouraged me to enter for a scholarship tenable at Pembroke College, Oxford, and a little to my surprise, and I daresay to his, I won it. My grandfather was not so much gratified as overwhelmed by the news, and he embraced me with shaking arms.

He must have been as embarrassed by the contact as I was, for he recoiled slightly, as if he had let his emotions get the better of him.

'Everything I had hoped for is coming true,' he said. 'A pity your grandmother is not alive, poor woman. She lived long enough to suffer the disappointments and hardships of life, but not to enjoy the consolations.'

He arranged for me to have a generous monthly allowance and equipped me with numerous papers, including an Egyptian passport giving my date of birth as 12 June 1938, and my place of birth as Resznitz. I felt that I had by now earned the right to know more about myself than he had been willing to impart, and I asked if he was sure that I had in fact been born in Resznitz.

He seemed to be saddened by the question.

'Has Carla put some nonsense in your head?'

'She gave me to understand that I was born in England.'

'The facts are as stated in your passport,' he said, and brought the conversation to an end. He became ugly when he turned peremptory, and I was sorry I had brought the matter up. He, for his part, must have regretted his peremptoriness, for he came home unexpectedly early and we had cold drinks together on the terrace. It had been an unusually hot day, even for Egypt, and it remained hot even though the sun was beginning to set. There was not a breath of wind to disturb the limp fronds of the palm trees around us. The blood-red sun seemed to fill the sky and bathed the city in a golden glow. It was my favourite time of day because apart from the dramatic effects of the sunset there was usually an evening breeze, which seemed to thrust life back into one's nostrils. One died at noon and underwent a form of resurrection in the evening, but this evening was different. I felt utterly lifeless; so did grandfather, and he almost collapsed into his chair.

'I'm beginning to feel my years,' he said, then added quickly, 'I am not old in years, only in experience, but experience can also weigh a man down.'

I almost asked him how old he was, but did not wish to seem presumptuous. He could not have been much over sixty, but his face had lost its taut, rounded quality, and his skin hung loosely about his mouth and neck, his complexion was blotchy and his hands were becoming shaky. There were also his thick glasses, which functioned not only as an aid to vision but as a barrier between him and those about him.

I had found him warm and affectionate when I was small, and cold and distant as I grew older, but I gradually came to suspect that what I took to be coldness was really a sort of diffidence, and that he kept his distance because he was not quite sure how he would be accepted. There was, apart from his slight size, no obvious reason for his diffidence. Carla had told me more than once that he had been a brilliant student and had 'a string of degrees as long as your arm'. Everywhere one went he was treated with deference, 'Yes, Herr Doktor', 'Certainly, Herr Doktor', and government officials in Egypt approached him with something like awe, as if he was a minor deity. He was, by most standards, a successful professional man, but something had happened at an earlier stage in his career to break him, and I somehow associated that something with my mother, which was another reason why I regretted having raised the question of my birth earlier in the day; but he raised it himself now.

'I'm sorry for being so sharp with you this morning. You asked a reasonable question and you're fully entitled to an answer. I promise you, you'll know everything in good time. I was only cross with Carla. She should have known better than to fill your mind with nonsense. That woman is not to be relied upon.'

After that he became almost genial, and he told me of a grand tour he had made across Europe when he was about my age just before the First World War.

'There was always trouble in the Balkans, but apart from that you could travel anywhere without impediment. Father had a bit of money in those days and we were able to travel – by train, of course – like English milords. The carriages were like drawing-rooms.'

I asked what was to stop him making a further tour. We could perhaps travel together.

'I haven't the time,' he said. 'Besides, Europe is no longer Europe, and the places which mean most to me I'll never be able to see again. In any case, it would be no pleasure for you to have a decrepit and bad-tempered old man as a companion.'

He told me about his father, who had been a substantial landowner and a loyal and patriotic German. His tenants were Livonians or Russians, but he set up a German-language school for their children and sent the best of them on to universities in Germany, and they returned – those that did return – as super-Germans. 'Everyone has the capacity to become a German,' he said. As far as he was concerned, there could be no higher status. He sighed. 'I also used to be very proud of being German, and used to think it gave one a sort of hereditary grace. Now it's beginning to feel more like a hereditary disease. It would be nice if you could become an Englishman.'

It sounded a slightly absurd thing to say, as if he was urging me to become a doctor or a lawyer, as he must have realized himself, for he quickly added: 'I'm not suggesting that you should consciously make the effort, or pass yourself off as an Englishman, but there are English attitudes worth emulating.'

'Such as?'

'Casualness, lack of intensity, a limited preoccupation with the past, cheerfulness in the face of adversity. I suppose it all mounts up to an unquenchable optimism that everything will come right in the end. I used to envy the English milords I met on my travels before the first war, but never liked or admired them. They didn't seem to be quite human. I really got to know Englishmen only after the last war, when they were in Germany as conquerors. Triumphs can bring out the worst in people, but they came without arrogance, swagger or vindictiveness. They were not always very efficient, and drank rather a lot, but somehow they always got things done.'

'Aren't the Egyptians similar in a way?'

'Yes, except that they don't drink, they do not always get things done, and they don't think it particularly important that they should. No, it would be nice if you could become an Englishman.'

His voice faded away.

It was dark now, a blue, soft, velvety, fragrant darkness so thick as to be almost palpable, which seemed to muffle the noises which usually filled the Egyptian night, or perhaps it seemed quieter because there was no breeze to carry the noise.

Usually when I found myself in my grandfather's company and had nothing to say I felt compelled by the silence to say something, if only some banality about the weather, but now, for the first time, the very silence between us was in itself a form of communication. I think had I remained in Egypt I would have been able to regard him not only as my *locus parentis*, but as a friend and companion. Perhaps he was nervous of the possibility, which is why he began to open out only as I was about to leave.

—— *Chapter Two* ——

In my last term at school I had applied myself to my work, and especially to European history, with more than usual assiduity, and when I surfaced from my immersion in the eighteenth century I was startled to find myself overwhelmed by the twentieth.

Although grandfather had a large library and subscribed to a variety of journals, he never bought a newspaper, which I ascribed to his frugality until I noticed that he only switched on the radio to listen to music and he seemed to have either a lack of interest in contemporary events or a distaste for them. I seemed to have inherited his attitudes, and were it not for my friend Gerald I might have had only the vaguest idea of what was happening in the world about me.

Gerald and I had made elaborate plans to tour Europe together once our exams were over. He was not what our headmaster called 'scholarship material', and his father expected him to go into his business. Gerald himself had other ideas which had not yet quite crystallized. 'My grandfather used to say you leave too many hostages to fortune by planning too far ahead. I'll worry what to do with myself when I get back from Europe.' He had already bought a car, and we had finalized our plans when he phoned to tell me that he might have to cancel them.

'The bloody business about the canal has upset everything,' he said.

The nationalization of the Suez Canal was something which had impinged even on my consciousness, for Cairo went wild for a week, but I couldn't see what it had to do with us.

'Father's afraid this could be the end of everything, and he doesn't want me to leave Egypt for the time being.'

'The Jews are a jittery lot,' Markham once told me, and I could now see what he meant.

I toured Europe on my own, by plane and train instead of by

ferry and car, stopping at Rome, Florence, Venice, Vienna and Paris, and was too engrossed in galleries and museums to pay much attention to current events, so that when I – the prospective Englishman – landed in London I found myself in a country on the brink of war with Egypt, and by the time I settled into Oxford I was an enemy alien.

Oxford, even with its clogged thoroughfares, was a wonderland to me. An Englishman would, no doubt, have taken it all for granted, but to me it was the stuff of legends. So was Venice, but Venice had been a disappointment. I had arrived on a hot and steamy day and found a small room in a modest *pension* in which I could hardly breathe. Nor was there relief to be found outside, for the streets were so crowded one could hardly move, the air was oppressive and the canals stank to heaven. Oxford, on the other hand, was – apart from the traffic – exactly as I had imagined it, the mellow buildings grouped round green lawns, the cobbled courtyards, the quiet lanes, the cheerful taverns and tea-shops, the soft, moist air. One could breathe and move without effort. What added to the pleasure which I took in my surroundings was the belief – instilled in me by my grandfather – that I had arrived among the elect, but if others felt the same they carried their feelings lightly, for they were relaxed, convivial, even a trifle boisterous, and displayed a light-heartedness which I had never encountered in Germany or Egypt, and which was almost infectious.

The Suez crisis, however, spoilt things, especially for someone as apolitical as me.

I knew no one in Oxford, but arrived with a letter of introduction from the headmaster of my school to a former pupil from Bahrein called Rashid, a postgraduate student at St Anthony's College.

He was of average height, slightly built, with a sallow complexion, a thick, black moustache and a deep voice which did not quite go with the rest of his person and did not seem to belong to him.

His first words were: 'You have come at a bad time.'

'In which way do you mean?' I asked. The question immediately placed our relationship on a wrong footing.

'In which way?' he said. 'Haven't you heard there's a war on? Don't you know that your home country is the victim of Zionist,

27

imperialist aggression? Where have you been?'

He was active in the Union of Arab Students and was involved in organizing a constant succession of protest meetings, demonstrations, rallies, marches. I went along as a curious onlooker or, at best, a sympathetic observer rather than as an active participant, and he was pained by my detachment.

'I know you are not Arab, but you are Egyptian. Don't you see it is all wrong?'

I explained that I wasn't even Egyptian.

'I know, but you are an Egyptian national and you went to school in Egypt. Your blood should be boiling. Or are you afraid to say anything because you are German?'

That was certainly part of the answer. Germany's treatment of the Jews had been touched on by different teachers at different times when I was at school in Germany, and I had also read a great deal on the subject, yet what I acquired as a result was not so much a sense of guilt as one of reticence. Perhaps I saw some mitigation in the fact that I had not, after all, actually been born in Germany, and that I had had my early upbringing in Latvia, but whenever the word 'Jew', 'Israel' or 'Israeli' was uttered in conversation, not only was I disinclined to voice an opinion, my mind somehow failed to formulate one. I had already become aware of this in Egypt and had ascribed the failure to ignorance, but this was certainly not the case by the time I reached England and it was clear that my mind had developed a sort of filter to exclude awkward matters.

The ferment and *angst* aroused by events in the Middle East did not quite go with my picture of Oxford and it seemed to me an alien phenomenon generated by alien groups. Moreover, I had come to Oxford to study and not to demonstrate or protest. I was impatient to get down to work, and if the detachment which Rashid complained of had not come naturally I think I would have tried to acquire it. As a result, any fraternal obligations which he may have had to introduce me to Oxford society were allowed to lapse.

I had been largely on my own during my school days in Egypt and was again largely on my own in Oxford, and if I made friends at all they tended to be my seniors. One friendship in particular flourished after very unpropitious beginnings. I was reading Modern History, and one of my tutors, Mitrofanoff, a tall, aristocratic-looking figure with a broken nose and silvery hair, denounced me as a fraud almost at our first encounter.

'Your origin is German, your nationality is Egyptian, your manner is English, but you speak Russian like a native. Out with it, Neumann, who or what are you?'

'Newman,' I insisted.

'Come, come now, you weren't born Newman.'

'I wasn't born Neumann either and as Newman is the name I've adopted I'd prefer to be called by that name, if it's all right with you, sir.'

'Where were you in fact born?'

'I'm not too sure.'

'What do you mean, you're not too sure?'

'That's the plain fact of the matter, sir.'

'What does it say on your passport?'

'Latvia.'

'Russia, you mean.'

'No, sir, Latvia.'

'Latvia was Russia and is Russia.'

'Not when I was born, sir.'

'The very name Latvia is an aberration, sustained by German predators. It may not be part of the Russian heartlands, but before this course is over I feel confident that you will agree that it was and is part of greater Russia.'

He himself was an émigré and had left Russia shortly after the revolution. His family, he told us more than once, had owned vast estates. 'I could ride at a gallop for two days and two nights, and sometimes did, without leaving the family's domain.' It was all, of course, lost. 'I wouldn't begrudge it to the Bolsheviks if they only knew how to handle it, but my grandfather got more out of the soil with illiterate serfs than the Bolsheviks have ever done with all their plans and planners.'

He lived in a shabby Victorian house in North Oxford which, with its icons and religious bric-à-brac, looked like a cross between an antique shop and a shrine, though overall there hung, like a secular incense, the ghost of meals past.

He had worked as a chef in Paris in the twenties and was still a superb cook, but if everything about the ambience was Russian, the drink was Scotch.

'Don't let anyone tell you that Russian food can only be

enjoyed with vodka,' he said. 'Vodka is all right for those who seek oblivion, but civilized drinking calls for Scotch.' He however managed to obtain oblivion even with Scotch, and he would become in turn merry, then soulful, and finally tearful – before passing out altogether.

His family had been ruined by the Bolsheviks and many of his relatives and friends murdered, but he was, or said he was, pro-Communist without being Marxist.

'I think you have to be a Jew to understand Marxism,' he said. 'I certainly can't make head or tail of it. Happily the Russian generation of Soviet leaders, as distinct from the Jewish ones, has made only a half-hearted attempt to implement it, and they have given Russia an authority, stability, power and international standing it has not enjoyed since Alexander I.'

When I mentioned my own family background, he said:

'Ah yes, German colonialists. I should imagine you rarely heard a word of Russian at home.'

'The servants spoke Russian.'

'They would, but no doubt everyone else spoke German. That's the trouble with the Germans, they're as bad as the Jews. Many of them came in with Catherine the Great, some even before, but they remained incorrigibly German. Trade was in the hands of the Jews, industry in the hands of the Germans. One must say this for the Communists, they've given Russia back to the Russians, which may explain why it's the mess it is.'

He had been teaching the same course for years and was obviously tired of it, so that he welcomed every opportunity to stray from the subject, which I did not particularly mind, for his conversation was often illuminating and he could be hilariously funny when he spoke about himself, for with all his aristocratic airs he tended to present himself – a trifle unconvincingly, I thought – as a cross between Oblomov and the Good Soldier Schweik.

'It's the only way to survive, dear boy. When people feel they can laugh at you, they are less likely to cut your throat. The one thing you must never do is to give the suspicion that you're laughing at *them*, which, of course, I do all the time. Having a deformity helps, and if I hadn't fallen and broken my nose, I'd have had it done professionally. I also cultivated a lisp for a time.'

We were by then on first-name terms. He called me Harry, and asked me to call him Mitri, which was a relief, for I usually stumbled on Mitrofanoff.

He observed that I seemed to have few friends in Oxford.

'Not surprising, really. You're old for your age, most Englishmen are young for theirs. It's their redeeming quality, they never grow up. I once came upon one of my colleagues unannounced – an old man with an international reputation as an authority on Slavonic languages – and found him on all fours, playing with an electric train. He didn't even have the excuse of children or grandchildren. He had bought it for himself as a Christmas present, and offered to let me work the signalling equipment. If dons are like that, what is one to expect of the undergraduates?'

My contemporaries were perhaps not quite as childish as he suggested, though insofar as they were I should have liked to join the fun, but I was never asked, and I began to wonder if there was something about my appearance or manner which made people keep their distance. Did I have stale breath, or body odour? I used to shower or bathe twice a day in Cairo and although the primitive sanitary arrangements at the college made it difficult to maintain the habit, I still bathed at least once a day, and if anything I was obsessively clean. Was I perhaps too clean – washed out? Was I deficient in body odour? Was it perhaps my bookishness? I did have a habit of carrying a book round with me everywhere I went, and (except when dining in hall) would prop it up against the sauce bottles when I sat down for a meal, but I had only developed the habit because a book was company of sorts.

There were any number of societies and clubs, political, religious, cultural, social, and some with no apparent purpose whatever. I was not interested in politics or religion. I did try something called the Tolstoy Society, but found it full of thin, earnest women with lank hair who talked through their noses, and I did not feel encouraged to try anything else. I also went along to one or two Union debates and, although the topics discussed were serious enough, the speakers were frivolous, even facetious. I wouldn't have minded the frivolity if I could have joined in, but most of the jokes seemed to be private, and I gradually came to realize that to enjoy Oxford socially one had to enter as part of a group, from the same school, or the same town,

31

or the same religious denomination, or, if one was foreign, from the same country or region. I did not fit into any group. I would not have been regarded as a Latvian by Latvians, a German by Germans, or an Egyptian by Egyptians, and I was painfully slow in becoming the Englishman my grandfather wished me to be.

During my first year, however, I was sustained by the very novelty of Oxford, its ceremonies, its caps and gowns, its crested blazers, its buildings, the sound of bells on misty Sunday mornings, and snatches of Evensong from this or that chapel, its eccentrics and eccentricities and, indeed, my simple pride in being in the place. It suggested that I had done something with my life, and might yet do more. By the second year I came to take much of it for granted and was left with little to temper the ache of loneliness.

I derived considerable satisfaction from my studies and the praise heaped upon me by tutors, but it was no compensation for my social isolation, especially as the end of the term approached and the moist night air echoed with boisterous laughter and the sound of merry-making and merry-makers.

Then one afternoon an attractive, if scruffily dressed, young woman, with blue eyes and a pretty upturned nose, came up to me and asked if I wanted to buy a ticket for a dance.

There are thousands of students in Oxford, but certain faces stand out, and although I had never made her acquaintance, I had seen her before a number of times, and once I looked up from a book in the Bodleian to find her staring at me with a half-amused expression.

I was slightly startled by her approach, and she repeated the question in a loud voice, as if I was deaf.

'Would you like to buy a ticket for a dance?'

'A dance?'

'You know, you put your right foot in, you put your left foot out, you do the hokey-cokey and waggle it all about, that sort of thing, and I'll be there, so you can't possibly refuse.'

She didn't mention the date, the venue or the price, but it would have been unchivalrous to say no, and in any case I was cheered by her insistence, and I not only bought a ticket but eventually turned up at the dance. There was a small band, which made a loud noise out of all proportion to its size, and a large and boisterous crowd. Some of the chaps couldn't keep their feet, which, given the nature of the occasion, was no disadvantage. I stood by the door for about ten minutes feeling very self-conscious, for apart from anything else I wore a very ornate waistcoat which caused some of the dancers to falter in their step, and not a few of them commented on it in loud voices and uncomplimentary terms. Of the pretty ticket-seller with the upturned nose, however, there was no sign, and I was about to leave when I felt a hand grasping mine, and I was pulled into the centre of the floor.

'Shall we dance?' she said.

It wasn't quite a dance, but merely a matter of bouncing up and down to the beat of the band. I was fascinated by the movement of her ample breasts, which threatened to escape her blouse. She said something to me, which I couldn't hear above the noise, and she repeated it in a loud voice:

'What's the matter? Have you never seen a pair of tits before?'

I heard her that time, so did everybody else, for at that moment the music suddenly stopped, but before I could answer a long-haired figure with a red beard like a gruff Jesus pounced on her and pulled her away.

There were a number of unaccompanied girls in the place, some of them rather attractive, but I hesitated to approach them, possibly out of fear of rebuff, and because I wanted to be free to get back to the ticket-seller. I not only liked her appearance and personality, but her uncouth turn of phrase.

My knowledge of Englishwomen was derived partly from contact with the genteel, rather remote English maiden ladies who taught me English literature and drama at our Cairo school, and partly from my reading of Jane Austen. The word 'tits' emanating from that dainty, red-lipped mouth, therefore, had an overwhelming effect on me. I had stumbled upon another England and another sort of Englishwoman, and I urgently wanted to know more of them. Perhaps she had had the same effect on others there, for although I kept stationing myself at strategic points to be at hand when she was free, somebody somehow managed to grab her first and the evening was almost over before I finally got hold of her.

She looked at me rather coldly and held me at arm's length. I asked if I had done something to displease her, and she said:

'You're a bastard, aren't you?'

33

It was not the sort of proposition with which one could easily argue.

'I should imagine I am,' I said, 'but what makes you ask?'

'All those girls hanging around – couldn't you have asked one of them to dance? They weren't all ugly, and even if they were, it wouldn't have killed you to bob around with one or another of them for a minute or two, instead of standing around in your fancy westkit like a stuffed dummy.'

'I'm sorry, was that expected of me? I didn't know.'

It was difficult to talk above the noise and we went to the pub next door. I had a little glass of sherry. She had a great overflowing mug of beer, and every time she raised it to her mouth a frothy moustache formed on her upper lip. I could imagine hair growing on her chest.

'I don't suppose you've been to a dance before, have you?'

'Not this sort of thing, no.'

'And women frighten you a little bit, don't they?'

'Frighten? No, I wouldn't say frighten, but they're a little outside my experience.'

'I thought so. You're a fairy, aren't you?'

'A what?'

'A fairy.'

It says something for my sheltered upbringing and my innocence that even at the age of nineteen I wasn't quite sure what she was talking about, but her meaning became clear as she went on, and I felt bound to assure her that I had the normal equipment of the normal male.

'I'm sure you have, but for all I know you may use it as a pipe-cleaner.'

She put her hand on my knee. 'Does this do anything for you?'

'Yes.'

She moved her hand upwards.

'And this?'

There was no need to answer. I was breathing heavily and must have turned red, for she said:

'You know, I think you're a virgin.'

'You make it sound like a form of original sin.'

'It *is* a form of original sin. No man is an island. Any man who forgoes a pleasure which is his to enjoy makes the world a less happy place.'

34

Although she had probed me for the most intimate details about myself, the only things I learnt about her were that her first name was Sue and that she was a student at Somerville College.

I phoned her the next day and asked if I could speak to, or leave a message for her, but it must have been a vintage year for Sues. The college porter said there were at least a dozen and asked me for her surname. I didn't know it, but said she was dark-haired and blue-eyed and had the most enchanting upturned nose.

'I'm sorry, sir, but I have a poor eye for noses.'

'She has a large bosom.'

'Bosom, did you say, sir?'

'Bosom.'

'We have more than a few whoppers in this College, sir; in fact, without wishing to boast, sir, Somerville is famous for them.'

I suppose I should have gone down to lay siege to the College until she emerged, but I had a rather difficult essay to complete for a rather demanding tutor, and I took my inability to contact her as a sign that I should get down to work.

She, for her part, must have taken my supposed indifference as a challenge, for I emerged from my lodgings one evening to find her waiting for me. The situation reminded me a little of Markham, except that I welcomed her importunity.

'Aren't you going to ask me in?' she said.

'I was about to go out.'

'Do you have to?'

As a matter of fact I did, but I still went back in and, at her request, poured her a large brandy.

'I thought you'd try and phone me,' she said.

'I tried to, but your College is full of Sues, and I didn't know your surname.'

'Didn't you? It's Cohen.'

'Cohen?'

'You seem startled. I'm Jewish, does that frighten you?'

'Not in the least.'

'As a matter of fact I thought you were Jewish yourself.'

'What made you think so?'

'Your cock, actually.'

'My what?'

'You heard. I didn't see it, but it felt distinctly Jewish, though, of course, you could be Moslem, or even American – '

35

'Why American?'

'Because Americans are nipped in the bud – albeit without ceremony, at birth – didn't you know?'

She was full of such arcane bits of wisdom.

I had never received any guidance on the subject, but I presumed that as she had taken it upon herself to invite herself into my rooms, the normal courtesies of Oxford life required me to 'enter in unto her', as they say in the Bible, but the blunt and off-hand manner with which she approached the subject of sex tended to defuse it. I had, as I said, already discovered that she was no Austenian heroine, but she was so far outside my experience of women that I was not quite sure what to make of her.

The only woman I knew as a woman was, of course, Carla; otherwise my knowledge was derived from books and from conversation with Gerald. He rarely spoke about anything else and explained that good Jews, like good Moslems, rarely consort with females of their own class except with a view to marriage, and his contacts with women were, therefore, limited to prostitutes.

'It's ideal,' he said. 'You come, you have your fun, you pay and you go. The only possible drawback is that you can sometimes come away with a dose of the clap.'

He offered to take me, and even pay for me, but I was put off by the thought of the clap, and I suppose the same thought must also have affected my response to my visitor. Anyhow I failed to rise to the occasion and when she rose to leave, she said:

'You *are* a fairy, aren't you?'

'I thought you had satisfied yourself to the contrary.'

'I've satisfied myself that you have a cock, and a big one at that, but fairies have cocks, you know – they may not deserve them, but they do have them.'

She had to go on to a tutorial and so did I, but I asked if we could meet again.

'What for?'

'I like your company.'

'You don't act as if you do. Forget it.'

But I didn't want to forget it, and I wouldn't have been able to even if I tried, for if I had failed to make use of her company when

I had it, I yearned for it when it was no longer there. I must have been moved by curiosity more than lust but I phoned her almost daily; she never returned my calls. Then one day I must have caught her by the phone for she answered in person, but when she heard it was me she told me to go and fuck myself, which, as rebuffs go, sounded fairly final and it left me feeling disheartened. Then, just as I was beginning to despair, there came a card out of the blue, which I still have, and which I have always intended to frame. It bore the message: 'Miss Sue Cohen requests the pleasure of your company to an ORGY. Dress/Undress Optional.' The date was a Sunday some two weeks ahead.

I was to receive rather more important messages in the years ahead, but I can recall none which brought me greater jubilation. It was, apart from anything else, the first time in my life that I had been invited to a party, and this promised to be more than a party, an initiation rite. Hitherto I had passed among my contemporaries as a sort of ghost. Now, at last, I was about to become part of living Oxford.

When I received the card a muffled bell rang somewhere at the back of my mind to suggest that I might be otherwise engaged, and the Sunday was nearly upon me when I remembered that I was expected in Edinburgh that weekend as the guest of a Dr Graham, who had worked with my grandfather in Vienna. I had been looking forward to the weekend, for my grandfather rarely spoke of companions or friends and I had always thought of him as a man alone, and I was eager to meet Dr Graham if only because the more I thought of grandfather the more of an enigma he became, and I felt that an encounter with a former colleague might help me to understand him, but I could not give such thoughts priority over the promise of an orgy, and I phoned him with some faked-up excuse about exams ahead for which I was ill prepared.

'I understand, I quite understand,' he said. 'I was a student myself, you know. Bring your books and papers here and I'll see that you're undisturbed,' and put the phone down. In the circumstances I felt I had no alternative but to go up as arranged, but I planned to leave Edinburgh early on Sunday morning so as to be back in Oxford in good time for the party.

It was a desolate weekend. Dr Graham, a rotund, white-haired figure, kept proffering large glasses of whisky and talking in a

semi-intelligible accent about Freud and Jung and 'other im-
mortals'. 'Your grandfather,' I heard him say (or thought I did),
'could have been an immortal if he hadn't buried himself in some
obscure Russian forest.'

He must have found me an inattentive listener, for as he was
talking I could see Sue in different postures and various states of
disarray: Sue on the bed, Sue on the floor, Sue in the bath, Sue
dangling from a chandelier.

I left him immediately after breakfast early on Sunday morning. As I approached the border it began snowing slightly, and
then heavily. By the time I reached Yorkshire the roads were
impassable.

I abandoned my car, trudged to the nearest village and tried to
phone Sue. All the lines were down. If I had not been numb with
cold I might have cried.

It was Wednesday before the roads were clear, and by the time
I reached Oxford the term was over, Sue had gone home and
there was no one about who could tell me where home was. It
was only then that I sat down and wept.

I later wondered if I had not used the onset of the snows as an
excuse to *avoid* my destiny. I liked Sue's sprightly company and
the promise of instant seduction, but the promise may have
remained attractive for as long as it was unfulfilled, and perhaps I
was afraid of fulfilment. After all, I had had her alone, on my
own, in my own rooms, ready and willing to do anything I asked,
for had she not volunteered her own presence? And yet I had
kept my distance. With one such opportunity forgone, and
another almost wilfully lost, I came to wonder whether I was the
man I thought I was. Could Sue have been right after all? Was I
a fairy? Or was I apprehensive about the thought of getting
emotionally involved with a Jewess? If not, why did I go up by car
when I could have gone by plane? Why did I go at all? I did have
an old-fashioned habit of keeping appointments and sticking to
arrangements, but I could have allowed myself an exception on
this one occasion, and I didn't. Moreover, once stuck in the snow,
why didn't I abandon my car and try to continue the journey by
train? Didn't it suggest that my car meant more to me than Sue?

There is nothing quite as desolate as an Oxford college on a
foggy winter's night after its inmates have scattered for Christmas. I had made no plans for the holiday in the hope that

38

something or someone might turn up to make it bearable. Sue had turned up for a happy moment, but I had virtually turned down the hope of companionship she offered, and the empty rooms, the empty corridors, the silent, empty quads, almost symbolized the desolation I felt in myself.

I had dutifully offered to spend Christmas with my grandfather, but he had written to say that he would be away and all I could see ahead was several weeks of solitary confinement. Being alone in a crowd is one thing, for one somehow obtains an oblique companionship from the mere presence of others, but being alone on one's own is quite another. I was afraid I might become suicidal, when I received an unexpected invitation from my aunt Carla.

—— Chapter Three ——

I had kept in touch with Clara intermittently over the years after she complained that I only sent her Christmas cards:

'. . . you're all I've got, Heinschein, and I want to know everything about you, how you're doing at school, what friends you're making, what your plans are. Nearly everyone I knew is dead, so letters are company for me. I save them all and read and re-read them, and I want you to write to me at least once a month. . . '

I didn't have all that much to tell her but I did as she asked and wrote regularly once a month, until her letters to me began to fall off and I wrote every two or three months, till by the time I got to Oxford I was only writing about once or twice a year, while she hardly wrote at all. The invitation to spend Christmas with her, therefore, came right out of the blue and I readily accepted.

She had moved to Frankfurt and I expected to find her in some small back room, but the Germany I found bore no relation to the Germany I had left some six years earlier. Shops were full, traffic was heavy, people seemed well-dressed and well-fed, perhaps even over-fed, and Clara lived in a spacious, well-furnished, centrally-heated flat. She had dyed her hair a bright red, and at first I thought she wore a wig, for her hair used to be short, but now it went down to her shoulders. She had a well-paid job with a large American company, and her lively, girlish manner made it difficult to believe that she belonged to my grandfather's generation; but if he was old for his years, she was young for hers, and her new-found prosperity may also have retarded the onset of age.

But the change in Clara was not merely due to the change in circumstances. She had found a boy-friend, a large, cheerful, red-faced American called Chuck, who drank a lot and who was an executive of the firm she worked for. He came for dinner one evening and stayed the night, and the thought, and perhaps even the tremors, of what was happening next door, kept me restless in my lonely, celibate bed. If Sue had been around at that moment, I think I would have satisfied her that I was anything but a fairy.

I presumed Chuck would be with us over Christmas itself, but he had to return to America to be with his wife and children. I had never envisaged my aunt as a German butterfly, but she seemed to be content with her role, indeed she bloomed on it.

We had Christmas dinner together, just she and I, a delicious meal, with abundant wine in front of a blazing fire (she had central heating *and* an open fire, an unheard-of extravagance).

I was oddly aware of her even before we sat down for the meal. I helped her to set the table, and when our hands accidentally touched, something like a tremor ran through me.

When we were at table, and after we had had a glass or two or wine, she said to me:

'And has our little Heinschein got himself a girl-friend yet?'

'Not yet.'

'I'm surprised. You're a good-looking boy, and nearly twenty. What are you looking for?'

I leaned over and took her hand.

'Someone like you,' I said. There was a glint in her eyes, half-amused, half-mischievous, and after looking at me for a moment she rose from the table and began to unbutton her dress.

'What are you waiting for?' she whispered.

I began pulling off my clothes, while she stretched herself out in front of the fire almost like some sort of offering. For a woman of her age she was in remarkably good shape.

'You *are* a big boy,' she said, 'but then you always were, even as a child.'

I tried to ease myself into her.

'Not yet,' she said, 'save it,' but the moment she touched me I overflowed, and I felt like a little boy who had spilt his helping of trifle at a rather grand party.

'You're too excited,' she said. 'We'll try again later.'

And later things went according to plan. As they did the following morning, the following afternoon and the following night. Christmas took on a new meaning for me.

I had planned to return to Oxford before the New Year, but in

41

the event stayed till Twelfth Night. I might have been tempted to stay till Easter if Chuck had not returned. In fact when he did appear and Clara fell upon him with open arms, I experienced my first severe pangs of sexual jealousy. What right had this large, red-faced alien to defile my beloved aunt? Clara must have sensed my feelings, for when she drove me to the airport she said: 'You're much better than Chuck, and bigger,' which I thought was in poor taste, and which did not entirely mollify my feelings. She also urged me to come back to Frankfurt, and to come often, but there was hardly any point in doing so while Chuck was around.

When I returned to Oxford I returned to my senses with that purposeful sobriety which often assails people after a prolonged debauch. I was tempted to contact Sue, but I was by now more than half-way through my degree course, and I was afraid to do so. 'You are well in line for a First,' Mitri had told me, 'unless you take active steps to avoid it,' and contacting Sue would have been about as active a step as I could have taken.

What pained me was the fact that she did not try to contact me. It would not have been sensible to look for temptations, but I would, I think, have forgiven myself for yielding if temptation had come looking for me. I thought I could recognize her in every face I saw. I looked out for her in the Bodleian and other places she used to frequent, but there was no sign of her, but I did not dare to go down to her College, for I was afraid I would find her.

That spring was the sunniest and most prolonged I could remember, full of soft sound and fragrant whispers, and my loneliness and isolation were borne in upon me by every tinkle of laughter. I could hear the thrust of boats on the river and the strum of guitars, and trees sighing under the weight of their greenery. I could contain myself throughout April and much of May, but then one evening, at the end of a torrid day, when Oxford was awash with the glow of the setting sun, I told myself that a Second and a fuck therewith was better than a First and yearning therewith, and cycled over to Somerville, only to find that she had sat her Finals and had left the previous day. I returned to my rooms feeling that I was fated to take a brilliant First, and a brilliant First I took. Who was it who said, 'Show me a First and I'll show you a leper'?

I not only got a First but, what was perhaps more important, I obtained a major research scholarship enabling me to remain in Oxford for a further three years.

I had gone up to Oxford with only a vague idea as to what I might do when I had finished, and had considered the possibility of taking up law. After about a year, I thought I would prefer a University job if possible, and now, with a first-class honours and a research scholarship, such a possibility was clearly in sight.

I had a conscience about my grandfather, for I had only travelled to see him once since I had left Egypt, and he was too shaky to come and see me, but I felt that my triumphs made up for my lack of attention, and when I cabled him the news he wrote:

'What you have told me was no more than I expected. Since you were a small child, I always felt that you were something special, with special abilities, special qualities and a brilliant future. I have no doubt that you will make the most of it, and that given your great gifts and powers of application, you will have much happiness and success ahead. Your grandmother would have been very happy and very proud. You are a great compensation for all the disappointments we have suffered, and I know that you are too wise to let it all go to your head. God bless you, my boy.'

Mitri did a dance when I told him the news.

'This calls for a celebration, don't you think?', and he took me out to dinner at the Randolph, which made a change from the smell of stale cooking and the oppressive atmosphere of his home.

'Now that you've conquered Russia, so to speak, you must make yourself a quiet corner all of your own.'

I had already thought of that and was entertaining the possibility of writing about the development of Lithuanian trade.

'No, no, my boy, stay clear of Lithuania. It's too full of Jews, and Jews mean complications. You will have to learn Hebrew script and Yiddish to get at the sources, and even if you do you'll stumble on material which you will be unable to utter and which no one will publish.'

'Why not?'

'It's not even fifteen years since the war, and Jews are still a taboo subject. You may write of their positive qualities, which are

43

many and well-founded, but you daren't touch upon anything negative, not yet. Save that for your old age. In the meantime, avoid Lithuania and Poland. Try Karelia.'

He too prophesied happiness and triumphs ahead.

'My God, I envy you. When I was your age I was often suicidal. I could face up to the dangers which accompanied the Russian revolution, but not the loneliness, poverty and squalor which followed. To be an undergraduate in Oxford – to be an undergraduate anywhere – is no great joy, for it offers the maximum of temptations with the minimum of restraints, and the years are full of momentary pleasures and lasting regrets, but with a good degree behind you, and greater maturity, you can really begin to enjoy the place. At your age Oxford is paradise.'

The hopes he and grandfather had for me – certainly their hopes about my happiness – were not immediately fulfilled.

The period of history I had planned to research was already sufficiently covered, and I was encouraged instead to look into the development of the Soviet banking system, and if my research work and the occasional meetings with my supervisor offered some satisfaction, I derived little joy from anything else, and the next few years were among the dreariest of my life.

My grandfather had provided me with a generous allowance while I was an undergraduate. When I qualified I felt I should be independent, but found that once I had paid for my lodgings and food I had little money left for anything else. There had been times in my childhood when I was on the verge of starvation, but then everyone around me was equally hungry, but now for the first time I felt the actual pinch of poverty, so that, for example, I had to forgo coffee after lunch because I often lacked the few coppers to pay for it. There was, of course, no question of buying books, and if I wanted to read a paper I had to wait till I could get hold of a copy in the Senior Common Room.

To an extent it was controlled poverty because I could, *in extremis*, have cabled the old man for funds, and I could imagine what it must have been like to be not only destitute but without an avenue of escape from destitution. I finally found my escape not through resort to my grandfather but by taking a part-time job with a crammers' college which prepared students – mostly foreign – for entrance to British universities. It was a curious institution, manned by superannuated dons, unfrocked priests, old soldiers who hadn't had too good a war and were having an even worse peace, writers suffering from writers' block, and research students like myself unable to survive on their grants. There was a high turnover of students and an even higher turnover of staff, and there was about the staff-room a permanent smell of stale gin, stale tobacco and stale urine which we ascribed to the presence of a gentleman we called the Oldest Inhabitant, a gnarled figure with a beak of a nose, the only one among us actually to wear an academic gown, possibly to hide the fact that he had no academic qualifications. He could be found asleep at most times of the day or night, in a grease-covered armchair in a corner of the Common Room.

One day I was sitting at the table, working, when I looked up and saw him staring at me with one large, bloodshot, disapproving eye. He reminded me at that moment of a debauched eagle.

'What are you doing, young man?' he demanded.

'Marking papers.'

'Thought you were. A waste of time. These lads aren't here to study, they use this place as an occasion for a fuck, a quick fuck or a slow one, as the case may be, but that's all they're here for, to fuck.'

And then, having delivered himself of his Delphic utterance, he slumped back into sleep.

A week or so later, I was sheltering in a doorway from the rain when I saw him splashing along through the puddles, his shoulders hunched, his knees bent, his hands in his pockets, and I called out to him. He turned to look at me. There was rain falling from the brim of his battered homburg on to his nose, from which it descended in a straight line to his waistcoat. There was also water running along the furrows of his face. He was almost the embodiment of a wet afternoon.

'Aren't you going to come in from the rain?' I said. 'You'll get drenched.'

'I am drenched,' he said, and continued on his way, though at an accelerated pace.

The next day, he apologized for not stopping to talk:

'You see, I have this regular arrangement with a young lady. At my age, you've got to keep your member in regular use, otherwise it seizes up altogether. She normally charges the earth,

45

but I send her my students, so she fits me in by way of commission. She'd fit you in as well if I put it to her.' And such was my isolation that I nearly took him up on his offer.

Mitri was on an extended sabbatical in America, so that I could not even look to the hospitality and companionship he used to offer. On the other hand, as I was no longer an undergraduate, I was less conscious of the cliques and groups and societies and clubs on every side of me and, therefore, less troubled by a sense of exclusion.

My supervisor, Dr Kluger, a brisk, dapper figure in well-cut suits and a taste for double-breasted waistcoats, which gave him a slightly archaic look, confined our contacts to the business in hand, never asked me about myself, never talked about himself, and never asked me up for as much as a sherry, but he was very encouraging and, at his recommendation, I was invited to address a seminar, organized by one of the clearing banks, on East European trade. It was held in a large London hotel and, when we broke up for lunch, one of the participants, a tall, dark-haired figure called Mr Rich, who, indeed, looked it, invited me to join him for a drink. He complimented me on my paper, and said:

'I take it you know Russian.'

'Reasonably well.'

'Any other languages?'

'German and Arabic, a bit of French.'

'That's enough to get on with.'

I had noticed before that Englishmen were unduly impressed by anyone familiar with a language other than English. At school in Cairo even the clots were bilingual, and some of the boys spoke three or four languages. My grandfather spoke six, and even Clara spoke four. Rich himself knew only a bit of 'opera Italian', as he put it, which he had picked up while serving in Italy during the war. He had also served two years in Egypt, but the only thing he had picked up there was malaria.

He asked me so much about myself, my experience, my background, my aspirations, but said little about himself. The gathering was composed of bankers, academics and financial journalists, and I took it from his well-cut suit and immaculate appearance that he was not an academic, and probably not a journalist. I suppose I should have asked him who he was, but that, as I had already discovered, was a hazardous thing to do when moving among people with a claim – or who believed they had a claim – to eminence, and it was only after the gathering had dispersed that I discovered he was a director of Eissenmacher's, the merchant bankers.

I was puzzled by the interest he had shown in me, but had not otherwise given much thought to the encounter until a few weeks later, when I received a letter from him. It was oddly phrased: 'I don't know if you've ever given thought to the possibility of a career in banking, but if you have, perhaps you might like to come down to see us and talk to us.'

In those days, anyone who took an Oxford First was allowed to think that the world was his oyster and that he could be almost anything he wished, and although I had amused myself with thoughts of various careers, I had never entertained the thought of entering a bank, nor did I feel my training equipped me to be a banker, but I was, nevertheless, flattered and intrigued by his letter and readily accepted his invitation.

I thought I would be meeting him privately but, after a preliminary chat, found myself ushered into a boardroom lunch, presided over by the Chairman, a diminutive, pink-faced, white-haired figure with a nicotined moustache, called Lord Firwood. The meal was pleasant enough, the wine was superb, and we discussed everything under the sun except my future – if any – with the company, and I returned to Oxford feeling deflated and nonplussed. Presumably Rich had exceeded his authority in the offer he made me, but then he hadn't strictly speaking made me an offer in the first place, and perhaps I had read more into his letter than it contained. Or perhaps he had made me an offer but his colleagues felt that I was not really the man for them. I may not have deported myself with sufficient grace, I had drunk too much or too little, I had eaten too briskly, or my conversation was not sufficiently stimulating, or perhaps my breath smelt. When I examined myself in the mirror that night I wondered, not for the first time, whether there was something about my appearance or manner which caused people to distance themselves from me. I was uncommonly tall and had a slightly woebegone look, but otherwise I seemed fairly normal.

The following afternoon the Oldest Inhabitant (whose actual name was Breecher) said to me:

'Had an upset?'

'Why, do I look upset?'

'You always do, but today you look even more upset than usual. If it's any consolation to you I'm upset myself. They've taken her away.'

'Taken who away?'

'The young lady, the consolation of my old age. They arrested her and her young man for keeping a disorderly house, or something of that order. I was nearly run in myself. I'll have to find somebody else, not all that easy at my age, you know.'

But it could not have been too difficult either, for a few days later he said to me:

'Are you out of your place all day?'

'Most of the day.'

'Ah! Would you mind if I dropped in for an hour or so?'

'By all means, when I got home in the evening.'

'No, not in the evening, in the afternoon, when you're out. You see, I live with my sister, the old cow, and – well, you understand.'

I did, and handed him my spare key there and then, but I completely forgot about the arrangement and, coming home one afternoon, I found him and a stout, middle-aged woman in what used to be called 'a compromising position'. Compromising or not, it was certainly indelicate. I took one look, muttered an apology and fled.

'You might have knocked,' he said to me reproachfully the next day.

'I'm sorry, I completely forgot.'

'You're not entitled to be absent-minded at your age.'

I came to regret the arrangement, for apart from the fact that I had to hesitate, cough loudly, ring the bell, and knock on the door before entering my own rooms, I had to throw open the windows to let the atmosphere of frayed lust, stale urine and perfumed sweat disperse. Then amidst all this there came a letter from Carla with the happy news that Chuck had finally abandoned his family and had moved in with her as a permanent resident. For the first time in my life I began to feel sorry for myself.

About three weeks, or perhaps even a month, after the lunch – I had tried to drive the occasion from my mind – I received a letter

48

from Rich apologizing for not writing sooner, and formally offering me a job. He mentioned a salary so large that I at first thought it was his telephone number and such was my state of dejection that as I read and re-read his letter I kept asking myself, what did they want *me* for? When I told Kluger about it the next day, he seemed to share my feelings.

'You got an offer from Eissenmacher's?'

'Yes, sir.'

'The merchant bank?'

'At what level?'

'Fairly senior, to judge by the salary.'

'I hope you don't think I'm inquisitive, but do you need the money?'

'Who doesn't?'

'Indeed, but I was somehow under the impression that you had money behind you, but then one does fall into the habit of thinking that anyone who isn't English must have money, if only by way of compensation. I'll tell you why I asked. You're one of the most promising students I have and I think there is a definite future for you in academic life, though, of course, not much money . . .'

What he was really offering me was the choice between genteel poverty and gross riches. I must have disappointed him, for I unhesitatingly chose riches.

I left a paper behind on his desk, and when I turned to retrieve it, I thought I saw him looking at me with a mixture of envy and chagrin.

That evening, by way of celebration, I took Breecher out to dinner.

'Well,' he said, 'it's good to have friends in high places, but once you're installed you'll forget you ever knew me.'

'Oh, no, I won't.'

'Oh, yes, you will, and if I was in a high place I would want to forget I ever knew myself. In fact, even friends in low places forget me.'

His normally aggressive tones turned doleful.

'As a matter of fact, I used to be in a fairly high place myself. Mayor of a cathedral town, Governor of the choir school, prison visitor, but I had this unfortunate habit – but I don't want to bother you with the details.'

49

I didn't want to be bothered with the details, but after gazing into his gin for some seconds, he went on to bother me with them all the same.

'Everybody's got something to hide,' I said.

'I'm sure they have, only they manage to keep it hidden. Ah, people will tell you, there's one thing about ruin and disgrace, you get to know who your real friends are. What you get to know is that you've no real friends. Drop old Breecher a line, if only at Christmas.'

—— *Chapter Four* ——

There is nothing like a high salary, a carpeted office in a tower block, a battery of telephones and an attractive secretary to give a man a good conceit of himself.

At first I would sit in my swivel chair, gaze out at the panoramic view below and ask myself what I was doing there, but what began to give me confidence was the sight of an elegant young woman, with magnificent legs, taking down every word I uttered and then returning them to me in an immaculate typescript. The typescripts, indeed, may have added to my confidence more than anything else, for they made my every pronouncement seem Delphic.

I had to prepare abstracts on the economic situation of most of the East European countries we traded with, list their principal imports and exports and give my appreciation of their credit-worthiness. To update my information I had to have frequent meetings with trade attachés, which usually took the form of lunches, and I became familiar with every expensive restaurant in London.

I rented a furnished flat in New Cavendish Street, round the corner from the BBC, which was convenient, for after a year or so in the bank I received frequent invitations to comment on East European trade on BBC news programmes.

The Chairman heard me one evening as he was being driven home, and I was summoned to his room.

'That was you on the wireless yesterday, was it not?'

'Yes, sir.'

'Thought the name rang a bell. Been with us long?'

'Over a year.'

'Hope you don't mind my asking, but what exactly do you do here?'

And I told him, after which he may have read my reports for the first time, or read them with new eyes, for I was again summoned to his presence.

'I like the way you handle things, Newman, very clear, very neat, to the point. Could you do the same for Brazil? Very big, Brazil, country of the future.'

'It is a little outside my field, sir.'

'Shouldn't take you long to mug it all up, bright young man like you.'

'I might need an assistant.'

'By all means. Have a word with Rich. He'll fix you up.'

But it wasn't as straightforward as that.

'I should have warned you about the old man,' said Rich. 'He's a bit past it and doesn't know what's happening. Brazil isn't Russia. We've got people on the spot there, and always have had, who know exactly what's happening, sometimes even before it happens. Forget about it; I'm sure he will.'

And he did.

My responsibilities, however, grew not because of any whim of the old man but because of the increase in trade with the eastern bloc, and instead of preparing background reports I was increasingly involved in negotiations with trade officials and spent half the year in planes and hotels, which could be pleasant enough if one found oneself in Budapest, but which could be bleak and dispiriting if one found oneself in Warsaw or East Berlin.

And again, in the midst of busy negotiations I would suddenly become aware of myself, working out agreements involving millions of pounds affecting the livelihoods of thousands of people, and feel uneasily that this was all some big mistake and that fortune had pushed me into a role for which I was not equipped. At what point, I wondered, would I come to accept that I had not been advanced to my position in error, or through the whims of friends or the influence of relatives, and if I had got anywhere at all it was through sheer ability and hard work.

I suppose my doubts about myself persisted because while I enjoyed a certain success in business I was, in other respects, an abject failure.

I am not sure how the belief entered my head – perhaps it was derived from American films – but somehow I assumed that attractive secretaries were fair game, available not only for work but for pleasure. My own secretary was called Iris, and about a month after I settled into my job I asked if she would care to come out to dinner.

She looked up in surprise:

'Are you talking to me?'

'Who else?'

'I'm sorry, I thought you were dictating a letter. I'm afraid I can't. I have an ailing mother in Haslemere who waits up for me, and she gets worried if I'm home late.'

I thought of asking her out to lunch instead, but with her expensive clothes and exotic perfumes she didn't look the sort of girl who lived with an ailing mother in Haslemere, and I took it that her excuse was a polite way of saying no.

Some months later, I was ascending in the lift to the top floor when a young girl entered with some folders under her arm. It is possible for people to share a railway carriage for hours on end without exchanging a word, but it is difficult to stay silent within the more intimate confines of a lift, even though the journey may only take seconds, and after searching my mind for what to say, I asked:

'Are you new here?'

'Yes.'

'Who do you work for?'

'Everybody.'

'What do you do?'

'Everything.'

We found ourselves in the same lift again on the way down, and in an inspired moment, I said: 'We'll have to stop meeting like this,' at which she smiled.

I took her out to lunch that day. Her name was Sylvia, and she had long, blonde hair reaching down to her back in the style made famous some years before by Brigitte Bardot, but she did not have the same voluptuous build and, in fact, looked slightly pinched and undernourished.

'Are you one of the bosses?' she asked.

'I'm not a director, if that's what you mean.'

'But you're on the eighteenth floor, aren't you?'

'Yes.'

'So you must be a high-up. How come you're so high up at your age?'

'I'm not as young as I look.'

'But you can't be over thirty, can you? Are you one of the

family? I don't mean you yourself, but did you marry one of the Eissenmacher girls?'

'Unfortunately not. In fact, I'm not married at all.'

'You're not?'

'No.'

'Funny. When a high-up asks me out, he's usually married.'

I asked her if she would like to go out for a run in the country over the week-end.

'Oh no,' she said, 'my boy-friend wouldn't like it,' and then added with a smile, 'But he can lump it, can't he?'

When I called for her the following Sunday morning, she tottered out on high-heel shoes as if she was going to a cocktail party.

'Haven't you got walking-shoes?' I asked.

'What for?'

'Walking.'

'Walking. Haven't you got a car?'

'Of course I've got a car, but wouldn't you like to walk once we're out in the country?'

'I don't want to get great, big, heavy calves like a Russian woman athlete.'

She looked askance at my Morris Minor. Presumably she had expected something bigger.

In the event, I could have done with something bigger. Her skirt was very short and as we drove along the bumpy country road, the rub of her thigh against mine made it difficult for me to maintain a straight course, or to drive at all. I pulled up under the shade of a large tree and asked if she wanted to have a walk over the meadow.

'A walk? In these shoes? How can I?'

'I didn't actually mean a walk.'

'I know what you mean, but I don't want to get myself muddy. Do you know what it costs to clean a dress these days? – and they always ruin it in the cleaning. Besides, if you're after what I think you're after we didn't have to come out all this way for it, did we? I mean, haven't you got a place of your own?'

The thought had occurred to me, but I was by now English enough to associate pleasure with rusticity, with fields and woodlands. Even if I was no shepherd, there was something nymph-like about her, and I should have liked to make love to her

54

in the meadow, earthiness to earth, under the open sky.

We tried to get to grips in the car but, given the length of my legs, it was impossible and we drove on to an expensive hotel where we had lunch and then went upstairs to bed.

It was all pleasant enough, but not Arcadian.

One afternoon she came into my office looking somewhat downcast.

'Popeye has it in for me,' she said.

'Popeye?'

'Personnel. I had to do a bit of shopping. There's nothing in the City, at least nothing that *I* could wear, and I went up West. You know what the traffic's like and what with one thing and another I overstayed my lunch-break. Well, you wouldn't believe the fuss he made. It's not as if I've all that much to do in the first place. I mean most of the time I'm just sitting around polishing my nails.'

I went to see Popeye, as she called him, a heavily built man with greying hair and floppy jowls, and I explained that she had been anxious to buy a birthday present for her mother, and that she had stayed away longer than intended.

It wasn't the excuse she had given me, and it was an odd experience hearing myself telling lies for no good reason. He listened impassively.

'I understand,' he said.

The next morning Rich called me into his office.

'Look, Newman,' he said, 'you're doing a perfectly good job, as long as you do the job you're doing, but you have no business to meddle in any other department. If you wish to bring anything to the attention of Personnel, send me a memo, and I'll deal with it.'

I left his room feeling as if I had received six of the best.

Even with the success I had attained and the standing I enjoyed in the bank, it was not difficult to shatter the little self-confidence I had.

The Chairman entertained the West German Ambassador to a boardroom lunch that day, and I was the only member of the staff present who was not actually on the Board. I was no great conversationalist, but fairly adept at introducing some pertinent remark during breaks in the conversation, and could speak with ease when it came to matters of trade. That day there were many awkward silences and Rich kept looking in my direction with a mixture of anxiety and hope, but I couldn't open my mouth. I couldn't eat either, and when I returned to my office I couldn't get down to work.

The next day I stayed away from the office, which I sometimes did when I had an immense amount of material to digest, for I always found it easier to work in isolation, but that morning I stayed away because I couldn't face the office.

I slept late, had a hot bath, but didn't shave, possibly because I couldn't face myself, and dressed very slowly, feeling oddly conscious of the weight of my limbs. I went to a nearby restaurant and ordered a coffee and croissant. I had *The Times* and the *Financial Times* under my arm but did not open them, and sat around till the coffee got cold and undrinkable. I picked up my papers, put the croissant in my pocket and walked to Regent's Park. It was a summery day, the sky was bright blue and the cherry trees were in bloom. The park was shrill with children and dogs, but I tired very easily and went back by taxi.

The phone was ringing as I opened the door. I let it ring, undressed with some difficulty and got into bed.

I don't know how long I slept. I was wakened by the door-bell, and shuffled slowly downstairs to open the door. It was Sylvia.

'Where have you been? We missed you. They've been phoning for – ' She broke off when she saw the tears streaming down my face, helped me up the stairs and put me back into bed.

I don't know if I had been overwhelmed by a sudden and severe bout of the 'flu, or a nervous breakdown, or both. I would have been content to get by with aspirins, but Sylvia insisted that I see a doctor, who tapped me and prodded me, examined my eyes and my tongue and my urine, and finally concluded that all I needed was complete rest, and to aid the process he gave me some pills. I don't know what was in them, but I felt what little strength I had ebbing out of me, as if my finger-ends were leaking, every time I took one, yet I did not lapse into sleep. Instead I was transported backwards to an earlier incarnation, to fields and forests all covered in snow, and I seemed to hear Tchaikovsky's music in my ears. The details varied. Sometimes I saw bent, black-clad figures, sometimes horses, sometimes a dog or a cat, but the snow-covered landscape was always the same, and so was the music, and I would come to convulsed with cold, as if I had been naked in the snows, and Sylvia would come into bed to warm me up. She had moved in by then as a permanent resident: I don't know how I would have survived without her.

She told me that I was visited in the course of my illness by both Rich and his wife, Giselle, who must have brought the better part of a flower-shop with her, for I opened my eyes one evening to find banks of carnations on either side of my bed, as if I had been lying in state.

Once I stopped taking the pills my recovery was fairly rapid. Rich had a place in the country and he suggested that I might wish to go there to convalesce, but I was impatient to get back to my job and I suggested to Sylvia that she might wish to get back to hers.

'Job?' she said; 'I ain't got none,' and it was only then that I discovered that she had not bothered to obtain leave to look after me and, as a result, had been dismissed.

'I'll have a word with the office manager,' I said, and even as I was speaking I had the odd sensation that my life was moving round in smaller and smaller circles, for did not my previous word with the office manager set off the whole cycle of events which had brought me to bed? I had a word with Rich instead. He didn't know who Sylvia was, and I explained that she was the young woman who had been looking after me.

'And you mean she works in this building?'

'Yes.'

He seemed surprised by that, even perturbed, but he had her reinstated.

Whoever said that two can live as cheaply as one couldn't have paid the bills. Until Sylvia moved in I had thought I was well, even extravagantly paid, but she found my rooms poky and my whole style of living cramped.

'You want a place where you can give a party or swing a cat. I mean even Popeye's got a five-bedroomed house.'

We eventually found a sizeable flat in St John's Wood which was well within my price range, but once she started ordering furnishings and furniture we moved well beyond it, and I again found myself assailed with money worries. I had, of course, had money worries while I was a research student in Oxford, but they arose out of simple poverty. My new worries came with comparative wealth, and they worried me. I managed to handle millions on behalf of the bank with unerring competence, but didn't know how to handle the few thousand I earned myself, and though I continued to get sizeable increments and generous bonuses, my debts continued to grow in proportion to my income.

I found her choice of decor a bit garish. The dominant colour was a bright green, which assailed the eyes as one entered, and which seemed to glow in the dark. The furniture was also rather better to look at than sit in, but I got used to it all, and once we were installed we decided to throw a party.

It was less than a success. I invited my colleagues and their wives, while Sylvia invited her friends, and the mix didn't work, especially as her friends took over the party and put on records of a sort, and at a pitch, which made conversation impossible. Also several of them got drunk. One girl spewed up her innards, another began to take her clothes off, which in itself was not an unwelcome diversion for she was very shapely, but, at the same time, a young man tore open his fly and they began to fornicate in the middle of the floor.

After everyone had left, which they did in something of a hurry, Sylvia said apologetically:

'I don't know who he was. I didn't invite him, honestly I didn't.'

A few weeks later the Chairman died. The funeral was private, but there was a memorial service in the parish church adjoining his estate. I was invited to attend. I wasn't sure if Sylvia was included in the invitaiton, but she had no wish to go in any case, and I went on my own.

It was an august occasion. We were addressed by a Bishop, and there were famous banking names, Barings and Rothschilds, Kleinworts and Schroeders, Warburgs and Bischofsheims on every side.

There were also some very attractive young women who did not quite go with the sombre setting, whom I took to be members of the immediate family.

After the service, Rich asked if I could give him a lift home. He had come with Giselle but she wanted to go on to visit some friends in the country and was taking the car.

There were any number of people with faster, more spacious cars who could have given him a lift and I took it that there was something behind his request, which, of course, there was, but it took him some time to get it out, like a man suffering from dyspepsia trying to bring up wind.

'Newman,' he said, 'I hope you think of me as a friend.'

I sometimes had doubts on the matter but said that I did.

'Perhaps even more than a friend.'

I wasn't quite sure what sort of status that represented. Perhaps he meant patron, but again I didn't argue and he went on:

'As you know, I pride myself on having an eye for talent and I haven't picked a dud yet. It was me who brought you to Eissenmacher's and you have fulfilled my hopes in almost every respect, But' – and he paused – 'I must say when Giselle and I came away from your house-warming party we were both a little worried.'

'I'm sorry about that. Things got a bit out of hand. It wasn't a planned performance.'

'Oh no, no, no. Good heavens, no. Giselle thinks I'm an old fuddy-duddy and that that's the sort of thing one has to expect when one moves among young people in London. And not only young people. I once had to eject a very senior colleague who drank more than was good for him and exposed himself in front of my guests. Giving a party can be a hazardous thing, and I must say we enjoyed your party very much. Splendid evening – '

'You mean memorable.'

'Well, it was that, too, but we did come away a little worried because – if you will forgive me for saying so – you combine skills, amounting to genius, in one area of life, with callowness in almost every other. Can I ask, have you any ambition?'

'I wouldn't have joined the bank if I hadn't.'

'Quite. Yet you don't give the impression that you have, because a truly ambitious young man is selective in the company he keeps.'

'Are we talking about Sylvia?'

'Oh, don't misunderstand me, she's a lively and attractive young woman and as an occasional companion one wouldn't have a hard word against her – none of us, after all, lead blameless lives – but people are beginning to think of her as your wife. I don't know if you've met the new Lady Firwood. A scrubber, straight off the streets, but then Firwood can get away with it because, of course, he's an Eissenmacher and was born at the top, but people like you and me, who have to make our way to the top, have to be more choosy. You're an attractive young man with a good education and brilliant prospects. There were two or three Eissenmacher grand-daughters in the church. Didn't you cast your eyes over them with more than a passing interest? They've not only got the name and the money, they've got looks. I can't promise you'd get anywhere with them, but that's the sort of thing you should be aiming for.'

He left me in a troubled state of mind. What he said was true. I was impossibly callow and the proof lay not in my liaison with Sylvia but in the fact that I had listened to him in silence. I should have thrown him out of the car.

When I got home that evening, I was half tempted to propose to Sylvia, if only as an answer to his presumption, and I might have done so had I not found an unsightly young man in the lounge drinking my malt whisky from a beer mug. I didn't ask who he was, or what he was doing, but simply told him to fuck off, and in those very words. He looked at me as if he hadn't heard right.

'I'm Syl's friend.'

'I don't care who you are, get out before I throw you out.'

He looked towards Sylvia by way of appeal, but she was herself too startled by my demeanour to say anything, and he fled without finishing his drink.

It was, as far as I could remember, the first time I had raised my voice, and I was pleased with the effect. I would have to do it more often.

— *Chapter Five* —

A few months after the new Chairman took over there was a shake-up in the senior management of the bank and Rich became Chief Executive. I didn't expect the change to affect me one way or the other, but a shake-up of middle management followed and I was asked if I would like to take over the Cologne office.

It would have been promotion of sorts, and it certainly entailed a higher salary. It would also have meant a move out of my specialized slot into more general banking experience, which I would have welcomed, but I had attained a certain emotional and social equilibrium, bordering almost on happiness, and a move to Germany would have meant another disruption.

Nor was I quite certain what to do about Sylvia. I could, given the informal nature of our relationship, hardly insist that she accompany me to Germany, and I half suspected that Rich had engineered the whole move in order to bring about what might be called a judicious separation.

Sylvia was used to my frequent absences abroad, and when I told her that I had been asked to go to Cologne she thought I might be away for a matter of weeks.

'No,' I said, 'it'll be rather longer than that.'

'Months?'

'Longer than that.'

'You don't mean for good?'

'No, but I would be away for three or four years, maybe five.'

'Well, that's as near to for good as counts, isn't it? What'll happen to this flat, then? And what'll happen to me?''

'Wouldn't you like to come with me?'

'To Germany? Not on your life.'

'What do you suggest I do?'

'Do what you like, but if you expect me to traipse after you to Germany, you've got another think coming.'

I was involved that day in an endless succession of meetings, and I couldn't even see her at lunch-time, and when I got home in the evening I found her packing.

'What are you up to? I shan't be moving until after the New Year.'

'Aren't you? Well, I'm moving now.'

'It's not even certain that I shall be moving at all.'

'Isn't it? Well, I am. I should have done it before, only I thought – '

'You thought what?'

'Never mind what I thought.'

I could see her distress and felt distressed in turn. I wanted to put a comforting arm around her, but wasn't sure how she would take it. Instead, I said:

'I'll stop here if you want me to.'

'Go, go. Forget about me. I'm bloody sure I'll forget about you.'

A car hooted outside, and she quickened her pace. I tried to help her shut her case.

'No, leave it alone. I'll manage.'

'Then let me carry it for you at least.'

'Will you do me a favour and fuck off!' and half carrying and half dragging her case, she clattered down the stairs and out into the night.

I looked around at the empty flat, and it suddenly seemed very, very large. And when I went to bed, it seemed very cold.

I was fortunate in the fact that I have never had problems with falling asleep (though I sometimes did have problems in staying awake), and thus wherever I found myself, no matter how uncomfortable the bed and strange the surroundings, I dropped off as soon as my head touched my pillow. Now, however, I spent a sleepless night, turning this way and that, asking myself how I could let a stranger order my life. My job wasn't worth that much to me, no job was worth that much to anybody, and when I got to the office the next morning I told Rich that I did not, after all, wish to take up the job in Cologne.

'Pity,' he said, and that was all. He was often sparing in words, but I hadn't expected him to be that sparing, and felt slightly put down.

Sylvia didn't report for work, which didn't surprise me, but when I went to her flat in the evening none of her friends knew where she was, or where she could be contacted. I then phoned her mother, who received my call with impatience.

'She's probably off with one of her boy-friends. Don't ask me which one or where to. She never tells me anything.'

Yet, though I had achieved nothing and had forgone promotion, I returned to my flat with a slight feeling of accomplishment. I had asserted myself.

I had mentioned the offer of Cologne to my grandfather, but letters to Egypt take time in reaching their destination, and about a week after I had turned down the offer I received a cable: ADVISE NOT REPEAT NOT ACCEPT LETTER FOLLOWS.

I knew exactly what lay behind it. He was satisfied that I had become the Compleat Englishman, and he was, no doubt, afraid that if I returned to Germany, even for a few years, I might revert to my origins. I cabled back to assure him that his advice had been taken even before it was received.

A few months later I was, rather to my surprise – for the area was quite outside my field of experience – asked to accompany the Chairman and two of the directors on a tour of Saudi Arabia and the Gulf States, and I arranged to travel to Cairo first, to spend a few days with my grandfather, and to join them in Riyadh.

I had neglected my grandfather shamefully since I had left Egypt, but excused myself with the thought that he didn't seem all that keen to see me. Whenever I suggested a date for a visit he replied that it would be awkward, which was reasonable enough while he was still head of a large government hospital. He was now retired and semi-mobile, but still came up with excuses that he might not be free, or that he didn't want to put me to the bother or expense of the journey, and I could only conclude that he was embarrassed by growing decrepitude.

This time I did not write to suggest a date and told him simply that I was coming. He sent his Mercedes to meet me at the airport, and as I got in I was startled to find that it already had a passenger, and a most unwelcome one at that – Markham.

It was nearly ten years since I had seen him, but he didn't appear to have aged at all, and almost blended in with the grey upholstery.

'How nice to see you,' he said.

I was too surprised to answer.

'Don't suppose the old man told you that I'm working for him.'

'You? Working for my grandfather?'

'He's nearly blind, poor chap, as you must know. I'm his amanuensis. More than that, his eyes and ears really. Been with him for a year nearly. He got into quite a flap when he heard you were coming. You won't keep him up too long, will you? He tires so easily.'

There was something about the very presence of that slight, smooth, reptilian figure which made me feel uneasy, and I even found it difficult to talk to him. We travelled in silence for a while, then he said:

'London to your liking?'

'Yes, on the whole.'

'I gather you're doing very well. The old man's very proud of you. Your letters keep him going. He's not in top form, I'm afraid.'

And he wasn't. The house itself prepared me for his appearance. It was sadly dilapidated, with peeling paintwork, warped timbers and broken shutters. Most of the rooms were in darkness, with dust-covers over the furniture, as if he was preparing for a long journey, and I found him hunched in a wheelchair in a corner of his study. My first instinct was to rush over and embrace him, but he looked slightly apprehensive, as if afraid that I might do just that, and I grasped his hand. His face was swollen and glossy, as if covered in grease.

'You shouldn't have bothered,' he said.

'I was passing through Cairo anyway.'

'Then you should have passed on.'

We had, for all the years since I last saw him, little to say to each other. He asked me about my work, but I could add little to what I had already told him in my letters.

'Have you friends?'

'Not many.'

'No, I wasn't good at making friends either, but one doesn't need many. One good friend is really all one needs.'

He added, *à propos* of nothing, that Carla had been to see him, 'with a loud American'. He seemed distressed by the memory of the visit.

After we had been together about half an hour his head began to droop. He seemed to be falling asleep. I was afraid he might topple out of his chair and called Markham, who wheeled him to his bedroom.

'He's like that all the time, poor man. Lapses in and out of sleep. But he's all there when he's awake, and he can be pretty testy. He had a stand-up argument with his sister, or rather he would have done if he'd been able to stand up.'

'What was it about?'

'Money, I should imagine. It's about the only thing which agitates people of that age. Handsome woman, his sister, in a manly sort of way.'

I remained in Cairo for two days. I could have stayed longer, but I saw no point in it, for it was obviously a strain on the old man to have me there at all.

'Hates visitors,' said Markham. 'It took him a week to recover from his sister.'

I was sorry I had come, though, of course, I'd have felt guilty if I hadn't, and I was at least able to satisfy myself that whatever misgivings I may have had about Markham, he was a conscientious, and even devoted, servant. He drove with me to the airport. 'I don't know when you hope to come again,' he said, 'but I shouldn't leave it too long – not if you hope to see him again.'

A few hours later I was in Riyadh.

When I was asked to join the tour of Saudi Arabia and the Gulf I naturally presumed it had something to do with my knowledge of Arabic, but I soon discovered that my function was rather more humble.

We were treated to lavish, Arabian-Nights-style banquets wherever we went but, as the Chairman observed, it was 'mutton, mutton everywhere, without a drop to drink'. We did not, however, go thirsty, for as the most junior member of the party I had been entrusted with the baggage, and the baggage contained a large and varied supply of alcohol, which finally answered the question of why I was there.

On our last night in Riyadh the Chairman gave a very private party behind locked doors in his hotel suite for members of our party and about a dozen or so guests. It was all very merry but I felt a little out of it and he waltzed over to me, glass in hand, and said:

'Anything the matter, Newman? You look as if you've had your balls jammed in the lift.'

65

'It's not that, sir – '

'No Sirs here, it's after office hours. The name's Edward.'

'Well it's like this, sir – '

'Edward.'

'Edward. I keep asking myself what the hell am I doing here.'

'I often ask myself the same question, especially when I can't get hold of a drop of the hard stuff, but you're a promising young man, and this is a promising area. If you're a specialist in this game you can't get very far, and certainly not to the top. I want to get you away from the wretched People's Republics and into the Middle East. I wouldn't want to be stuck here for more than a week at a time, but God, there's gold in them there dunes. You could do very well here, and I'm sure you would, only – to be perfectly frank – I sometimes have the feeling that your heart's not in banking. We offer you opportunities which any young man would have given his balls for, but you turn them down.'

'Do you mean Cologne?'

'I do indeed. It may not have been a major operation, but you would have been in charge, and it would have given you a chance to show your mettle.'

'I had a private reason for turning it down.'

'Dammit, I had private reasons for not joining the bank at all. I wanted to be an explorer, but most of my uncles kept having daughters. The old man did rather better and had three sons, but one of them went mad, another got killed. There had to be an Eissenmacher in the bank, if only as a mascot, and so I went in. I had no options in the matter.'

'But, with respect, I did. I'm not an Eissenmacher, so I didn't have to go to Cologne. I don't even have to stay in the bank.'

'But you're not thinking of leaving, surely?'

'Well, if you don't think my heart's in it, perhaps I should.'

'Now, now, Newman. My remark was not a reflection on your competence. My heart's not in the bank either, but I think you'll agree that I'm doing a reasonable job. I only wish you'd look less miserable. Have another drink.'

'I've already had a few.'

'Have a few more. The old man – who wasn't the fool he looked – used to say, never trust a man who stays sober at a drinking party, he's trying to steal a march on you.'

And he picked up a dimpled Haig and poured it into my vodka.

66

I had found my few days in Arabia not only depressing but confusing, for all the Arabs one met not only dressed alike and looked alike but they nearly all had the same name, which, all things considered, was not surprising, since they were all members of the same ruling family, but I couldn't tell them apart.

When we got to Bahrain, however, things livened up a bit, for as we stepped off the plane I saw a face which not only looked different, but which I actually recognized. It was Rashid, and as soon as he saw me he rushed forward and grasped my hand in both his. I was pleasantly taken aback by the warmth of his greeting, because our last encounter in Oxford, some ten years before, had been distinctly chilly.

'You two know each other?' said the Chairman in surprise.

'Of course,' said Rashid in his deep voice, 'we are old friends from Oxford' – after which I was regarded with new eyes. This time I was asked to attend all the meetings, most of which were presided over by Rashid, and although I had only a few occasions to open my mouth, the contributions I did make were considered useful.

I was, therefore, not surprised when towards the end of our stay one of the directors, Malcolm Beatty, a sad-eyed, soft-voiced Scot with shaggy eyebrows, said to me:

'I don't know if the Chairman mentioned this to you, but he wants you to join my department. Is the Middle East up your street?'

'Hardly. I lived in Egypt as a boy, but apart from picking up a bit of Arabic, I know very little about it.'

'It's not unlike Eastern Europe, you know. You deal with governments, or rather with members of the ruling families, and public corporations rather than private companies. Things here in Bahrain are comparatively straightforward, but otherwise you have to learn the language behind the language, if you know what I mean. They're very courteous and like to be amenable, and you often think you've reached an agreement on one set of terms, when you find them putting forward quite another. Also, some of them have ways of doing business which, if you haven't worked in the area, you may find questionable, but the possibilities are tremendous. Would you be interested?'

'I would certainly like to think about it.'

The next day we were having drinks together when he said to

me, *à propos* of nothing, 'I hope you don't mind my asking, but you wouldn't be Jewish, would you?'

I was so taken aback by the question that I wasn't sure how to answer, and he went on:

'It's your name, you see.'

'My name? Doesn't Newman sound English?'

'Of course it does, and no doubt it is, but it's the sort of name people who change their names go in for. Also, you seem to speak every language under the sun.'

'Is that also a Jewish trait?'

'Oh yes, they're marvellous linguists – been around, you see.'

'So have I.'

'Exactly, which is what made me ask.'

'Are you trying to say that if I'm Jewish I can't work in your department?'

The very suggestion seemed to distress him.

'No, no, no, don't put it that way. Christ, the Eissenmachers were Jewish at one time, everybody knows that. I've worked with Jews all my life, but you must understand the Arab mind. Their market is huge, and the competition is fierce, and, other things being equal, they prefer to deal with people who aren't Jewish.'

'In which case I may be the wrong man for your department.'

'You mean you are Jewish?'

'I'm not, but I'm not prepared to work under such terms.'

'Pity.'

An hour or so later, I was joined by the Chairman.

'Now, what's all this nonsense Beatty's been telling me?'

'I wasn't aware that you imposed religious tests on your employees.'

'Religious tests? What religious tests? My grandfather was a Jew, or at least he was born one. I'm C. of E. but my wife's a bloody Papist; my children, insofar as they're anything at all, are agnostics. Winston, the head of our legal department, is a Jew, and a practising one at that. Haven't you noticed he only eats fish? I thought he was a Papist, but it all came out when he invited me to his daughter's wedding. I don't care a bugger if you're a whirling Dervish, but if you want to do business with these fucking wogs, you've got to humour them. I sometimes think you should be in the church, not in a bank, and even in the church you have to learn to compromise. You've turned down Cologne, now you're turning down Arabia. Do you want to be stuck where you are all your life?'

'I haven't complained.'

'But *I'm* complaining. I like young men to be ambitious, to grasp at opportunities when they're there, to make them when they aren't. Now listen, this is an order. Beatty's due to retire in another two years and needs a good man to replace him. I want you to be that man, and I want you to join him right away.'

'That's hardly practical, sir.'

'All right, take a few months to wind up the affairs of your department.'

'I also need a successor.'

'Right, take six months, but I want you to be with Beatty by the summer, and I want you to sit in at meetings of his department as soon as you get back.'

It wasn't usual to come across a man who knew how to give orders. Even Rich, who knew how to handle people, gave orders in such a way that one felt one was doing him a personal favour by complying, and indeed, he looked grateful if one actually complied. When the Chairman gave orders one was not disposed to argue, not because he was Chairman, but because of his absolute confidence that they would be obeyed; and obey them I did.

He and his two colleagues returned to London the next day. I had planned to do the same, but on an impulse flew on to Cairo.

Markham was startled by my unexpected arrival.

'You should have told me you were coming and I'd have met you at the airport.'

'I'm sorry, I hadn't really planned to come. How is he?'

'Resting, rather fitfully, I'm afraid. He keeps crying out in his sleep. Who is Inge?'

'A daughter.'

'He has a daughter?'

'He had.'

'Strange. He was showing me some photographs recently. His brothers, sister, his wife, you – he never mentioned a daughter.'

I went into his room. He was fast asleep, and breathing heavily.

'He's hardly stirred for the past twenty-four hours.'

'Have you called a doctor?'

'You should know how he feels about doctors. He's one himself, after all.'

'But he's hardly in a state to tend to himself.'

'That's what I told him, but he won't allow a doctor to set foot in the house. He has a nurse, of course. He was like this before, shortly before you came as a matter of fact, but then he sat up and asked to be taken for a drive in the country. That's about the only pleasure he has left, poor man, he likes to be driven at speed, with all the windows open, and the wind stirring his hair – though his hair's all going, if you've noticed.'

I had noticed, and his head was covered with sores.

'I think you should call a doctor.'

'It would only upset him and, if I may say so, you're upsetting yourself. He's in good hands, we're all very fond of him and are doing our best to make him comfortable.'

I stayed the night, and when I came into his room the next morning he was sitting up in bed being fed a soft-boiled egg by an Arab servant.

'I heard you were here, but why? Haven't you enough to keep you busy?'

His voice was reassuringly firm.

'I was passing this way and I wanted to see how you were.'

'You were only here a few weeks ago. What sort of changes did you expect?'

He was, in fact, painful to look at, but I was cheered by his very sharpness. Yet I was reluctant to leave him, for I was certain I would never see him again, and I thought, I hoped, he might wish to talk to me. He might have been physically decrepit but he seemed mentally alert and could not have been unaware of his condition. I was familiar with his taciturnity and his desire to draw a line through the past, but was there nothing of which he wished to unburden himself as his end approached? Did he wish to take all his secrets to the grave? I was not restless with curiosity about my origins, though perhaps I should have been, but I was curious about his silences. It was all very well to dismiss what Carla had told me as nonsense, but as he was unwilling to fill in the details himself I had nothing better to go on. I tried to approach the matter by asking him about Carla's visit, at which his face clouded over.

'It was very painful. I thought I knew my sister, but I didn't, or

70

rather there was a side to her which I hadn't discovered, and it was a very unpleasant discovery; but let's not talk about it.'

There was precious little else he was willing to talk about, and with the ghost-like presence of Markham hovering in the background it wasn't easy to converse at all, but I felt I could not leave Cairo empty-handed and, at the risk of upsetting him, I said:

'Don't you think I should know rather more about my past than I do know?'

'That's why you came here, isn't it?' And he leaned over to give me a reassuring pat on the knee. 'I promise you, you will know everything you want to know – and perhaps even more – in good time.'

This time I stood my ground.

'But, with respect, grandfather, that isn't good enough, is it? We live three thousand miles apart. We haven't been meeting that often and I don't know what opportunities there will be for us to meet again – '

'Especially if I should drop dead in the meantime,' he interjected.

His new-found acerbity made me wonder if my worries about his health were not perhaps misplaced. Anyhow, he refused to be drawn.

'He's not as shaky as he looks,' said Markham as he saw me to the door. 'He could outlive us all yet, and probably will.'

Chapter Six

I had only been away a few weeks but I somehow didn't feel the same when I got back, and things didn't look the same, and I wondered what could have brought on the change. Was it my meetings with my grandfather, the intimation that he was about to fade out of my life and that I would soon be left in the world on my own? Was it the exalted view which the Chairman had of my abilities? Or was it simply the change in climate?

I had spent three weeks amid bright sunshine under blue skies; I returned to grey skies and rain, and when I opened the door of my flat and switched on the lights I shuddered at the hideous hues, the ugly furnishings, the grotesque furniture, the very memories which they evoked. I quickly switched the lights off, locked the door, and went to sleep in a hotel. The next day I put the flat and its contents on the market. I came to wonder how I could have lived there at all, and at the entire liaison with Sylvia. Loneliness makes for strange bedfellows.

I was nearly thirty, a man of some means, and I wanted a place of my own, but did not have sufficient confidence in my own tastes to know what to buy and how to furnish it, and I asked Rich's wife, Giselle, if she could help me. I had been entertained in her home a number of times and I liked everything about it, possibly because I liked everything about her. She was a tall, long-necked woman who looked elegant even while bent over the kitchen stove in an apron (but then she had an elegant stove and elegant aprons). She had the same sort of colouring as my aunt Carla, the same greenish eyes, the same reddish hair and regular teeth, but there was something coarse and earthy about Carla, whereas Giselle represented everyone's idea of an English lady, which doesn't mean to say that she always behaved like one. One heard the most bizarre accounts of her private life, but these, if anything, added to her charms.

When I told her what I wanted she said: 'I wouldn't buy a flat in the first place. Flats are for illicit liaisons and confirmed bachelors, and I can't see a young man with your prospects staying a bachelor for long. Why don't you rent something furnished until you find a wife and then, of course, you'll have to fall in with her tastes.'

And I went down on my knees, and took her hand.

'Will you marry me, then?'

'If I was a younger woman – '

'I don't want a younger woman, I want you – '

She got down on her knees and kissed me on the lips.

'You're very gallant, and very attractive, but you don't know me and you could do much better. Besides, what would my husband say?'

If her husband hadn't come in at that moment, I am sure she would have allowed me to make love to her on the carpet. Indeed, she seemed disposed to let me do so even though he had come in.

'You're interrupting us,' she said to Rich without moving her eyes from mine. 'Go away.'

'Sorry to be disobliging,' said her husband, 'but have you forgotten? We're having guests for dinner.'

And I took her advice and found myself a furnished flat, or rather she found it for me, in South Kensington, near the Albert Hall, and, by way of a house-warming, we made love together in the four-poster bed in the main bedroom.

'I don't know why you're so confident that I'll marry soon,' I said, 'I keep looking for another Giselle.'

'Don't look too hard, my love,' she warned, 'or you might find one.'

A few weeks later, a little to my surprise, I received an invitation to the wedding of the Chairman's daughter. The ceremony itself was to be held in the church adjoining the family estate, and the reception in Firwood Hall.

I had been to the Hall before, but only once. It was at the outing to the estate held annually for bank employees and their families. We swam in the swimming-pool, played cricket with the village team, had cucumber sandwiches and tea, followed by trifle and ice-cream. It was all, as a colleague observed, like a Sunday-school treat, and I didn't go again.

The wedding was rather different. The church was too small to

73

contain all the guests and, again to my surprise, I was honoured with a reserved place, as if I was one of the family.

The bride, a tall, magnificent woman, towered above her father, and was followed by a long line of bridesmaids, dressed as tiny little Bo-Peeps, and a column of page-boys dressed as grenadiers. There were flowers everywhere, round the columns, on the pews, on and around the pulpit. The sunny morning lent itself to flowery outfits. There were flowers, real and artificial, on hats and bosoms, and, of course, flowers in lapels, and it was difficult, at first sight, to tell where the flora finished and the fauna began.

The reception was not actually in the Hall itself, but on the back lawn. There were gallons of champagne, which I have always felt to be an over-rated drink, and as I was looking around for a glass of spirits one of the Maids of Honour came up to me and said:

'Can I help you? You look lost.'

I looked under the brim of her straw hat and found myself gazing into the most beautiful blue eyes I had ever seen.

'Actually, I wouldn't mind a glass of vodka, or spirits of any sort.'

'I don't think there's any here, but if you come inside I may be able to find a bottle.'

I followed her into the deserted building, along a hallway into what must have been the library, where she pulled a bottle of vodka from what looked like an antique globe.

'Do you mind drinking from the bottle?' she said. 'I'm too tired and lazy to find a glass.'

Nothing daunted, I sat down, unscrewed the cap and took a long swig. She sat down opposite me, took off her hat and tousled her hair.

'My God, how I hate hats. How I hate weddings.'

I offered her a swig.

'No, no, thank you. No, wait, perhaps I will,' and she took rather more than I thought was good for her.

'Are you the bride's sister?'

'I am, worse luck. Ugly, isn't she?'

'Do you think so?'

'Looks like a horse. So does her husband. He's a dago, you know. Argentinian. Met at the Badminton Horse Trials. You begin to look like a horse if you spend all your time with horses,

74

you know. I prefer cats. I wouldn't mind looking like a cat. I wouldn't mind *being* a cat. I wouldn't mind being anything if I could only get away from this horrid place. Can I have another swig?'

'No, no, I don't think you had better.'

'Why not, it's not yours?'

'I don't think it's good for you. You're far too young to be drinking vodka, especially from a bottle.'

'How old do you think I am? I'm absolutely ancient.'

'What do you do?'

'I'm still at school, worse luck, the oldest girl in the place. I'm nearly nineteen, but father won't let me leave until I get my A-levels. I'll probably have to stop there forever.'

'What do you want to do?'

'Open a home for stray cats, if I had my way, which I won't. What do you do? You're in the bank, I suppose, everybody's in the bank. You're not a relative, are you, because I've seen you before somewhere.'

'At your grandfather's memorial service.'

'Are you married?'

'No.'

'Would you like to run away with me? I do so want to get away from this place.'

Our conversation was suddenly interrupted by the intrusion of a tall, gaunt woman in a large hat, whom I recognized as her mother, and without a word to her daughter, or as much as a nod in my direction, she took her by the arm and yanked her out of the room.

I went outside and rejoined the guests. Rich, sweating profusely under a grey topper, came over to talk to me.

'I don't know if this is the place to raise such things, but I need to go abroad tomorrow and I may have no other opportunity to do so, but I must say I am disappointed . . .'

I couldn't hear what he was saying. I couldn't hear what anybody was saying. I had, for the first time in my life, fallen in love, and with a schoolgirl at that. I had read about it in novels, heard about it in songs, seen it depicted in innumerable films and plays. There were moments when I had thought I was in love with Aunt Carla, or Sue or Sylvia, or Giselle, but this was, as they say, the real thing. It didn't involve bodily contact. One didn't even have to touch hands. Mere contemplation of the person was enough. I searched for her – I say 'her' because I didn't even know her name – until the company dispersed, but it wasn't all that important that I didn't find her. It had been sunny in the morning and hot at noon. By the time I drove home it was overcast, but I was hardly aware of the clouds, for my whole being was suffused with a glow.

I had a huge stack of papers on my desk which I had hoped to go through, but hard as I tried to focus my attention on them, my mind bounced off. I could see those blue eyes everywhere. I finally gave up, had a bath, and fell asleep in the water, and nearly drowned in the process, with those eyes still before me; and if I had drowned that night I would have died a happy man.

When I woke the next morning, it all seemed like a dream, and I might have concluded it was a dream but for the fact that papers, or at least the popular ones, were full of pictures of the wedding and gossip about the guests, including the Maid of Honour I had met, whose name, I discovered, was Lee and who was in her final year at Cheltenham Ladies' College.

Beatty asked me if I had been there and I said I had.

'I thought I saw you in church, but you vanished after that.'

'I went to look for a real drink.'

'And did you find it?'

'I did.'

'You might have shared it, you know. The champagne was like gripe-water. We had to go to the local before we could find anything worth drinking.'

I managed, as the day proceeded, to get down to work, but with the greatest difficulty, and, as soon as my secretary was out of the office, I phoned Firwood and asked for Miss Eissenmacher. A pompous voice answered.

'Which Miss Eissenmacher, sir? There are three of them – sorry, two.'

'Lee, please.'

'You mean Miss Felicia, I take it.'

'Yes, please.'

I could hear slow steps echoing down the corridor, and more rapid steps echoing back up, and a woman's voice answered.

'Who is that?'

'My name's Newman.'

'Who do you want?'

'Lee.'

'She's not available,' and the phone was clamped down.

I had expected something like that. Instead I wrote to her at the school. She replied a few days later:

'Are you the marvellous man with the vodka bottle at the wedding? You must be. Please come and see me. Let me know when you're coming and put up at the Queens Hotel. I'll get out to see you somehow.'

I followed her instructions to the letter, and waited in the lounge, with a bottle of vodka beside me by way of identification. It is strange how when one looks for a face one can see it in every face one sees. I wasn't sure what to expect, and half feared that she might turn up in a gymslip and a pudding-basin hat, and when she did appear, though not in school uniform, I was still slightly taken aback by her outfit.

I suppose I still had that picture of her in the puffed-up petticoats and the large straw hat, the dainty shepherdess of my Arcadian dreams. She now appeared in a pair of jeans and an over-large jersey, but her eyes hadn't changed, and I took her hand and pulled her against me.

'Not here,' she said, 'this is Cheltenham. Let's go up to your room.'

I had thought of waiting for her in my room, but reminded myself that she was, after all, still a schoolgirl and I felt it wasn't the decent thing to do. I still wasn't sure if it was the decent thing, even though she had suggested it, but I threw caution to the winds, and hand-in-hand we dashed up the steps.

It didn't take her long to get her clothes off, for she didn't have anything on under her jersey and jeans, and as soon as she was naked she busied herself undressing me.

'Am I the first?' I said.

'The *first*? I'm nearly nineteen,' and it became clear that, for all her tender years, she had very considerable experience.

It was heavenly but extravagant. It would have been enough just to see her. I had hoped that she might stay the night, or at least for a meal, but she pulled her clothes back on and rushed out.

'Can't. Must get back before I'm noticed. What's your name by

77

the way? I couldn't make out your handwriting.'

'Harry.'

'Harry what?'

'Harry Newman.'

'Bye, Harry, you will write again, won't you?'

She kissed me and fled.

I wrote to her almost every day, and she replied with equal frequency. Then one afternoon I was at a meeting when I was called out by my secretary for an urgent call.

'Can you meet me at the Kingsley Hotel, Bloomsbury?'

'When?'

'Now. The school's visiting the British Museum and I managed to sneak out. They won't miss me for an hour or so.'

'I can't. I'm at a meeting.'

'But you *must*. I'll die if you don't.'

I rushed back to the meeting, mumbled an apology and rushed out.

She was almost tearful about my hesitancy, but otherwise looked as delectable as ever. She wanted us to go upstairs but I was in a hurry and she was in school uniform, and it was out of the question. I bought her tea and an eclair, which seemed to mollify her slightly, kissed her forehead and fled.

I came to realize that what success I enjoyed in my professional life was largely due to my complete failure in private life, and I was able to absorb immense quantities of information because I had nothing else to absorb me. Now that I was at last beginning to live I became more lackadaisical in my work. I didn't remain in the office to pore over papers till six, seven or eight in the evening, but dashed out the moment my secretary placed the cover over her typewriter. In the office I spent long hours writing private letters, and even when I was actually working I found it difficult to keep my mind on my work. No one as yet complained, but no doubt they soon would.

What worried me rather more was that my letters were interfering with *her* work.

'I've got another beastly exam in two weeks' time,' she wrote, 'and I shall plough it this year as I ploughed it last. But it doesn't matter. Nothing matters except you, and the thought of you, and your marvellous, marvellous letters. I live for the post. If a day passes without a letter, I die. I can't eat, I can hardly drink, I can't study. And when one does come, I can't study either. I rush away, lock myself in the lav. and read and re-read it, every loving line.'

I wrote back to suggest that she owed it to herself and her family to pass the exams, or at least to make an effort to pass them, and that it might be better if we stopped writing to each other until her exams were over.

The result was an anguished phone call the following morning. I had given her my home number, and suggested that it was not a good idea to phone me in the office, for I had a new secretary, a prim woman in her forties, who said nothing and noted everything, but, not for the first time, she ignored my suggestion.

'Have they been on to you?'

'Who has? What do you mean?'

'Mummy, daddy, the headmistress, somebody, because you sound as if they have. I don't know if I'll pass the beastly exams, but if you don't write I won't even be able to sit them. I'll die, I mean it, I'll die – '

'I understand, would – '

'I mean it, I shall, I'll die – '

'Can we talk about it later?'

'No, not until you promise to write.'

'I'll be home by six.'

'I can't phone at six. I shouldn't even be phoning now. I'm supposed to be in class. Promise you'll write.'

'I promise.'

'Every day?'

'If possible.'

'Promise you'll write every day.'

'I promise I'll write every day.'

'And that you still love me?'

'Of course I do.'

'Then say it.'

I looked uneasily at my secretary, who was examining her nails with more than usual intensity.

'*Say* it.'

'I love you.'

'And always will.'

'And always will.'

A few days later I received a phone call from Lady Firwood

asking me if I could meet her in the bar of the Charing Cross Hotel. It came at an awkward time, but it was not the sort of invitation I could refuse.

I arrived in time but she was already there, with a cigarette in one hand and a brandy in the other.

'Ah,' she said, 'now I know who you are. You were the young man with the bottle.'

'I hope it's not the only thing I'm known by.'

'It's a start. I'm sure you're busy, so let me get straight to the point. It's Lee, a beautiful child, but as you must have observed at a glance, a child. She is very much in love with you, which is understandable for I can see you're a charming young man, but as you probably don't know – and there is no reason why you should – it's something that afflicts her every year, and about the same time of the year. Like cyclical malaria. I can almost tell the date from the onset of the attack. One year it was a bus-driver, another, a tennis-coach, so that I thought her aspirations were rising, but the third it was an ice-cream vendor, so obviously they were not. I must say that in this instance she at least shows taste. Presumably she's seduced you – '

'Hadn't you better ask her?'

'My dear young man, I hope you don't think I'm trying to interrogate you, I'm just presenting you with the sad facts of the case as they really are.'

'How did her earlier liaisons resolve themselves?'

'In the case of the bus-driver it was fairly simple. His wife waited for her outside school and threatened to cut her throat – and his. In the case of the tennis-coach it was even simpler. He was a pouf, and she tried to cut her wrists. In the case of the ice-cream vendor we had to buy him off.'

'In this instance the situation is rather more complicated, because you see I'm not married, I'm not a pouf – '

'And I wouldn't attempt to buy you off.'

'But are you trying to scare me off?'

'Yes, in a sense I am. As you must know, my husband thinks the world of you. Given the right wife, or even the right girl-friend, you could have a brilliant future. She could be your ruin.'

'Wouldn't she be the ruin of anyone else she might marry?'

'Depends on whom she marries, if, indeed, she should prove constant enough to marry at all, which I sometimes doubt. If she marries one of her second cousins, or someone like that, with lots of money and not too much sensitivity, she mightn't do too much harm, and might even do some good. You two would be mismatched in every way. She has no education, no intelligence, never opens a book, hardly ever reads a paper, doesn't know what's going on in the world – '

'And what she really needs is some well-endowed, well-connected idiot.'

'That's about it.'

'Would I qualify if I had money?'

'Now you're being cynical.'

'What you seem to be saying is that it doesn't really matter whom she marries, as long as she marries within her class, but, if you'll forgive me, didn't her father marry out of his class?'

'I thought that might come up. He did, which is all the more reason why she should marry into hers. No doubt somebody must have told you, or you read it in the gutter-press, that I'm working-class. I only wish I was. My own father didn't do an honest day's work in his life. He debauched the daughter of a fairly well-to-do family and lived on her income while it lasted. When it was gone he abandoned her and me and, until I became an actress and managed to support her, my mother kept a lodging-house. I'm afraid my daughter has inherited something of my father's fecklessness. Edward and I have been fairly happy, but given the way our children have turned out – and, as you may know, I've also had trouble with my other daughters – '

'I didn't.'

'We have. Given the way our children have turned out, I'm not at all sure if Edward did the right thing.'

'You seem to be more worried about me, and even my children, than you are about your own daughter.'

'No, but a disastrous marriage would hardly ease my worries.'

'You appreciate your daughter and I haven't even discussed the possibility of marriage?'

'I do, but the possibility does exist, and I am anxious to forestall it.'

'For my sake as much as your daughter's?'

'For all our sakes.'

'Supposing I was to say that in spite of everything you told me I would be prepared to risk marriage if your daughter would have me?'

'I would say you'd be making a terrible mistake.'

She stubbed out her cigarette and rose. 'I'm sure we shall meet again, and if we do I hope we can forget we ever had this conversation. Edward doesn't know anything about this. I do hope there won't be any need for him to know.'

She held out her hand by way of farewell. I hestitated to shake it, but I did. It was cold and slightly clammy.

I continued as if the meeting had never taken place but asked the Personnel Manager for a change of secretary. He was surprised at my request. 'She's one of the most experienced women we have, speaks three languages and – '

'I know, she's wasted on me.'

I had to go to Poland the next day and was away for three weeks, half expecting that I would be out of a job on my return. Instead, I was offered a move to New York, and I at once smelt a rat. I wasn't sure if my relationship with Rich had got to the point where I could be perfectly candid with him, but I was willing to take the risk, and I said:

'Did anyone put you up to this?'

'What do you mean?'

'Did you discuss this with the Chairman?'

'Of course. It's a senior appointment and all senior appointments have to be cleared with him.'

'But why New York? I was to move in with Beatty.'

'I was under the impression you weren't all that keen on the Middle East.'

'I wasn't, but the Chairman gave me little choice in the matter.'

'The fact is something like an emergency's cropped up. We had a good man in New York, but he moved out and took some of our best chaps with him and we've had to take urgent steps to replace them. You'd be getting wider responsibilities, a higher salary – '

'And a chance to prove my mettle.'

He slapped his desk pad with exasperation.

'I don't know what gets into you sometimes. When I offered you Cologne, you presumably thought I was trying to wean you away from I-can't-remember-her-name. Who do you think I'm trying to wean you away from now?'

'The Chairman's daughter.'

'The Ch – . Which one?'

82

'Lee.'

'Oh God!'

He got up and walked round the room with his hands to his face.

'Oh God! That this should happen to you of all people. Don't say you've got entangled with her?'

'Go on, say it. She'll be the ruin of me.'

'Ruin isn't the word. She's beautiful, but quite mad, and she'll drive you mad as well.'

'Tell me honestly, didn't you know anything about this?'

'Of course not, how could I? And I shouldn't imagine the Chairman knows either, or he'd have told me. He tells me everything. Harry, I beseech you, take the New York job. It won't be vacant for another three months, but go now, tomorrow. Take! Flee! Fly!'

When I got back to my office the phone was ringing.

'Darling, this is me, Lee. I'm phoning from Cheltenham Station. The exams are over. I've ploughed them all, but who cares? Tell me you love me.'

'Of course I love you.'

'Very much.'

'Very much.'

'Forever and ever.'

'Forever and ever.'

'I'll be at your place by seven.'

She wanted to run away to France, to Italy, to America, 'anywhere to get away from this dreadful place'.

'It won't be necessary, my love. They won't clap us in irons, there's nothing they can do to us. What I'm going to do right now is to phone your parents.'

She was aghast. 'My parents!'

'They'll want to know what's happened to you.'

'They're not interested in me at all. All they want me to do is to pass beastly exams, and I hate them.'

She regarded the very suggestion as proof that my feelings had cooled and that I didn't really love her – 'If you did you wouldn't want to stop here for another minute.'

I eventually managed to reassure her and she calmed down sufficiently to wash her face and have something to eat.

'I suppose you're right,' she said with resignation, 'we'll have to phone them, but you still love me, don't you?'

'I adore you.'

'And you'll marry me?'

'Of course.'

She brightened up at that.

'Mummy won't like it,' she said (and she didn't), 'though daddy might.'

And he did. He was, in fact, delighted, and took me to his Club by way of celebration, where we both got pleasantly drunk.

'Couldn't have picked a nicer chap . . . fellow after my own heart . . . brilliant young man . . . Straight as a die . . . Great future . . . Only hope he knows how to keep her in hand,' and so on, as if he was speaking about a third party . . . 'Was afraid she might end up with one of her cousins, or someone like that . . . Family's full of idiots, you know . . . all that in-breeding . . . Absolutely delighted . . . Couldn't have picked a nicer chap . . . couldn't have done better . . . didn't think she could hold down a chap like that . . . More to her than I thought . . . afraid she might end up with a cousin . . . Family's full of idiots, you see . . . all that in-breeding . . . '

At a later, and more sober, encounter, he asked me something about myself.

'From what I hear, you were found in a handbag in Victoria Station, not that it matters, but people keep asking me about my prospective son-in-law and I feel a bit of a twit not being able to tell them a thing.'

And I told him my history as far as I knew it.

'So you mean to say you've no family at all?'

'None to speak of.'

'Well, that's a relief. I've never been able to hit it off with my children's in-laws – neither have my children, for that matter. The damned wedding's hardly over before they come round to borrow money, and when I lend it to them – even at favourable rates – they're always aggrieved when I ask for it back. I should warn you, though, once it gets known that you're marrying a banker's daughter you'll find relatives, or rather they'll find you. Ever tried to trace your family line?'

'No, never.'

'You will. It hits you when you turn sixty. Wife calls it the Forsyths' syndrome. I hope to give up banking in another five or six years and write a family history. Already have a chap collecting papers. I suppose you know how we started?'

'I've heard various versions.'

'Great-grandfather was a jumped-up Jewboy, from Germany actually, which is one thing we have in common. He was a toy-dealer who lent money to his customers to help them over their slack periods, and found that there was more money to be made from money than from toys. He made a bit, married more, but it was grandfather who made Eissenmacher's an international name, and father – bless him – who nearly unmade it. Couldn't say no to a relative. The third generation's the crucial one because by then there are so many relatives about that if you try to cram them all into the bank you can more or less stifle it. If you can survive that you're here to stay, and I think we're here to stay.'

Once it was clear that we were firm in our intentions and that we were determined to marry whatever happened, Lady Firwood withdrew her objections, and I was invited to dinner at Firwood Hall. We exchanged amused, conspiratorial looks as I entered, and she received me with almost extravagant warmth, as if to show that anything she may have said at our earlier encounter should be forgotten. She was a firm-jawed, handsome woman with alert, intelligent eyes, and I took a liking to her.

The large downstairs rooms were hardly used, and they had converted what had been the children's rooms into a compact flat for their own use.

There was an old, bent, white-haired butler who hovered about the place flicking flies with a napkin, and we were looked after by a young Spanish couple.

'The flat was my idea,' said Lady Firwood (whom I was now required to call Barbara). 'Edward's not very happy with it. It makes him feel as if he's come down in the world.'

'It's cramped,' said Edward. 'I like a bit of space above my head. When grandfather bought this place he had about a dozen clerks and was no more than a jumped-up moneylender. I employ over three hundred people and we've been forced to retreat into a rabbit-hutch.'

'We use the public rooms when Edward wants to impress some overseas client,' said his wife, 'but as you are virtually a member of the family I'm sure you don't object to roughing it with us.'

I didn't. Neither Lee nor I had much to say, even though we

both had too much to drink. We began with champagne, had hock with the fish and claret with the meat, and wound up the meal with port and brandy. We dined by candle-light, which seemed to bring out the lustre in her eyes. She wore a low-cut gown and her skin seemed to glow. The walls were panelled in oak, with candles in silver brackets. The cutlery was silver, the glass crystal, and the round table was polished oak. There was a glowing mellowness everywhere which seemed to reflect the glow within me. It was not merely that I had found a particularly beautiful wife but, after so many years in the cold, I had been received into the bosom of a particularly attractive family. It all seemed like a dream, and when I returned to London the next evening I was afraid to fall asleep in case I woke up to find it *was* a dream; but I dropped off very easily, for I had hardly slept at all the night before.

I was wakened some hours later by the sound of the phone. It was Markham.

'Sorry to disturb you at this unearthly hour. Been trying to get through to you for the past few days, but there's been no reply. I'm afraid I've got some bad news . . .'

— Part Two —

Part Two

— *Chapter Seven* —

'Dear Harry,

I have left this letter with Dr Ignatz Wolf, my lawyer, with instructions that it should not be sent to you until after my death, which, I fear, may not be distant.

I should, of course, have divulged all that I'm about to tell you before, but I have never had much courage to do so, and I have never been convinced that it's an advantage to know too much about one's past.

I come from a Westphalian family, a branch of which settled in Latvia as early as the 18th century, another branch settled in Russia, but wherever we were we always regarded ourselves as Germans.

I was one of eight children, seven sons and a daughter. Four were killed in the First World War. One died of typhus. A sixth killed himself. Only Carla and I remained.

I was trained as a doctor in Koenigsberg and served in a field hospital on the eastern front, where I was severely wounded. It took me about a year to recover and I was then sent with a medical mission to Turkey. I helped to establish a hospital and field stations in Mesopotamia and picked up a knowledge of Arabic, which was to stand me in good stead later.

After the war I resumed my medical studies in Vienna and became a specialist in diseases of the mind. I practised for a time in Dvinsk, where I became friendly with a Jewish family called Marcovitch, and in Riga, and in 1934 I established a small sanatorium at Resznitz.

The war and its aftermath left millions maimed, not only in body but in mind, and I was not short of patients. After one year I had to move from the small building in which I began to a larger one, and two years later to a larger one still, and I had already engaged an architect to erect an entire complex, when the war broke out and my plans had to be shelved. Even then I still had a few patients whose families could not be traced, and I continued to look after them even when they could no longer pay fees, but when the Russians came in I was forced to close down altogether.

While still in Vienna I married Herta, the daughter of an Austrian doctor. We had one child, Inge. The pregnancy being an extremely difficult one, my poor wife nearly died in the course of her protracted labour. She never recovered her health or her spirits and, in view of what was to follow, it might have been better to have stifled the infant in the womb.

Our daughter caused us anxiety from the day she was born. We were partly to blame for, being an only child, we over-indulged her, and as her mother was frequently in ill-health she was largely brought up by servants. Her behaviour grew worse as she grew older, and there were times when she made our life intolerable. Finally, in 1938, when she was eighteen, she left home and that was the last we saw of her. We understand she married and had a child, but we received no direct word from her on the matter. The one consoling thought I can offer you is that she was not your mother, and you are not her child, and it is in fact by no means certain that she did have a child, for she died in a fire about a year after she left home. I don't know what Carla told you on the matter, or what she may yet tell you, but the sad facts of the case are exactly as I have set them out.

The Marcovitch family traded in timber and flax, and had a *datcha* in Resznitz. The old man, Sender Marcovitch, helped me to set up my clinic. He died some years before the war and his business was taken over by his two sons and a son-in-law. When the Russians occupied the country they arrested both sons and, from what I understand, they deported them to Siberia. None of us knew exactly why they were arrested, but in the event the deportation may have saved their lives. The womenfolk and the children were less fortunate.

There was, as you must know, an *entente cordiale* between Russia and Germany, and as a German I was able to offer the family – which consisted of old Mrs Marcovitch, two daughters, a daughter-in-law and three children – some help and protection, but when the Germans invaded the following year all that changed. I was near enough to Poland to know what we had done and were doing to Polish Jews, and I feared that any influence I might be able to exert would be insufficient to save them. I therefore persuaded them to seek safety in a large barn in the forest which I owned, and where I thought I would be able to look after them. Two months later the barn was set ablaze. Anna, whom you may remember, snatched one child from the flames. You were that child. Everyone else perished. Your mother Sarah, *née* Marcovitch, is dead. Your father, Vladimir Bergmann, may still be alive, though all the efforts I have made to trace him have proved unavailing.

The story we spread was that you were our grandson. We could not, of course, bring you up as a Jew, but we were careful not to raise you as a Christian, and although I cannot expect you to forgive our silence, I hope you will believe me that it was only our love for you which kept us silent.'

I read the letter and re-read it several times. I prided myself on my ability to absorb difficult documents, but the more closely I studied this one the more confused I became. Every sentence was perfectly plain, but the sense of the letter as a whole seemed to elude me.

I phoned grandfather's lawyer, Wolf, but he seemed equally confused.

'Your grandfather left the letter with us about eighteen months ago,' he said. 'Most of our records were destroyed in the war, but he left no depositions, no sworn statements to support his letter. It is also at variance with his will, in which you are clearly described as the son of his daughter Ingeborg, and his heir. Between ourselves, I found your grandfather's behaviour in the last years of his life erratic, and I would not be disposed to pay too much attention to his letter. In fact, I wouldn't mention it to anyone else because it could give rise to complications when his will is published.'

It was not at all my impression that my grandfather's behaviour had been in the least erratic. He may have been physically frail, but he seemed to have his wits about him, which is perhaps why I found the implications of his letter so unwelcome.

I had been a Latvian, a German and an Egyptian, and I was finally becoming an Englishman, and did not want the added complication of being a Jew. I had nothing against being Jewish as such. The only two friends I had made before my move to London, Gerald in Cairo and Sue in Oxford, were Jewish. Some of the most admired figures in Oxford were Jewish. The contribution of Jews to history, for good or ill, was out of all proportion to their number, and even Mitri, who could not be regarded as a semito-phile, once said to me after a visit to Vienna: 'You can't imagine what a provincial backwater it has become, but then, of course, it was the Jews who made Vienna what it was.' There was something about the very fact of being Jewish which compelled attention, and I preferred to be anonymous. As a child, I felt burdened by the fact that I had lost both my father *and* mother, but then I had thought they had died in the war, like so many others, and had not been singled out as victims, which perhaps brought me to what may have been my main reservation. To be a Jew was to be a hereditary victim, to be burdened by history. The Germans were burdened by guilt, but I wasn't even quite German, and I was well on the way to becoming an Englishman, if only by grafting, and it was not unnatural while on the verge of a new life to resent the intrusions of an old one, and an old one, moreover, in which one had but a passive role. I didn't wish to be associated with so tragic a story.

I had told Lee about my past as I knew it before I received the letter, and even that reduced her to a paroxysm of tears; I hated to think what the whole truth might have done. I was about to be grafted, if not to olde England, at least to an English family of good standing, and as English in its ways and its eccentricities as could be imagined. We were to marry in a church which was almost a family chapel, and although there would have been no formal barriers to the marriage even if my past were known, there would have been psychological barriers, for how could the son of Vladimir and Sarah Bergmann stand at the altar of St Agnew's Church, Upper Firwood, and be united in matrimony to Felicia Eissenmacher at a Christian service? Did I not owe it to Vladimir and Sarah to be true to myself and their memory? And yet, if they were my parents, would they have wished me to forgo the true happiness I had finally discovered? I had not only found a wife in Lee, but parents in Edward and Barbara. I did not for a moment think I would be disowned if I said I was Jewish, but it might have affected the pattern of the future I saw forming ahead.

But I continued to be troubled by the letter, for if grandfather was not senile, what could have been his motives? And I recalled a conversation we had had shortly before I left for Oxford. He had been desperately anxious that I should shrug off my German identity, and what better way of doing so than by giving me a Jewish one? This seemed to be the only logical explanation, but I was not burdened by his guilt and, therefore, did not feel bound by his obsessions.

The news of my association with Lee must have appeared in the German press, for Carla wrote me a letter of congratulations. I wrote back to thank her and, without mentioning grandfather's letter, asked if she could tell me more about my origins because my prospective bride, not unnaturally, wanted to know more than I was able to tell her. She replied:

'Didn't Gunther tell you everything? He was always secretive, but I didn't think he was *that* secretive. It is all very sad, dear Heinschein, and if you want to know everything, I think you and your beautiful bride will have to come and see me, but in outline it's this. Your mother was a beautiful young woman, but wayward, and she ran away to England when she was seventeen or eighteen. I saw a lot of her while she was in Latvia – we were almost like sisters – but she did not write to me after she left, which upset me very much, and about a year later I heard that she had died in a fire in America. Gunther flew to America to find out what happened, and to this day I remember when he returned with you in his arms. I'm afraid I can't tell you anything about your father. To be honest, I am not even sure if Inge married – but your bride's family doesn't have to know that . . . '

I was not entirely satisfied with her account, for apart from anything else it differed in several material respects from what she had told me as a child, but I recognized that she had no cause to lie to me, and it was as far as I could take the matter for the time being, for other and more immediate problems were pressing in upon me.

Lee and I decided not to have a formal announcement about our impending marriage – or rather, I decided and she reluctantly agreed – because I could imagine headlines like GERMAN WAR ORPHAN MARRIES ENGLISH HEIRESS in the popular press and I had no wish to be pestered by reporters and photographers. All that could wait for the wedding itself.

'I think you're ashamed of me,' said Lee, pouting her rosebud of a mouth.

'Ashamed of you? You're the greatest thing that has happened to me, or could happen to anyone.'

'Then why are you being so secretive? Don't tell this, don't tell that. I haven't anything to hide, have you?'

'Look, my love, we're due to go to America in another few months. I've got to wind up the work of my department, or at least to hand it over in reasonable order to my successor. You've not only got all the arrangements for the wedding, but you must also go to New York to find a flat. You don't want to start married life in a hotel, do you?'

'It wouldn't worry me. I could start married life on a park bench.'

In fact, my efforts to avoid publicity proved futile.

There had been brief reports about Lee and me in the papers from about the time she left school, but they were sporadic. However, while Lee and her mother were in New York they were picked up by the American press, which the British papers in turn regarded as confirmation of the gossip they had originally published, and what had been a minor story came to be treated as a major one, with precisely the sort of headlines I had imagined. I could refuse interviews, but could not stop them from writing fantasies. These were sometimes amusing, occasionally irritating and often boring, and I eventually learned to ignore them, but about a month before the wedding there appeared an article in a German magazine, by a journalist called Schwarzwald, which I could not ignore. It was about my grandfather, and it alleged that he had been an ex-Nazi in the employ of the Egyptian government and that he had been murdered by Israeli secret agents.

The article was profusely illustrated and had pictures of grandfather as a medical student, as a doctor in the army medical corps, and outside his sanatorium with German officers. There were also photos of him in Egypt, and there were claims that he had worked for German intelligence before and during the war, and that his sanatorium was, in fact, a sort of listening-post for what was happening in Eastern Europe. I had no idea what was fact and what was fiction. It then, however, touched on something which I was afraid might have been fact.

94

Grandfather had left me over half a million pounds sterling. I gathered that his sanatorium had been profitable for a while, and that he had been well paid in Egypt, but still could not understand how he could have accumulated so large a sum. The magazine suggested that he had been entrusted with the money by a Jewish neighbour whose family had perished in the holocaust. But that was not the worst of it. It was alleged that he had actually betrayed the family to the Nazis.

The magazine was sent to me by Wolf, by special delivery, and I received it as I was about to set out for work. When I read it I phoned the office that I would not be coming in.

I re-read it, and the effect was shattering. I didn't normally drink in the morning, but I poured myself a large brandy and read it a third time. I didn't know what to believe and what not to believe. I felt that the idea that the ailing, elderly figure who had been working for the Egyptian government could have been involved in anything sinister was plainly preposterous, nor could I believe that, even if he had been a Nazi, it would have taken the Israelis more than twenty years to track him down, and that they would be interested in killing a blind and half-paralysed old man near the point of death. That part of the story, I was convinced, was pure fantasy.

But the rest? I had always thought of the old man as the soul of kindness, but he could be firm, even severe, and something of his sharpness was evident even in old age; but this was hardly proof that he was a monster. On the other hand, how did he amass that half million?

One thing seemed certain. If he was, in fact, a Nazi he would hardly have harboured a Jewish infant under his roof and passed it off as a grandchild. I had the choice between being the son of a Jew or the grandson of a Nazi.

But again, if he had been a Nazi, with all that money would he not have sought refuge in South America instead of somewhere as exposed and accessible as Egypt?

Then I thought of his letter again. Could not his claim that he had saved a Jewish infant from the flames be an attempt to exculpate himself in the eyes of posterity?

But difficult as I found it to believe his letter, I found it even more difficult to believe the Schwarzwald article. The one made him too much of a hero, the other too much of a villain. They

95

could both be wrong and probably were, but the more I thought about it the more confused I became. My mind was more attuned to ledgers than to life.

I picked up the phone to call Edward, but hesitated – and was surprised at my own hesitation. Was I nervous of confronting him with the revelations in the magazine? Did I have doubts about the extent to which I was accepted as a member of his family?

Giselle told me once: 'He may not have much Jewish blood in him, but it shows itself at odd moments and in odd ways.' How would he react to the possibility that his son-in-law's grandfather had been a Nazi?

I phoned him all the same, but he was not in the office and was not expected in till after lunch, and I put the receiver down with something like relief. A moment later, Carla called. Her voice was shaking; she, too, had just seen the article.

'It's not something to talk about on the phone. I am flying to London.'

She arrived in the evening, clutching a copy of the magazine like a truncheon. She threw off her coat, hat and shoes and had a large whisky before she could say anything.

'Could it be true?' I asked.

'I'm not sure. He was always secretive,' she said. 'He kept secrets from his wife, from me, from you, he may have kept secrets from himself.'

'But can you imagine the man we knew doing anything like this?'

'I know Germans – good, kind, family men, upright citizens, people of standing – who have done worse.'

We went through the article line by line. There were first the circumstances of his death. As far as I knew, he had died in a crash when his Mercedes went out of control. I had seen the results of the autopsy.

'A Mercedes does not normally go out of control,' said Carla. 'It could have been tampered with.'

'It's unlikely.'

'But not impossible.'

It was true that he worked for the Egyptian government, that much I knew myself, but it was as the director of a mental hospital. I had seen him treating patients. The article didn't say this. It mentioned that he was a psychiatrist, but implied that he was engaged in various nefarious activities, including the inter-rogation and brain-washing of Israeli spies. I just couldn't believe it. He had joined the hospital in 1952, and the spy-ring was not discovered until 1955, so he was certainly not brought over for such a purpose.

'Which doesn't mean to say that they didn't use him once he was there,' said Carla, 'and he was very nervous of strangers, even friends. Chuck and I went to see him last year, and he looked very uneasy, as if we had caught him at an awkward moment.'

'He was a sick man and half-blind, and in any case he had retired by then.'

'But he was very uncommunicative – '

'He was also uncommunicative with me.'

'That proves it. He acted as if he had something to hide. That's not only my opinion. Chuck thought so. And his house was like a castle, with guards and dogs – '

'If you noticed, all the houses in the neighbourhood had dogs. He was a helpless old man –'

'So why did he have to stay in that huge place? He could have come back to Germany, where Chuck and I could have looked after him. You should have seen his face when I said that. He began shouting at me, shrieking at the top of his voice. In fact, he wasn't as sick as he looked. There was something odd about the whole set-up, and that white-faced Englishman, what was his name?'

'Markham.'

'Sinister little creep. He tried to stop us from getting near him. If I hadn't held Chuck back he'd have knocked him down. I wanted to have a private word with my brother, but he wouldn't let him out of his sight, this Markham. I tell you, there was something going on in that place. An ordinary doctor doesn't live like that. He had something to hide. And don't forget he was a member of the Nazi party. There's a photo of the membership roll.'

'But no proof that he was an active member.'

'What do you want, a photograph of him in a Gestapo uniform?'

As we proceeded, I began to feel that where I had been looking for an advocate for the defence I had found a counsel for the prosecution.

'Did you quarrel as children, or something?' I asked.

'I don't remember him as a child. Don't forget, he was fifteen years older than me. I remember him as something of a father, and a stern father at that.'

We eventually came to the crucial passage, the betrayal of the Marcovitch family, and there, at least, I thought I might have her on my side, because while we both knew what the Germans had done to the Jews, it was difficult to believe that anyone with a spark of humanity could do this to a friend, and a friend moreover who had helped him; but even there her credulity was not strained.

'He was always mean, and may have been greedy, and greed has no limits. Did he really leave half a million pounds?'

'About that.'

'You didn't tell me.'

'I only heard about it myself a few days ago.'

'And you mean he left it all to you?'

And it quickly emerged that this was the real purpose of her visit: not the vindication of her brother's name but a share of his fortune. She felt entitled to it, she said, and as she made her point again and again, she seemed to undergo a transformation. Her eyes hardened, her face coarsened, her teeth, which I had always associated with a friendly, smiling personality, became menacing, her voice became shrill. If this was the real Carla, then perhaps the magazine had discovered the real Rhiner.

I wanted to get her out of my sight, and said I would arrange for an *ex gratia* payment.

'*Ex gratia* payment? Fuck your *ex gratia* payments,' and she banged down her fist on the table. 'That bloody money is mine as much as yours. More!'

'But, don't you understand? If grandfather was a Nazi it isn't mine either. I can't touch it.'

'What do you mean, you can't touch it? What'll you do with it?'

'I'll have to leave it with trustees while the matter is investigated. It may belong to the heirs of the Marcovitch family.'

'The Marcovitch family had no heirs. They all perished in a fire – even I know that. Look, if you've a conscience about using the money, I haven't. And of course you can afford to have a conscience. You're marrying an heiress – you didn't even have the decency to drop me a line and I had to read it in the papers. You're already ashamed of your poor relatives, even before you've got rich. Apart from anything else, I need the money. Chuck is so bloated with dropsy that he can hardly move, the poor bugger, and he's not even properly covered for medical insurance. And how would you like your posh in-laws to know that your grandfather was a Nazi? Eh? Ask yourself that.'

'Are you trying to blackmail me?'

At which she softened, or perhaps changed tack.

'For God's sake, Heinschein, I'm your Aunt Carla. Have you forgotten? I gave you your start in life, remember?' And, as if to refresh my memory, she gripped my knee. 'Would I blackmail you? But these things get out. The magazine's not on the streets yet, you know, but I suppose they must send advance copies to other papers, because my phone hasn't stopped ringing. Would I tell the story as I knew it? A thousand marks, five thousand marks, ten thousand, twenty. I didn't listen to any of them. I came straight here. But, my love' – and she began rubbing my thigh – 'I'm a war-widow with a small pension, and a boy-friend who was quite charming in his prime, but who now can't even make it stand. Oh, you're lovely, lovely – so big, so hard, so strong.'

We finally settled the matter in bed. I would make her a large *ex gratia* payment, and we would examine my grandfather's estate after the matter had been fully investigated. In the meantime, I promised her that I wouldn't touch it, and that she would get a letter from my lawyers to that effect. I was sorry to see her go.

It was disconcerting, while Carla's sweat and perfume still lingered in the air, to get a phone-call from New York.

'Darling, it's me, Lee. I tried to get you in the office, but you weren't in. Are you all right?'

'Of course I'm all right.'

'Are you sure you are?'

'Yes.'

'You sound impatient, it's not like you.'

'Lee, darling, I'm perfectly all right.'

'Listen, darling, I've found this marvellous, marvellous flat, with a roof-garden, would you believe it? They're asking the earth, and mummy says it's far too expensive, but I couldn't live

99

without a garden, and you did say we had to be in Manhattan – darling, are you there?'

'Of course I am.'

'I feel as if I'm talking to myself. It has nine rooms, which is not as large as you might think, because three of them are bathrooms, and there are ever so many toilets. I think Americans must be very dirty – or perhaps very clean – with weak bladders. Actually, one of the bathrooms is for the maid, and – darling, are you sure you're there?'

'I'm listening.'

'There is something wrong, isn't there? I can feel it.'

'Darling, I promise you I'm perfectly all right.'

'I'm flying back.'

'Don't be silly.' At which she began to cry.

'We're not even married and you're already scolding me.'

'But darling, I keep trying to assure you that I'm fine. There's no need for you to come back, not at this minute.'

'I would still rather come back. I feel unhappy and upset.'

Fortunately her mother was on hand to restrain her.

At that moment, the thought of Lee and a church wedding and a reception at Firwood Hall seemed strangely unreal. My new life had been overwhelmed by the old one before it had even begun.

I had never been entirely happy about my change of name, for it was a little like sailing under false colours, but grandfather obviously knew what he was doing, for it granted me a certain amount of respite. I had no doubt that the papers would sniff out the connection sooner or later, and by the time of the wedding they would be full of it. There were serious disadvantages to marrying a peer's daughter.

I eventually got round to phoning Edward, and he came round to see me right away. He knew German, and read the article without raising an eyebrow, and even with something like impatience, wondering, no doubt, what I was trying to tell him, until I mentioned that the subject of the article was my grandfather.

'Good grief! From all that you told me I thought he was some sort of saint.'

'So did I.'

I poured him a drink and he seized it gratefully.

'I wouldn't tell Lee. She's very excitable.'

'Do you believe it?'

'I don't believe anything I read in the papers, but you obviously do, and she might. She's got enough excitement to get on with as it is – perhaps too much. What happened to the money?'

'The half million? He left it all to me.'

'You make it sound as if it's bad news. Half a million is a tidy sum, you know.'

'But I can't touch it, of course.'

'Why not?'

'I would have thought it was obvious. The money may not have been his.'

'Why not? He owned a private sanatorium. I know of small clinics in London with a turnover of millions.'

'Latvia isn't London – and this was in the thirties.'

'But even if he only made ten thousand in the thirties and used it wisely, he could have been worth over a million now. If you don't want to touch it now, at least invest it in gilt-edged until the matter is cleared up.'

Once a banker always a banker. He went on to suggest ways in which I might double the money in five years without touching the capital, and I had to interrupt him in mid-flight to explain that that wasn't the problem.

'Think of the publicity Lee and I have already had – and the wedding is yet to take place. Can you imagine what will happen if news should get out that I am the grandson of a notorious Nazi? I know we don't have the same names, but it wouldn't be difficult to establish the connection.'

'I don't see the problem. Whatever your grandfather may or may not have done, you certainly were innocent. There's a skeleton in every family cupboard. Forget it.'

But he changed his mind when the article in the German magazine was taken up in the American press.

I asked Lee to come back and we postponed the wedding. This too made headlines. My phone both at the office and at home never stopped ringing. Lee suffered similar importunities. Photographers and television cameras lay in wait wherever we went, and we finally sought refuge in a remote cottage on Exmoor owned by a relative. That only added an element of mystery to the many fantasies already in circulation and, in any case, our cover was soon blown. It was Edward who came up with a solution.

'We need a man in Moscow. You could be the man.'

There was no absolute safety from the intrusions of the press even in Moscow, but Edward thought he had the connections to keep molestation at a tolerable minimum and perhaps to eliminate it altogether, and I readily agreed. I would have gone to the moon to escape persecution. Lee, for her part, would have followed me to the moon. She was only nineteen and I was twenty-nine. We were in no hurry to raise a family, so that we had no immediate need to marry. We would remain in Russia for a year or two till the matter had blown over, and would then return for a quiet wedding in England.

— *Chapter Eight* —

I had been to Russia before, indeed I had been to all the 'People's Democracies', and if I had taken the expression at its face value I would have acquired an abiding distaste for both people and democracy. As it was I acquired an abiding taste for vodka, for vodka just about rendered a stay in East Berlin or Warsaw or Moscow tolerable, and if I were to sum up my experience of People's Democracies it would be gloom tempered by intemperance. I used to find Moscow particularly unpleasant, hot and oppressive in summer, cold and impossible in winter, but I was dejected not so much by the climate as by the people I had to work with: dour, bulky men in ill-cut, ill-fitting suits who could display a semblance of bonhomie when the drinks began to flow but who otherwise seemed to conduct negotiations with formulae picked up from phrase-books, the most common being: 'I shall have to refer the matter to my superiors.'

Every major city has its own characteristic smell, which cannot be easily defined. The smell of Moscow is all too easily definable. It hits one as one arrives, and it is the smell of stale cabbage, though it may be merely the smell of stale, unhappy lives. It is at its strongest in hotels; it hovers over people and affects the very air one breathes, and even now it invades my nostrils at the very mention of Moscow. People often spoke to me of the 'barbaric grandeur' of the architecture and I took some pleasure in viewing the onion-domed churches (few of which served as such), but I found the many-pinnacled blocks of flats in Stalinist Gothic more imposing than impressive, for they looked more like fortifications than habitations. Their very size somehow added to the oppressiveness of the atmosphere and gave one a dark sense of foreboding.

I was not a particularly blithe spirit anywhere, but in Moscow I was completely alone, an unhappy stranger in an unhappy land, and if the Russians themselves were stand-offish I had found it difficult to mix with the hard-drinking, loud-voiced, guffawing expatriates and could not help noting that when I came among them their guffaws suddenly stopped, as if they had been laughing about me. In an odd way Moscow reminded me of Cairo, for there too the visitor remained apart, but while the segregation in Cairo was voluntary, in Moscow it was by order. One couldn't even meet in shops, for there was nothing in them worth buying unless one resorted to the special hard-currency shops catering for tourists, which were, of course, closed to Russians. And, finally, I could never relax in the place. Perhaps I had read too many stories about the secret police, but if I was not conscious that I was myself under scrutiny other people seemed to act as if they were, and the fact that they seemed ill at ease made me feel uneasy, and it is a measure of the harassment which I had suffered in London and New York that I now made for Moscow with something like relief.

I was not at all sure how Lee would take to the place, and at first she didn't. As her mother had suggested, she was not an avid reader, but she had seen a film of *Anna Karenina* and had expected Russia – with variations in detail, of course – to be substantially like the place described by Tolstoy.

She was disappointed from the very first day. We lived in a suite of rooms in the Sovietska Hotel, and I worked in a suite of rooms in the Metropole, while we looked around for something more suitable.

I was perfectly content with my working offices, but Lee was distressed with her domestic ones.

'The cold water is warm, and the warm water is cold, the rooms are poky and badly ventilated, the food is awful and the service is dreadful. Why did we have to come here?'

It was also wet. London or Manhattan in the rain can be fairly tolerable, even appealing, but Moscow in the rain, contemplated through the grubby windows of a chilly and rather drab hotel room, was no joy.

'I can now see why the Russian stories are all so sad. If I was Russian, I would want to kill myself. I've got half a mind to kill myself even though I'm English.'

We still had each other, but even that began to pall, at least to Lee, and I had the feeling that regular, well-ordered, untrammelled, licensed – even semi-licensed – sex was not entirely to her liking, and that she preferred the excitement – to use an expression I had heard – of 'a furtive poke in a dark corner'.

Her main pleasure was television, even though she rarely understood what was happening on the screen, for it was, as she put it, 'company of sorts'. She even took to watching television in bed, and as I liked to work or read in bed, we soon began occupying separate rooms, and it seemed for a time as if our marriage might be over before it began. It was saved by Mitri.

It was years since I had seen him, and his sudden appearance in a Moscow street made me think he was a hallucination brought on by despair. He recognized Lee before he recognized me (I wasn't even aware that they knew each other), and picked her up and cuddled her as if she was a doll.

'Your father told me you were in Moscow. I was aghast. Aghast. What are two frail little waifs like you doing in a place like this?'

We went back to our hotel, where Lee poured her heart out.

'I don't know why your father didn't speak to me before letting you come here. Russia is tolerable, even attractive, but Russian hotels are not. They are badly designed, badly run, badly maintained, and they bring out the cussedness in the Russian people. Russians are perfectly nice otherwise, kindly, helpful, if a bit feckless, like the Irish really, but employ them in a hotel and they will form a conspiracy against the guests. Leave it to me. I'll find you something – something special.'

And he did: his family's former town-house, or a part of it.

'These were only the servants' quarters, you understand. You're behind the green-baize door, so to speak, but it's nearly winter and the other rooms are impossible to heat.'

Once installed in our own home, Lee became a new woman. She had spoken about taking a Cordon Bleu cookery course, but proved to be a reasonable, if extravagant, cook. (She once used up half a bottle of malt whisky on a trifle.) We found ourselves a cleaning woman, an old babushka who reminded me of Anna, and whose name, in fact, was also Anna. She worshipped Lee.

'I haven't seen anyone so beautiful, so light, so graceful, in my life,' she told me. 'When she's around I find it difficult to work. I just want to sit and watch her. And she's a Baron's daughter, isn't she? I could tell at a glance. An aristocrat remains an aristocrat. My mother, may she rest in peace, worked for the Petrovs. Do you know the Petrovs? I think they're in America.'

We entertained, and were entertained, mostly in Embassies, and wherever we went a circle immediately formed round Lee. She had heard, or read somewhere, that half the Embassy staffs in Moscow were spies, and she asked every diplomat we met if he was a spy. 'I don't mean as your full-time job, but isn't it something you do on the side?' Not a few volunteered to become spies if it pleased her.

Again, she had heard that most Russian officials one encountered were secret agents of the KGB, and would approach them each with a disarming smile and say: 'I hope you don't mind my asking, but are you in the Secret Police?'

If she was the pet of the expatriate community, she was adored among the natives, and if I had any difficulties with officials, or even Commissars, she only had to have a word with them, and the matter was settled. Western businessmen, who had been banging their heads against closed doors, watched my progress with disbelief. I was aware I had acquired an ornament in Lee; it never occurred to me that she could be an actual asset and, as a senior official said to me:

'They should make you Ambassador, no, Foreign Minister. No one can say no to your wife.'

(It, of course, never occurred to a Russian that Lee could possibly be less than my wife, for, although they knew there was such a thing as adultery, regularized illicit unions were absolutely outside their reckoning.)

When the snows came and stayed, we were invited to the *datcha* of a Commissar, and we sledged, skated, made snowmen, fought with snowballs, got drunk, sang sad Russian songs and cheerful English sea-shanties, and we began to feel that Russia, once penetrated, offered friendships and pleasures to be found nowhere else in Europe. But the snows were too persistent, and one's soul began to ache for a glimpse of greenery, and we decided to take a holiday in the Crimea.

Arranging a holiday, even for us, was not a matter of merely picking up a phone and booking rooms. It took a few days to organize, and Lee complained that she was being spied on.

She had an obsession with spies, and I thought she was imagining it, but when I came home she asked me to stand behind the curtain and look out, and there indeed was a young man in a fur hat gazing up at our window.

'He's been there all morning,' she said.

'But what makes you think he's spying on you?'

'Because he keeps looking up this way all the time.'

'Let's have lunch,' I said, 'perhaps he'll go away.'

And sure enough, by the time we finished lunch he was gone.

There was no sign of him when I left for work the next morning, but a few hours later Lee phoned to say he was back. She had to go out to do some shopping but she was too terrified to leave the house. In fact, she was terrified to be alone at home.

I hurried back.

It was an awkward situation. It is not an offence, even in Russia, to stand on a pavement and gaze up at a house. He hadn't been making obscene gestures and hadn't actually followed her. I could hardly go up to him and demand: 'Excuse me, but would you mind not staring at our house.'

He left again after lunch-time, and the following morning Lee wouldn't let me go to the office.

'He'll be back,' she insisted, and I waited all day, but he wasn't, or the next day, or the day after, and we went to the Crimea and gave no further thought to him.

We went to Yalta. Russia remained Russia even under Mediterranean skies and amidst Mediterranean vegetation, but the very distance from Moscow and the balminess of the air enabled people to breathe a little more freely. They seemed more cheerful and relaxed. Hotel staff, we found, were relaxed to the point almost of being comatose, and the service was execrable, but the rooms were spacious and well appointed, the wine was good, the sea was blue and the beaches were clean, and even if we sometimes had to wait an hour or two for a meal the food was eventually served, and the caviar and sturgeon especially, were worth waiting for.

Lee recovered her high spirits and her frisky playfulness. She was like a child taken on an unexpected treat, eager and appreciative if a trifle shrill, and with her voluptuous build and her tiny bikinis she attracted crowds every time she appeared on the beach. A large white-haired Russian in a huge pair of droopy drawers went so far as to engage me in conversation.

'You from England?' he asked.

'Yes.'

'She also from England?'

'Yes.'

He puffed pensively for a while on a long cigarette, then he said:

'They make them different in England.'

Even the service improved (at least when we were served by men).

Lee threatened to sunbathe topless. I had to warn her that Yalta was not St Tropez and that she might cause a riot and court arrest. As it was, someone must have complained that she hid too little and exposed too much, for the Chief of Police appeared in person to survey the scene. He returned the next day with what looked like a delegation from the local Soviet, but if they had any complaints they did not address them to us.

We swam, played tennis, made love, went for long walks in the surrounding countryside and toured the battlefields of the Crimean War. Neither of us could recall a happier holiday and we considered the possibility of staying on in Russia after we married.

By the time we got back the snows had melted and it was spring, and Lee and I took a walk in Kremlin Park, which, with its towers and battlements and golden domes, looked like a setting for a fairy-story, but when we sat down for a rest there he was opposite us, on another bench. He wasn't wearing a fur hat, so I wasn't sure if it was him, but Lee insisted it was. And he sat there, unsmiling, hands deep in the pockets of a short coat, staring at us. I didn't know much about spying, but I thought it safe to assume that an actual spy wouldn't stare at his quarry in this way. He was obviously a young man who had taken an inordinate fancy to Lee.

'Can you blame him?' I said. 'I would have done the same' – which seemed to reassure her, and I got no more frantic phone calls.

Then, one evening, I came home to find her in tears. 'That young man,' she sobbed, 'when I went out this morning, he fell on his knees and started kissing my shoes!'

'I'll have to call the police,' I said.

'No, wait. I haven't finished. And he said he loved me, and lived only for the sight of me – '

'In English?'

'No, in Russian.'

'But you don't speak Russian.'

'You don't have to know a language when some poor man pours his heart out to you. I understood every word. He couldn't live without me, he said, could he touch me, could he kiss me.'

'What did you do?'

'I took him upstairs and we went to bed.' With which she broke down in a flood of tears.

'There's a limit to being the Good Samaritan, you know.'

'I know,' she wailed, 'and I can't forgive myself. What's going to happen?'

'What do you mean, what's going to happen?'

'He said if I won't let him come again he'll kill himse-e-elf.'

'Well, that might solve all our problems.'

'How can you speak like that? I thought you were understanding and good and kind. The best thing would be if I killed myself.'

'I'll tell you what. Let's all kill ourselves, but let's have supper first.'

And, still sobbing and sniffing, she began to prepare the meal. It arrived burnt at the bottom and salted with tears on top.

It was the end of a dream, but then I had never really regarded it as anything else, for I doubted if either of us were capable of forming a lasting association. I had enjoyed a year of happiness the like of which I had not known before and to which, in a curious way, I did not feel entitled, and now that it was over I had no quarrel with fate.

My most immediate regret arose not from the end of my affair with Lee but at the end of my association with her family. I had taken an inordinate liking to her parents. I sometimes asked myself if I wasn't possibly a snob at heart and my relations with the daughter gave me the feeling that I was an Eissenmacher of sorts; but the Eissenmachers weren't Howards or Cecils and, as Edward said more than once, 'We're parvenus'. I liked the parents not so much for what they represented but for what they were. I liked the conviviality and briskness of the father and the intelligence and good looks of the mother. I liked to be part of their set-up and, although I had felt that my warm feelings towards them were fully reciprocated, I did not think our relationship would outlast my liaison with their daughter. In fact, I was sure it wouldn't.

I could not resume my normal life as if nothing had happened, and the next day I phoned Edward to give notice that I was winding up my affairs in Moscow and that I would be leaving the bank. My call did not seem to surprise him.

'I think I know what's happened,' he said. 'Don't do anything, I shall be over on the first plane.'

'There is no need to do that,' I said. 'I am only giving formal notice that I shall be needing a replacement in another month.'

He arrived the next day with his wife. I tried to avoid her glance when I met them at the airport. He was full of apologies, and she full of recriminations.

I had, by then, moved into a hotel. I left them with Lee, and quickly retreated to my room. He phoned me later to ask if he could come round and see me, and, to my relief, he arrived on his own. He stood scratching his head for a moment and smiling at me sheepishly.

'Where does one begin? What does one say?'

'I'm not sure that one has to say anything. I am old enough to be responsible for, and face the consequences of, my own actions.'

'Indeed. You wouldn't have a drop of brandy in the place, by any chance?'

I didn't, but I ordered a bottle, and he poured himself a tumblerful. It was Georgian brandy, and not entirely to his taste, but he gulped it as if it were beer.

'You don't know what a day I've had. It began from the moment you phoned, and it's not over yet. I think I'll stop here for the night, if I may. The way my wife goes on, one would think I could have done something about it. If I had only had a word with her, if only I had had a word with you, if only this, if only that – '

'It wouldn't have helped. She had more than a word with me.'

'I know, she told me, but somehow she thinks that as I happen to be your employer, you would have listened. I suppose I should have warned you you were taking on a handful, but then what woman isn't? I took on a handful myself, but it's lasted reasonably well. Looking back on it now, it was a mistake to pay any attention to that hoo-ha about your grandfather. I can't see that it would have done you any harm, or the bank for that matter. You should have married as planned. It's a good father who knows his own daughter, but I think that if she had actually been your wife instead of your – your, er – consort – things might have turned out differently. I'm not suggesting you should think again – '

'I have thought again. I thought all night. That's why I moved out to a hotel the next morning.'

'Why don't you go away for a bit?'

'I intend to go away for more than a bit.'

When I got back to London, it was as if the whole thing hadn't happened. I had lost nothing, except perhaps a little self-esteem.

I knew I wanted to leave the bank, at least for the time being. I wasn't too certain what I would do when I left, beyond the fact that I wanted a clear mind for a period of stock-taking. But there was not all that much stock to take. The events of the past year had merely confirmed what I already knew, that I was adept at making a livelihood but not at directing my life, except that I wasn't at all sure that life was something which could be directed, for it had a way of taking its own course. The thought should have induced an attitude of resignation. Why struggle when faced with the inevitable? Except that the very inclination to struggle was perhaps also inevitable.

I wondered if I should, perhaps, go back to academic life. New universities were opening everywhere and old ones were expanding and, although I had not taken a doctorate, I thought my banking experience might count for something and that it might not be impossible to get a lectureship in applied economics. The drawback to any such scheme was that I had acquired tastes and commitments which did not go with the sort of salaries paid to university teachers, and my mind turned to the fortune left by my grandfather. And, almost as if provoked by the very thought of that money, there arrived through the post a heart-rending letter from Carla to say that Chuck was dead. But that, she was quick to add, was no tragedy, for he had been in such a pitiful state over the past few months that she had been tempted to put him out of his misery with her own hands. And even that was not the worst. He had left a sizeable fortune, every penny of which had gone to his wife and children.

'Why is everybody so unkind to me?' she asked. 'Do you remember how I slaved for your grandfather after the war, and how I nursed his cow of a wife? Yet he left all his money to you.

The bastard Chuck was even worse. When I met him I was still young, still attractive, and could have married again. He was already almost past it, but I gave him the best years of my life, kept home for him, washed his clothes, cooked his meals and put up with his sexual quirks, some of which you wouldn't believe (or perhaps you would – do you know, he would dip it in Nestlé's milk and have me lick it clean?). But the worst of it was the end, when he was a bloated, putrid, stinking mass. I had to wash him, feed him and drain him. His wife had had him in his prime, I when he was garbage. His wife could enjoy him, I had to nurse him. Yet his wife got his money and I his pus. May he rot in hell, as he rotted in life.

'I am suing the wife for a share of his estate. I hope that I don't have to sue you – the only person left who means anything to me at all – for a share of my brother's estate. It is nearly a year since we last met, and you said you would have the matter investigated. How long will the investigation take? I'm getting on, I'm sorry to say, and I need the money NOW.'

It is strange how events do not so much provoke one another as accompany each other in a predetermined pattern, for in the same post that brought her letter there came a letter from Wolf, grandfather's lawyer, to say that it was fully a year since the will was published, that no putative heirs had made any claims on his estate, and that there was no impediment in law to my use of the money. He added that grandfather had been left the equivalent of about £100,000 by a former patient and that he had no doubt that every penny in the estate had been lawfully and honourably acquired.

A lawyer remains a lawyer. I was not really interested whether grandfather had acquired his fortune legally or honourably, but whether he had betrayed his friends or not. I was aware that this was something which Wolf would probably find it impossible to establish, but I wrote back to ask him if he could at least find out whether grandfather had been a member of the Nazi party (as alleged in the German magazine article), and, if so, whether he had been an active member or not. I also underlined all the other allegations in the piece and asked him to see how far they could be confirmed or denied.

In the meantime, I sent Carla a further £5,000, which, I said, would be deducted from any sums she might receive in an

112

eventual settlement. She accepted the money with little gratitude and no grace.

'How long do you think I can wait for "an eventual settlement"?' she demanded. 'I am fifty-six and have only a war-widow's pension to live on. I'll expect to hear from you within the year. If I don't, you'll hear from my lawyers. I'm sorry to write like this to my little Heinschein, whom I have always loved, and who means more to me than anyone, but I have had too many disappointments to remain the patient, easy-going person I was.'

I was beginning to regret that I had ever been left any money at all, for I was yearning to put the whole matter of grandfather's history and grandfather's estate out of my mind, but it became clear that I would have been unable to do so even if he had died quietly in bed, and had not left me a penny, for Carla phoned me one morning to ask if I knew that a television company was making a film about him. They had asked her if she would be willing to co-operate and had promised her a fee if she did. It could not have been a large fee, for she had told them she wanted to think about it. 'I have nothing to hide,' she added, 'but who knows what they might dredge up? We can't stop them, I suppose, but what's the best thing to do?'

'Tell them to phone me,' I said.

They phoned that same day, and the call brought two surprises. The programme was being made not by a German company but by a British one, and the producer of the programme was someone I hadn't seen since I was a student, but whose name rang an immediate bell – Sue Cohen.

—— *Chapter Nine* ——

'You've spoilt it all, bugger you,' she said. 'I thought I had a scoop. That article about your grandfather aroused a lot of interest, but it was only little me who knew that he was your grandfather, and I thought here was a story that had everything. Notorious Nazi criminal. Whizz-kid grandson takes a brilliant First at Oxford, joins a bank and marries into the English aristocracy. Can you imagine the sort of footage we could have had? Egypt, Oxford, dreaming spires, death-camps, Firwood Hall, the Hon. Felicia Eissenmacher. Now you've spoilt it all by getting divorced.'

'You've got it all wrong, my dear, we weren't even married.'

'But you're no longer even friends, so half the point of the story is gone, but we've gone too far to turn back, which is why I brought you here.'

When she first asked me to lunch at a Soho restaurant, I hesitated, because I had no intention of letting my past be played out on television. On the other hand, I was curious to see her again, and in need of company, and I agreed. She had changed very little in the ten years since we last met, the same dazzling blue eyes, the same tousled hair, the same scruffy appearance, which was now *de rigueur* for anyone in the creative professions, but which had been less common when she was an undergraduate. She had helped to set the trend.

'You know, when I first heard that you were in a bank and about to marry a banker's daughter, I thought it couldn't be the same Harry Newman, for I saw you as an obscure don in an obscure field, teaching in an obscure university, and married to a tall, thin woman with a flat chest and buck-teeth who played the organ in college chapel on Sunday mornings.'

'And I had imagined you as a social worker, no, a sort of secular missionary, teaching blacks how to bottle-feed babies, or how to avoid having them in the first place, or perhaps as an actress, or maybe running a finishing-school for young ladies of good family, teaching them manners and deportment, that sort of thing. The only thing I didn't expect was to find you in the gossip industry.'

'Why the gossip industry?'

'If I may be frank, isn't the film you're talking about just so much animated gossip?'

'I sold it to the company as such, if that's what you mean. Perhaps I even thought of it as such initially, but – ' and she paused to unzip a briefcase she had brought with her. 'Have a look at these, my love, and tell me if it's mere gossip.'

It was a sheaf of documents, mostly in German, some in Arabic, and all appended with an English translation.

'You don't have to read them all. Just have a look at the top one.'

It was a photostat of grandfather's membership card of the Nazi party. There had been a reference to his membership in the Schwarzwald article, but it had been accompanied by a torrent of so many other allegations, some of them preposterous, that I had been able to brush it aside. Seeing the card on its own somehow amounted to an indictment.

'Well,' she said, 'do you still think it's gossip?'

'How long was he in the party?'

'I have no reason to believe he ever left,' and she pointed to another document which showed that he had been working for German intelligence throughout much of the thirties and until the German invasion of Russia.

'Would he have been trusted with such duties if he wasn't a Nazi?'

I didn't know what to say and, in fact, found it impossible to continue the conversation, or the meal.

'You look as if you could do with a drink,' she said, and filled my glass. If the drink had been hemlock I would have taken it.

'Is all this news to you?'

'Of course. Grandfather could be sharp and irritable, and he was always taciturn, but he was otherwise the soul of kindness.'

'And, no doubt, some of his best friends were Jews.'

'But they were. Our neighbours were Jewish. They helped him build his sanatorium.'

'You mean he was befriended by Jews. Not the same thing, is

it?'

'But they would hardly have done so if they had known him to be a Nazi.'

'Which merely suggests that he was quiet about it. But look, you seem to be taking this personally. He was only your grandfather. It's no reflection on you. I've never believed that the sins of the father must rebound upon the heads of the children.'

'It's not that, but I've cherished a certain picture of the man which you've come near to destroying.'

I was a little taken aback by the strength of my own reaction, and so was Sue.

'I'm sorry. I didn't really mean to show you all these papers now, and I wouldn't have done, but your crack about the gossip industry – ' She took my hand, which calmed me down slightly. 'There's a film I want you to see.'

'No, not now. I've had about as much as I can take for one day.'

'It's not what you think. You may find it a pleasant surprise.'

I was not quite in the mood for surprises either pleasant or otherwise, but I walked with her across Soho to a private viewing-theatre which had a well-stocked cocktail bar in an ante-room. She poured me a brandy before we went in, which made me suspect that the surprise she had in store might not be as pleasant as she suggested, and I braced myself for the sight of grandfather in a brown shirt with a swastika arm-band and jackboots. It was nothing like that, but I was still in need of the brandy.

The film was a succession of flickering shots, badly made and poorly developed, which looked as if they had been taken in a snow-storm, but, from the very first shot, it evoked memories so sharp, so clear, so poignant, that I almost cried out.

I couldn't have been more than six when I left, but I recognized everything. Resznitz, the Russian Orthodox church with its onion-shaped domes and the bearded priest, the Lutheran church with its tall spire, the cobbled streets, the fire-brigade depot, the market square and the public lavatory – I could almost smell it – and then the lake, the woods and – yes, there was my grandmother, big and fat even then. I not only remembered the setting, I recalled the very film. It must have been shown before, presumably by my grandfather. In fact, he must have taken it, for he didn't appear. And there was the sanatorium, presumably

before it was enlarged, and these must have been his patients –
no, they were his staff. And then a dancing bear! I must have
cried out in alarm, for Sue stopped the film and put on the light.

'Anything wrong?'

'No, I'm sorry, but you can't imagine what all this means to
me.'

'I can indeed. That's why I brought you. But are you sure
you're all right? You're very pale.'

'No, no, I'm fine. Let me see the rest.'

Yes, there was the dancing bear again. I thought I had actually
seen it in life, but it must have been on film. My earliest memory,
a shadow. And then a large, genial figure with a long beard and a
peaked cap. Was that old Marcovitch? In which case the young
men beside him were probably his sons, and the woman,
handsome but unsmiling, was presumably his wife. And then
Carla. There could be no mistaking her. She couldn't have been
more than twenty then. What a figure! What legs! What a smile!
And then building workers on scaffolding – the extension to the
sanatorium. Old Marcovitch again, with a young woman, his
daughter presumably, and his wife, still unsmiling, and then . . .
darkness.

I lit a cigarette and drank my brandy with a shaking hand while
they changed the reel. Sue sat on my arm-rest with her arm over
my shoulders.

'Do you recognize any of the people?' she asked.

'From my own recollections only grandmother and my aunt.
My aunt would be able to tell you who's who.'

'We'll have to bring her over.'

The lights dimmed again and I was back in Resznitz. A tall
woman in black with a smiling face. That must have been old
Anna before she was old, and two young men, her sons
probably. Then a tall figure appeared who made me sit up. Sue
stopped the film.

'Something you want to tell me?'

I asked her to play back the last few frames, and the man
reappeared. I had seen him before.

'On film, or in life?'

'I can't be sure, but I've definitely seen him.'

He appeared again later, and this time she held the frame. He
wore a white coat, which suggested that he was one of grand-

father's colleagues, but he did not quite go with the setting. There was something lordly and cosmopolitan about him: the way he held his head, the lofty bearing, the trimmed moustache. One could have imagined him in Vienna, Berlin, but not in a forest clearing at the back of beyond. But I still couldn't place him.

'Perhaps you'll remember as we go on,' said Sue.

The film resumed. The bearded figure of the old Jew again, surrounded presumably by his family, but with a new man among them, tall with cropped hair and a small beard, and looking rather less homespun than the rest. All the others smile into the camera. He is plainly not amused. Aunt Carla again, in boots and a fur coat, moving towards the camera. The rapid, jerky movement of the film made her, and everybody else, even the Marcovitch family, look Chaplinesque, so that one had to make an effort to recall the tragic ending to their story. And then snow again, the buildings dark and still amidst the all-engulfing white, which reached up to their windows. The tall Lutheran church, almost sinister in its white mantle, and the Russian church with its many domes, seemed to be sinking in the snow. And Resznitz Square deserted. And then, the forest, black and white, white and black, the branches motionless, the trunks half buried in snow-drifts. And the fields, great white ways, stretching without impediment in every direction. Not a soul in sight. Waggons buried in snow. Cattle staring forlornly from the shelter of a barn. And then – at which I almost cried out again – a large, black dog moving slowly and awkwardly across a snow-covered field. It couldn't have been my grandfather's. He didn't like dogs. Strange how the animals, the bear and the dog, the dog and the bear, were fixed in my memory, but not the people.

Then the sanatorium again, the extension now complete, with a large car outside, and the Marcovitch sons again, a dark-haired woman with a child in her arms and the tall, unsmiling figure I had seen before. The woods again; naked children swimming in the lake. And Resznitz once more, the market-square deserted, and then a long shot, as if taken from a tower or a roof, of soldiers, and then . . . darkness.

The lights came on again. I remained motionless for a time, saying nothing. Sue lit a cigarette but also remained silent. Finally I said:

'Looking at that man in that setting – did he strike you as a

Nazi?'

'No, not in the least, but I have seen films of Hitler in Berchtesgaden, playing with children, fondling dogs, and I also wouldn't have thought of him as a Nazi if I hadn't known him to be Hitler. And isn't there something odd about the whole set-up? He had one child, didn't he, your mother, and only one grandchild, yourself, and yet though his neighbours, his friends, his colleagues, his employees feature in the film, you don't and neither does your mother.'

'The film was presumably taken before the war, and I wasn't around yet.'

'It wasn't taken in one go. Most of it was pre-war, but those troops taken from a distance in the final long shot, they were German. I've been able to establish that, and the Germans only came in 1941. And, in any case, what about your mother? Did you see her in any of the shots?'

'She died when I was a few months old.'

'But presumably you've seen photos of her. She wasn't in the film even as a girl, was she?'

'She was in school in Germany, so she may not have been around.'

I wondered why I said that. That she went to school in Germany was true, I had that from Carla, but, as Sue pointed out, most of the film was taken in the summer when, presumably, she would have been home on holiday.

The very process of interrogation, I found, makes one act as if one has something to hide. I had also been mystified by the exclusion of my mother from the film, but, recalling grandfather's letters, I presumed that he had cut her out of the film to erase all traces of her existence; but I hesitated to say that. Here was a woman whom I had known only casually about ten years ago, whom I hadn't seen since, and who was intent on depicting my grandfather as Judas. Why was I talking to her at all? And yet a strange sense of intimacy prevailed between us, as if we had never separated, and I finally told her almost everything. I say 'almost' because I did not mention grandfather's letter, but that, in a sense, was something which I was keeping even from myself. In any case, the more I learned about him the less convincing it seemed. I did not, and could not, believe that he had actually betrayed the Marcovitch family, but it is unlikely that he strove

119

officiously to keep them alive, and very unlikely that he would have sheltered one of their children throughout the war years. He had obviously been anxious to shield me not only from Germany's past, but his own.

I asked her where she got the films.

'Does the name Markham mean anything to you?'

'Markham? From Cairo?'

'Was he from Cairo? He materialized here in London, slight figure, very pale, very smooth, rather sinister. He had heard from Schwarzwald I was in the market. I had to pay the earth for them.'

'Did he tell you how he came by them?'

'No, and I didn't ask. I was too glad to have them at all.'

I presumed he had helped himself to the films after grandfather died and had also fed Schwarzwald the cock and bull story about him being involved in the interrogation of Israeli spies. The distaste I had always had for that man, and which for a time I had thought misplaced, appeared to have been fully justified.

We went back to her place in a taxi, and she said:

'You looked so ill over lunch you had me worried. I got most of my information and documents from this chap Schwarzwald. You must have seen his article.'

'Of course I did, but I just refused to believe it.'

'Then why do you believe me?'

'He only quoted extracts while you came up with complete documents, and I suppose when the article appeared I was too preoccupied with too many other things. I was about to get married, to be received into the nobility as you put it, and to move to New York. All that's come undone. You caught me at a vacant moment; it was like strong drink on an empty stomach.'

'I'm sorry.' She kissed me on the lips and I felt something like life flowing back into me.

She lived in a large flat in St John's Wood, whose elegant furnishings did not quite go with her scruffy appearance. I had expected cane furniture, travel posters and guitars, and table-lamps fashioned out of empty liqueur bottles, the casual trappings of Bohemia, but here was leather and teak, glittering crystal, gleaming brass and expensive pictures in expensive frames.

The kiss on the lips had induced a pleasant sense of tumescence, but I immediately felt deflated at the sight of her abode. I knew that sex went with squalor; it hadn't occurred to me that opulence was a bromide, but she kissed me again and I lost my awareness of my surroundings. We didn't even make it to the bedroom, but made love in the middle of her Bokharan carpet with our clothes scattered about us.

'Now can you see what you missed?' she said, stroking my hair. 'Why didn't you come to my party?'

'Your party? God, you've got a good memory.'

'I'm Jewish, you know, we've got long memories, especially when it comes to slights.'

'Do you remember the weather? I was stuck in a blizzard in Edinburgh.'

'In *Edinburgh*! What the hell were you doing in Edinburgh when you were expected in Oxford?'

She seemed genuinely angry, as if it had all happened yesterday.

'I had every intention of coming back in time.'

'You did not. You were afraid of me. I should imagine you still are.'

'Why should I be afraid of you?'

'Because I'm Jewish and you're German.'

I was half tempted to tell her grandfather's version of my origins, but I did not think it appropriate. It is difficult to discuss a serious matter seriously when one is naked: a baring of bodies does not always lead to a baring of souls.

'Do you know, I almost cried with frustration when I couldn't get to the party.'

'I did cry – with distress.'

'I can't imagine it.'

'Imagination is obviously not your strong point. I took a shine to you. I'm not sure why. You're good-looking, but I've never attached much importance to looks, not in a man. I suppose it was your slight air of helplessness. You didn't seem to know where you were going, and what you were doing. You looked lost, and when you failed to turn up – '

' 'I failed to turn up because I *was* lost.'

'Don't interrupt me. When you failed to turn up I was beside myself. You hadn't phoned, no explanation, no apology. I had never been stood up before, and I half suspect that one of the reasons I jumped on the idea of making a film about your grandfather was my determination to settle old scores.'

'Isn't there such a thing as a statute of limitations? All this happened ten years ago.'

'What's ten years to a woman scorned? Nursing grievances is the nearest thing I've had to a full-time occupation.'

Her voice faded away as she – still stark naked – went into the kitchen to make something to eat. It was a frugal affair, a meal of herbs, for she was slimming, and looking at her over my grated carrots I recognized that she had good cause to slim, but the sight of all that voluptuousness made it difficult for me to eat.

'What's the matter, got no appetite?'

'Not for food.'

At which she got up and pulled a sweater over herself.

'Is that better?'

'Not much.'

She sighed and put on a pair of slacks.

'The trouble with you is that you've been deprived for too long. I can't see why people bother dressing when they've got central heating.'

As the evening progressed we each tried to catch up on the life of the other. She had the advantage of me in that she had culled a whole dossier on me from the popular press and, although I had to correct her on details, she had my story in outline, whereas I knew almost nothing about her.

She had joined a repertory company as assistant stage-manager on coming down from Oxford, from which she had progressed to working on television commercials (family connections had helped for she had relatives both in advertising and the film industry), and eventually she graduated to television itself. This was her first major programme – her 'make or break effort', as she put it.

'It's all been rather dull and uneventful. Nothing much to show for my thirty years – nothing much to hide either. And, oh yes, I got married, but let's not talk about that.'

But she did talk about it, and without prompting from me.

'He's an actor, quite successful, though his face is better known than his name. Makes his money advertising after-shave. That's why he married me, to get work in television commercials.'

'And why did you marry him?'

'Someone to show off to my family and friends. He's very

good-looking. We haven't quarrelled, or separated, or anything like that. We don't see each other often enough to quarrel.'

I told her about my own pseudo-marriage, without going into too much detail.

'She's very pretty, but from what I hear she's an imbecile – the company I work for is full of debs, so I know all about her. I wouldn't have thought she was your type at all.'

'What is my type?'

'Someone large, brash, assertive, intelligent and sexy – me, in fact. Are you sure you didn't go after her because she was the boss's daughter? I think – '

She was interrupted by the phone, and she remained in conversation for something like half an hour.

I took the dishes to the sink and washed up as she was talking, but the shrill screech of the phone, plus the subject matter of her conversation, killed the sense of intimacy which had built up between us.

'That was one of my spies phoning from Egypt,' she said. 'It seems that Schwarzwald's allegations were well-founded.'

'I wish you'd drop the whole thing.'

'Just like that?'

'I mean, who the hell was my grandfather? A small country doctor running a small private clinic in some neck of the woods. Who the hell cares?'

'I do, for one. You can't explain what happened to the Jews in Europe through a film on Eichmann or Heydrich, or anyone like that. The tragedy was too vast, the crimes too colossal for the imagination to grasp. I've watched dozens of these films, and they've left me stunned rather than informed. What I hope to do is to cast some light on the matter by telling the story of one man, who, as you say, was of no particular consequence, and his immediate victims, who were likewise of no particular consequence. I see your grandfather as Every German, and the Marcovitches as Every Jew.'

'Which means you're presuming his guilt to start with.'

'Only insofar as he's German, but I'm only collating the evidence at this stage; perhaps you could help me assess it.'

'I can tell you the idea that my grandfather was killed by Israeli agents is too crazy for words.'

'I'm not really interested in how he died, but how he lived. I understand he was involved in the interrogation of Israeli spies, which is rather more serious.'

'I don't believe that either.'

'You're accusing me of presuming his guilt, whereas you're presuming his innocence. Can't we just examine the evidence together and weigh it up for what it's worth?'

'And if he does prove to be innocent wouldn't that kill your programme?'

'I'll risk it.'

'What would it involve?'

'A trip to Cairo, perhaps another to Russia. They wouldn't take long.'

I had, as a result of the persecution I had suffered, acquired a distaste for the media, and especially television, but she had caught me at a loose end when I wasn't quite sure what to do with myself (and I had never been adept at doing nothing). She had satisfied me that I could not dismiss the programme she was preparing as mere gossip. She had come up with some disturbing information, and might come up with more, and I thought if I was around I might at least be able to see what use she would make of it and possibly forestall any abuse.

At the same time, while I liked her company, I was slightly nervous of being with her at all, for insofar as I gave credence to her discoveries about grandfather they seemed to confirm my belief that his version of my origins was false and that I was almost certainly German, while she was not only a Jewess but a Jewess of the most Jewish sort: loud, assertive, aggressive, restless and complicated. I was afraid of getting caught up with her, but my fears were outweighed by her enthusiasm and I found myself swept along. When an irresistible force meets an immovable object, the object ceases to be immovable.

—— *Chapter Ten* ——

I had lived in Cairo for over four years without ever being part of it. Our house was in one suburb, my school was in another, and I was whisked to and fro in a limousine without setting foot in the city. And the people I mixed with (insofar as I mixed with them) were hardly part of the city themselves. I didn't even share the same climate as the natives, for the house, the school, the very car, were air-conditioned, and finding myself now in the midst of Cairo I felt as if I had never been there before.

Sue's informant, a Dr Baddawi, lived a couple of miles from our hotel. She thought we could get there in five minutes. I, knowing something of Cairo's traffic, suggested we allow half an hour, but in the course of the half-hour we had gone less than half way, and we continued our journey on foot. Sue was enthralled with the teeming crowds, the clamour, the colour, the dust, even the heat.

'We'll have to film in Cairo whether your grandfather was innocent or not. It'll make the programme.'

We were half an hour late for our appointment, but Dr Baddawi, a plump, sallow-skinned figure in a white suit, brushed our apologies aside.

'You are early. I always expect people to be an hour late.'

Sue introduced me as Dr Rhiner's grandson, and he clasped both his plump little hands round mine.

'This is a privilege. Your grandfather often spoke about you,' which made me distrust him at once, for I couldn't imagine my grandfather doing anything of the sort.

He chatted incessantly while he made coffee. But once we each had a cup in hand there came an awkward silence, and Sue said:

'You don't mind that I brought Mr Newman with me?'

'No, no, no. It's an honour to have him here, but did we not agree that this should be a *very* private conversation?'

Sue looked uneasily in my direction, and I rose to my feet.

'I think I'll have a walk, if I may.'

'You'll find a very interesting mosque almost opposite,' said Baddawi, 'one of the oldest in Cairo, but do finish your coffee first, there's no hurry.'

The mosque was a crumbling ruin and, as the roof was in danger of falling in, it had been closed off to the public. I lit a cigarette, and as I did so I thought I could see a figure, also with a cigarette in his mouth, watching the flat from which I had just emerged. Shades of Moscow! But then I noticed other figures similarly employed, or unemployed. Either half of Cairo was engaged in spying on the other half, or leaning on a corner with a cigarette in one's mouth was the principal local pastime.

I waited for about half an hour and when Sue failed to appear I walked back to the hotel. She must have found a short cut for I found her waiting for me in the lobby. She was full of apologies.

'I'm sorry about that, but he was nervous of talking to me at all.'

'Why? What's he got to be afraid of?'

'Several things. As a state employee he shouldn't be talking about a security matter, and as a doctor he shouldn't be talking about his former patients. But the long and the short of it is this. He worked with your grandfather at the hospital about the time they broke up the spy ring and he remembers very clearly two young men, both of them students, being brought in for treatment.'

'They could have had a breakdown.'

'That's quite possible, and there may, in the event, have been nothing more to it than that, but they were kept in a special building to which only your grandfather had access. Baddawi had helped to treat all his other patients, but neither he nor anyone else was allowed anywhere near these two, and even the nurses were employees of the security services and not the hospital.'

'Reasonable precautions, wouldn't you say, given that they were spies. What I want to know is, was my grandfather involved in their interrogation, as Schwarzwald alleged? Did he have them brain-washed?'

'He thinks he may have done. Did you know your grandfather had received a decoration from the Egyptian government?'

'He was entitled to it. He had set up the whole hospital.'

'Baddawi thinks it had something to do with the spy-ring. The head of the security services, whom he knew personally, was at the ceremony.'

'When did all this happen?'·

'About fifteen years ago.'

'I don't trust memories to go back that far, and in particular I distrust Baddawi. Why is he telling you all this in the first place?'

'Why do you think? Money.'

'I don't know how much you've paid him, but I'll find you a dozen people to attest to grandfather's innocence for half the sum.'

The next day she came up with yet another revelation. There had been a large colony of German doctors and scientists in Egypt at the time, and it seemed that my grandfather had kept clear of them all. Didn't that strike me as significant? I had to confess that it didn't. There was something contrary and uniquely Jewish about her logic.

'Look,' I said, 'he went out to Egypt to start a new life. Some of these chaps were ex-Nazis, and not all that ex at that, and he wanted to have nothing to do with them. Now if he had been part of their set-up you might have been at liberty to draw conclusions, but what you are trying to say is that the fact that he stayed clear of the Nazis is in itself a proof that he was still a Nazi himself. What sort of reasoning is that?'

'The reasonable sort. He was anxious to avoid suspicion.'

I sighed and tried again.

'Let's put it at the most cynical level. Let's agree that he was a Nazi right up to the end of the war, but once he saw the game was up he wanted to make a new start, if not for himself then at least for me. If he'd been someone of consequence in the party, with something to hide, he wouldn't have waited till 1952 to make a run for it, he would have fled right after the war, and not to Egypt, but to Bolivia or Argentina or Brazil, like Eichmann, Barbie and the rest.'

'I'm not suggesting he was in their class.'

'Then what are you suggesting?'

'That your grandfather may not have been the figure of contrition you think he was; I am not at all sure that he turned over a new leaf, as you think he had.'

'Will you be having Baddawi on screen?'

'Of course not, we won't even be able to name him.'

'So there won't be an opportunity to cross-examine him.'

'No, but there will be every opportunity to refute his evidence, if we should find any evidence to refute it.'

The next few days she toured Cairo and its surroundings selecting film locations and securing the necessary permissions, while I busied myself in the University library. I had vague recollections of the spy trials, for they took place while I was still in Egypt, and I was able to locate the newspaper reports without difficulty. Thirteen Jews were arrested, two managed to escape, another committed suicide while in jail, and the others were put on trial. I tried to obtain a transcript, which was impossible, for most of the hearings were in camera, but, searching further, I came upon a statement from the Minister of Justice that two of the accused had been found unfit to plead and had been admitted to hospital. As a famous historian once said, most secrets are to be found in print.

I presented Sue with a copy of the statement.

'Puts Baddawi's testimony in a new light, doesn't it?'

'It doesn't disprove it.'

I felt like putting my hands round her pretty neck and throttling her.

'But don't you understand that the onus of proof is on you? You are dealing with a man who has never been charged in any court of law, or even before an ad hoc tribunal, and all you have against him is rumour and hearsay. Schwarzwald went round the Middle East with jangling money-bags making it known that he was in the market for evidence, and you're doing the same.'

'I'm in the market for all the evidence, not only for the prosecution. You don't seem to understand what I'm after. I'm not trying to apportion guilt. All I'm going to do is to present what evidence we have and let viewers judge for themselves.'

'I'm not a lawyer, but there is such a thing as inadmissible evidence, and I would say that not a little of the sort of evidence you're accumulating would not be admitted in any British court of law, or, for that matter, an Egyptian one. The only hard fact you've had to work on is that at some time in his remote past he was a member of the Nazi party, but you can't go on from that to say that he was an unrepentant Nazi who had betrayed his friends in Latvia and had been involved in brainwashing Jews in Egypt.'

'But I don't intend to do that. For example, I've just discovered that the two young men in prison were released some years ago, and I'm trying to follow them up, and their families. It won't be easy, for they all assumed new identities and left Egypt, but one never knows. The marvellous thing about working on this sort of programme is that it's full of surprises.'

The most surprising thing about the programme, as far as I could see, was that she was allowed to work on it at all. Perhaps I had been spoilt by my Oxford training and my experience in the bank, but I was used to dealing with people who, in the main, knew what they were doing and how it was to be done, whereas here I had stumbled upon someone who bumbled along with cheerful self-assurance but who was somehow saved from the worst effects of her incompetence by a guardian angel. I supposed that as she was only playing with shadows it didn't really matter, but what, I wondered, would happen if she had been, say, a doctor?

I had not really intended to collaborate with her on the programme but now I felt compelled to continue out of incredulity, or rather from sheer fascination at the way she went about her work. There was madness in her method, but I was finally able to convince her that any charges which may have arisen against grandfather out of his years in Egypt were decidedly not proven. He may have been a Nazi, perhaps even an unrepentant one, but there was no evidence that his sympathies or antipathies were allowed to affect his work at the Cairo hospital. In that respect, at least, my visit to Cairo had not been wasteful.

While I was there I tried to contact Markham, but was not surprised to discover that he had vanished without trace; but I did manage to find Ahmed, who had been grandfather's housekeeper, and he told me: 'He steal everything: books, papers, films, cameras, gramophone. He come with truck and take everything. I tell police but they do nothing.'

The next stage of Sue's programme promised to be less fraught, but I approached it with a certain degree of foreboding, for she had arranged to interview Carla in London, and I was deputed to look after her. Carla had always been unpredictable and tended to become more so as she grew older, and I wasn't quite certain how she would act or what she would say, but I need not have worried, for on this occasion at least she turned out to be the Carla of my dreams.

She had been booked into an hotel, but when I met her at the airport she said:

'Why a hotel? Haven't you room in your place, or am I too old for you, my little Heinschein?'

She was, by her own dating, nearly sixty, and beginning to look her age, but I didn't want to upset her – or perhaps I didn't want to deprive myself – anyhow I took her home, and she threw her arms round me as soon as we were alone.

'Oh, you don't know how I've been aching for you. When I heard your marriage was finished I was sad for you, but happy for Carla. Here, let me touch you, I could suck you dry, my juicy little Heinschein. I'll show you your Aunt Carla is never too old.'

I had never had any serious doubts on that score.

Before we began filming Sue wanted her to see the Resznitz film, and she screamed with excitement at the very first frame.

'Ah, I haven't seen them since the war. Gunther was very good with his camera. If he hadn't been a doctor, he could have been in Hollywood.'

Something of her excitement communicated itself to me, though it was only a matter of weeks since I had seen them last. Here they were again, as etched in my memory, the churches, the bearded priests, the cobbled streets, the fire-depot, the market square, the sanatorium, and I prepared myself for the next frame – there it was, the dancing bear. When we came to the people, Sue held each frame so that my aunt could identify them. I was mistaken in believing that some of the figures were patients.

'No, no, no,' she said, 'they couldn't have been patients. He wouldn't have filmed his patients. It would have been unethical. And it's all in the open. The patients were nearly all locked up in a special wing. He only dealt with very serious cases. People came to him as a last resort.'

She identified each of the Marcovitch family in turn.

'That's the old man. He wasn't that old but he looked old because of his beard. And his wife, what was her name? Zelda, I think. Gave herself airs, a bit like my sister-in-law. And that's the oldest son, can't remember his name. That's the youngest, Moshe, flashy little rascal.'

'Why do you say that?' I asked.

'I'll tell you sometime. He was friendly with your mother.'

'With my mother?' I said. 'You didn't tell me anything about that.'

'Oh, it was nothing serious, Heinschein, she had lots and lots of friends and he was only one of them. But his parents weren't happy about it, neither were hers.'

'Because he was Jewish?'

'Not only because he was Jewish, because he was helpless, but the fact that he was Jewish didn't help and the fact that she wasn't didn't either. Poor Gunther, what he went through.'

'He looks American,' said Sue.

'He liked to think he was and tried to dress for the part. Look at that bow-tie and the two-tone shoes.'

He, in fact, looked like a city slicker who had dropped in on his country cousins.

'And that's the second son – Jacob, I think he was called. And, ah yes – the son-in-law, Vladimir. Gives me the shivers.'

'He looks rather attractive, in a sinister sort of way,' said Sue.

'Oh, he was attractive all right, but not half as attractive as he thought he was. He could never keep his hands to himself.'

Then the tall figure I had not been able to place came on, and her voice softened, even quivered, at the sight of him.

'Ah, that's Dr Apteker.'

'Who exactly was he?'

'One of the doctors – he was only there for about a year. Prince Charming. Wasn't he beautiful? He only came to Resznitz because he was running away from a woman, or rather her husband, and probably left for the same reason. He could still be alive, you know.'

When we finished she waited for more, but there was none to come.

'Oh, but there is,' she insisted, 'much more. He took a film of my wedding, and Inge, and there's none of you, Heinschein. He took film after film of you and me together. This can't be all.'

'It's all we have,' said Sue.

I suggested that Markham had perhaps been selling her the film in parts to whet her appetite in the hope of a higher fee for the next instalment. Sue, for her part, was satisfied with what she had. 'I'm not interested in a family saga. All I need is a few clips to give us the feel of the place, and what we have is more than enough.'

She filmed Carla that afternoon. My aunt had painted her hair a blood-red and was wearing a frilly blouse with a high neck and a well-tailored two-piece suit. Her disappointments may have been numerous and heavy, but she was nothing if not resilient, and a talented actress to boot, and I felt oddly proud of her as I watched her perform.

'My brother, Gunther, should have been a priest. He never lived for himself. When he was young it was for his parents and friends, when he was older it was for his patients, they worshipped him. He did not have a happy family life. His wife was an invalid and his daughter – well, she was very young and very pretty, and not very sensible. I suppose she did not like living in a small Latvian village.'

'Can you tell us more about her?'

'There isn't much to tell. My brother spoke very little about her. I know she had a child whom he brought up as his own, but that's all I know.'

'What happened during the war?'

'He tried to continue as if nothing had happened. He was a doctor, you see, and didn't think in terms of enemies or friends, only in terms of need . . .'

By the time she had finished one had the impression she was talking about St Francis.

'Your aunt's a natural,' said Sue.

'Did you believe everything she said?'

'I don't have to. I shall be cross-cutting her with Schwarzwald.'

'You seem to work on the principle that if you have two liars contradicting one another you've arrived at the truth.'

'Was she lying?'

'She may for all I know – and, indeed, for all she knew – have been telling the truth, but it was certainly not the truth as she saw it.'

Schwarzwald was a large man with thick glasses and heavy jowls and he recognized me even before Sue had introduced us. He spoke perfect English with a German accent.

'I know you from your graduation photo,' he explained.

'Where did you see my graduation photo?'

'Does the name Markham ring a bell? Apparently your grandfather left him most of his personal possessions. I, of course, knew of you as his grandson, but the fact was not germane to my article, and in any case I heard you were about to marry and I didn't wish to cause you any added disturbance.'

He paused, as if expecting an expression of gratitude, but I had none to offer, for he had caused me disturbance enough. Instead, I asked him how he came to write the article in the first place, and his little mouth puckered in an apologetic smile.

'I have my sources, which I must protect.'

'Did Markham tell you anything?'

'Markham? He had nothing to tell. He tried to sell me some films but they were of no particular interest to me, but I did buy a number of photographs, which you may have seen with the article.'

I sat in at the interview, which was unremarkable for his contribution consisted largely of an almost verbatim restatement of his magazine article, though in answer to some questions about my grandfather's death he said: 'I, of course, have no proof that he was killed by Israeli agents, but it can be shown that his death, and especially the violent way in which he died – his car caught fire and he and his driver were burnt to a cinder – caused panic among other Germans working for the Egyptian government and many of them left shortly afterwards.'

However, in answer to further questions, he allowed that there may have been nothing sinister in the fact that grandfather had treated some of the spies in his hospital, and he agreed that there was no absolute proof that he was involved in their interrogation.

I found him as unconvincing as I had found Carla, though his ponderous demeanour did give a certain spurious weight to his testimony, and Sue was pleased with the interview. Otherwise she suffered a succession of setbacks.

She had sent a young man to the Wiesenthal Documentation Centre in Vienna to see if he could dig up any new information on grandfather, and he came back with a raging hangover, but nothing beyond the information she already had.

More seriously, she had planned to film in Resznitz but couldn't get permission to come near the place.

'It must be in or near a security zone,' I said. 'Half of Russia consists of security zones. I could have told you that.'

She herself ascribed it to the fact that one of her colleagues had filmed in Russia without permission, and had returned with some unflattering footage. 'We're all having to pay for his bit of bravado,' she said glumly.

She then tried to get into Russia as a private tourist, but failed to get a visa at all, by which time she was almost in despair.

'Doesn't your company ever abandon a programme as impractical?'

'They do all the time, but this is my first major programme and I don't intend to give up and, fuck it, I won't.'

It was strange and unsettling to see her on the verge of tears, and I suggested that I could possibly go to Russia for her. At which her lovely eyes cleared. It was worth making the offer just for that. I had to add quickly that there was no certainty that even I would be allowed to go anywhere near Resznitz, but my offer gave her hope and she threw her arms round me in a suffocating embrace.

I was not acting out of mere chivalry. It was now nearly three months since I had left Eissenmacher's. I was still being paid, but the payments wouldn't continue forever and I would soon be running short of money. There was, of course, the fortune which my grandfather had left me, but if my lawyers were satisfied that it was mine legally I was not at all convinced that I had a right to it morally, and some of the evidence unearthed by Sue suggested that I had not. I was not at all sure if the matter could ever be finally resolved, but the only hope of doing so was in Resznitz. Even so, I hesitated. Was it grandfather's repeated warnings about turning up the past? Was it my own fears of what the past might hold?

At the same time, the sight of the Resznitz film had whetted my curiosity. Sue was surprised that I had not revisited the place when I was actually living in Russia, but I had had more than enough to preoccupy me during that chaotic year and the thought of doing so had never entered my mind; but now, having so to speak revisited Resznitz as a child, I was eager to revisit it as an adult, and my eagerness, in the end, outweighed my hesitancy.

But I, too, found difficulty in getting permits. I phoned a senior official in the Soviet Embassy whom I had known very well, and his first words were: 'Ah, Mr Newman. Is it true that you have left Eissenmacher's?'

'No, I haven't left, at least not yet. I'm on leave.' But my status in his eyes was clearly diminished and when I told him what I wanted he replied coldly that I had come through to the wrong department. When I got through to the right department the official was even less helpful. 'Write to Moscow,' he said, and put the phone down, and I decided to expedite matters by phoning Mitri.

'It can't be done, dear boy,' he said. 'I know the area very well. Used to have estates round there. They won't allow you within a hundred miles of the place – unless, of course, I should be able to find the time to go with you.'

He found the time and got us the permits.

'I don't know how you do it,' I said.

'It's quite simple really. The Russians, finding the present drab and the future forbidding, have rediscovered their past. Haven't you seen them rebuilding and refurbishing churches and monasteries all over the place? They'd refurbish me if I gave them half the chance, for I'm regarded as a venerable relic. And, of course, I'm one of the few émigrés not to breathe fire when the word Communism is mentioned. I'm aware of its faults, but as far as Russia is concerned it has its virtues and I have never been afraid to describe them.'

I introduced him to Sue and she was charmed, not so much with what he had to say as his manner of saying it, and as I had told her that I would in no circumstances appear on screen she almost signed him up there and then to give his impressions of Resznitz when we returned.

'He's better than a visit to Russia,' she gushed, 'he *is* Russia. I intend to do a programme on him when he gets back. He's a natural.'

We had arranged to fly to Riga and as I was strapping myself into my seat he said to me:

'Refresh my memory, dear boy, but you're not, how does one put it, associated with that Eissenmacher girl?'

'Don't you read the papers?'

'Not if I can help it.'

'No. I'm afraid that's all finished.'

'I thought it had. You will forgive my presumption for having raised the matter in the first place. The trouble is I've never been able to acquire the detached attitude which the English don has towards his students. Don't forget we were serf-owners until not so long ago, and one is born with a congenital tendency to direct, or at least intrude upon, the lives of others. Moreover, as you must know, I have spent most of my academic life in America, where students snatch at strangers to lay bare their innermost selves and where teachers are treated as lay psychoanalysts. Exposure is overdone there, but I sometimes feel that privacy is overdone here, don't you?'

'I'm not sure.' I should, perhaps, have uttered something more positive in favour of privacy, for he went on:

'Very attractive, that television girl. Would I be mistaken in believing there's something between you?' And he put a hand on my knee. 'Forgive my intrusions, dear boy. Old men live vicariously on the lives of others, insofar as they live at all.'

'We're friends,' I said.

'She's Jewish, you know.'

'I could be Jewish myself.'

'So could we all, and so was our good Lord, but that's a little beside the point. They seem to control the media.'

'She's a very minor producer. This is her first major programme.'

'But the people who own the company, aren't they Jewish?'

'They may be.'

'I'm fairly certain they are. In America they seem to control absolutely everything. It's getting to be the same here.'

We had a car waiting for us at the airport and we continued from Riga by road. I had been over those roads twenty-five years earlier: they were as empty now as they had been jammed then, but otherwise little seemed changed.

'I am grateful you persuaded me to keep you company,' he said. 'I'd almost forgotten what it is to drive along roads uncluttered by advertisements, and look at those skies, how open, how high, how clear, with nothing ahead to impede the eye. I do love flat lands.'

But our sense – or at least my sense – of euphoria began to fade as we approached Resznitz, though in fact I was there before I knew it, for it had become a sizeable town with factories, a hospital, several large and very ugly housing estates. It had changed out of all recognition. Even the cobbled market-place had vanished. The sanatorium, however, was still where it had been, in its own grounds, though surrounded by a high fence. It had been taken over as a holiday home for writers.

'I gather it was a lunatic asylum,' said Mitri. 'Very appropriate.'

I remembered it as being much larger and more austere, and it used to be painted a chilly white. Now it was cream-coloured, the window frames were bright yellow, and with the elaborate wood-carvings on the eaves and gables it looked almost Tyrolean.

Mitri was anxious to visit one of his former homes before he saw anything else, while I was anxious to visit the writers' home, and before we parted he offered a word of advice:

'You've lived here before so I shouldn't have to tell you. Beware of using Russian save *in extremis*, for if they see you've taken the trouble to understand the language they'll regard you with suspicion. Play the dumb Englishman. It helps.'

The warden of the writers' home, a large woman with a smattering of English, and more than a smattering of a moustache, showed me around. She said she was from the locality and that she had worked in the place as a child.

'I work in dairy,' she said, patting her udder proudly, 'make butter and cheese. This was clinic. It belong to a German doctor, a Nazi.'

'Didn't he in fact help the Jews?'

'The doctor? Help Jews?'

By way of reply she took me to a small clearing in the woods a few hundred yards from the house.

'Here is stables, store-house, barn full with straw. Over there in the woods the Jews have *datcha*, and when the Germans come they hide here, in barn. The men run, and the women and children hide here, five women, four children. One night Latvian counter-revolutionaries who work for doctor come and spread benzine on building, and start fire, and all burn.'

'Did no one escape?'

'Escape?'

'Run away.'

'Yes, a woman and child, and child is on fire, but is still running, and they run after him and the woman and beat them to death and throw them into fire. And there is nothing left, only ashes.'

'When did you find all this out?'

'I'm a child, I live here. Everybody knows. The men talk about it. When partisans come they catch the men and hang them, but the Nazi doctor is gone.'

It occurred to me that if she had actually worked in the sanatorium she might even have remembered me, and I asked her if there were any children about the place.

'Yes, small boy, and he go back with doctor to Germany.'

'Whose child was he?'

'His daughter. She goes before the war, but the child remain with father.'

'You're quite sure about that?'

'Sure. I am ten years old, I remember everything.'

I asked her if she remembered old Anna.

She was taken aback by the question, for while I mentioned that I had been to Resznitz before, I had given no hint of my association with the doctor or the sanatorium.

She remembered old Anna very well, she said, in a rather cautious voice, but wanted to know more about myself, and I said my people had known the Marcovitch family.

'The men go away,' she said, almost implying they were deserters. 'The women and children die in fire.'

'Did all the men go away?'

'All, all.'

She seemed disinclined to continue the conversation and brought the visit to an abrupt end. Before leaving, however, she asked me to sign the Visitors' Book. I did as she asked, but while flicking back the pages I noticed, or thought I noticed – for the writing was almost illegible – the name of Apteker.

'You know him?'

'I've heard of him, but he's not a writer, is he?'

'No. He is a doctor. He work here before the war.'

As far as I could make out, the date of the visit was 1957, but it was quite impossible to decipher the address.

'Did you know him?'

'I remember him. He is very nice man,' but that was all she could tell me about him.

Although the authorities discouraged contact with local inhabitants, I tried to engage people in conversation, which wasn't easy. They tended to shy away and even when they were prepared to talk they were nearly all newcomers to the vicinity, so that they had nothing useful to relate. I did, however, meet one old man – I thought of him as such, but it emerged that he was only in his fifties – who spoke without inhibition, especially after I presented him with a bottle of vodka. He remembered both my grandfather and the Marcovitches. The latter, he said, only came to the neighbourhood in the summer, and had all died in a fire shortly after the German invasion, and he too believed that grandfather was a Nazi, but he did not suggest that he had any part in the death of his Jewish neighbours. His mother, he said, had worked for Rhiner in the laundry of the sanatorium, and used to clothe her whole family with discarded items of apparel. He remembered a small boy in the place who was the doctor's grandson and who went back to Germany with him towards the end of the war. He also recalled seeing the Rhiners' daughter. He had no doubt about the date.

'It was just before the darkness came,' which was his way of referring to the initial Russian occupation of the country, and he could describe exactly how she looked and what she wore and what she was doing. She had been lying out in the grass at the back of the sanatorium playing with a child. It was a hot summer's day, her skirt was pulled up and she had provoked his first erection. The memory of the scene, he added, gave him an erection even now.

I asked if he remembered old Anna. Very well, he said. She had only died about ten years ago, and had gone mad towards the end of her life. It was the result of working in a mad-house, he thought. His mother, who was still alive, had also gone slightly funny. And then, almost by way of an afterthought, he added: 'Anna's two sons were hanged, you know, after the Germans left.' He wasn't too sure of the reasons because there had been a lot of hangings and shootings at the time, and in fact not many of the local inhabitants had survived.

Mitri, who had been searching the area for family retainers, had reached the same conclusion.

'Nearly everybody I knew was old enough to have died a natural death, but one might have expected to find children or grandchildren, but whole villages have vanished. Most of the people round here seem to have been brought in after the war.'

He had also been shown round the sanatorium by the warden, who had given him almost precisely the same account she had given me, and in precisely the same words.

'It was a recitation,' he said, 'as if she had learnt it all by heart.'

139

I returned for a second visit, lingering in the corridor and spending some time in the grounds. The warden was away and I was accompanied by her assistant, a red-faced, thick-set man who followed me uneasily and watchfully, as if I might make off with some of the books or furniture. I wasn't sure what I was looking for, ghosts perhaps, echoes, something which might remind me that I had spent my early childhood there, but it was as if all traces of our stay had been exorcised. Perhaps I might have felt different if I had returned in the winter, for my most vivid memories were of snows and silence, but as it was my time had been wasted. I had found nothing which would have enabled me to confirm or deny the stories about my grandfather. I must have looked fairly distressed, for Mitri said to me:

'I wouldn't be too upset about the sins of your grandfather, dear boy. I daren't tell you what my own forbears were up to.'

'It isn't as simple as that,' I explained. 'If I had known for certain that he was in fact a Nazi I'd have been able to live it down by now.'

'Have you any reason to believe that he wasn't? Please do not quote your own feelings about the man, for they certainly would not constitute a valid reason.'

'Have you met any Nazis yourself?'

'A great many, and not always German ones at that. I was in Intelligence during the war, and was involved in their interrogation. The most innocuous-looking people, some of them. One was a plump, soft-voiced major, with the bearing of a bishop, who had personally ordered the massacre of two hundred Jewish children in an orphanage. He didn't even try to deny it. I'm glad to say that when they hanged him the gallows snapped, and he had to be hanged again.'

I had a copy of grandfather's letter in my briefcase and, almost on impulse, I let him see it. He read it first with his glasses and then without, as if impaired vision might somehow improve his understanding, for he was obviously finding it difficult to take in.

'A crude attempt at self-exculpation,' he said finally.

'Would he have made it posthumously if it was just that?'

'He could only have made it posthumously, otherwise he might have had to answer some awkward questions. Do you really think you're Jewish?'

'I could be.'

140

'Do you *feel* Jewish?'

'Not particularly. No.'

'Exactly. You mustn't forget that I stem from twenty generations of Jew-baiters, without of course being one myself, but I
can still sense a Jew at fifty yards. No, forget it, my boy, you
couldn't possibly be Jewish. I know Jews and Jewishness are all
the rage these days, but you mustn't feed yourself on illusions, or
think that you can somehow exonerate your grandfather by
masquerading as a Jew. And it's not only a question of my
instincts on the matter. You must have heard the warden with
your own ears. Everyone perished in that inferno. No one
survived and no one had a chance of survival.'

'But didn't it all sound like an authorized official account?'

'Yes, but just because an account is authorized and official it
doesn't necessarily mean that it's untrue. The truth is sometimes
told even in the People's Republics, and even by official
spokesmen. The question one has to ask oneself is whether the
spokesmen could have had any motive for distorting the truth.
Oh, no doubt they may have embellished some details, but there
can be no doubt that the Marcovitch family perished in the
flames. You are not, never were, and could not be, a Jew.'

'You make it sound as if it should be a source of reassurance, if
not outright jubilation.'

'Well, frankly, between ourselves, as goy to goy, isn't it? One
does meet so many Jews who try to hide the fact – '

'Does one?'

'My dear boy, your own bank is full of them. The Eissenmachers have been trying to pass themselves off as Christians for
generations. Oddly enough, the only one who still insists he's a
Jew is father Eissenmacher, but that, I suppose, is his way of
claiming kinship with our Lord. There was a branch of the family
in Russia before the Revolution. One of them married a remote
relative of mine in Kazan Cathedral, if you please, and his son
became an Abbot. Another member of the family, Serge, helped
to finance the Russian Revolution. Let me be perfectly frank. We
were brought up to regard the Jews as infidels and children of
Satan. I did not share those feelings, for I had no contact with the
Jewish masses, but being a staunch adherent of my own faith I
admired the tenacity with which they stuck to theirs. The Jews I
didn't care for were the de-tribalized variety, the ones who tried

141

to pass themselves off as something else, like the Eissenmachers and others.'

'May you not have resented them possibly because you feared their competition?'

'They weren't competitors, dear boy. They were bankers, traders, industrialists, we were land-owners. No, I resented their presumption,' and he leaned over and gave me a reassuring pat on the knee. 'Your sentiments are commendable, dear boy. You're a child of your generation, and your generation knows only of the wrongs done to the Jews. I do not underestimate them for a minute, and certainly as a German you are entitled to any guilt feelings you may have on the matter. It was the Jews who were the main propagators of German culture in Austria, Hungary, Bohemia, even Russia, which is one of the reasons why they were resented. They should have been made a privileged species but instead they were hounded and finally killed; but there is no reason why any Russian should have a conscience about them. Jews in the mass spoke Yiddish. If one met a cultivated Jew he generally spoke German or French, and if he did deign to speak Russian one could be more or less certain that he was a Bolshevik. The Jews may not have been responsible for the Russian Revolution but it could not have triumphed without them. You may ask where are they all now, the Trotskys, the Kamenovs, the Zinovievs? But then revolutions do have a habit of swallowing their own children, which is perhaps the best thing that can be said for them.' And he patted my knee again. 'I do hope that you will not let this candid exchange impair our friendship. I do not expect you, or anyone of your generation, to agree with me, but I have the feeling that your children might.'

— *Chapter Eleven* —

I was confident that the television programme would be a fiasco which, with any luck, would be dropped before it reached the screens, for Sue had very little solid information to work on, or work with, but she was clearly a dab hand at building bricks without straw and she managed to produce a film of fifty minutes' duration which, while amounting to nothing, was never dull and was sometimes exciting. At first, it looked like an indictment, but then it became a quest. Whenever the pace of the story threatened to falter she brought in Mitri, who functioned as a sort of resident oracle. He was, with his confident, assertive manner, his off-shore accent, his aristocratic mien, and his elegant, eloquent hands, a natural performer, and his performance, indeed, was to launch him, at seventy (or perhaps more), on a new and lucrative career as a television personality.

I breathed a deep sigh of relief when the programme was over. It may have brought Sue and me together again, but while it was being made it impaired our relationship, sometimes almost to breaking point.

When we returned from Egypt she had moved out of her flat and into mine, but her last words before she fell asleep, and the first when she woke, were about the programme. Often she did not sleep at all but would lie through the night staring upwards, as if the different sequences were being flashed on the ceiling, and, indeed, when her sleeplessness began to infect me, I almost thought I could see them myself. Her approach, and especially her inclination to jump to firm conclusions on very limited evidence, involved us in frequent altercations, and when I tried to resolve them with an embrace I found her cold and unresponsive. Even when it was all finished and ready for presentation she was so worried by its reception that her insomnia became more persistent and acute. Thus, when it was eventually shown and acclaimed I thought we might finally be able to put my grandfather behind us and assume a normal existence, and for a while we spent an idyllic fortnight in the South of France, where the words television or Rhiner or Resznitz were never uttered.

When we got back Sue was invited out to lunch by a publisher, who offered her a substantial sum to write a book on my grandfather, which she readily accepted. She generously offered me half her fee if I would consent to act as collaborator. This, I felt, was where I had come in. It looked as if my grandfather would be around to haunt me for the rest of my days.

I was by then back in Eissenmacher's. They had treated me with great generosity over the matter of paid leave and after a few months I was beginning to feel that I was receiving alimony.

A week or so after my return from Resznitz Edward asked me to lunch at his club.

'Tried to get hold of you before. You seem to be everywhere except London. Frankly, I thought we might have heard from you by now.'

He was, of course, right but partly because I was preoccupied with Sue's programme and partly because I was still embarrassed by my memory of events in Moscow I had hesitated to contact him. I had also hoped to clarify the question of my gandfather's legacy, but the more I knew the more it seemed likely that I would not be able to touch it. The matter was, therefore, settled by my circumstances. I would have to return to the bank because I needed the money.

Edward was delighted with my decision, almost as if the whole misadventure with his daughter had been his fault and he felt that he had been forgiven.

'Lots happening all over the place. We need you everywhere.'

And I was sent almost everywhere, now to Tangiers, now to Tehran, and most frequently of all to Riyadh, Dubai and Kuwait, moving from pressurized cabin to air-conditioned lounge, from air-conditioned lounge to air-conditioned limousines and from air-conditioned limousines to air-conditioned hotels, along a corridor insulated from the normal world and peopled with slight, short-haired figures in mohair suits with Gucci cases in their hands. The trend towards slightness was, I suppose, set by the Japanese. Fat men were either too wise to subject themselves to such a regime, or too heavy to survive it, but I began to think of myself and my fellow-travellers as part not so much of an international jet-set as of a skeletal club, and my experience imbued me with a yearning for ordinary, moist, English-type air, ordinary food and ordinary human beings.

Beatty, whose department I had joined, said I was lucky.

'When I began working in the area, malaria was as common-place as the common cold is here, and more often than not you could also go down with yellow fever or the Black Death or some such thing, and you travelled along dust-tracks in temperatures of a hundred-and-twenty in the shade, except that there was no shade for miles around. I'm surprised any work got done at all, because a chap had to keep himself topped-up with alcohol to survive.'

Alcohol was, in fact, an important element in survival even now, and I had passing fears of becoming an alcoholic. I was a moderate drinker in London, but now consumed immoderate quantities, partly to while away the tedium of the plane journeys and partly because it was free. One met very few people who were not in a position to drink themselves to death, if not at their own expense then at the expense of their companies. Yet they would always sit up when the free booze came round, with a look of eager anticipation, like children about to be offered a treat. I would have a couple of vodkas before the meal, a bottle of claret with it, and a couple of brandies to follow, and I would arrive at my destination in a glowing stupor. Others looked the same, and we called it jet-lag.

I was, by now, too senior to hazard being caught with bottles in my bag in a prohibited zone, but I always had the telephone number of somebody who knew somebody who could keep me supplied. It was, I suppose, a little like looking for an abortion in the good old days when it was still illegal.

Sue, for her part, was busy burrowing her way through the musty archives of Central Europe in her second quest for Rhiner, and frequently when she was at home I was away, and vice versa, and I said to her: 'We can't go on not meeting like this.'

Then one day I returned from an exhaustive and exhausting tour, which had taken me as far as Karachi, to find that she was gone, without a message as to where she might be reached. I phoned her husband, but he also was away, and I wondered if they had done the dirty on me and eloped.

145

Sue had said to me on more than one occasion, 'You'll have to meet my husband,' in the way that girls in the old days used to say, 'You'll have to meet my family.' I was not particularly happy about the prospect of the encounter, if only because I was not entirely happy about the role of 'the other man'. Each of us had vaguely raised the question of divorce and marriage from time to time, but we were both too busy to do anything about it. Her husband, for his part, was not pressing for a divorce, so we all let things drift. Then one evening Sue and I went to a rather grand party given by her television company. I went to the bar for drinks and when I returned I found her in animated conversation with a large, robust figure whom I had not met before but whose face had beamed at me from many a colour supplement. It was Len.

He gave me a bone-crunching hand-shake when Sue introduced me and put an arm about me, as if he was grateful to me for having taken over his marital responsibilities.

'So you're Sue's new guy. I've been dying to meet you.'

He spoke with a mid-Atlantic accent. He was rather better looking in the advertisements than in life. In the former, he looked healthy, lean, tanned. In person, he was pale and flabby with rings under his eyes and the beginnings of a double-chin. He had the dark hair and immaculate grooming of a twentyish hero, but he was beginning to acquire the posture and build, if not yet the manner, of an English butler.

'What do you think of her television programme?' he asked. 'Great, wasn't it? I'm proud of her,' and he gave his wife a hug which she did nothing to resist and which made me feel jealous. She had tended to speak of him in an off-hand, even dismissive way, which had satisfied me that their marriage was finished, but seeing them together filled me with doubts and unease.

Sue also made occasional threats to introduce me to other members of her family, as if it was an ordeal she was anxious to get over and done with, but she never got round to it and I, for one, did not press her.

I usually made it a rule to phone her once or twice a week, if possible, but Pakistan's telephone system was not all it should be, and I found it impossible to get through. It was not too difficult to incur Sue's displeasure and I wondered if she was angry with me because I hadn't contacted her, but the day after I got back she phoned me in a slightly woebegone voice, which I did not quite recognize as hers, to say that she was with her mother.

She had called me from some improbable places in her time, but never from her mother's, and I said, with understandable surprise:

'What are you doing there?'

'It's a long story. I'll tell you when I see you.'

Which was how I came face to face with her entire family in one fell swoop: her mother, her brothers, her sisters-in-law, but not her father, who was dead, which was in fact why her family happened to be together in the first place. Sue herself was not only not religious, but, if anything, anti-religious, and summed up her philosophy with the words 'I don't know if there is a God, but I hope to God there isn't.' Her family, however, were deeply observant, and they had assembled in her mother's house for the traditional week's mourning. She had warned me to come with a hat. The only hat I actually owned was a white straw hat which I wore during my trips to Arabia and the Gulf, and which I felt would not have been appropriate for a house of mourning. I therefore went out and bought myself a bowler, but as soon as I appeared Sue broke into a fit of uncontrollable laughter, which alarmed her family and embarrassed me.

The house was large, almost a mansion, standing in its own grounds in Brondesbury Park. The rooms were spacious, but over-furnished, with rugs on top of carpets, and large leather armchairs, a vast leather sofa and an obstacle course of pouffes and footstools and coffee-tables, and chandeliers which evoked memories of the neo-Moorish palaces in Jeddah. The mother herself was short and dumpy, with hair painted a platinum blonde and bright blue, over-mascara'd eyes set in a pouchy, pampered face. She was flanked by her two sons, both dark-haired, dark-suited and dark-humoured. Both were tall and good-looking, but one was heavily built and the other slight. The heavy brother had a slight wife, called Dora. The slight one had a large wife, called Doreen.

I didn't know if Sue had told them who or what I was, but once they had got over the embarrassment and alarm of her laughing-fit and after I had taken off my bowler and put on a skull-cap proffered by one of the brothers, I was received with friendly interest, especially by the mother.

'It's not often Sue invites a friend home,' she said. 'When she was younger she used to bring all her friends home – and what friends. I was ashamed to have them in the house. Now that she's older, she's ashamed of me. It's Oxford what did it.'

'Wot done it,' said Sue.

'A lot of good Oxford did her. My husband, bless him, didn't go to Oxford, he didn't go to university, he hardly went to school, but he built up a nice business. We brought up a nice family, we have a nice home – look at it, it's nice, isn't it?'

I looked uneasily at Sue and agreed that it was.

'The boys did go to university, but thank God it didn't do them no harm. Stanley here's an estate agent, and Morris is an accountant.'

We exchanged nods.

'But Sue was the bright one – not that the boys weren't bright, but Sue didn't have to be bright, and she was, and she hasn't done much with herself. Do you know her husband?'

'I've met him.'

She leaned forward and whispered in my ear, as if she was confessing to a private misfortune – which perhaps she was.

'An actor. More out of work than in work. She could have had anybody.'

A few minutes later a whole throng of visitors descended, many of them looking oddly like her mother, and the house filled up. Sue got out of the chair and beckoned me to follow her into another room, which, to my surprise, turned out to be a small, book-lined study. From the first impression I had of the house I did not readily associate it with books, let alone a study.

'I'm sorry about my mother.'

'What have you got to be sorry about? She's a dear.'

'She's an embarrassment, but it should make you glad you've never had one. I'm sorry to drag you here. I felt if I didn't see an intelligent face I'd burst, but you've done your duty and you don't have to come again.'

'What do you mean? How long does this thing last?'

'A week.'

'And you've got to stay here all that time?'

'I'm afraid so.'

'Good God.'

'Hard to be a Jew, isn't it? It's not so bad for them, they at least believe in it.'

'Then what are you doing here?'

'I believe in my father. This was his retreat. He'd lock himself away from the rest of the family, and in particular my mother.'

'I'm impressed by the books.'

'Don't be too impressed. They're in hand-tooled leather most of them. He was a collector rather than a reader, but he half believed that if he was surrounded by them something of their contents would seep in by osmosis.'

I put a hand on her breast.

'Not now, my love. I haven't washed for days. Save it for when this is all over.'

I had to go abroad again a day or so later and when I returned she was back in her own flat. I was about to ask her why she had moved but she was clearly not in a state to be questioned.

It was about five in the afternoon, cold and misty outside and not all that warm and bright inside. She looked as if she had just got out of bed, which in fact she had, and was still wearing a dressing-gown. I was going to switch the light on, but she asked me not to:

'I don't want you to see my face, otherwise you'll turn to stone.'

She took off her dressing-gown and sat up in bed while I put an arm round her.

'You looked fairly cheerful last week.'

'That was last week, and I didn't feel particularly cheerful even then. In any case, these things take time to sink in.'

'Is Len not about?'

'He's also taking time to sink in. I wish he'd sink into the ground. He's making a drinks commercial in the West Indies, and didn't even come back for the funeral – the bastard.'

'I thought Len was close to your father?'

'He was close to his money, and no doubt hoped to be remembered in his will, but in fact father parcelled all his money out years ago, most of it to mother. I bet she'll remarry within a year, the old cow. She's not unattractive in her grotesque way, and she's worth a packet.'

'And she's got some charm, you know.'

'Has she? It's lost on me. Perhaps you should marry her. She was certainly impressed with you. She was on to me the minute you left – "So good-looking, such nice manners. Who is he? What does he do? Is he single?" She'd have you like a shot.'

'Which at least suggests she's got good taste.'

'I've never been able to forgive father for marrying her. I suppose he needed the money, but God, there must be easier ways of making it. He could have picked pockets or robbed a bank or something.'

'She must have been very pretty when she was young.'

'Maybe, but her whole family was *grob*. Do you know what *grob* means? Gross, ignorant, coarse. But the marriage worked reasonably well, which it usually does when there's a bit of money about. I adored my father. He was very proud when I got into Oxford, but began to worry when I was twenty-one, twenty-two and still single because I was mixing with all these goyim, first in Oxford then in television – and he was afraid his precious Susan might come home with one. When I was twenty-five and still single he had something like a breakdown. He said it was due to business difficulties, but I also had something to do with it, which is probably the main reason why I married Len – '

'Is he Jewish?'

'Just about, but he keeps it dark. Anyhow, I brought him home as a trophy, which gave father five happy years, in spite of his ill-health. Otherwise, I've been a lousy daughter, lousy wife, lousy everything.'

She began weeping softly, and I pressed her against me. It was now quite dark.

'God, how I envy you,' I said, 'even your grief. When my grandfather died my main feeling was one of exasperation, for it came at an awkward time. I've never experienced grief, not real grief.'

'Have you experienced love?'

'I think I have.'

'Then you'll experience grief.'

I made her something to eat, but she wouldn't touch it.

'Have you eaten at all during the past week?'

'Not much, but I can afford to lose weight.'

I found the thought that she should be concerned about her appearance at all slightly reassuring, for she looked a mess. I suggested that I stay the night.

'No,' she said, 'I think you had better leave. I'll be all right.'

I kissed her on the forehead, and left with something like relief. The sound of her wailing followed me along the passage and rose to a crescendo as I waited for the lift. I went back and let myself in.

'I can't leave you like this.'

'Why not? I don't want to see anybody. I don't want to be with anybody.'

I didn't argue, but went to the bathroom and ran a hot bath. I then lifted her, half-struggling, out of bed, tore off her nightdress and dumped her with a loud splash into the water. It must have been hotter than she had expected and she may have thought I was trying to murder her, for she began screaming hysterically, but she calmed down when I ran the cold water tap and started to soap her breasts. I washed and scrubbed her thoroughly, shampooed her hair and dried her, and she fell fast asleep in my arms. I lifted her into bed, tucked her in, and was making myself something to eat when I suddenly remembered that I had a reception to attend at the Egyptian Embassy. I looked at myself. I was half drenched from the struggle in the bath. I went to the wardrobe and selected one of her husband's many suits. It was a bit short in the leg, but otherwise fitted me perfectly, and thus attired I went out into the night.

When I saw her the next morning she was a new person; still pale and thin, but her voice had recovered its confident tone, and something of a sparkle had returned to her eyes. When I bent over to kiss her she wrapped my tie round her hand and pulled me into bed on top of her.

'Oh dear,' I said, 'on an empty stomach.'

'That's the best time for it,' she whispered.

When it was over she said to me: 'Shouldn't you be working?'

'Why? Do you call this play?'

'Seriously, though.'

'I've taken the day off.'

'What are you going to do with it?'

'Nothing. It's something I haven't done for a long time, nothing, and I thought you and I might like to do it together.'

She sat up and stroked my hair.

'You're in an oddly flippant mood.'

'I am, aren't I? I wonder why? I suppose it's because it's a working day and I'm not working.'

'I thought you loved your work?'

'You get to love what you can't avoid.'

'Come off it, you don't have to work if you don't want to – you're loaded. There's nothing wrong with being rich. As a matter of fact, I was fairly rich myself till Len blew it all.'

'So when are you going to be shot of him?'

She swung her legs out of bed. 'Right now. I'm going to see a lawyer.'

But then, as she was pulling on her bra, she paused:

'Wait a minute! Have you in fact proposed to me? I don't want to be shot of one husband before I'm sure of another. And I want you to do it properly, on your knees.'

'On my knees? Are you sure? I'm wearing my best suit.'

'I know, but I'd like to see you perform a genuine act of self-sacrifice – like denting the crease in your trousers.'

And I got down on my knees, held her hand, and proposed. My position, as Lord Chesterfield might have put it, was slightly ridiculous, for she was only wearing a bra, but she accepted. Then, as she was buttoning her blouse, she said:

'You know, I must be mad. Here we are, about to enter into holy wedlock, but all I know about you is your name, the fact that you went to Oxford and work in a bank, and that you have a big cock.'

'Isn't that enough to get on with?'

'Seriously, though.'

'Seriously though, you know about as much about me as I know about myself.'

'And you're not really interested in finding out, are you?'

'Not really.'

'You must have had a very unhappy childhood.'

I thought about it for a moment. I suppose I didn't have a childhood to speak of, for childhood presumes parents and the presence of other children and I had neither one nor the other and didn't know what the company of children was till I came to Germany, but I didn't recall being unhappy, and the first time I experienced anything like grief was when I left Anna, and even that was a numb grief, for there was too much happening at the time and I would not let myself believe that the parting was permanent.

'No,' I said, 'insofar as I had a childhood at all it was not unhappy, but you could say it was different.'

152

'Then it must have been unhappy, for children hate to be different. Your grandfather must have been very strict.'

'What makes you say so?'

'He was strict with himself, that much I've already discovered, and he was strict with his daughter. Cut her out of his life in the same way that he had cut her out of the film. You could see the way it jerks along where he cut her out. I think I let him off lightly in the television film. He must have been a monster. Your lack of interest in your past is unnatural. I think he cauterized something in you, if only your sense of curiosity. Have you never felt there was something odd in his very tendency to hold things back? Didn't it make you feel that he had something to hide? Innocent men aren't secretive.'

I didn't think that was true, but I was provoked by her remarks to take her to my flat and show her grandfather's letter. As she read it a wide grin spread over her face.

'Do you actually find it amusing?'

'No, it's all very sad, but it explains everything. You were afraid to discover you were a Jew. You remind me of Len in a way, except that Len knows he's Jewish and tries to hide it, while you think you have an option on the matter.'

'But don't you see, if the letter is true then I have been fed on lies, and once one is dealing with liars it is difficult to know what the truth is. If you think he was a Nazi, would he have risked his life to save a Jewish child? And if I was Jewish, would he have kept me in the dark about my antecedents?'

'He would if he got attached to you. I know of other such cases.'

'Nazis sheltering Jewish children?'

'Perhaps he wasn't a Nazi.'

'But what about your documents?'

'People change. Why didn't you show me this before?'

'There wouldn't have been much left to your television programme if I had, would there?'

'On the contrary, there would have been another twist to the story. This'll all have to go into the book, you know. As a matter of interest, did your in-laws know about this?'

'In-laws? Which in-laws?'

'The Eissenmachers.'

'They weren't in – '

'All right, they weren't in-laws, but don't be pedantic, you know who I mean.'

'No. I've hardly told anyone.'

'But did the Eissenmachers make no enquiries? When my brother Stanley proposed to Doreen, her family – who are pretty big in the rag trade – hired a private detective to look into his past.'

'The Eissenmachers are not in the rag-trade.'

'And they made no enquiries?'

'None as far as I know.'

'There's aristocratic nonchalance for you, but I can see why you didn't tell them anything. You were about to be received into the bosom of olde England, or at least pseudo olde England, and you felt that your Jewish past might affect your reception. Perfectly understandable. Most people would have done the same, except that I somehow always thought that you were a cut above most people. I had a great many friends in Oxford, but all on the make – possibly because they were nearly all Jewish or Welsh – young barristers with the glow of fees in their eyes; aspiring journalists peddling dirt about their friends to Fleet Street; budding politicians with their eyes on the Commons; would-be actors preening themselves for the footlights. You were the first person I met who seemed wholly devoid of ambition. They also aspire who only stand and wait. In fact, you were not only ambitious, but you didn't think you had to push. In fact, I don't really know you, do I?'

But she moved her possessions into my place all the same. We drank a bottle of champagne and set up as man and wife. This, as I reminded myself, was the third time I had set up home without the benefit of clergy, or even marriage.

A few months later I was at home, working, when Sue came into my study:

'Wouldn't you like to become Jewish? I mean you're already as good as a Jew in the one place that counts,' with which she gave my penis a playful tug.

I knew exactly what had inspired the question. I had attended the Barmitzvah of one of her nephews the previous day in my bowler hat and had been accepted as one of the tribe throughout. A great-aunt had even addressed me in Yiddish, to which I answered in German, which more or less confirmed my status, and Sue was obviously anxious that her family should not be disillusioned.

'It's partly that,' she admitted, 'but the fact is – ' she hesitated, 'I'd like to marry in synagogue.'

'*In synagogue*!?'

'I know, I know. We're both confirmed agnostics – '

'I may only be a confirmed agnostic, but you're a raging, blaspheming, God-baiting atheist!'

'I know, and I wouldn't have felt this way while my father was alive, but I owe it to his memory. He was a pillar of his congregation, you know, a founder member.'

'Did you and Len marry in synagogue?'

'Good God no. Can you imagine it? But the fact that we didn't upset father very much – '

'So you want to bring me into synagogue by way of expiation –'

'It's not only that. I know it's perfectly irrational, but I somehow have the feeling – Oh hell, I'd just like a traditional wedding, and I would like to go up the aisle in white with a bouquet in my hands and have the massed throngs on either side oohing and aahing over me. I've been to so many registry office weddings, and they were all so colourless and tame and, what is more to the point, none of them have lasted, not even mine.'

'My dear, you want everything: atheism and the benefit of clergy, a goyish husband and a synagogue wedding.'

'But you don't have to stay goyish, especially as you're not absolutely certain that you are a goy in the first place.'

'What do you mean?'

'You could convert – not only for my sake, but out of reverence for your grandfather's memory.'

'Where does my grandfather come into it?'

'You said yourself, he wanted you to be a Jew, even if you weren't.'

'Look, my dear, whatever my grandfather may or may not have been, the one certain thing I can say about him is that he's dead, and unlike you, I have not the slightest feeling that the dead have a claim on the living. Do what you like for your father's memory, but don't start embroiling me in worship of the dead. It's enough that I'm a pseudo-Englishman. You would not wish me to add to the deception by becoming a pseudo-Jew. More-over, while I believe wholeheartedly in all that Englishness

155

entails, I lack the Englishman's reverence for believers or belief, and I don't feel equipped to marry even in church, let alone in synagogue.'

'All right,' said Sue, 'have it your way, you bloody goy.'

— Chapter Twelve —

Len may not have been much of an actor, but it seemed to me that he had a promising future as a blackmailer.

That the marriage between him and Sue had broken down irrevocably was obvious to all concerned, and neither of us anticipated that there would be any difficulty with the divorce, but he must have thought there was money to be made from the fact that I was 'a banker'. Sue pointed out patiently that there was all the difference in the world between a banker and someone who worked in a bank, even at fairly senior level, but he would not be convinced.

'He's forty, you know,' she said, 'a crucial time in the life of an actor. He's too old even for minor romantic roles, and in another few years he'll be too old even to be advertising after-shave. I suppose he can look forward to advertising denture powder, or walking-sticks, or trusses, but the poor bugger probably needs the money, so we'll either have to run him down on a dark night or pay up.'

What made the matter urgent was the fact that she was expecting our first child, and she showed a surprising determination that it should be born in wedlock. I pointed out that I was born out of wedlock myself, but this thought had hardly blighted my life.

'The least you can do for a child is to provide him with a full complement of parents, and I want to do just that,' she said.

I was quite prepared to pay Len £5,000, for I reckoned that it would cost us that much at least to deal with a contested divorce, but he wanted more, 'much more', and I said: 'Fuck him, not a penny more.'

'That's all very well,' said Sue, 'but you've already fucked me.'

'Yes, but I'd rather father a bastard than give in to one.'

In the end, he withdrew his objections and I suspect that Sue leant on her mother or brothers to come up with the extra, and we married some six weeks before our child – a boy whom we called Jacob – was born. I had hoped he might be a girl.

Even before he was born Sue said, rather defensively: 'Everybody gets circumcised these days, even women. I can't think when I last saw a common-or-garden foreskin.'

I wasn't against the idea of circumcision as such – I was, after all, circumcised myself, as Sue kept reminding me – but I was unhappy at the idea of religious ceremonies and blood-rites, and we finally compromised by bringing in a surgeon who was also a licensed *mohel*, or circumciser. I, being a goy, had to take a back place at the whole ceremony, which I was quite happy to do. Our own modest home was too small for the occasion, and it was held in Sue's mother's house in Brondesbury Park.

'My boys are always on to me to move into a small flat. So was my husband, bless him, but he was foreign, you see, and they've taken after him. I want a big place so when the family have celebrations I've got room for them all, thank God. This was my mother's house, you know. We changed it a bit, pulled down this part, and added another, and maybe a bathroom or two, but I want one place where the family can meet as a family. My boys, bless them, are both doing very well, but you should see their homes – no room to swing a cat. Here you can have a *bris*, a barmitzvah, even a wedding, if it's not too large, and I'll tell you something else, I want Sue to have this place when I'm gone, because if I left it to my sons they'd pull it down and build a block of flats in its place, but I think like Sue – she thinks like me.'

I became rather fond of the dumpy little woman (though I thought she would have been a good deal more attractive if she had allowed her hair to assume its natural silver), and, largely at my behest, Sue and I adopted the habit of eating with her on Friday nights. The fare was ample, even extravagant, but never less than delicious. There were usually other guests at the table, a widowed brother or sister-in-law, and things got on merrily enough until Sue decided it was feeding time for young Jack, but instead of going upstairs she would have him down at table with us and whip out one massive breast and then another, to top him up, at which all conversation stopped.

'I wonder what's the matter with these people?' she would say.'Haven't they ever seen a child being fed?'

Nor did she limit herself to the semi-privacy of her mother's home: she fed him on trains, buses, at an anti-pollution rally in Trafalgar Square, at a Promenade Concert in the Albert Hall, in pubs, cafés and restaurants and, on one memorable occasion, at a Jewish wedding. She was (she would be) right in the front pew, and just as the Rabbi began to address the young pair on the responsibilities of married life, he noticed that all eyes, including those of the bridal couple, were turned away from him, and when he himself turned to look he lost track of his theme and had to begin again. The infant was by then of a size, if not of an age, to sit down to a meal with a knife and fork, but if Sue believed in something she believed in it with a vengeance, and I suspect that if I hadn't taken a stand on the matter she would have breast-fed the lad at his Barmitzvah.

We had acquired a three-bedroomed flat, which we both thought would be sufficient for our needs, but neither of us anticipated the amount of clutter which could be caused by a solitary infant. My fancy alighted on a sizeable, five-bedroomed house with a large garden. It was in good condition, the price was reasonable, and Sue liked the size and shape of the rooms and almost everything about it, but, in her eyes, it had one serious drawback: it was almost within walking distance of her mother.

'I'm not afraid of your mother,' I said.

'I think there's something on between you and the old girl,' she said, and in a sense there was. I had been (or thought I was) afraid of family entanglements, but once I became entangled with Sue I began almost to cherish them, and to my eyes her mother symbolized the whole concept of family, its closeness, warmth, the feeling of mutual awareness, mutual concern and mutual dependence. Sue had described it all as stultifying , and much as she loved her father, she said that she did not really begin to breathe till she left home.

'You don't have to be Jewish to want to assert your own personality,' she said. 'But somehow it's only Jews who have a conscience about it, and I went back home at every opportunity –'

'But who forced you?'

'Nobody *forced* me. I felt forced by my own sense of guilt, and I blamed them for making me feel guilty. The love you find in the Jewish family is always tempered by guilt and resentment, which wouldn't be so bad if it was limited to the lifetime of one's parents, but it continues in enhanced form well beyond the grave. You can still admire it, and harbour a soft spot for the old girl, because you've never been enveloped by it. You think I'm making a fetish of it, but when we lived twenty miles away I felt I had done my duty when I saw the old girl once a week, but if she lives round the corner I'll feel obliged to pop round every day, and what's worse, she'll be popping round here every day.' Which she did, but, in fact, she made herself extremely useful as a baby-sitter while her daughter was involved in an endless succession of shopping expeditions.

I also became friendly with Sue's brothers, a pair of dull though amiable men whom she dismissed as morons. They were far from that, but they lacked the vivaciousness of their womenfolk. I found their wives' names confusing, for Doreen, who sounded small, was large, and Dora, who sounded large, was small. The latter was always expensively groomed and might have been beautiful but for the fact that her mouth and teeth were far too large for her face.She was also restless and seemed to be here, there and everywhere at once. She knew, or said her father knew, the Eissenmachers, and she was a little in awe of the fact that I was nearly one myself (if only by marriage), and I suspect that she wondered how anyone who could have aspired to such a status could have married someone like Sue. Doreen was large, pink, blonde, but well-proportioned, and could, especially when wearing a low-cut dress, have done well as a barmaid, or as a model advertising dairy foods, for she had good teeth, a highly-coloured if coarse complexion and bright hazel eyes. She was not quite as genial as she looked, for she was short-tempered, especially with her children, and could bawl them (and her husband) out even in the presence of guests.

'She's common,' said Sue, 'but I like being with her; I feel small next to her.'

The drawback to dinner at the Cohens was that they had the segregationist habits of the Edwardians, and after the meal the ladies would find themselves in one room and the gentlemen in another. I, of course – though I sometimes made efforts to escape – had to join the men, which was a bore, for if their cigars were good the conversation was dull, and it was confined, in a season, to cricket and, in and out of season, to the ups and downs of the stock market, possibly in the hope that I might let some inside information drop in the course of our exchanges. I was not, in fact, privy to such information. I thought I had a sound appreciation of the movements of foreign currency and occasionally backed my judgement with money, but lost fairly heavily; I had to learn that such fluctuations were due less to the pressure of economic forces than to the whims of the market, and for all my years in banking I was still unable to anticipate such whims.

The onset of motherhood had taken Sue a little by surprise and she had spoken of having the infant 'nipped in the bud', not because we were unmarried at the time but because she wanted to have her book behind her before she assumed family responsibilities; but she was thirty-two already and such talk, as she realized herself, was absurd. And so the boy had not only brought us the joys of family life but had removed, for the foreseeable future, the apprehension which the very thought of the book had stirred in me. But if Sue was, for the time being, disposed to leave the past alone, it intruded upon me from another direction. Carla kept belabouring me with letters and phone calls demanding that the question of grandfather's legacy be settled once and for all. She had given me a year's grace, after which I had sent her a few thousand pounds. Now a further year was up and she let it be known that she was no longer prepared to be fobbed off with 'petty cash', as she called it. Her phone calls became more frequent, threatening, even hysterical. She often called me at the bank, and I was not infrequently interrupted at important meetings to face up to her barrage of demands.

'This is Carla,' she would always begin. 'What's happening? When are you going to pay up? Whose money do you think it is? You're robbing a war-widow, do you know that? Do you want your bank to know about it? I'll tell them, don't you think I won't.'

There is no uglier language than German when uttered in heated, insistent tones. It amounted to blackmail, and I finally told her to put her claims in writing and I would get my lawyer to see to it, which seemed to take her aback.

'Is that all you have to say?'

'What do you expect me to say?'

'I don't expect you to say anything, I want you to pay up, now,

161

at once.'

'I would rather my lawyer handled it,' I said, put the phone down and asked my secretary not to accept calls from her any more.

A few days later her claims arrived, and she not only demanded the entire legacy but interest for the delay in settlement. My lawyer reproved me – indeed I reproved myself – for my initial generosity and said it had compromised my position; he suggested a payment of £30,000 by way of settlement. It left me in a dilemma. I had invested grandfather's money in government securities which were by now valued at over £700,000, so that it would not have been difficult to part with £30,000, except that I was still not convinced that I could touch the money at all. My attitude exasperated my lawyer.

'I thought we had settled all that.'

'From the legal point of view.'

'Not only legal,' he insisted, 'not only legal. I showed you that the money was honourably acquired. I have the documents – I *showed* you the documents – '

'But suppose he was a Nazi – '

'Who wasn't? I have Jewish clients who have accepted millions by way of reparations – '

'They were entitled to them. Who am I to claim reparations?'

'You are claiming nothing. You are trying to disown something which is yours. What are you going to do with the money? Are you going to leave it untouched to accumulate forever?'

That certainly was a pertinent question, and if I had been at all consistent I would have passed the money over to some fund for the benefit of the victims of Nazism. I told myself that I was reluctant to do so because I was reluctant to reconcile myself to the thought that my grandfather had in fact been a Nazi, but it may have been a matter of simple cupidity. It is not easy to part with a fortune: it was as much as I could do not to dig into it. In the meantime, if only to play for time, I told my lawyer to proceed with the offer in the near certainty that Carla would turn it down, which she did.

'She is playing into our hands,' he said, rubbing his plump hands. 'Now she'll get nothing.'

As fate would have it she didn't even get that, for a few days later I was leaving the office when I noticed headlines about a

162

plane crash. I picked up an evening paper and read the gruesome details without in any way thinking that they could have anything to do with me, but Carla was on that plane and there were no survivors. But that was perhaps the least ironical part of it. She had died intestate and, as her only heir, everything she had was left to me. Unto him that hath shall be given. It all seemed so unfair that I kept asking myself not so much why fate had done this to her, but why it was doing this for me? Was it fattening me up for some sacrificial slaughter?

When I was a child, my aunt had represented all that was bright and beautiful, and as I grew older I saw her as a sort of lush, engulfing earth-mother, and I might always have had a deep affection for her were it not for grandfather's legacy. The prospect of money made her a different person, and towards the end of her days she was but a menacing voice, rasping, demanding, hateful, and I should have greeted her death with relief; yet I did not know myself even here, for after the sense of shock had passed I was filled with remorse, even guilt, and it seemed to me as if I had been high-minded at her expense – if indeed I had been high-minded at all. I asked myself if I had not used her brother's past as an excuse to deprive her of her rightful share of his fortune. My feelings, however, eased a little when it transpired that my aunt was not quite the penniless, luckless war-window she had claimed to be, for she left property worth nearly £200,000.

I sold her house complete with its furniture and furnishings and arranged for letters, papers, family photographs and the like to be sent on to me in London. They arrived in a trunk while I was abroad, and when I returned home one evening I found Sue sitting on the floor surrounded by papers and photographs. 'This is a treasure-trove,' she kept exclaiming, almost hysterically. 'I don't have to write the book. It's all here, half written for me, and illustrations too.'

There were letters from Carla's brother as a medical student, letters from the front, letters which he had sent to his parents, all in a neat, controlled hand which enabled anyone with even a modicum of German to read them. They all suggested a very earnest, if somewhat stuffy young man who hoped to be a medical missionary, and who probably would have been one but for the war. They did not suggest the making of a Nazi. All this, I

163

discovered by merely scanning the letters Sue had in her lap. There were many others, neatly packed in boxes in careful, chronological order. But what intrigued me even more than the letters were the photographs, hundreds of them, mostly faded. They had been kept together in albums but had come loose in the course of transit. I sat down to have a look at them and was immediately transfixed by one particular photo which stared out at me from the pile. It was of a mother and child, or rather of a woman and child. The woman was Carla. The child was almost certainly me.

—— *Chapter Thirteen* ——

I don't know how far husbands keep secrets from their wives. I had only two secrets from Sue: the first was my grandfather's legacy. Secretiveness about money comes as second nature to bankers. I never discussed what went on in the bank at home, and Sue would no doubt have been bored by it if I had, and I treated grandfather's money as if it was the money of another client. The other concerned my liaison with Carla. It wasn't a secret in the sense that it was something I was strenuously trying to hide, but neither was it something I felt bound to confess. Neither Sue nor I were in the habit of discussing our past affairs. Where I was concerned there was, in any case, little to discuss – and the matter had never come up. Now she took one look at the photo and said:

'That's you, isn't it?'

'I think it is.'

'And that's your Aunt Carla. Could she have been your mother?'

'I hope not,' I said, 'she was the first woman I slept with.'

At which a wide grin spread over her face. 'You dirty mother-fucker.'

She not only had a coarse sense of humour but a grotesque sense of occasion, and when she saw I was far from amused she said:

'You don't really think she could have been your mother, do you?'

I wasn't sure what to think. She had always tried to make out that she and grandfather didn't quite belong to the same generation but it was clear from her papers that she was seventy-four when she died, which would have made her about forty when I was born, so that although it was unlikely that she was my mother it was well within the bounds of possibility. What really worried me was the fact that while she had often taken me

165

through her family album she had never shown me that particular photo before. Why had she withheld it from me?

'Well, it's not particularly flattering, is it?' said Sue. 'Have a close look. If you were a woman – and even if you weren't – would you want anyone to see you looking like that? It makes her look soppy. The trouble with you is that you're going through a delayed Oedipal phase. You never knew your mother, so you're letting your imagination feast on your aunt. You're not only guilty of mental incest, but mental necrophilia. I don't know what gets into you sometimes.'

The fact of the matter was that neither did I, but I was shaken by the photo and I somehow had the feeling that if it did not contain a truth it somehow pointed towards it.

I had had a particularly gruelling day at the office, and had been cheering myself up on the way home with the thought of a large malt whisky, but I forgot the whisky and my weariness, and sat down beside Sue to go through the papers. One box was marked Koenigsberg, 1914-20; another Berlin, a third Dvinsk, a fourth Hamburg, a fifth Frankfurt. There were over a dozen of them, the many stations of her cross. I opened the first and began reading.

'I thought you weren't interested in digging up your past,' said Sue.

'Not when you have to look for it, but if it lands on your doorstep it's a different matter.'

I barely ate that evening and hardly slept that night, and when I came down for breakfast I found Sue in her nightie poring over the letters as if she had not been to bed at all.

'Bless your aunt,' she said, 'bless her, and all her friends and relations. They wrote so neatly and intelligently.'

I dipped into the boxes again and only broke off because I had an urgent meeting first thing in the morning, but I might as well have stayed at home, for I found it impossible to concentrate on what was being said by others and had nothing to say myself. Again I didn't know what had come over me. It was as if my aunt and her past had invaded, indeed taken over, my life in revenge for the way I had neglected her. The odd thing was that although she had often spoken of herself as a jackdaw, the accumulation of letters showed a streak of sentimentality which I had not hitherto associated with her, or, indeed, with the rest of the family. It was as if I was discovering them all for the first time. I began wondering whether I shouldn't ask the bank for a period of unpaid leave so that I could get through the papers without interruption.

I had returned there as Beatty's no.2 in the Middle Eastern Department, as it was grandly called (as if it was a division of the Foreign Office), with the understanding that I would succeed him when he retired. The job was fairly senior and highly paid and one heard suggestions that it had been given to me as a reward for cohabiting with the Chairman's daughter for a full year, and that if I had stuck it out for a further year I might have been elevated to the Board. Beatty's retirement age, however, came and went but Beatty himself remained, and I felt slightly betrayed. 'Our interests in the area have grown by leaps and bounds,' he explained, 'and I have been asked to hang around for another year or two yet to keep an eye on things.'

But as far as I saw it, the fact that I had allowed my domestic circumstances to affect my professional responsibilities had counted against me. Up to the age of thirty I had been regarded as an up-and-coming young man. Now, at thirty-four, I was thought of as down and going. I was never certain of my own feelings, even about my work, and the fact that I was again thinking of taking unpaid leave suggested I was even more disgruntled than I thought. I did not, however, proceed with the idea and instead asked if I could anticipate my annual leave and take my holidays right away. Rich was surprised by my request, for it was April and, as somebody observed, it was too late for skiing and too early for surfing.

'Nothing wrong, I hope.'

'No, nothing. Some domestic matter has cropped up and I should like to deal with it without further delay.'

Some hours later I was called into the Chairman's office.

'Hear you're taking leave.'

'Annual holiday.'

'Passover, that sort of thing?'

'No, that's over.'

'Wife's Jewish, isn't she?'

'Very much so, I'm afraid.'

'Nephew of mine's going back to the fold – after three generations. Don't know what's happening to the family.

Thought you'd like to know she's getting married, Lee I mean. Don't much care for the chap. Not sure if she does. An Earl, Irish. Good with horses, not much good with anything else, but there we are.'

I was surprised to feel a pang of regret at the news. I hadn't set eyes on the girl since I had left her that day in Moscow, and she had rarely come to mind, yet was I pining over the thought that I could have been that Earl if only I had played my cards right? No, I was perfectly happy with Sue, but ideally, I suppose, I should have liked Sue as a wife and Edward as a father-in-law (except that I couldn't quite see him married to Sue's mother). I would have liked to be part of his family, not because he was Chairman and an Eissenmacher, but because he was himself. He was the sort of Englishman grandfather must have had in mind when he expressed his adoration of the English, languorous in some ways, brisk in others, combining the dilettantish air of the amateur with thorough-going professionalism, relaxed, convivial, straight-forward, yet never quite the innocent he looked. Giselle told me that she was convinced that he had more or less engineered my liaison with his daughter. 'Why do you think he took you to Arabia that time? He called it a familiarization trip, but he wanted to familiarize himself with you, to get the measure of you, so to speak, and I think he was impressed. And why do you think you – a comparatively junior employee – were actually in the church at the wedding? He hoped you'd run into his daughter, and it all worked out exactly as planned. What he didn't reckon was that you'd run out on her so soon. He was very upset when it happened, almost cried on my shoulder.'

I didn't know if it was true, for Giselle had a lively imagination, but the thought of it drew me even closer to him, and the news he gave me now was an intimation that our special relationship – if, indeed, it had existed at all – was now finally and formally at an end. The thought sent me home in a slightly dejected frame of mind, but I brightened up at the sight of my wife, my child and the prospect of an untrammelled six weeks to work on the papers.

It was now some two years since Sue had signed the contract to write her book, but she approached it in fits and starts, with rather more fits than starts. Now, with the treasure-trove before her and my anxiety to proceed, she brought in a nanny and was free to apply herself fully to the task in hand.

I had a book-lined study in which I used to work at home, but it was far too small for our needs. Our garage, however, was large and we had it converted into a workroom, with two separate tables, a large filing cabinet, typewriter and copying-machine. We worked together and the weeks flew by as if they were days. It was like being back as a graduate student in Oxford, but without the loneliness or poverty. We were immensely helped by Carla's orderliness. We opened a file for each correspondent, and others for anyone who featured in the letters with any frequency, and filled in cross-references as they arose. We also had the photographs carefully stacked. Those we could identify we filed right away. Others became identifiable through their own words, or through references to them in other letters, and, after about a month, we had built up a fairly coherent picture of grandfather's family, prosperous but, for all their prosperity, rather frugal, churchy, starchy, philistine, pompous. I came to wonder how they could have had a daughter like Carla and, to judge from their letters, they must have wondered themselves, for she was a source of concern from her earliest days. The concern turned to something like despair as time went on, and the last letter from her mother ended with the words: 'God knows we did our best for you, why do you treat us like enemies?' I was surprised, in the circumstances, that she held on to the letters, for she had obviously not taken them to heart.

'It's nothing to do with taking them to heart,' said Sue. 'Once you get into the habit of holding on to things you can't throw anything out. I've still got my mother's letters to me, semi-literate though they are – '

The only personal letter I had ever saved was the one from my grandfather and it was not so much a letter as a testament. 'Was she hoping to re-read all this in old age?' I asked.

'No, holding on to letters is a proof that you've lived, that you've meant something to someone, that the past isn't completely past.'

'Given what she's been through, poor woman, she should have been grateful that the past was past.'

'Oh, I don't know. Listen to this. "It can only be minutes since I left you, but I have already begun counting the minutes till we should meet again. I don't know if I shall ever post this letter, but writing to you makes me feel almost as if I'm talking to you, and sometimes if I sit back and pause I think I can even hear your voice and see your smile. Can I be going mad? If so I pray that I should stay mad . . ."'

I listened with something like disbelief. I was aware that my aunt could inspire lust. It hadn't occurred to me that she could ever have inspired such tenderness.

'How old was she then?'

'About eighteen, I would say, to judge from the date. I never got letters like that, but then most of the chaps I went out with were medical students and other semi-literates. Ah, I live in the wrong age.'

I concentrated on the letters from grandfather. At first he wrote only in answer to some enquiry from her, or when he had news to impart, such as his engagement and marriage, but later, after their parents died, he seemed to have assumed their admonitory duties and sent her a letter a month, almost without fail.

When we entered the twenties I searched every line of the letters for some hint of his political attitudes, but the nearest thing to them were the occasional remarks about Viennese Jews, which could possibly have been construed, and which Sue did construe, as anti-Semitic. One referred to a popular newspaper which, he said, was Jewish-owned and which, he complained, 'was poisoning the minds of the people'. Another suggested the Jews owned Vienna, but this was said not so much by way of complaint but as a piece of incidental information. Carla tended to be litigious even then, and he warned her not to engage a Jewish lawyer. 'It's a straightforward case which any competent man can handle,' he wrote. 'The Jews may be bright, but they're expensive.' But such asides did not, even in Sue's eyes, make a man a Nazi. And, as I pointed out, there were any number of derogatory references to Frenchmen, Hungarians, Russians, Poles, Serbs, Greeks, Turks and Arabs, and if grandfather possibly did dislike Jews, it was part of his general distaste for mankind.

Letters from my grandmother, written in a tight little crabbed hand, were few and far between, and they were usually provoked by impatience or anger:

'. . . really, Carla. It is not for me to tell you how you should conduct your life, but I think I should remind you that your brother is a doctor and not a banker and although he is, thank God, now doing quite well he has incurred heavy debts which he must pay off, and frankly I think you have been abusing his generosity. I don't know how many Marks he lent you, but I do know that you haven't repaid him one, and I don't think you have a right to ask for further "loans", as you call them, until you have at least made an attempt to repay what you owe him . . . Needless to say Gunther doesn't know I'm writing, and I don't usually make it my business to interfere in these matters, but this has been going on for far too long, and must stop . . .'

My aunt seemed to have been born with money troubles and there were numerous letters from tradesmen demanding payment, and more than a few from lawyers. Grandfather sometimes chastised her for her extravagance in carefully measured tones, and also pointed out that he wasn't a bank, but he never demanded actual restitution and only showed something like anger when he received a large bill for expenses which she had incurred in his name.

'The man had the patience of Job,' I said. 'Can you really imagine him as a Nazi?'

'No,' said Sue, 'but I couldn't imagine him joining the Nazi party either, and join it he did.'

He rarely touched on external events, either because he chose to ignore them or simply because he thought they would be of no particular interest to his sister, and he almost never mentioned politics or his political views. If he was a member of the party, I was convinced he must have been an extremely inert one, but then we came upon a name which tempered my conclusions – Gottfried Hanau.

Hanau appears to have been the great love in Carla's life, and she had a whole box of his letters. She met him through grandfather, and he was not only an active Nazi, but a rabid one. He wrote to her with some regularity, but his letters were in no sense love-letters, even if they contained the occasional term of endearment. They were full of dark fulminations against the Jews as 'poisonous', 'corrupters', 'blood-suckers', 'parasites' and, most chillingly of all: 'Germany will never be Germany till we have got rid of this lot.' No document which Sue produced was quite as damning as the thought that my grandfather could have

171

been on terms of friendship with such a man, and that they were friends was patently clear from grandfather's own letters:

'We were short of everything, especially time, and we could only treat those wounded who we thought had a reasonable hope of recovery. Gottfried and others were therefore more or less left for dead. That he eventually recovered was a miracle which neither he nor I nor anyone else could explain. I can only ascribe it to will-power. He himself sees his recovery as proof that he was saved for some great destiny, and he may be right . . . '

There was only one occasion when he seemed to distance himself from his attitudes, and, even then, not completely:

'Gottfried has been with us for the past few days. He has become excitable and has some strange ideas and seems to blame all our troubles on the Jews, but he is full of enthusiasm and has boundless energy and I am sure we shall hear a lot more of him in the years to come. He spoke warmly of you . . . '

I followed Hanau's career through his letters with morbid fascination, and watched him rise from *Haupteinsatzleiter* to *Gemeinschaftzleiter* to *Hauptgemeinschaftzleiter* and even on to *Kreisleiter*, or major. He met Hitler and Goering. He moved from Munich to Berlin. He acquired a large apartment.

Then suddenly, silence, with no more letters from Hanau, but a torrent of letters from everyone else. The letter from her brother did not mention Hanau at all, and was curiously short:

'What can I say? I can only repeat what father used to say in such a situation. Who knows the ways of God? It may all be for the best.'

He was in Resznitz by then and he invited her to come and stay with him.

The abrupt end to the Hanau correspondence mystified Sue, and she presumed from the many letters of condolence ('a loss not only to you and me', wrote one friend, 'but a loss to the fatherland') that he had died suddenly or been killed in an accident, but I had by then acquired a sort of Who Was Who in the Nazi party and I was able to establish that he had been murdered in the 1934 purge of Brownshirts. Revolutions, as Mitri liked to remind me, consumed their own children, and Hanau had not been consumed a minute too soon.

Grandfather's membership of the Nazi party dated from the previous year and I ascribed it to his friendship, indeed his infatuation, with Hanau, and even if he had some passing sympathies with the aims of the party I thought it unlikely that they would have survived the purge.

The death of Hanau must have left my aunt severely shaken. Grandfather's letters were full of medical advice and even grandmother wrote in solicitous terms to enquire after her health, adding: 'I miss him very much so I can imagine what you must be going through. It all reminds me of the terrible losses we suffered in the war, but we owe it to our loved ones to look to the future . . .'

There was also a letter from Marcovitch:

'Your brother told me about your sad loss. I remember seeing you together and you seemed so happy, and your brother was so happy for you. The old get used to their misfortunes, but for the young they are very painful, but being young their wounds can heal . . .'

We then turned to the letters from Inge, the woman I had thought of as my mother, and they helped to brighten the gloom. She was born in 1918, an event which brought a touch of animation to grandfather's letters which I had not noticed before and which he was unable to sustain for long. He did not refer to her with any great frequency, and when he did it was in terms of exasperation rather than endearment, and almost every term of praise was qualified by a complaint: 'She is intelligent for her age but wilful' . . . 'lively but disruptive' . . . 'pretty, but I'm afraid rather spoilt'.

It all became a little wearying. Then when she was about ten she began writing herself. Things immediately livened up and the correspondence, with breaks here and there, continued for the next ten years.

'How can such a dull man have had such a delightful child?' said Sue. 'They're a joy.'

Her spelling was poor and her hand was childish even as she grew to maturity. She was perceptive, uninhibited, gay. She was

173

not only bright in herself, she cast light on everything about her.

'I think mummy likes being ill, for she can be kind and understanding when she's in bed, but when she gets on her feet she snaps at everyone, and especially daddy, as if he had no business getting her on her feet. She doesn't like noise and she doesn't like a mess, and she says I'm messy and noisy. Everybody hates her. Daddy walks around looking as if he's got a pain in the head and says nothing. She keeps complaining that he spoils me, but he hardly talks to me . . . '

Then there was a letter on the death of Hanau:

'They never said anything to me, of course, they never do. They forget I'm sixteen and think I'm still a child, but I picked it up anyhow, and ran to my room and cried myself to sleep. Poor, poor Gottfried. I was in love with him myself, so I know how you must feel. Poor, poor Carla. He used to come here every Christmas, as you know, but he hasn't been here for years. I asked father why he doesn't come any more, and he told me not to bother him with nonsense. Had they quarrelled? I shall miss him terribly.'

A little later, there came a reference to the Marcovitch family:

'You will know the Marcovitches. They're Jews, but very nice. They have three sons, all of them good-looking, especially the youngest, but they're all a good bit older than me, and pinch my cheek and chuck me under the chin, as if I'm a child. They're only here in the summer and they'll be gone in another week, and I'll be back in school in another two weeks. I hate school, but I hate it here even more when the Marcovitches are gone and there's no one here except papa, mama, the lunatics and the nurses. If it wasn't for poor Schutzi I would go mad myself.'

Schutzi was her dog: large, black and shaggy. He featured with her in several photographs, and I recognized him at once as the dog of my memories and the dog I had seen in the film moving cumbersomely through the snow.

'He's very sad, Schutzi, [she wrote in one letter] but then so is everybody else. I think it's the long winter and the deep snow, and nearly everybody is old, or looks old. Two nights ago I was wakened by loud voices and rapid footsteps in the corridor, and the next morning the police were here and daddy looked very white and upset, and mummy, who had been up and about in a fur coat over her dressing-gown, is back in bed. They say some poor soul hanged himself. Can't blame him, can you?'

We began to feel sorry for her:

'Please come for Christmas. You can't imagine how awful it will be without you, what with mama ill, and papa in despair, and snow everywhere. He always buys me generous presents, but they're not everything, and oh, I'm so dying for company. Do you think madness is catching? I'm being serious, because I have the feeling I'm going mad every time I come to Resznitz. It isn't so bad in summer, but I dread Christmas. Please come . . . '

That particular Christmas, however, turned out to be less bleak than she had anticipated:

'I'm sorry you couldn't come, because you would have loved it. There's a new doctor in the place, tall, blond, handsome, called Apteker, and I fell in love with him as soon as I saw him. I think he's Jewish, but doesn't look it. He livened everything up and made even mama smile – for a while. All the nurses are in love with him and they turn quite human when he's around. When the holidays were over I couldn't bear to tear myself away . . . '

Her passion for Apteker proved impermanent, for the following summer she wrote:

'Will you promise not to breathe a word about this to anyone? I shouldn't even be telling you, but if I don't tell somebody I'll burst. I'm in love again. And guess with whom? I'll give you a hint. You met him last summer and said yourself he's very good-looking, like a girl. Remember? That's right, the youngest Marcovitch boy. He's Jewish, but what does it matter, and he has a girl-friend, or had, because he said he's not going to see her again. He said he can't live without me, and I don't know what we're going to do. His family don't know anything about it either, and of course he daren't tell

175

them. You must remember his father with the beard, like a Rabbi. Can you imagine what he would say? And can you imagine what mama would say? As for father, he'd lock me up with his lunatics, I'm sure of it, so I don't know what we'll do. Dear, dear Carla, what would you do? '

At first we thought that what dear Carla did was to shop her, for the letters suddenly stopped, but it soon became clear that they stopped because she was actually staying with Carla. The girl had presumably become too much for her parents, especially as she had by now left school, but the aunt proved a most inadequate guardian, for at the end of 1937 she received a terse telegram: MESSAGE INCOMPREHENSIBLE PLEASE EXPLAIN, followed by a letter:

'What do you mean you don't know where she could be? She could hardly have vanished into thin air. If I can't entrust my child to my own sister whom can I trust? Did she not mention her plans to you at all? Must I worry about her on top of everything else? I thought you were having a telephone installed. What is your number? Will you be good enough to phone me? I intend to come to Koenigsberg without delay.'

Sue and I immediately concluded that the girl had eloped with young Marcovitch, except that, as far as we knew, Marcovitch had gone to America, whereas we could only find one further letter from her in an envelope postmarked Maida Vale (London). It was brief, confused and undated:

'Dear Carla,
    You mustn't be angry with me. Too much has been happening and I'm all in a tizzy. I'll write again when things settle down.'

Presumably things didn't settle down, for as far as we could discover this was her last letter.

'No marriage, no husband, no children,' said Sue. 'What was she doing in London? Where was Marcovitch? Had he abandoned her? Had she abandoned him? Why the silence?'

We had to put such questions aside for the time being, for a major new character had come on the scene, one Gerhardt Buchbinder, who must have swept my aunt off her feet, for there were only two letters from him, neither of them particularly passionate, before letters came flooding in congratulating her on her engagement and her impending marriage. She was forty by then, so it wasn't a minute too soon. The arrangements might, of course, have been accelerated by an untimely pregnancy, but there were numerous photos of the wedding, taken in May 1938, none of which suggested that she was, or recently had been, with child. According to my own papers I was born in June of that year.

'Well,' said Sue, 'that puts you, or rather her, in the clear.'

I wasn't sure. My papers could have been forged, because once one is provided with a sham identity one can never be certain where the sham ends and the truth begins, and I wanted to see what other surprises the letters had in store.

Carla rarely mentioned her late husband, and seemed reluctant to discuss him when he was mentioned by others, as if he was some deep secret, and I suspect that the secret lay in his lowly rank and the fact that he was more than ten years younger than her. He was an *Unteroffizier*, or sergeant, in the regular army when they married, and an *Oberweichtmaster*, or sergeant-major, when he was listed as missing four years later.

By then, her correspondence had begun to peter out, no doubt due to the disruptions of war and the fact that she was always on the move. Of events in Resznitz during the crucial months of June to October 1941 there was never a word, and barely a reference to the German occupation.

There was a letter from grandfather which must have been written shortly after Buchbinder had been listed missing:

'There has been so much suffering and death that yet another misfortune can sometimes pass unnoticed, but Herta and I were profoundly moved by your sad news of poor, dear Gerhardt. We saw and knew so little of him, and he was so young, but he was a good, kind man and we knew how happy you were together. Perhaps he may yet turn up. We should not live on false hope, but we cannot live without hope. I cannot even come to see you because the winter is dreadful and it is impossible to move, and it is almost impossible to get a travel permit, but I shall try . . . '

I found it a compassionate and sensitive letter, and even Sue was moved to tears, 'which doesn't mean he couldn't have been a

Nazi,' she added quickly. 'Here was his poor sister, after so many disappointments, finally married, and hardly had she settled down to married life before she was widowed. I've never suggested that he was devoid of feeling. He was naturally sorry for her. Damn it, she was his sister, and Buchbinder was his brother-in-law, and he may have been troubled by the thought of having the wretched woman back on his hands. What *I'm* looking for is a show of compassion for someone who wasn't a relative, or even a German – a Jew, in fact.'

She found it a little later.

—— *Chapter Fourteen* ——

'Dear Carla,
  A voice from the past, Hirsch Apteker, remember me? I was a colleague of your brother Gunther and often stayed with him in Resznitz and as you may know he saved my life when he helped me escape from the Nazis. A mutual friend gave me your address and told me that your brother is alive and working in Egypt. It all sounds too good to be true. Do you know where I might contact him? '

It was hardly more than a note which I nearly overlooked, but I jumped with excitement as I read and re-read it. Sue couldn't see what the fuss was about.
  'Read it, the first sentence,' I said.
  'I've read it.'
  'But don't you see? It answers all our questions. Would my grandfather, would anyone, betray his closest Jewish friends and then save the life of a Jew who was only an acquaintance? He wasn't a Nazi, he couldn't have been.'
  'But what about his membership of the Nazi party?'
  'Bugger his membership of the Nazi party. It doesn't mean a thing.'
  I was surprised by my own vehemence; so was Sue. Was it because I finally saw grandfather's fortune as mine, and she was questioning my right to it? I, however, calmed down and pointed out that grandfather had only shown a passing awareness of what was going on in the world and mightn't have known what the party stood for – if he had in fact joined in the first place, for Rhiner was a fairly common German name and she might have got hold of the wrong one.
  'But is Dr Gunther Rhiner all that common?'
  'We can have it checked, but it's obvious, isn't it? Whether he was a member of the party or not it did not affect his attitudes and

179

conduct as a human being. Look, I'll be honest with you. There was a time when I was myself half convinced that he could have been a Nazi' – and it was then that I told her about the fortune he had left and my suspicion that he might have obtained it by dubious means. She seemed curiously unmoved by the revelation, and didn't even ask why I hadn't told her before. I suppose I had expected a good Jewish daughter from a good Jewish home to throw up her hands and go wild at the thought of all that money lying idle and untouched, even unmentioned.

'Seven hundred thousand pounds,' I said. 'Do you know what that means? '

'No, not really. Money's never meant much to me, but then I've never been short of it. I hadn't thought it meant all that much to you.'

Neither had I, but I couldn't hide the fact that I was trembling.

There were now two main leads to follow: the London letter from Inge, and Apteker. Sue took the former in hand, while I turned to the latter, but first I wrote to my German lawyer asking him to check how many Gunther Rhiners there were in the German medical register for 1933. He did more than that and checked the German, Austrian and Czech registers and came up with seven, including two who were born in the same year as my grandfather. That was all I needed; I felt that grandfather had been completely vindicated and that, as far as he was concerned, the case could rest. And this time Sue raised no objections.

I should have been conscious of a sense of accomplishment, even triumph. Yet all I could feel was the slight fillip to the ego one gets on finishing a tricky crossword. Some sort of ceremony was called for and I opened a bottle of champagne, but the very sound of the cork popping was hollow.

'To the memory of a good and innocent man,' I said, holding up my glass. Sue raised her glass, gulped it down, wiped her mouth with the back of her hand, and got on with her work. It was all an anti-climax, possibly because only part of our quest was over. The main question still had to be answered. Who or what was I? If grandfather had saved Apteker he could conceivably have saved me, which, as Sue pointed out, meant I was Jewish.

'And you know, I somehow always had the feeling you were. Jew can sense Jew as dog can sense dog.'

If the thought had worried me when I first read grandfather's letter it didn't worry me now, for I was virtually Jewish by contagion, but it was far too early to draw such conclusions, for all the evidence suggested that the Marcovitch children had perished with the Marcovitch womenfolk; but I thought that the final answer to this question might be provided by the elusive Apteker.

His address in the Resznitz visitors' book had been completely illegible, but I was able to make out his address on his note to Carla. That note was written eighteen years ago and if he was a contemporary of Carla's he could well be dead, but I wrote to him in any case. At the same time, I hired a young man to scour the medical registers of Europe to see what he could find.

My letter to Apteker remained unanswered, but the young man came up with several useful leads, showing that Apteker had been trained in Koenigsberg and Vienna, and that he had practised in Sweden from 1944 to 1951 and had then moved to New York. He was even able to find me his New York address. In New York, however, my enquiries were regarded with suspicion.

'Who are you? What do you want to know? Why do you want to know? He hasn't been here for years.' I had evidently touched on a phase in the man's career which they didn't care to talk about. I was involved in countless transatlantic calls before I could get to the source of their hesitancy, and it was this: Apteker, apparently, had been a well-known Communist and had lied about his past to get into America, and, as a result, had been deported to East Germany three years later. This helped to explain something which had troubled me. How did Apteker manage to get into Resznitz after the war if it was in a security zone? Had he been in a position to pull strings like Mitri? I now had an answer: he was a trusty, a Communist, one of them.

I kept looking at his picture over and over again and the carefree impression it gave did not normally go with Communist sympathies. He was clearly no common-or-garden Bolshevik. Sue thought I was becoming obsessed with him. 'You've found the man you'd have liked as a father,' she said. 'Frankly, he looks a bit like a dago to me. I've never been able to trust a man with a moustache, especially a neat moustache.'

I had numerous East German contacts from my banking days, but they greeted my enquiries about Apteker not so much with suspicion as with silence. I should have remembered from my earlier experience of the People's Republics that there was little to be obtained through phone calls and even less through writing, and I considered the possibility of flying to East Germany to see what I could do in person when my enquiry agent discovered that Apteker had defected to the West during the 1956 upheavals in East Berlin. 'He was sixty-four when he defected and in poor health,' he added, 'so it is quite possible that he may no longer be alive. I have examined the relevant records in West Germany but found no reference to him, but I understand he had friends in Sweden and am making enquiries there . . . '

In the meantime, Sue had struck gold. She had found the marriage certificate of Ingeborg Henrietta Rhiner, spinster, of Lisson Grove in the Parish of St Mary Le Bone, and Maurice Marshall, bachelor, of the same address. 'That's not all,' she added triumphantly. 'I went straight on to the address in Lisson Grove and, would you believe it, I found an old woman who actually remembered her. "How can I forget?" she said. "Oh, she was a picture, she really was, and a bit saucy too." I then asked about Marshall, but she couldn't remember a thing about him. "How could I? She had boy-friends coming and going all the time. Some of the neighbours complained. I didn't. Good luck to her, I said."'

She could, however, find no trace of a birth certificate either in the local parish records or in Somerset House. We considered three possibilities. First, that for some reason she had never registered the birth; second, that she never had a baby, against which we had to put the insistence not only of grandfather but also of Carla that she did; finally, she may have emigrated shortly after her marriage and had her baby in America, which was more or less confirmed by her elderly neighbour.

'Oh, yes, she was in the family way. Not surprising, really, the way she carried on. She had these fellers coming all times of the day and night. The neighbours all complained, but then they would, wouldn't they? I didn't. Good luck to her, I said. Then, one day, she's gone, and that's the last I see of her. I suppose she owed a bob or two for the rent. Well, we all did in those days.'

'Our search is as good as over,' said Sue as we drove home. 'We've more or less cleared your grandfather, and we've found your mother.'

'I wouldn't be so sure about that.'

'You wouldn't? Christ, if the poor woman was to materialize before you, throw her arms round you and cry "My son! My son!", would you be satisfied then?'

'But the point is, she hasn't materialized before me. You've found her wedding certificate, which is one thing, but we haven't yet seen a birth certificate – '

'Didn't you hear what this woman just told us?'

'Yes, that she was pregnant, but there's many a slip between cup and lip. She could have had an abortion. She could have miscarried. The baby could have been still-born.'

'You're prepared to consider every possibility except the likely one. Your aunt saw the infant, didn't she?'

'She saw *an* infant. We have found no one who actually set eyes on the mother and child – '

'You're a snob, that's the long and the short of it. You're not too happy with the sort of mum we've discovered, she's a bit down-market for your taste. You knew she was pretty, you were hoping for a bit of class. Instead you've found somebody who might have been willing to show her knickers to help pay the rent. In a way I can understand your feelings, it makes me see why you were reluctant to start looking in the first place.'

'I'm perfectly prepared to reconcile myself to anyone we may find, but we shouldn't rush to conclusions.'

'You were prepared to rush to conclusions where your grandfather was concerned long before you had anything to go by –'

'I had my knowledge of the man to go by. I've no personal knowledge of this woman. Let's wait at least till we find out more about my purported father, what's his name – Marshall. He could still be alive, and if he is he could tell us everything.'

'We have no clue to his whereabouts at all. We should be satisfied with what we have. As Lady Bracknell might have said, to look for one parent is a sign of filial concern, to look for both verges on greed. We'll find him in good time, but I should warn you, if your mother was the sort of girl I think she was, your father may have been a pimp.'

It was with this thought in mind that we began searching through police records for the immediate post-war years – Sue, I noticed, applied herself to the search with rather more zeal than I did – and a little to my relief, and her disappointment, we found nothing.

The next logical step would have been to resume the trail in America, but something happened to make that impractical. Our second child was fast on the way. The baby, a girl, was born prematurely, and we called her Gertrude, for no better reason than that her mother had made her name as an amateur actress playing that part in an Oxford production of *Hamlet*. The child, though under-weight, developed rapidly, but it had been a difficult pregnancy; Sue remained bed-bound for over a month. She was not quite herself even when back on her feet, and remained wan, thin and pale, with lank hair; she ate little and tired easily.

We had a nurse for the baby, an au-pair for the older child and a woman to help with the cooking and cleaning, so that when the baby was about three months old I thought I could safely go on to America. It was, in retrospect, a thoughtless thing to do, and I left with a feeling of deep unease, but Sue herself had urged me to go. 'I'll be all right,' she insisted. 'What do you think I am, a baby? Let's get this matter out of the way. If you don't go, I shall.'

I flew straight to Chicago and the next day I managed to find the full story of the hotel fire in the newspaper files at the Central Library. It was, as I suspected, or rather feared, not an ordinary hotel, and one of the porters, a religious fanatic, had set fire to the building in the belief that he was doing the work of God by destroying a den of iniquity. It was on a winter's night. The city was deep in snow and the fire appliances had found it difficult to get to the blaze. The building was an inferno by the time they reached it, and twenty-one bodies – eight women, twelve men and a child – were found among the ashes. There were brief biographies of the women victims (but not of their clients). The child was not Inge's and there was no reference, either in the report of the fire or the inquest, to the fact that she was a mother. It had all happened in the early hours of New Year's Day 1939.

Inge had been last seen by her London neighbour about March 1938, and if she had had a baby it would have had to be born some time during the next few months, and not later than the end of September. I began searching through the local records. Marshall was a very common name in Chicago and I had only got as far as June when I got a phone call from Sue. She sounded distraught.

'There's a man outside been watching the house,' she said. 'He was here yesterday and he's been here again today. I could see him from the bedroom window, and I'm frightened.'

For a moment I thought I was back in Moscow and listening to Lee Eissenmacher.

'Is he there now?'

'No, but he may come back, and I'm frightened.'

'He won't come back, I'm sure, but phone me again if he does.'

'Will you come back if he does?'

'Yes, if necessary, of course I will.'

Which seemed to reassure her and she put the phone down.

I should have taken warning both from the character of her message and her tone of voice and arranged to fly back there and then, but having come all this way I wanted to return with the birth-certificate in hand. I was also anxious to see what I could discover about the mysterious Maurice Marshall, and I was confident that even if British police records had yielded nothing, the American ones would be more fruitful. But the next day I received a phone call from Sue's sister-in-law, Doreen. 'You'll have to come back,' she said tersely, 'Sue's in hospital.'

'Why? What's happened.'

'I wish I knew. I shouldn't think it's anything physical, but we'll talk about it when you're here.'

I flew back on the first available plane, racked with foreboding and guilt. Sue was in hospital, heavily drugged and lapsing in and out of sleep, and failed to recognize me in her waking moments.

'She tried to kill herself,' said Doreen.

'Kill herself?'

'An overdose of something or other, they're not quite sure what. I think she swallowed everything she had by her bed. The Filipino girl called me. I brought her straight here and they pumped her out.'

The next day she opened her eyes and started when she found me sitting beside her.

'What are you doing here?' She sounded less surprised than displeased, as if I was trespassing.

'What are *you* doing here?'

She had apparently been asking herself the same question. She had no recollection of what had happened.

'All I remember is panic and fear and then oblivion. Did I really take an overdose?'

'That's what they tell me.'

'I can't believe it, can you? It's not me, is it?'

Her recovery was rapid and she was out of hospital within the week, but the doctor insisted – I suppose rightly – that she could do with a holiday, and we left the children in the charge of Doreen and went on a cruise.

It was a disaster. Somebody once observed that the true test of a marriage was how a couple felt about each other when they were doing nothing, in which case our marriage was a flop. The weather was cool and grey in the English Channel, cold and stormy in the Bay of Biscay with almost everyone on board heaving up their innards, but we comforted ourselves with thoughts of sunshine once we reached the Mediterranean. It never came. It rained in Gibraltar, poured in Naples, and when we reached Venice it was under two feet of water. But that was perhaps the least of it. We found as soon as the ship left her moorings that we had booked berths in a floating old-age home. The average age of the passengers must have been about eighty and the talk was all of doctors, hospitals, medicine and what they ate at their last meal and what they might be eating at their next one, though meal-times were occasionally enlivened by the sound of this or that passenger giving his last gasp and sinking under the table. Sue and I became testy and irritable with each other and with everyone else. I, a modest drinker, became a heavy one; Sue, a modest smoker, was like a chimney. The cruise lasted three weeks; had it lasted four we would have jumped overboard.

We returned to a crisis.

The nurse had gone over to Doreen's house to help her look after the children. Our Filipino au-pair remained to look after the house and we assumed that while we were away her boy-friend would move in with her, which he did.

When we returned all the blinds were down and all the curtains were drawn, which made me think they were away, but when I tried my key in the door it wouldn't budge. The door had been bolted from inside. I pressed the intercom and a frightened voice answered:

'Who that? Nobody in.'

186

'It's me. What's up?'

At which there was a rapid trot of footsteps in the hall and she unlocked, unbolted and unchained the door and almost fell into my arms crying.

'Oh, Mr Newman, I'm so glad you here. A big man come to the door. He come here last night and come again this morning and he look angry you not here.'

'Are you here all on your own?' asked Sue.

'No, Berto is upstairs. He afraid to come down. He come twice, very big and very angry.'

'Did he say who he was?' I asked.

'He ask if you live here. I don't say nothing and shut door.'

'Was he tall and thin?' asked Sue.

'No, not thin. He big and fat and he speak a funny English.'

I looked uneasily at Sue, but she seemed a good deal less troubled by it all than I was. We managed eventually to calm the girl down and to prise Berto out of his redoubt. He was slightly more coherent.

'He phone yesterday morning and ask to speak to you. I say you no here. He ask when you come. I ask who he is. He say is not important and I put the phone down. Then last night he come again.'

'How do you know it's the same person?'

'He have the same voice. He come again this morning, but we don't open the door and he begin to shout.'

'Why didn't you call the police?' asked Sue, and he shrugged his shoulders uneasily: he had his own good reasons for not calling the police. I wondered whether in the circumstances we shouldn't leave the children with Doreen for another day or two.

'You're beginning to sound like my mother,' said Sue. 'I want the kids back here. The house doesn't feel the same without them.'

And we brought them back, but I spent a restless night, shocked into wakefulness by every sound, and I kept shuffling up and down the stairs to make sure, and doubly sure, that every door was bolted and every window locked. And even the next day I jumped every time the phone went or the door buzzed. It was as if the nervous hysteria which had seized Sue when I was in America had been transferred to me, and I called in a security firm to fix up the house with an elaborate system of alarms. By the time I got the estimates, however, I had calmed down, and I put the whole matter aside.

In the meantime, we resumed our researches and began by recapitulating our findings to date. We agreed that we had established the innocence of my grandfather and that, in the absence of any information to the contrary, we felt we could more or less close his file. We also agreed that his version of my origins was a fabrication contrived for my benefit, and that whoever was my mother it almost certainly was not Sarah Marcovitch. But who was it? Sue had thought that she had settled the matter by her researches in Lisson Grove, but my own researches in America, far from confirming it, had left the whole matter open.

We went through the rest of Carla's papers, but, as I suspected, they threw no new light on the matter. I had at the very outset of our work written to Yad Vashem, the supreme Holocaust authority in Jerusalem, to ask if they had any information on the Marcovitch family, but they had none and it was safe to assume that neither of the older sons nor the son-in-law had survived. There were only two people who, if they were still alive, might be able to help us. One was the youngest Marcovitch brother, Moshe, who had emigrated to America before the war, and the other was my grandfather's colleague, Apteker. I already had one young man trying to follow up Apteker. I now engaged another to follow up Marcovitch.

Sue felt she had enough on my grandfather to begin the actual writing and she applied herself to it with enviable energy and speed, and page after page flew from her typewriter. She was, of course, immensely helped by Carla's papers, but I felt that she was over-using them, and that what had been intended as a biography of my grandfather was becoming a social history of the Baltic Germans. She had written twenty pages merely to set the scene, and another hundred before my grandfather was even in uniform. She had pronounced literary ability and it all read well, but she had yet to acquire the first rule of the craft, which was an ability to exclude, and I warned her that at the rate she was going her book would be over a thousand pages.

'So be it,' she said, 'the bigger the better.'

In the meantime, my own researches, or rather my own researchers, proved disappointing. Apteker seemed to have vanished without trace, and, while my American researcher had come up with innumerable Moshe Marcovitches, none of them was the Marcovitch I was looking for. I was tempted to leave the matter there, especially as Sue's preoccupation with her book had left me with more than my share of domestic responsibilities.

We, of course, had nannies (consecutively rather than concurrently) for the children, but none of them stayed for long, and those that did stay exacted such terms that we were (or rather I was) more or less their servants.

My responsibilities in the bank had also become more demanding, but at the end of the day I still managed to beat my secretary in the rush to the car park, and the whole question of who was, or was not, my mother, gradually faded from my agenda.

Then, early one evening I returned from work to find Sue entertaining a large, white-haired man in the drawing-room. His nose was broken, his suit was baggy, one shoulder was higher than the other, and one eye was larger than the other. He rose unsteadily to his feet as I entered and extended a huge, hairy hand.

'I am Marcovitch,' he said in a hoarse voice.

I stopped in my tracks.

He was as far removed from the idea of a ghost as may be imagined, but the very sound of his name made me feel as if I was looking at one. I also felt a quiver of alarm, which may have been due to his very size and his ungainly stance, for he looked as if he might topple over on top of me. Sue, however, was a picture of composure, with a cup of tea in her hand as if she was entertaining the Vicar.

'Mr Marcovitch was here some months ago when we were away,' she said, 'but he was kind enough to come back. Would you like some tea?'

I poured myself something more formidable than tea before I could regain my composure or even my voice. He looked so unlike the Marcovitch men in the pictures I had of the family, I wondered if he was not an impostor. The two older brothers were tall and the third one was short, but all three were slightly built, while here was someone like an all-in wrestler gone to seed, with a neck like a tree-trunk.

'Are you from Resznitz?' I asked.

'Dvinsk,' he said. 'We have house in Dvinsk and *datcha* in

189

Resznitz.'

I asked him how he knew about me.

'Yad Vashem,' he said.

He had only left Russia some months previously and had begun his searches almost from the moment he got off the plane. If I had doubts about his identity, he had even more about mine. Sue had told him that I was from Resznitz, and he said firmly: 'Is no Newman in Resznitz, not before war,' at which I told him something about my history and explained my change of name.

'You Rhiner's grandson?' he said disbelievingly. 'So you the boy he bring from America. I remember. Your mother die in fire. Very sad. A beautiful girl. Dr Rhiner is not the same when she die. He is good German. Not his wife. She is Nazi. But your mother is beautiful girl. I remember the day you come. Very sad.' He seemed on the verge of tears.

Later in the evening he took out some photos from a small case. 'This is the last time the family is together,' he said. Both Sue and I had seen copies of it before, but we did not interrupt him and he went on to describe each of the figures: 'Here is my older brother, Avner. He is working with my father in business. He is dead. Here is his wife, Hannah, she is dead, and their little boy, Sasha, he is dead. This woman is my sister, Sarah, she is dead. Here is her husband, Vladimir, he is dead. Here is my wife, Fruma, she is dead, and our little boy, Hersh, he is dead. Here is my mother, she is dead and my father, he is dead. Here is me, I am living, and my younger brother, Moshe, he is maybe living, maybe dead. Photograph is taken before he go to America.'

'Have you tried to find him?'

'Sure. I ask everybody, but nobody know, so maybe he is dead.'

'Thirteen people and only two survived,' said Sue. 'Did they all die in the war?'

'No, father die before. Bad heart. Avner die in Russia. Vladimir die in bed. Everybody else die in Resznitz. Moshe is maybe living in America, but maybe he is dead,' and he went on to tell us the whole story.

He was born in 1911, the second son of Sender Marcovitch, and, after studying in some sort of Talmudical college, he entered his father's business. They were traders, dealing mainly in flax and corn, and were joined in time by his brother-in-law, Vladimir

Bergmann, and a certain amount of conflict developed between them because, as he put it: 'Vladi wants very much, very soon,' by which he meant that he had expected to become a partner in the firm as soon as he married into the family. I interrupted to ask if his younger brother, Moshe, was also in the firm. He scratched his massive jaw for a moment before answering.

'Moshe is good-looking but is good-for-nothing – he likes girls too much and when he is nineteen, twenty, father give him money to go to America. Avner thinks is big mistake, Vladi thinks is big mistake. Then I think I also go to America, or maybe Argentine, or Shanghai. Everybody is selling their shops and houses and is going everywhere, and when everybody is selling nobody wants to buy. Vladi says go, go, Avner and I will look after everything. Go. And Fruma also says we go. She has brother in Argentine and he ask us to come. And father is better and we are all packed. I have tickets and we see doctors and we got needles here in arm and all is ready, and we all have new clothes. I am dressed like English gentleman. Then father dies, the war comes and nobody goes. Only Moshe he is gone before and is maybe alive, maybe dead.'

When the Russians occupied Latvia their business, in common with all other such enterprises, was taken over by the local Soviet, but they continued to work for it as state employees for a time until one day, without warning, he and his brother were arrested and sent to Siberia.

'What about your brother-in-law, Vladimir?' asked Sue.

'Wait, I come to Vladi.'

His older brother, Avner, was taken ill in the course of the journey and died a little later. He, Jacob, worked in a labour battalion and managed to survive his ordeals. After the war he made his way back to Latvia. It wasn't easy for there was general chaos, public transport was at a standstill, and he made much of his journey on foot. It took him three years to get back to Dvinsk, and what had been a flourishing Jewish community had been turned into a charnel house, but he found a few survivors who told him that when the Germans came in his family had fled to Resznitz. When he got there he found two other survivors who, like him, had been deported to Russia, and who had returned to search among the ruins for their families, 'but no one is living'.

Yet he did not despair entirely, for he knew that my grandfather had remained in the vicinity throughout the war, and he thought he might have helped them. 'They say he is Nazi. Perhaps he is Nazi, but he help my family before, when the Russians come in.' And he found that he had indeed given them refuge in a large barn on his estate. 'They are there for maybe four months, my mother, my wife, my brother's wife, my sister, and four children – my sister now have little boy. Then one night there is fire, the building is full with straw and everything burns very quick. The forest also burns. In the morning no one is living. I have picture.'

Sue had left us for a minute to see to dinner, and he showed me the picture: eight bodies laid out in a row, three of them children, and all charred beyond recognition. Some of them, indeed, were so badly charred that they had lost all human shape.

When we sat down to dinner none of us could eat. Nor did we find it all that easy to speak. Sue, who had been fighting back tears for much of the evening, suddenly excused herself and fled from the room. She returned a bit later looking pale but composed. We had, while she was out of the room, lapsed into Russian, but we now reverted to English. I asked if he remained in Resznitz after the war.

'No, is nothing in Resznitz. In Dvinsk they tell me Vladimir is Communist big-shot and I go to see him, but he is not in Dvinsk, and I go to Riga and I work in shipping line. I am clerk.'

In Riga he remarried and began to build a new life. A few years later, while working in the port, he saw his brother-in-law coming down the gang-plank of a liner. 'It is many years since I see him but he is not changed, and I see from his shoes and valise that he is very important, because he has leather shoes and leather valise, and he wears a good coat, English stoff. He looks at me and says nothing, and I say I am Jacob, Sarah's brother, but he says nothing and goes away in a taxi; then maybe ten years later I hear he is dead.'

He was looking tired and drawn and Sue asked him if he would like to go to bed.

'No, no,' he said, almost with alarm, 'I must got to hotel, I have medicines in hotel.'

I offered to drive to the hotel and to bring his medicines over, but he wouldn't hear of it, and I drove him into town. He was staying at a seedy little place in Bayswater, and I suggested he would be much more comfortable with us.

'No, no,' he insisted, 'I am going back tomorrow, my wife is worrying about me.'

When I got home Sue was sitting up in bed, red-eyed and bleary-faced.

'That settles it all, doesn't it?' she said, as if talking to herself.

I wasn't sure what she meant.

'I had been coming round to the view that your grandfather's version of events was the true one, that you were the child of the Marcovitch girl and had been rescued from the barn – '

'I couldn't have been. There were no survivors, he said so himself, and showed me a photo of the remains.'

'Where? Here?'

'When you were in the kitchen.'

'And I suppose you scrutinized them all without batting an eyelid? '

I looked at her for a moment wondering what I could have done to bring this on, but she continued:

'I was half convinced, more than half, that you were Jewish, possibly because I wanted to be convinced, but obviously you're not. If you had even one drop of Jewish blood in your veins you couldn't have behaved with such detachment.'

I wasn't aware that I had behaved with detachment. I certainly hadn't felt detached, even though I was myself by now convinced that I could not be Jewish, for Marcovitch had confirmed Carla's story.

I had been deeply moved not only by what Jacob had had to say, but even by his incoherent way of saying it. One did not have to be either a Jew or German to be affected, though in a sense I was both. For the first time – possibly because my origins had been finally established – I became conscious of a feeling of guilt, as if I had personally contributed to the tragedies he described. If I had shown any detachment earlier it was possibly because I had given myself the benefit of every doubt and had suspended myself in an emotional limbo, in which I was neither Jew nor German, nor even, as Sue would have said, perceptibly human. Now I felt German guilt and was near enough to Sue to experience something of her grief. I doubt if I was capable of the sort of emotional display she may have expected, but as it was the deep feelings which stirred me were suddenly tempered by her onslaught, and distress gave way to consternation.

Sue was not herself. Her recovery had obviously not been as lasting nor as complete as I thought, and the visit of Marcovitch had brought on a relapse. She needed two or three Mogadons before getting to sleep, and while she slept I moved all the pills from her bed-side drawer into mine.

When she came downstairs the next morning she was lurching around like a drunk and looked white and ill, and she did not resist when I almost carried her back up and put her to bed.

'We can't go on like this,' she said haltingly. 'We'll have to separate. I can't go on living with you another minute.'

⸺ *Chapter Fifteen* ⸺

Our quest was over, but I was sorry that it had ever begun, for I saw it as a cause of her breakdown. Her doctor thought the same, and when he brought in a psychiatrist he made the same point.

'The mind becomes as vulnerable as the body, especially after a difficult pregnancy,' he explained. 'She was not really in a fit state to cope with the sort of situation this man represented. She seemed to have entered into the lives of the victims as if she was trying to experience their torments – in fact she was experiencing them.'

I thought the matter was rather more complex.

Sue used to make as many jokes about her goyish husband as I did about my Jewish wife, and our exchanges almost became our standard act at parties, yet I sometimes felt that while my asides were (or were meant to be) good-humoured, those of Sue had an underlying bite, as if at bottom she felt that no matter how lightly she treated it her marriage to me had been a cardinal sin. I was, of course, aware of the deep Jewish tribal feeling against exogamy, and I had met people in London and New York whose parents had quite literally mourned for them as if they were dead because they had married out of their faith. I personally was readily accepted by Sue's family, partly, I suppose, because, goy or not, I was preferred to her former spouse, partly because my identity was blurred and, as her mother put it, 'you can never tell – I know people who was Jewish even where they thought they wasn't', from which she concluded that as I had no proof that I wasn't, I almost certainly was. And finally, there was the fact that I was fairly successful and rich. 'If you'd been poor there would have been trouble,' said Sue. I had not actually bought an indulgence but I had, so to speak, acquired one through prosperity.

As a result, Sue gave the impression that she could live as cheerfully with my goyishness as I with her Jewishness, but there were moments of strain which I feared might become more pronounced as our children matured. What, for example, would happen when Jacob became barmitzvah? 'There's nothing to it,' said a colleague who also had a Jewish spouse, 'nothing to it at all. You don't even have to be there. All you have to do is to pay for it, and if your bank balance can take it, you can.' But still the very thought of it filled me with vague apprehensions.

Yet, with all the banter, Sue must – as she said herself – have cherished the hope that somewhere in the course of our researches we might stumble upon some detail which would show that I was a Jew. Instead, we had merely confirmed that I was not only a goy, but a German goy at that, and who should confirm it but a scarred victim of German atrocities, a living witness to all that Jews had been through.

Doreen, who moved in with her own children (and two cats, a dog and a hamster) to look after the household, put a comforting hand on mine and told me not to take her seriously. 'Her old man was like that, so is her brother. They all go off their chump from time to time. The old woman's the only sane one among them, and she's getting senile.'

The first time Sue was in hospital she was there for a week. This time she was in a psychiatric ward for over a month, and only regained something of her spirits after a prolonged spell of analysis. It says something about the state of her health that she submitted herself to such treatment without argument, for she was dismissive of psychiatrists, psychiatry and especially psycho-analysis and described the calling as 'the last resort of cranks and charlatans', or at best would refer to psychiatrists as 'good doctors gone to seed'. At first her misgivings did not seem wholly unfounded for, although she gradually became less tearful, all the sparkle seemed to have gone out of her. She managed to look after the children and cook meals, but seemed to be moved by habit rather than anything as positive as will-power. Psychiatric illnesses may be as serious as any other, but somehow they do not evoke the same ready sympathies as even minor physical illnesses, and I found myself getting impatient with her. The large, bland woman shuffling dolefully round the house was not the woman I had married, but gradually the real Sue began to emerge, as if she had been hibernating within herself, and it was a wonderful thing to behold.

She had been ill from beginning to end for about a year and

both Rich and Giselle had been very understanding throughout; when Sue began to show signs of responding to treatment, Rich suggested that we could both do with a change.

'Not an ocean cruise, if that's what you mean,' I said.

'No, I had something far more drastic in mind. Would you like a spell in New York? I'm sure it would do Sue a lot of good.'

In some ways it did, in others it didn't, for she developed something akin to religious dementia.

I had been slightly apprehensive about the move because Sue, even in her prime (especially in her prime), would not have been considered – to use Rich's expression – 'a good company wife'. Now good company wives are useful anywhere, but indispensable in America, where a man cannot hope to rise to a senior post without a helpmeet worthy of the grade. Sue had a good education and good looks. She was well-read and could be witty, but she was unpredictable. She was no respecter of persons, had a limited sense of occasion, and there was no telling what sort of riposte even a casual remark might provoke. Nor could she be induced to be pleasant, or even civil, to people she didn't care for. She didn't suffer fools gladly and, indeed, didn't always suffer the wise either if, as often happened, she failed to be impressed by their wisdom. She also had an aversion – whether as hostess or guest – to what she called 'compulsory entertainment'. Then there was the matter of dress. Sue had expensive taste, but was an expensive accumulator rather than an expensive dresser, for she often picked up 'a little something' which took her fancy, but she rarely fancied it long enough to wear it, or tired of it after donning it once or twice, and we had to have a large house if only to make room for her accumulations. She had some magnificent evening gowns and, when she did make the effort to dress up, she could look not only regal but overwhelming. In the main, however, she was content to romp around in jeans, and with her unruly mass of hair, which reached her shoulders at the back and sometimes obscured her vision at the front, she looked like a superannuated teenager. She had changed in some respects as a result of her illness. Her penchant for up-market scruffiness, however, remained the same, but unfortunately she could no longer get away with it, for, partly because of her age, and partly because she had been – and to an extent still was – on drugs, she had put on weight. It troubled me rather more than her in

197

London, but I wondered how she would take it in New York.

In the event, she took it in her stride, and even joked about it. There was a reception for us shortly after we arrived, and she remarked on the neat figures and dainty shapes of the other wives. 'I don't know how they do it. The women of fifty look like thirty, and the women of thirty have the slim hips and rosy complexions of teenagers.'

Having reconciled herself to her size, however, she began to assume the persona that went with it, and became almost a caricature of the Yiddishe Mamma. She used to be an omnivorous reader and would go through *The Times* and *Guardian*, the weekend reviews and a book or two in the course of a week, and her conversation, if occasionally foul-mouthed, used to be informed and witty, but her talk now was all of nurseries and schools and of childhood ailments, and recipes and food and the cost of everything, so that when she came out with a word like 'fuck' – which she occasionally did – I thought I could hear the voice of the Sue I first knew and loved and felt like embracing her.

We rented a house on Long Island Sound, as spacious as ours, with large rooms and a large garden, but there the similarities ended. For a start, most of the rooms seemed to be bathrooms and it had a vast, ultra-modern kitchen with dials and controls which hummed, whether in use or not, like a power-station, and at first Sue was afraid to set foot in it. The furniture too was ultra-modern and better to look at than to sit in (and, on reflection, it was not all that great to look at), but the surroundings were lovely, and we were part of an estate which included its own swimming-pool, sauna, squash-court and tennis court, so we could not feel that we had been short-changed by the move.

Sue's size may have been one reason for her drift towards religion. The other was our son, Jacob – or Jackie, as we usually called him. He was now four and, on the insistence of his mother, we sent him to a local Jewish nursery, partly because it was within easy reach (as were others), partly because his mother wanted him to have Jewish friends. He hadn't been there a month before he began to ask why we didn't light candles on Friday night, or attend synagogue on Saturday morning.

We were perfectly happy to comply with the candles, but on Saturday mornings I played golf while Sue normally pottered around in the garden. But I soon discovered that she was leading a secret life, that she had bought herself a hat – a *hat!* – something she had never previously worn in her life, and was attending synagogue with our son.

In due course we were invited by a neighbouring family to a Friday night meal. The setting was splendid: silver candelabras, English china, Irish crystal. The meal was good; the wine, thick, sweet and heavy, was execrable; and the conversation, which ranged mostly round the school, the synagogue, the Rabbi and his sermons and the spread of anti-Semitism, matched the wine.

'We'll have to invite them back, and you know what that means, don't you?' said Sue. What it meant was another set of cutlery and crockery and the separation of meat and milk. I could still have cream in my coffee after a meat meal, but I had to have it furtively in my study, as if I was giving myself a quick fix of heroin. I felt like a stranger in my own house.

Then I began to discover other people in a similar plight. One actually worked in the bank, another worked for our auditors, a third was a lawyer, a fourth was an Italian opera singer who had a home not far from us. We formed a sort of goyim anonymous and would meet from time to time for a drink and to exchange horror stories.

My bank colleague said that in the olden days when a Jewish girl married out of the faith she stayed out, and words like synagogue, religion, kosher, Rabbi, were never mentioned except by way of execration. Now they seemed to want to have their cake and eat it.

'When I first brought Sarah home and my mother saw she was Jewish she wasn't too worried, until she found she was religious. "She'll make your life a misery," she told me, "she'll want you to convert, she'll drag you to synagogue." Well, it wasn't quite as bad as that. She didn't even suggest I should convert, for she knew my feelings about that, and she hasn't dragged me to synagogue. But Jesus, have you ever eaten kosher meat? It's salted and washed, washed and salted and watered till it's drained of any taste it could have. It's not so bad when I'm in town, and I can sneak out for a meal, but when we're on holiday with the kids I forget what a full-blooded steak tastes like.'

Alvin, the auditor, had a worse complaint. 'I don't mind my wife's cooking, especially her fish. I don't even mind her meat. It's her relatives I can't stand. I've got a father and a mother, four sisters and a brother, and if it wasn't for Christmas I wouldn't see them from one end of the year to the other, but her family, they're always either eating with us, sleeping with us, or both. I've been married twelve years and I don't think we've had our house to ourselves yet.'

At which Franklin, the lawyer, interjected, 'That's not so bad. When my in-laws come round, they expect not only free bed and board, but free legal advice.'

But the worst horror story came from Carlo, the opera singer. He had married a girl, an heiress, who came from a religious home. She did not insist that he convert but her father did, which he was perfectly prepared to do, and he was undergoing the necessary religious instruction when he was told that there would come a point when he would have to be circumcised. 'And I say to my father-in-law, Signor, I say, you go too far. My soul I sell to anybody, but my body she is sacred.'

After which, I felt that I was getting off lightly. Nevertheless, I was beginning to feel, after a while in New York, that the whole world was becoming Jewish, and Orthodox Jewish at that, until I discovered that the process was not all one way. I had a secretary, a pert little girl called Alice, who was all dark eyes and dimples. Her father was a Rabbi, and she had been sent to a girls' seminary in the belief that at seventeen or eighteen she would assume the role of the Jewish mother throughout the generations and settle down and breed. She had other plans and, after winning a scholarship to Barnard, she joined the bank, where she was regarded with something like awe as one of the most efficient people around. In fact, the general refrain in the building when one encountered some insuperable problem seemed to be: 'Leave it to Alice.'

'She's less of a secretary than a boss,' someone warned me. 'You have to have everything carefully thought out before asking her to take a letter, no umming or erring, and you can't send her out to do the occasional bit of shopping for the wife. It would offend her sense of corporate loyalty to be engaged in anything wasteful.'

I thus regarded her with apprehension, but I quickly came to admire her many qualities, her alacrity, her presence of mind and her ability to respond to events without waiting for directions, so that there were moments when I felt almost redundant. She was good and she knew she was good, but did not flaunt her knowledge. And she was good to look at. Impeccably dressed and impeccably groomed, the mere sight of her was enough to brighten a grey morning. She also had good legs, which she rarely hesitated to display and, when taking dictation, she would sit up against me, as if she was hard of hearing, and this sometimes impaired my sequence of thought.

Secretaries were regarded as fair game in Manhattan, but I was nervous of entanglements, and besides I was conscious of my role as semi-ambassador from head office and felt bound to be on my best behaviour. But towards the end of the year we had a rather lavish office party and I found myself sitting next to her with a bottle in my hand and a funny hat on my head and an arm round her shoulders.

'It's taken you a long time to get round to this,' she said.

'Not at all, I've only been here fifteen months.'

'I get it. You work on the instalment plan. A year to get your arm round my shoulders, three round my waist, four to get your hand on my knee. By the time you start getting warm I'll be too old to enjoy it.' She looked at me with an amused expression not unmixed with derision. 'You're afraid of me, aren't you?'

'I was afraid – '

'I don't mean Alice, the super-secretary, I mean Alice, the woman. I noticed the way you keep looking up my skirt, half yearning to put your hand up but more than half afraid that if you did you mightn't get it back.'

'You're perfectly right about the yearning, but what you call fear is nothing more than natural restraint.'

'I find such restraint unnatural.'

'Does every chap you work for try his hand?'

'Some try their hand, some their foot, not a few have tried their heads. I sometimes have the feeling that the male sexual organ is becoming obsolete in America, but I work mainly with senior staff and perhaps they have good reason to keep their privates private.'

'I promise you, if I should ever throw off restraint I shall hide nothing from you.'

'Don't misunderstand me. I wouldn't want you to feel obliged to rape me or anything like that – '

Our cosy tête-à-tête was interrupted by the intrusion of a large, red-faced man. 'Forgive me pulling rank, old boy,' he said, 'but it's against the rules of the game to work on your own secretary at a Christmas party. You can't monopolize this little woman both at work and play.'

Shortly after the New Year I was dictating a letter to her when our eyes met, and we both smiled and both knew what we were smiling about.

'Do I do it now?' I asked.

'Only if you feel like it.'

'I always feel like it.'

'In which case you'll have to come round to my place after work.'

'You only function after office hours?'

'How else?'

'I am sorry. I thought we were talking about spontaneous lust.'

We eventually did get into bed with each other, not so much out of lust, or even curiosity, as the feeling that it was something we had to get over and done with before we could enjoy normal relations. I was afraid that it might lead to emotional entanglements, but the whole incident was almost clinical in character. She told me, even as she was undressing, that she had a regular boy-friend, and, indeed, there was a photo of him by her bed, which may have been intended to put me off my stride, but it didn't. We embraced, we stripped, fused and parted, and when we met again the next morning it was as if nothing had happened.

Sue was unwell at the time, and I should have experienced some guilt feelings; if I didn't it was probably due to the fact that she had engaged a coloured girl so attractive and voluptuous that I half suspect she was brought in as bait, and I believe that by yielding to a lesser temptation I was able to guard myself against the greater one.

While not unhappy in America, we encountered difficulties we would not, I think, have had to face in London. When Jackie was six, Sue decided to send him to a Jewish school in the neighbourhood. It was within walking distance and, moreover, it had a good name, and was set in pleasant surroundings, but about a month after he started he came back in tears and asked if it were true that he was a goy. Sue wiped away his tears and said it was all nonsense.

'You know I'm Jewish, you know my mother is Jewish, you – '

'But is daddy Jewish?' At which there was an awkward silence.

'N-no,' she said after some thought, 'but daddies don't have to be,' which he seemed to accept as a perfectly reasonable arrangement, but Sue returned with a new vehemence to a matter she had raised before. She wanted me to convert to Judaism.

'We've been through all that before, I know, but the last time we discussed it I wasn't the least religious myself – '

'In the *least* religious? You were anti-religious, a blasphemer, a virulent deo-phobe.'

'I've changed.'

'Yes, but I haven't, and even if I had, I'm not going to become a Jew simply because our son has been needled by young bigots. On the contrary, if such bigotry is part of the faith it's a good reason to stay outside it.'

I felt America was partly to blame. England was nominally a Christian country, but its character was largely pagan, whilst America, though nominally secular, was steaming with religious fervour, and if a thorough-going atheist like my wife could be affected, what would not a prolonged stay do to our children?

I had initially been asked to go out for a three-year stint. When it was up Rich asked me to stay on a fourth. 'You've been doing a first-class job,' he said, 'and it won't be easy to replace you.'

I assured him that on that score, certainly, there would be no difficulties, for I had an assistant called Dubin, a Cambridge chap, who had only been with me for about six months but who seemed perfectly capable of holding the fort and, if necessary, of taking over altogether.

'He's very young and inexperienced,' said Rich.

'He's learning fast. If he has a fault at all, it is that he's a little too eager, but he'll relax as he gets older. I can also pick a winner, and I assure you Dubin will be all right.'

Dubin was not, in fact, all that young, and I suspect what lay behind Rich's reservation was the fact that Mrs Dubin – pale, earnest and withdrawn – was not 'a good company wife', but that, in my opinion, was no great handicap.

Apart from the domestic reasons which made me anxious to get back to London, I found New York too restless, shrill, cosmopolitan, colourful, exciting, and perhaps, at thirty-eight, I was already too old for it. Also, I had been rather afraid of Alice, for although I was glad to have her around, she tended to provoke yearnings to do something wild and irresponsible, not so much during working hours but during weekends when I was, so to speak, trapped within the bosom of my family.

On Saturday mornings, Sue and the children went religiously to synagogue and I, as religiously, had a round of golf, but the golf club itself was a sort of secular synagogue. Most of the members were Jewish, and the bar did a roaring trade in Coca-Cola and chilled orange juice.

When I got home I had to change into banker's grey because we usually had guests for lunch and the talk was all of synagogue, Rabbis and schools. It was at such times that I became conscious of the stirrings, and it seemed to me that I was yearning not so much to run away with Alice as to run away from Sue. But even that wasn't quite the case, for I loved my wife, or at least the woman my wife used to be, and ideally I would have liked to take her out of her kosher, matronly self. And again, it must have been the very atmosphere of America which had induced such thoughts, for they died the moment we returned to England.

If I didn't always understand my wife, I am not sure if I quite understood myself, because, though I was troubled by our own Sabbatarian meals, I enjoyed those with her mother, and it was not merely because I liked her cooking, for Sue was also a good cook. I suppose it was because I was a guest in her mother's house and I could regard the whole scene as an observer, whereas at home I was required to be a participant. Moreover, Sabbatarianism and all that went with it seemed to go naturally with the old woman's personality and surroundings, whereas in my own home it seemed artificial, possibly because it was, in the last resort, the home of an unrepentant goy, and the fact that my wife happened to be a repentant Jewess was not enough to alter the situation.

Before we left New York we had a long argument about the education of the children. Sue wanted to send Jackie to a Jewish school. Her case for doing so in New York was that it was the best school in the area. There was, in fact, no Jewish school within reasonable distance of our London home, and she said: 'I don't mind delivering and collecting. I like to get out of the house first thing in the morning. Besides, as you know yourself, Jackie likes being in a Jewish school.'

'Even though they bait him about his goyish father?'

'Oh, that was just some stupid child of a stupid mother.'

'What makes you think there are no stupid children or stupid mothers in London?'

'I promise you, if that sort of incident should recur, I shall remove the boy from the school without a moment's hesitation.'

It recurred sooner than either of us expected, in the very first term in fact, and we moved the boy to a local prep school. He hadn't been there a month before he came home in tears saying he was teased because he was Jewish. I began to feel that goyim who marry Jewesses shouldn't have children, but we couldn't keep moving the boy from school to school every half-term, and we decided he would have to learn to live with his disabilities, and when our daughter turned five, we sent her to the same school.

With two growing children and living-in help, our home began to feel rather cramped, or so Sue claimed. It seemed a spacious enough home to me, but I think she had acquired the American habit of moving house from time to time, if only to assure oneself that one had come up in the world, or even by way of a change. There was a time when women would soothe their jaded tempers by buying themselves a new hat; now they bought a new house. I did not, however, discourage her, for I was involved in a great deal of air travel and she agreed to look for something within easy reach of Heathrow; but then, in the middle of her searches, her mother became critically ill and she virtually moved in to look after her while I remained at home with the children and the au-pair.

It was not a satisfactory arrangement, for I had to be away a lot, and we moved our home temporarily to Brondesbury Park. The irony of the situation was not lost on Sue. She had spent the better part of her life running away from her mother, and now, when she might have made good her escape, she became her prisoner. The illness was never diagnosed and, for a time, it seemed as if it might prove fatal, for her breathing was erratic and at night her temperature climbed to unheard-of heights and, although she pulled through, she was no longer the same person. Where she had been elderly but robust, she was now old and senile. Fond though I was of the woman she had been, I had very

205

little sentimentality about the woman she had become, and I suggested to Sue that we should put her in a home. Her brothers agreed and undertook to pay their share of the costs, but Sue wouldn't hear of it.

'She would die in a home.'

'She's not very much alive here.'

'But at least she's in familiar surroundings, among familiar people.'

I wasn't at all sure if she was in the least conscious either of her surroundings or of the people who surrounded her. She didn't know who I was and kept referring to me as Albert, and did not always recognize Sue, and spent most of the day propped up in a chair, dropping in and out of sleep.

One evening, Sue was upstairs with the children and I was reading a paper when I became aware that I was being subjected to critical scrutiny, and I looked up to see the old woman staring at me and almost quivering with agitation.

'Is anything the matter?'

'The matter? I'll say there is. Just you wait till father hears of it. And he will you know, because I'll tell him.'

I muttered some words of apology, which, however, failed to mollify her.

'It's no good saying you're sorry now. Father will hear of it. See if he won't.'

Her voice was oddly firm and assertive, even threatening, though the threat lay in the probability that she could continue like this for years. Sue, of course, bore the main brunt of her senility. I could understand the pangs of conscience she had felt about a father she adored, but not about a mother she scorned.

'Your brothers would be perfectly happy to put her in a home,' I said.

'My brothers would be perfectly happy to put me in a home as well,' she said. 'Let's not talk about my brothers.'

The old woman cast a blight over our existence. It was difficult for us to go out, and impossible to entertain. She had a large house, but she would seek out our company wherever we were, following us from the dining-room to the drawing-room, to the kitchen, and even to the bedroom. She had a television in her own room, but preferred to join us downstairs to offer a commentary on what was happening on screen. I think it was the

206

television which kept her going, especially late-night films, and her memory, if faulty in every other respect, was faultless when it came to recognizing old film-stars, and she not only knew who they were, but what they'd been up to. 'Veronica Lake – looks so nice, doesn't she? Threw her mother out of her own home, the bitch . . . Rita Hayworth, wasn't she a picture, *nebbich* . . . I don't like to think what's happened to her. It's all those husbands, you see. Marry once, twice, three times, but she's never stopped marrying . . . Look, Lana Turner. She's got a nerve showing her face on television. Did I tell you . . .?'

If she could have been offered a constant diet of vintage Hollywood, she might have remained lucid, but when we switched off she became querulous, acrimonious and paranoic. 'Wait till father hears of it' became her constant refrain, and we all speculated on what it was that father would hear of. She also carried a small box of hair-clips, safety-pins, odd ear-rings and other bits of junk which she referred to as her jewellery and would never be parted from because she feared we had designs on them. (She did have several valuable pieces of jewellery, but they were in a bank vault.) She insisted on doing her own cooking because she was afraid we might poison her, which we wouldn't have minded but for the fact that she set herself alight on several occasions and once nearly set fire to the house. When I prised the matches from her grasp and put the gas-lighter out of reach, she warned me in no uncertain terms that 'father would hear of it'.

Sue began to lose weight rapidly after we moved in with her mother, which I at first found reassuring, but when she continued to lose weight I found it worrying, for she was becoming gaunt. The only comfort I could draw from the situation was that with all her responsibilities she rarely had time to set foot in synagogue, and when it came to Yom Kippur I told her she didn't have to fast, because looking after her mother was penance enough.

One morning, Sue phoned me at the office to say that her mother had disappeared, which I might have treated as good news but for the certainty that she would reappear. In fact, she was found wandering down Kilburn High Road in her carpet slippers, and Sue was able to reclaim her from the local police station none the worse for her brief adventure. She lost all sense of time, and took to shuffling round the house at all hours of the day or night. Once she wandered into our bedroom and nearly caught us *in flagrante delicto*. Another time, she wandered out into the night. She was, by then, known to the police, who picked her up, wrapped her in a blanket and brought her home, at three in the morning.

I marvelled at Sue's toughness and resolve, but she couldn't go on like this and I feared she might have another nervous breakdown. I told her finally and firmly that if she would not consent to letting her mother go into a home I would have both her and her mother certified. By now she was no longer disposed to argue, and neither was anyone else in the family.

It was the ever-resourceful Doreen who undertook the formidable task of delivering the old woman into safe custody. She told her she was taking her on holiday and helped her pack, and she went quite willingly, even cheerfully.

'I'll have my hair done first. I always have my hair done before I go on holiday.'

And Doreen took her to the hairdresser, where she had a champagne rinse, and a manicure for good measure.

'Am I going to Bournemouth?' asked the old woman. 'I like Bournemouth.'

'No, mother, you're going to a quiet place in the country.'

'The country? I don't know if I like the country. They're full of old women, country hotels.'

'But it's got large grounds and a lovely garden.'

'That should be nice. I like gardens. All my friends have sold their houses and moved into flats. I can't understand how they can do it. I couldn't live without a garden. It has a large garden, has it?'

'Very large.'

'That should be nice. I like gardens.'

And off she went with much kissing of children, grandchildren and cats and dogs, and a peace descended on the large house so profound that my ears rang with it.

I suppose we should have run for it, but we tarried and, late one night as we were preparing for bed, a large car pulled up outside and the old woman emerged in the company of a policewoman and two police officers. She had hitched a lift with a lorry and the driver had taken her to the nearest police-station.

'Father will hear of this,' she said.

I felt that Sue had done everything that daughterly duty required and a bit more and, at my insistence, we moved out and Doreen (plus menagerie) moved in.

'She'll do the old woman in, I promise you she will,' said Sue. 'That'll solve all our problems.'

I wasn't sure what she did, and I never made it my business to enquire, but a few nights later the old woman died quietly in her sleep.

—— *Chapter Sixteen* ——

When the father died, the family had remained in mourning for a week. That, however, was in deference to the old woman's wishes; now that the old woman herself was dead, they proposed to remain in mourning for a night. Sue, however, would not hear of it. 'Do what you like,' she said, 'but I'm sitting *shiva* for a week,' and, thus shamed, her brothers had to follow suit.

And so she and her brothers sat on low chairs in mourning, while Dora and Doreen came in to look after them and the many visitors who came to comfort them. They chose the mother's house as the venue, which was just as well, for the torrent of visitors was unending and continued by night and by day. It hadn't occurred to me that one small, unremarkable woman could have so many friends and acquaintances and that they should all wish to honour her memory. After grandfather's funeral five or six colleagues and senior government officials came to offer their condolences, and that was about it. There were about a dozen people at Carla's funeral, none of whom I had met before and who dispersed almost as soon as she was in the ground. The Jews took death rather more seriously. Sue had not been on particularly close terms with her brothers, but being forced into each other's company for a week and suffering a common loss, they seemed to develop a new relationship. Cousins and second cousins twice-removed, some of whom they had not seen for years, descended from remote ends of London. Old quarrels were forgotten and old friendships renewed.

'If it wasn't for funerals,' said Sue, 'half of the family wouldn't be on speaking terms with the other half.' The whole experience seemed therapeutic. Sue had put her book aside as a result of her illness, and had seemed nervous of getting back to it (apart, of course, from the fact that her mother's condition had left her without the peace of mind to do so). But once the period of mourning was over she returned to her work with a new determination, and within a matter of months she had completed the first draft.

She asked me to go over it for her, which I did with pleasure. I marvelled at her skill. She was a natural writer, and brought out the many complexities of my grandfather's character without, however, losing herself, or the reader, in excessive psycho-analysis. She touched on my part of the story in rather greater detail than I would have wished, but it was all relevant to an understanding of the man. She was particularly perceptive in her treatment of his last letter to me, and regarded it as the one instance where he had allowed the wish to be father to the thought. But she did not think of him as flawless, and found him unimaginative, pompous, censorious and xenophobic – a fairly typical German who, while not subscribing to Hitlerism, felt no compulsion to question or challenge it, even from his secure Latvian haven.

I thought she gave excessive prominence to his work for German Intelligence, and that she had exaggerated his import-ance and influence. As a good German he no doubt gave the *Abwehr* what help he could, but he was no master-spy. What was perhaps a more serious fault was that she quoted early family letters with excessive frequency and at excessive length, for they were not particularly relevant, and as the book was, in any case, rather on the long side, I suggested a number of cuts. She rejected them all. 'Wilhelminian Germany', she said, 'was almost as interesting as Edwardian England, and the letters are full of it,' and the publisher shared her view.

'I had almost despaired of ever receiving this book,' he said, 'but it was worth waiting for. I had only asked for the story of one rather paradoxical individual, and she captured a whole epoch.'

And, for a moment, I was envious of my own wife.

The following year I turned forty, and by way of a birthday present Sue gave me a portrait of myself in oils. I had not thought of myself, and indeed had not been thought of, as a young man for years, but the portrait bore unkind intimations of middle-age and a *gravitas* which I hope had more to do with my person than my personality, for I had gained weight, and whereas I had been tall, thin, even cadaverous, I was now large and perhaps even portly. If I was only furry, said our daughter, I would look like a bear. It was a full-length portrait and I am fairly certain Sue had commissioned it because she wanted something large to go over the fireplace of our new home, which was a huge, ramshackle Victorian edifice, overlooking the Thames at Taplow, a sort of poor man's Cliveden.

Her mother had divided her various effects among her family, and had left Sue the furniture, which she promptly sold. With the help of her sisters-in-law, she ransacked the auction rooms and antique shops of London and the Home Counties to fill the reception rooms with Victorian furnishings and furniture, and what I had fondly thought of as a home began to resemble a department of the Victoria and Albert Museum. Yet, after regarding it all with distaste, and then with tolerance, I gradually began to like it. I only put my foot down when she began to display an excessive interest in my wardrobe with suggestions that I would look good in a Prince Albert coat.

'And perhaps a stove-pipe hat?' I said.

'No,' she said, 'high hats look silly, but long coats give dignity to a man, so does a beard.'

I rather feared that I might return one day to find her in crinolines, and she did have an evening dress which would not have been out of place in a Victorian drawing-room, but, in the main, she continued to romp around in jeans.

The place was almost ready for occupation when she discovered that there wasn't a synagogue for miles around, and she became strangely agitated, as if the absence of a synagogue would leave our new home unhallowed and unblessed. She found that there was a synagogue in Reading, but it was not within walking distance, and she was quite adamant that she wouldn't travel on the Sabbath, at least not to synagogue. I couldn't see that there was any urgency in the matter, for we had sent Jack to Clifton College, which had a Jewish House. As for Gertie, it was my impression that Jews had never paid much attention to the religious upbringing of their daughters. Sue had received no Jewish education at all, but she was determined that her daughter should do better, and found a retired clergyman, a Revd Pilchig, a dear little man, with smiling eyes and a tiny beard, to give her private tuition. At first, he travelled up from London by train, and when he found that too tiring Sue installed him in a small, nearby cottage and engaged him virtually as family chaplain.

But that was not the end of it. Jews, I discovered, have a ready instinct for the presence of other Jews. She found any number in and around Taplow, and got the Revd Pilchig to conduct services on Friday nights and Saturday mornings in our lounge, so that even if we couldn't go to synagogue the synagogue, so to speak, came to us. I didn't actually take part in the services, but I lit candles, put out lights, ran errands, and otherwise made myself useful, and I began to feel that any Jewish woman who wanted to keep a really kosher establishment should have a goy as a husband.

I was also deriving more satisfaction, or at least suffering less frustration, from my work in the bank than I had in the recent past. I was widely praised for my stint in New York, but although I had received an increase in salary on my return, it was not what I would have called promotion. I was a senior executive, on the board of several subsidiaries of the bank, but there was no obvious prospect of climbing the next rung to the main board. I was not an Eissenmacher, and being an ex-would-be Eissenmacher was no recommendation. I did not have the ability of Rich, nor a company wife like Giselle. I was in a rut, and a colleague by the name of Cobham said to me: 'I can't help noticing that you don't come into the office while the cleaners are still about and that you leave with the general stampede at five, that you avoid the avoidable foreign trips and when you do go, you stay away for two or three days instead of the mandatory fortnight. Moreover, you've put on weight. In fact, you show all the symptoms of the happily married man. You're looking at one now, and if you look hard enough you may see yourself twenty years hence.'

And I looked, and saw a heavily built figure with greying hair, a bushy moustache and sad eyes whom the secretaries called Tapper, to distinguish him from another middle-aged executive they called Pincher, though Pincher could sometimes tap and Tapper sometimes pinched, and both seemed to spend much of their day doing *The Times* crossword. ('It's the principal preoccupation of the staff,' Rich once observed, 'but any man who can complete the crossword in the course of a morning is well worth his hire.') Looking at him, I could see all that lay ahead – home to a couple of stiff whiskies, a good dinner and then two hours' sleep in front of the television screen before walking the dog and retiring finally for the night. Beyond that lay a small place on the south coast, or perhaps the Costa Brava, old age, infirmity and the sleep of sleeps. When he was younger, Cobham had lived for his children; now his most active time of the year was January, when he buried himself in travel literature. He had had a 'good war' and had emerged with the rank of major and the Military Cross, and he planned his annual holiday as if it were a military operation. His wife was active in the Royal Society for the Prevention of Cruelty to Animals, and she already had an OBE. 'She'll be a Dame yet,' he said, but he had no such ambitions for himself. I, too, was deriving more satisfaction from my wife's career than my own.

But then things began to move. The Chairman, who had often spoken of plans to retire to write the centenary history of the bank, actually announced that he would stand down. There was an Eissenmacher cousin on the board whom we thought would be his successor, but he was passed over in favour of Rich. Rich had told me more than once that they would one day have to reorganize the whole structure of the bank and, although he promised me nothing, his rise to the top gave me the hope that I might eventually rise with him. It was nothing more than a hope, but it added excitement to an area of life which had almost degenerated into routine. I began to experience a happiness which made me feel almost guilty. I would ask myself what I had done to deserve it and kept bracing myself for some incident or disappointment which might end, or at least disrupt, it.

Then one night I was sitting reading when I was startled by the sound of the phone. I don't know why I should have been, for it was hardly an unfamiliar sound, but there seemed to be an oddly menacing tone to it, an intimation of bad news.

It was Marcovitch. I almost dropped the receiver when I heard his voice. I couldn't understand why I was alarmed. Was I afraid for Sue? For myself? Was it the emotional havoc which his last visit wrought? He must have sensed the tremor in my voice, for he asked:

'Is all right?'

'Yes, we're all fine,' I said haltingly.

Sue came in at that point and when she heard who it was she asked him to come and stay for the night.

'No,' he said, 'is too late.'

'Come tomorrow.'

But he had arranged to fly on to New York in the morning and we agreed to have breakfast with him at Heathrow airport.

Sue seemed totally undisturbed about the prospect of the meeting, but it gave me a sleepless night, and I thought I could understand why. First, although Sue seemed to have recovered completely from her breakdown she could be unpredictable and I was not at all sure how she would react to a further encounter with Marcovitch, and for my part I was afraid that it could lead to the reopening of an issue which I had thought had been finally settled. There were, of course, some still unresolved questions, such as the identity of my father, but I felt no overwhelming compulsion to resolve them. I was no longer afraid of the past (insofar as I ever was) but I was becoming a little bored with it.

We both got a shock when we saw him, for he had lost the sight of one eye, and his massive head was shaking.

'I am flying to big meeting of Jews from Dvinsk. My wife isn't letting me go and I am running away,' he said, in tones which made him sound like a schoolboy on an escapade. He didn't seem fit to travel and Sue urged him to spend a few days with us before resuming his journey.

'No,' he said, 'the meeting is tomorrow. I must go now. I come and stay when I come back.'

'We should have made more of an effort to stop him,' said Sue after we saw him through to passport control. 'He's a sick man.'

'If his wife couldn't stop him I don't see how we could,' I said, but when I got to the office I phoned Alice to keep an eye on him.

She was mystified by the call.

'Who is he? What is he?'

'A sick and tragic old man.'

'So what's he coming here for? What do you think I am, some sort of nanny?' But she nevertheless agreed to pick him up.

Later that day, as we were about to sit down for dinner, the phone went. It was Alice. I somehow knew it would be. Marcovitch had arrived in a state of collapse and had been rushed to hospital. I immediately began phoning around for a flight, while Sue packed my bags.

'Do you think I should come with you?' she asked. 'I feel oddly responsible for him – as if he's a member of my own family.'

I felt exactly the same, but there was no point in us both going.

215

When I reached the hospital, he was fast asleep with his mouth open, and deathly pale. I remained at his bedside for over an hour before he stirred, and when he opened his eyes he blinked at me without recognition, and even with something like alarm, but he seemed to relax slightly when I began speaking to him in Russian. Alice had already taken the liberty of going through his papers as soon as he was in hospital and phoned his wife, only to find that the poor woman was herself an invalid and could hardly move. We now looked through his papers again to see who his contacts were in America.

He had a whole list of names, addresses and telephone numbers. Several of them were out of date, three of the people were dead, and of the others contacted only two sounded as if the name of Marcovitch meant anything to them; both arrived at the bedside at the same time, stout, breathless, elderly men in tight suits, carrying baskets of fruit. They both chatted to him in Yiddish, which he could take in, but he couldn't answer, and they both turned to me to enquire about his state of health. They must have taken me for his doctor, and I explained I was from Latvia myself, and that I knew his family.

'How could you?' said one. 'It's foity years since dey was all killed. You don't look much more than foity yourself.'

'My family was friendly with them.'

'What's your name?'

'Newman.'

'And what was it before that?'

'Rhiner.'

'I don't know no Rhiners, do you, Sammy?'

'No.'

'But I didn't know everybody. Dey was princes, de Marcovitches, you know, princes. I woiked for dem. I was lucky. I wanted to better myself, and you couldn't do dat with de Marcovitches, all de best jobs went to de family, so I came here. If my family had been princes, what happened to dem would have happened to me.'

'Do you know what we called dis guy?' said the other man. 'Samson. He was as strong as any tree oder guys put together. I wanted to marry his sister, but she wouldn't look at me. I didn't have class, you see. Well, maybe I didn't have class, but I had *mazel*, which is why I'm alive and she isn't.'

216

I asked them if they knew his brother Moshe.

'Moishele, sure, who didn't know him? He was de broder dey didn't talk about. But listen, Sender Marcovitch had five kids – '

'Six – '

'Five.'

'What are you telling me? Dere was Avner, right, den Jacob, den Moishele and the two girls. You're right. He had five.'

'But I only knew of one girl,' I said.

'Two. One married Yuri Bergmann's son, the big *sheigetz*. De oder married – well, if you don't know it's better you shouldn't know.'

'You mean she married out of the faith?'

'She didn't even marry – he was married already. Happens all de time dese days, but den, in de toities? It nearly killed de old man. She was de oldest. The apple of his eye, a queen. De long and de short of it is, he spoilt her. No one was good enough for her. De joke was, he was waiting for de King of England, what was his name, to propose. And de guy she went off wit was no prince. What's de old saying? Pride comes before de fall.'

I pressed them for details, but they could only offer rumour, and conflicting rumour at that. One said she had had a child, the other was sure she hadn't. One believed she had eventually married the man, the other thought she hadn't. But on certain things they did agree. She was about twenty at the time and was taking voice lessons, when she ran off with her teacher, a married man.

'He wasn't even Jewish,' they whispered in unison.

Neither of them were sure what had happened to her but one added:

'What could have happened? What happened to everybody? Living wit a goy didn't help, not wit de Nazis.'

Jacob had suffered a fairly serious heart-attack and the doctors thought he might have to remain in hospital for weeks, but they didn't reckon with his will-power or resilience, and he was on his feet in a matter of days. He was embarrassed to be a cause of inconvenience.

'Is first time I'm in hospital,' he said. 'I have bullet here, and here, and break head, an arm and leg, but I'm never in hospital.'

He had hardly opened his eyes when a stern-looking woman with a clipboard in her hand came round to settle the question of payments. Alice had posted a bond which had now expired and I assured her I would meet any further expenses he might incur. She looked me up and down. I had arrived in my Sunday clothes – a turtle-neck sweater and rather threadbare jacket – and she seemed unimpressed by my creditworthiness.

'Do you know what it costs to stay here?'

I didn't, and when she told me I almost became a patient myself, but I picked up the phone and arranged a transfer through the New York branch of the bank, which seemed to reassure her, and in a way I was grateful for the opportunity to make amends.

It was of course impossible for Marcovitch to attend the Dvinsk reunion, but the reunion in a sense came to him, for once it became known that he was in hospital he had a constant succession of callers. They came laden with baskets and hampers and bouquets and bottles until his room began to resemble a provision store. They chatted endlessly, though their voices not infrequently faded out into tears. They opened bottles of vodka and drank over old times. Doctors and nurses who tried to check the press of visitors and the length of their stay were ignored. A harassed hospital administrator threatened to call the police.

'This is getting to be like an Irish wake,' he complained.

Marcovitch pushed a glass of vodka into his hand and tried to calm him down.

'Here is my friends. Forty years I am not seeing them. Maybe I am not seeing them again never.'

That night he had a relapse and died the next morning. I flew with his body to Israel.

There was a surprisingly large turn-out for the funeral. Most of the people seemed to know each other, but there were several individuals who didn't look part of the crowd and stood a little away from the rest. Among them was a slight, well-dressed figure in dark glasses and with a broad, flowery band to his straw hat, which looked too colourful for the occasion, and, to my surprise, when the body was in the ground he stepped forward, took out a small prayer-book from his pocket and said *kaddish*. When he was finished, I was moved by curiosity to ask who he was.

'Me? I'm his brother, Moshe,' he said.

I stood looking at him, dumbfounded.

'His brother, Moshe,' he repeated. 'He had two brothers, an older one, Avner, and a younger one, Moshe. I'm Moshe. But who are you?'

It was too complicated a matter to discuss amidst the tombstones under the blazing sun. The widow had invited several of us back to her flat and I offered him a lift in my car.

'No, no, no,' he almost screamed, 'I had a word with her before, but it's all right, you go without me.'

We drove instead to the Intercontinental Hotel nearby, where he made a phone call before rejoining me.

'You staying here?' he asked.

'No, I'm in the King David.'

'The King David, huh? You must be doing all right. But you still haven't told me who you are. Where are you from?'

'Resznitz.'

'Resznitz, did you say? You don't look like you're from Resznitz. You don't talk like you're from Resznitz. What's your name?'

I thought for a moment of giving him my grandfather's name, but felt that it was perhaps too soon for such revelations.

'Newman.'

'It must have been Neumann, or something like that. I don't remember nobody called Neumann, but I left Latvia two or three years before the war, and my memory is not what it was. You knew my family? You couldn't have done. You look too young. They all died in the war, except Jacob.'

'I knew of them, and I met Jacob a few months ago.'

'Here in Israel?'

'No, in England.'

He sighed a deep sigh.

'That's irony for you. I've been here five years nearly, and I didn't know he's living till I hear he's dead.'

'You could only have been a young man when the war finished. Didn't you try to find out what happened to your family, to see if there were any survivors?'

'Listen, I'm not as old as I look even now. Sure I thought of going to Russia, going to Germany, going here, going there, and I even had a bit of money by then, so I could afford it, but to tell you the honest truth, I was ashamed. I don't know why I'm telling you all this. You may be a *lantsman*, but you're still a stranger, but that's the truth of it, I was ashamed. I wasn't even sure if I should go to the funeral, and I was glad you gave me a lift in your car, because everybody there must have been asking, wasn't that Moishele, the *ganef*, Moishele the *shikse kricher*? I asked myself, if I did start looking and did find somebody, a brother, a sister maybe, a nephew, a cousin, would they have been glad to find *me*? If they was dead, they was dead, and if they was living it was the least I could do to make them forget they ever had me as a brother.'

I was almost moved to tears by his confession and felt slightly ashamed that I should be holding so much back while he was unburdening himself of everything. Perhaps it was his slight size and general air of vulnerability which made me take to him, perhaps it was his candour, but he was not at all the shifty little shyster I had imagined. He was still a good-looking man and, with his white hair and tanned complexion, looked almost distinguished; far from being brash or flashy, he seemed rather retiring.

Immediately below us was the Mt Olives Jewish cemetery, and he kept pointing to it repeatedly.

'That's where I should be. There's something wrong with the world when Avner and Jacob are dead, and I'm still alive.'

I was curious to know if he ever attended any of the annual reunions of Dvinsk survivors.

'No, never. Who goes to reunions? People who have something to show for themselves, to exchange pictures of children and grandchildren. What have I got to show for myself? A Rolex watch? Gold cuff-links? A hand-made suit? People are no longer impressed with such things.'

'Did you never marry?'

'Young man,' and he put a manicured hand on my knee, 'my trouble is I never stopped marrying. Did nobody ever tell you?'

'No.'

'We lived in Dvinsk, but we had a holiday place in Resznitz, and there was a doctor in Resznitz – I don't know if you ever met him, they say he was a Nazi, but I don't believe it. Anyway, this doctor had a daughter, bright blue eyes, blonde hair. She wasn't Jewish. Nearly all the *shikses* were blonde from what I can remember, but they was a sort of cold blonde, if you know what I mean, almost white, but her hair was the colour of straw, warm, shiny. You only had to look at her and it was enough to take you through the day. Perhaps I was greedy, but I wasn't satisfied with just looking, I wanted to feel the cloth, if you know what I mean. You wouldn't think it looking at me now, but I was a picture of a boy then. All the girls was after me, and so was she. What I didn't know then was that she was after everybody, but I was very young, and not very sensible, and we decided to go away together. Father, *nebbich*, already had his fill of *tzores*, and I didn't want to kill him, so we had to be very careful about it. Business wasn't too good at the time either. I wasn't much use in Dvinsk, but father thought I might be able to do something with myself in America if he gave me a bit of money. Anyway, so I left to go to America, and she left to visit an aunt in Germany, and we both met up in London, and after a bit we got married.'

'You mean you married the doctor's daughter?'

'I just told you I did.'

'Didn't she marry somebody called Maurice Marshall?'

'And who do you think Maurice Marshall was? Almost the first guy I meet tells me, with a name like Moshe Marcovitch you'll never get anywhere, not in England, change it to Maurice Marshall. So I changed it. And I can tell you it didn't help a bit, because whatever name I had I went with it, and it didn't help in business. It didn't help in marriage either. It didn't work out. You see, the little money I had was spent, and she didn't have all that much, and I couldn't find work, but all that wasn't so bad, we could have managed. But then she decided to find work, and I didn't want that. I mean a young woman like that, no man could leave her alone, and the trouble was she didn't mind not being left alone. She came back at all times, and some nights she didn't come back at all. So we didn't go hungry, but how was I to think she made the money? I was afraid to ask. But anyway I meet a nice woman, or not so nice, but her father gives me a job as a traveller thinking maybe I'll marry her, which gives me the chance to get back to my wife, for a bit, here and there. It was all a bit awkward, because the woman who thought I was going to marry her thought it was about time we married, and so did her father. What made it even more awkward was that they were living in Manchester, and my wife was in London, and I was killing myself racing from one to the other, and trying to do a bit of business on the side while I was at it. What I didn't know was

221

that my wife was also doing a bit of business on the side. At first, I only had my suspicions because I kept finding clues about the place, like a pair of men's *gatkes* in the bedroom, or a pair of somebody's teeth in the bathroom, but I don't ask questions, if only because I was too sure of the answers. But one night I come home and find her in bed with two men, one of them a bearded Yeshiva *bachur*, and he hadn't even taken his hat off. Well, you can forgive a woman once, twice, but you can't go on forgiving her all your life, and I said to her, "You know this can't go on," and I think she saw I had a point, for a few weeks later she moves out and moves in with a red-haired student.'

'And that's the last you saw of her?'

'That's the last I saw of her, that's the last I hear of her, till I read about the fire. I didn't even know she was in America.'

'Didn't she have a baby?'

'It wouldn't surprise me if she did, in fact it would surprise me if she didn't, but whether she did or didn't, I had nothing to do with it.'

He began plying me with questions and I felt compelled to tell him about my grandfather.

His eyes widened, then he shook his head.

'No, no, we can't be talking about the same guy. This guy was a shrink. We didn't call them that in those days, but that's what he was, a shrink, and he had this private sanatorium – '

'I know. He was my grandfather – '

'But he only had this one daughter – '

'And I was her child.'

This took some time to sink in.

'You Inge's boy? What do you know? I could have been your father – in a way I am. I can't remember if we ever got divorced. Did Jacob know? I don't suppose he did.'

'Oh, I told him.'

'Yes, but he didn't know I was her husband, none of them did. I think Vladi guessed something was going on, but he kept it to himself. It's the only favour he did me – if it was a favour. Well I suppose it was – I'm alive, which is what counts, isn't it? He got through the war, you know, he's the type that always does. I'm surprised that Jacob did. He was as strong as a horse, Jacob, but he didn't have much up there. It was the daughters who had the brains. One married Vladi, and the other – what's the use of talking? You could have *tzores* without Hitler, and we did. What poor father went through in his life I can't tell you, but at least he died before his children, which is something.'

The sombre recollections brought tears to his eyes. 'Mind you, you didn't have to be Jewish to have *tzores* – though I suppose it helped.' The thought seemed to brighten him a little. 'Your grandfather had more than his share, I can tell you, starting with his wife, and then Inge.'

'Was his wife so much trouble?'

'A pain in the ass. Mind you, she had a lot to put up with. He wasn't the innocent little doctor you thought he was, he wasn't the little innocent doctor *I* thought he was, till I got to know his daughter. She told me a thing or two. I couldn't believe it, maybe I shouldn't – she had a good imagination, but she was the apple of his eye. What that poor man didn't go through because of her. I was supposed to be the black sheep of my family, but compared to her I was an innocent.' And he spent the next ten minutes justifying his conduct, as if I had accused him of turpitude. 'The trouble is, I was the youngest, and I didn't get a look in. Father already had Avner and Jacob in the business, so there wasn't much I could do anyway. Then Vladi came in, with plans to reorganize this, and reorganize that, and I see once father is gone I'd be out, which is why I planned to go. The whole Inge business came later. I could never have worked with Vladi in any case. I saw through him and he knew it. Everybody's after money, but he was after nothing else, and he thought we had it, so he was always sniffing round my sisters. And he had a college education, which was all what counted as far as father was concerned. It was father what fell in love with him, not Sarah. Oh, she married him all right, there weren't all that many eligible guys around – not with a college education.'

'Did you know he was a Communist?'

'Father didn't. I did. But who wasn't in those days? There was a crowd of them, Vladi, Apteker, others.'

I sat up at that.

'Apteker, did you say?'

'The shrink. He was in Resznitz for a bit. He was everywhere for a bit, including America, until they sent him packing. He was a Commie, you know, but didn't look it. Vladi and the others had sunken cheeks like Lenin and looked as if they lived on bread and vinegar, but Apteker was a picture of a man, more like a film-star. I don't remember seeing him without women round him. Even in America, when they had the deportation hearing, he was living with this actress, I can't remember her name, and when he left she went with him, to Germany or Russia, wherever it was. And all his patients were signing petitions, we need him here, you can't let him go, and in fact when they did finally pack him off there was women throwing themselves out of windows all along Park Avenue.'

'Have you seen him since?'

'All this happened fifteen, sixteen years ago. I don't even know if he's alive.'

'You don't know of anyone who might know?'

'Well, there's this actress he was living with, what's her name? As a matter of fact I saw her on television the other night, an old film, a very old film, so she couldn't be all that young herself. Now, what was her name? Houston, that was it, Linda Houston. She was before your time. She's almost before mine. Houston, that was her name.'

As we were talking we were joined by a large, handsome, dark-haired woman. He introduced her as his wife. 'She's from Brazil. She don't speak a word of English, and I don't speak a word of Portuguese, so we never have nothing to quarrel about,' he said. 'I'll tell you something, when you're young you ask yourself why the old *cackers* you see, who can hardly stay on their feet, want to live on, but I can tell you, I've had more happiness in my old age than I've had in the rest of my life.' And he leaned forward and patted his wife's ample thigh affectionately. 'And it's all because of her.'

Sue's mother used to have a saying: 'The more you know, the more you don't know,' and I could see what she meant. Nearly everything Moshe told me had merely added to my confusion. If he wasn't my father, who was? What was more to the point, could Inge have been my mother? Carla had insisted that she was, grandfather that she wasn't, and the timing suggested that he may have been right, for Moshe last saw her early in 1938, she was dead within the year and, according to the papers, she had been on the game for some months before that. When could she have had the child? And if she had had a child would the fact have passed unnoticed?

I kept asking myself the question all the way home, and an alternative version of my nativity began to form in my mind; or rather, the version which had occurred to me when I first set eyes on the picture of Carla and child, returned. Was it not possible that Carla was, after all, my mother, and that she had dumped me on her brother so that she might be free to marry Buchbinder?

There were two obvious arguments against this theory. The scheme would necessarily have had to involve my grandmother, and the relationship between her and Carla was at best cool, and not infrequently hostile. Nor was she, in fact, all that close to her brother and, although he was clearly capable of deception, I could not imagine him, and even less his wife, involving themselves in an elaborate charade for the sake of Carla, unless they were so shaken by the scandal which had surrounded their daughter that they may have wished to salvage what they could of the sister's reputation.

Then there was Carla herself. She was capable of anything, but would she, knowing me to be her son, have encouraged the sort of relationship which eventually developed between us? And, if I were her natural child, would she not have reclaimed me once she was widowed?

But, if she wasn't my mother, and Inge wasn't, who was?

I had phoned Sue about my encounter with Maurice Marshall *né* Moshe Marcovitch, and she kept plying me with questions as soon as I returned. 'What's he like? Was he the flashy little rascal I imagined? What does it feel like finding a father?' And I had to explain to her that, far from having found a father, I had probably lost my mother.

'But she was in the family way a good ten months before she died,' said Sue. 'We have that on the evidence of her own neighbour. And remember your aunt met your grandfather when he returned from America with the child.'

'My aunt *said* she met him.'

'You mean she could have been lying, but why?' And as she thought about it she must have reached the same conclusion as I had. She had found the thought amusing the first time round. Now that it appeared to be a real possibility, she was appalled.

'It's unlikely,' I said. 'I can't imagine that even my aunt was that depraved, and she would have needed the co-operation of my grandparents, and I can't see them playing along.'

'I don't know. Your grandfather took his duties as head of what was left of the family very seriously. His sister had already had more than one disappointment, and he may have been afraid that if he didn't take the child off her hands, he would have her on his hands for life.'

'But my grandmother wouldn't have had anything to do with it, I'm sure of that.'

Neither of us saw any point in speculating any further on the matter. We would have to settle upon an authorized version of events to which we would adhere in the absence of definite evidence to the contrary, and we chose the most likely version, namely that I was the son of Inge Rhiner. It was the version we gave to the children (without, of course, the embellishment that my mother had died in a brothel fire), and which Sue embodied in the final draft of her book.

The quest, as far as we were concerned, was over.

—— *Chapter Seventeen* ——

When Rich was appointed Chairman of Eissenmacher's and spoke about reorganizing the bank, I thought my place on the board was as good as assured, but a new board was appointed which consisted largely of members of the old. It included, however, three new names, two of them from outside the bank. The third was Dubin, my successor in New York, who was a good six years younger than me. I think I would have suffered the disappointment of non-promotion better if Dubin had not been my junior.

Dubin was the son of a Jewish baker and, like me, he had been one of Rich's protégés and (or so it was rumoured) one of Giselle's lovers. I suspect that I was brought in principally for my facility with languages and, I liked to think, for my ability to reduce complex figures into simple language. Dubin, if anything, had a facility for reducing simple language into incomprehensible jargon, but he had taken a First in maths at Cambridge, and had qualified as an accountant before going on to take a degree in computer sciences, and Rich had charged him with reorganizing the accounting system of the bank.

He must have accomplished his task to everyone's satisfaction, for he was spoken of with awe by seniors and juniors alike, though for my part I had to admit that I found his computer print-outs a source of vexation and confusion. I felt that I had – at forty-two – already outlived my epoch. I had always been afraid of machines, and the machines and the machine-minders had taken over.

I toyed with the idea of leaving, for I was – with grandfather's legacy – wealthy enough to set up in business as a very minor merchant banker on my own; but if I had the money I lacked the confidence, for I was no longer certain how I would fare in the new and mysterious world of high technology. And so I remained where I was, senior, but not very senior, highly paid but not highly regarded, not quite a Pincher or a Tapper, but doing routine jobs, in a routine way.

In the meantime, Sue was enjoying a new career as an author. Her publisher had almost given up hope that she would ever deliver the book he had commissioned, but now that he finally had it in hand he was delighted with it, and before her first book was even in print he invited her to write a second, 'about the Marcovitch family, perhaps, one would like to know more about them, or your husband, or his aunt. Now there was a character, his aunt.'

Completing an actual book was, to my mind, akin to securing a stake in eternity, and I daresay I would have been jealous of my wife even if I had been on the up and up. Now that I was in decline, it almost hurt.

When the book was published, critics were almost as enthusiastic about it as her publisher. What was perhaps more to the point, it sold in substantial numbers and, thus emboldened, she decided to take up her publisher's suggestion and to write a book on the Marcovitch family. I reminded her that what had made her book a success was the treasure of letters amassed by my aunt. There was no prospect that she would find anything like it again, and I wasn't sure if she would find anything more about the Marcovitches than was already contained in her first book. She was, however, determined to try and, after phoning Moshe – who didn't sound in the least enthusiastic about her plans – she flew off to see him in Jerusalem.

Idleness is the mother of mischief and so, as a matter of fact, is failure. A few days after she left, I was coming out of a meeting at the bank when I bumped into Alice. The meeting had been a prolonged affair, and I was half-dazed by the complexities of the matter we were discussing and the accumulation of cigarette and cigar smoke and, at first, I thought I was seeing things, but it was her all right, as pretty and as pert as the first time I had set eyes on her in New York. I asked her to join me for lunch, but she already had a lunch appointment and we arranged to meet for a drink after work. It was only then that she told me that she was moving – indeed, had moved – to London. I was at once delighted and apprehensive; delighted at the thought of having her around, apprehensive at what her presence might do to my marriage, but on balance delight predominated.

'Why didn't you tell me this before?'

'I had no reason to believe you'd be interested.'

'*I* wouldn't be interested?'

'You never wrote to me or phoned me after you left. The only time I heard from you was when that poor man turned up and almost died on my hands.'

'Yes, but there was no point in keeping contact while you were in New York, but if you're going to be here in London it's another matter. I'm delighted you're here. Delighted.' And I gave her an affectionate tap on the knee. She seemed almost to recoil, and at that moment I realized that there was another man, perhaps even a husband, though she had no rings on her fingers to show for it, but I immediately changed tone. 'What are you going to do here?'

'The same as in New York. Work.'

'Here in the bank?'

'Here in the bank. Didn't anybody tell you? I'm Sol Dubin's secretary.'

She had to say no more. Dubin had obviously engineered her transfer. I had entertained a similar thought when I was in New York but lacked both the nerve and the seniority. 'A name on the door rates a secretary on the floor,' as they used to say in America. The lad hadn't waited long to exercise his prerogatives. I had heard that his marriage was on the rocks. I didn't know if Alice was the cause, but she was certainly the compensation. He had separated from his wife and they were presumably living together. She certainly would make a good company wife, or mistress. With a consort like that I could see him succeeding Rich as Chairman. I went for the train with my tail between my legs. So much for my apprehensions, so much for the delights.

When I got to the station there was some hold-up on the line. I liked to be home on time to read to my daughter, and I phoned her not to wait up for me.

'But I don't mind waiting up, I *like* waiting up.'

'I'd rather you didn't. I'll tell you a longer story tomorrow.'

'Promise?'

'Promise.'

I had for a moment toyed with the thought of phoning my sister-in-law, Doreen, who had just divorced her husband, to ask if she would like to meet me in town for a meal, and perhaps more than a meal, but there is nothing like the lisping voice of one's own child to clear the soul of lechery. It however became clear that the hold-up was not a minor one and that there would be no train to Taplow, or anywhere near it, for hours. I took the announcement almost as a licence, and went to a phone box.

'Harry! How nice to hear from you. What can I do for you?'

'Shall I get straight to the point?'

'Please do.'

'I'd like a quick fuck.'

'Oh Harry, how sweet of you, but why didn't you ask me when I was available, when I was right in the next room to you? I was dying to have you in my bed, between my legs, but didn't you know I have a boy-friend?'

'No. Did you insert an advert in the personal column of *The Times*? How should I know?'

'Didn't Sue tell you?'

'Tell me what?'

'I'm living with Len. Her father would have been happy. I'm keeping him in the family.'

I put the phone down, and as I did so I could see a familiar figure waiting impatiently to make a call. I recognized her even if she wasn't looking in my direction, and I almost cried out. It was Sylvia, more substantial in build and more elegant in dress than I had seen her before. It was undoubtedly her. Fate had intervened to compensate me for my disappointments.

I went out of the kiosk and stood before her.

'It's me, Harry. Don't you recognize me?'

She looked at me unsmilingly for a moment, then said:

'You've put on weight, haven't you?'

'So have you,' I said. 'It suits you.'

'It doesn't suit you,' she said, and went on to make her phone call.

Failure begets failure. I could see myself becoming a fully paid-up member of the Pinchers' and Tappers' Club.

As the days passed I became conscious of a deep feeling of demoralization and blamed Alice as the prime cause. Her presence in an office twenty yards along the corridor from mine – her presence in London at all – was a misfortune. She was friendly enough and always greeted me with a smile, but her eyes no longer radiated the look of adoration which used to greet me in New York. I also couldn't help noticing that my own secretary's attitude to me had become more casual and less deferential. She used to arrive smartly attired and carefully made-up. Now she frequently looked as if she had just fallen out of bed, and would occasionally appear in the office in a sweater and jeans. Her work used to be immaculate, and if she made more than an error or two in a letter she would retype it. Now, she would bleach out the fault or type over it, and when I complained she would say:

'I don't mind retyping if you want me to take all week, but if you want the letters today that's the best I can do.'

And finally, since the reorganization I was rarely invited to set foot in the boardroom. Although I was not on the main board I used to be called in for consultations, and hardly a week passed in which I wasn't invited to join some guest or other at a boardroom lunch. Now all that was over. I had been given my chance to shine and, as far as Rich was concerned, I hadn't shone brightly enough. For the first time in his life he had picked a dud. If Rich was disappointed in me, I was in a way disappointed in myself. I was never quite sure how I functioned. I didn't seem to have a mind or soul of my own and merely reacted in response to expectations. While Rich thought I was a genius I acted like one, and now that he regarded me as a spent force I performed like one.

I kept pondering on my train journeys to and from work, and especially from work, at what point my decline had begun. I tended to ascribe it to the change of guard at the bank, but in reality it had begun somewhat earlier, about the time I discovered who, or rather *what*, my mother was. Sue and I kept repeating that we didn't believe that the sins of the fathers, or mothers, rebounded upon the heads of their children, and we both agreed that heredity was bunk; yet the thought that one's mother was a feckless whore, even if absorbed subconsciously, could not do much for one's self-confidence. My nightly mood of despondency rarely survived the train journey, and once I stepped over the threshold into my own home, amid the solid furniture and the heavy furnishings, I felt a different man, as if I had been infused with the spirit of earlier tenants. Or perhaps it was merely the reassuring sight of my full-length portrait over the drawing-room fireplace, me at my zenith. I was already beginning to live on my past glories.

In the meantime, Sue kept extending her stay. I thought that she would be able to see everyone there was to see within a week, or at most two, but she had now been away for three weeks, with no hint as to exactly when she might return.

She used to phone me last thing at night three or four times a week, but would never touch on her work. 'This is me trying to unwind,' she would say. 'If I'm going to talk to you about this Marcovitch or that, my mind will spring back into life and I'll never get to sleep.' Instead she would ask me about Gertie and the au-pair and the house and the cat and the dog. Almost as an afterthought she might ask me about myself. I couldn't help wondering what there was to keep her in Israel all this time. She had, after all, been unfaithful to her first husband, so there was more than a chance that she could be unfaithful to the second one. I never spoke about my work, but there is an unmistakable odour to failure, as there is to success, and she could not have been unaware that my standing in the bank was not what it used to be. Even my daughter was treating me with more than her customary disrespect.

There was also a time when our black labrador, a clumsy old bitch we called Gladys, would come bounding over to me with howls of joy and streams of saliva. Now when I entered, she would raise her head sleepily, give me a woebegone look, and return to her slumbers.

One day Cobham came into my office and said his wife was away and that he intended to celebrate the occasion with a night on the town. Would I like to join him?

I had always thought of Cobham as one of the cheerful failures in the company and the fact that he now, for the first time, asked me out, suggested that he saw me in the same light. I hesitated to accept because apart from anything else I wasn't quite sure what he meant by a night out.

'Dinner and a few drinks in the club,' he said, 'and then I know a little place where they have some very pretty girls. It's a bit pricey, but they know all the tricks of the trade, and they're worth every penny.'

'You mean a brothel?'

At this a pained look came into his eyes.

'Can you see me going to a brothel? No, this is a private place. You have to be a member.'

Although I admired most English institutions I had never

become Englishman enough to join a club. I was not what Dr Johnson would have called a clubbable man and, insofar as I yearned for company at all, it was the company of women. Cobham, on the other hand, was a member of three or four clubs and I suspect they were a means of getting away from his wife.

He took me that evening to something called the Oddballs Club and I expected to find it teeming with eccentrics, but there were few people about and they were mostly staid, grey-haired men in dark suits. The place did have a well-stocked bar and we depleted a good part of that stock in the course of the evening. We had a lot to talk about and after we had been drinking for a time he said to me, à propos of nothing:

'Do you know the Jews are coming back?'

'What do you mean?'

'The bank. I mean it always was Jewish but the Eissenmachers were giving others a look-in, but Rich is due to go in another year or two and you know who'll be taking over, don't you?'

'Dubin.'

'Exactly. Funny thing is, when you came in nearly everyone thought you were Jewish. Thought so myself, especially when you nearly married what-do-you-call-her. They say the Welsh are on the make but they're not a patch on the Jews, but then I thought no, you couldn't be one of them.'

'Why not?'

'Too relaxed. And you enjoy a drink like the rest of us. There's something to not being at the top, or anywhere near it, but the Jews don't know that. Here's to you.'

When we rose to round off our evening we were both unsteady on our feet and, although we were only going a couple of hundred yards down the road, we thought it was best to take a taxi.

The vision of pretty girls which Cobham had evoked earlier in the day kept dissolving in the alcoholic haze which had formed in my head, and vanished altogether when we reached our destination, for it was like a dentist's waiting-room, full of middle-aged men reading magazines from a pile on a table in the centre, and the only woman about was an elderly harridan dispensing drinks from a small bar in the corner.

We had obviously come at a busy time and I was disposed to leave.

233

'Wait till you see them,' Cobham whispered. 'They're beautiful, every one of them. You'll have the time of your life.'

I picked up a magazine and settled into a chair and fell asleep almost immediately.

I don't know how long I slept but when I awoke I looked at my watch and realized with a start that I only had minutes to catch my last train to Taplow, and dashed out into the night.

Normally I travelled home on the 6.20 when the train was full and there was bustle and chatter, and some of the passengers had had a few drinks while others were looking forward with cheerful expectancy to an evening at home; but now the train was almost empty. A grey mist filled the compartment and seemed to penetrate my very soul. I don't know how I would have felt if I had actually entered the unholy of unholies recommended by Cobham but the very fact that I had thought of doing so weighed me down with contrition.

When I got into my car at Taplow station I felt like driving into the river, but then, as I turned for home, I noticed lights blazing in almost every room though it was nearly midnight.

Sue was back.

I felt the worse for wear and probably looked it, for she seemed a trifle taken aback by my appearance (or possibly the hour at which I appeared), but she had the good sense to utter no word of reproof. For my part, I felt more than a little aggrieved that she had been away so long, but again felt this was not the time to say so. Yet I immediately became aware of a certain distance between us, which I ascribed to the fact that she had just returned from her Jewish world of torment and *angst* while I had been immersed in my goyish one of conviviality and booze.

'You look very tired,' she said, 'and I feel very tired. I've so much to tell you I don't know where to begin. Shall we talk about it in the morning?'

In spite of our weariness, however, neither of us could sleep. I lay awake in my bed and I was aware that she was lying sleepless in hers; then she said in a faraway voice, as if in her sleep:

'Has something happened?'

'No, nothing. We missed you. I didn't think you'd be away so long.'

'I didn't expect to be away so long. You used to be away all the time.'

234

'I suppose I'm not used to the reversal of situations. But, tell me, has something happened to you?'

'What makes you ask?'

'Do you remember when Marcovitch came here, you suddenly turned on me; I remember your very words: "If you had a drop of Jewish blood in your veins you couldn't behave with such detachment." In fact I was deeply moved by the very appearance of the man, but suddenly I felt a distance between us which at the time I ascribed to your ill-health, but perhaps it's more fundamental, for I felt it again this evening.'

'Which shows you should never trust your instincts. Certainly I was wrong to trust mine, because I'm almost convinced you're Jewish.'

Chapter Eighteen

'I thought we had settled the question of my origins once and for all,' I said.

'So did I, but did you know that old Marcovitch had had two daughters?'

'Of course I did. I told you all about it when I got back from Jacob's funeral! She was the older of the two and had a breakdown.'

'You didn't tell me – because I suppose you didn't know – that she had also had a child.'

I stopped, dumbfounded.

'Who told you that? Moshe?'

'No, he refused to discuss the matter, and in any case he wouldn't have known, but did you stop to talk to Jacob's wife?'

'Of course I did. I was with her for some time.'

'She told me. You sat there in a collar and tie mopping your brow and hardly saying a word.'

'It was a hot day. She has a small flat and the place was crowded with people I had never met before.'

'So I don't suppose you know she was from Resznitz?'

'She told me she was from Dvinsk.'

'She was a maid in the Marcovitch household and was with them in Resznitz every summer. She's not Jewish, as I suppose you know, which is how she survived, and Jacob married her after the war.'

'And she told you about the daughter?'

'I had heard about the daughter from others, but she knew a few things which they didn't, for not only was she virtually a member of the family, she was friendly with a male nurse in your grandfather's clinic. It wasn't easy to get it out of her because she wasn't all that eager to speak, and she didn't speak a word of English. It all had to be done through an interpreter, which made her even more reluctant, but after calling on her almost every day, and helping her with cooking and cleaning – the poor woman is an invalid, as you know, and can hardly move – I built up a friendly relationship with her and I eventually persuaded her to put everything on tape. They're all in Russian, so you'll have to go over them for me.'

We had abandoned our attempts at sleep and were sitting over coffee in the kitchen. Sue thought we could leave the tapes for later in the day but I was impatient to hear them. She had brought an entire case-load of tapes, all carefully numbered. She could be as methodical in her work as she was chaotic in her day-to-day life. She gave me the appropriate tape and I slotted it into the tape-deck of our hi-fi.

Our set was a very elaborate one, for we both loved music, but the voice which came out at us from every direction of our living room, wheezy, tired, and slightly muffled, was anything but musical.

'I felt bad about putting her to all that trouble,' said Sue, 'for she was very unwell, but I had to have everything she could remember, for she's the final witness, and I must say, unwell or not, once she started she was determined to go on. You can't imagine the stoicism of that woman.'

She began by talking about herself. She was from a peasant family of twelve children and was born and brought up in Resznitz, and first came to work for the Marcovitch family when they took a house in the neighbourhood for the summer. She was only about ten at the time. When she was thirteen, she went to live with them in Dvinsk and remained with the family till the German invasion ten years later. She remembered the head of the family as kindly and gentle, 'like Santa Claus', and the wife as a snob and a tyrant, and she thought that what eventually happened to the oldest daughter was 'a punishment from God'.

'She not only liked to keep her family apart from other families and wouldn't let the children bring friends home, but she kept Esther apart from the rest of the children. She spoke Yiddish with the rest of the family, but she spoke German with Esther. She travelled with her to Vienna and even Paris. The others never went farther than Riga. Esther had a room of her own like a salon, with books and pictures and a piano and a gramophone. The others had bare walls. Not that the others complained, for Esther *was* different, and they were proud of

237

her. She was graceful and beautiful and talented and seemed to belong to another world. I wasn't allowed to come near her, but when I grew older I was allowed to handle her clothes, to iron them and put them away, and they had a different feel to them. If they were cotton, they were a finer cotton, if wool, they were a finer wool, and she had silks and satins. And then two things happened. Esther began to have singing lessons with a famous teacher from Riga, and she found a boy-friend. He was a young lawyer, in a tight suit, called Vladimir, who must have had some business dealings with the old man, otherwise I don't know how he could have met her, or what he could have been doing in the house. The mother, of course, was unhappy about it. ''His father's a cobbler,'' she kept saying, ''he's nobody.'' ''But he's a bright young man,'' said the old man, ''he could become somebody.'' And he did, may he roast in hell.

'I distrusted him. I hated him, because, if you'll forgive me, when he thought no one was looking he kept on grasping my bottom. I had a big bottom, even then, and he made me black and blue. And, if you'll forgive me, he didn't stop there. I daren't tell you where he stopped, or would have done, if I'd given him half the chance, the filthy swine. Anyway, he couldn't have got far with Esther, for one day she runs off with her singing teacher, a white-haired old man, married, and a German. I don't know if she ran away with him or ran away after him. The thing I remember most clearly from that time was that the father's beard turned white almost overnight. One day he was a youthful, attractive man, the next day he was Santa Claus. Then about a year later she comes back in an ambulance, tearful, a mess. That was the last time I set eyes on her.'

I stopped the tape.
'When did all this happen? She doesn't mention dates.'
'She's vague about dates throughout, but you can work it out for yourself. Your grandfather established the clinic with the help of old Marcovitch in 1935, and I should imagine that it was one of the reasons why he financed the clinic, so all this must have happened a year or so earlier.'
'Not necessarily. He could have financed the clinic as a

straightforward business investment, so she could have gone in some time later.'

'Not much later, because she was about twenty when she had the breakdown and she was born early in the First World War.'

'Was she pregnant when she got back?'

'Wait, let her go on.'

We returned to the tape.

'We used to go to Resznitz every summer. At first they rented a house and then they built one. It was never a happy time because none of us could forget about Esther in that clinic on the edge of the forest. The old man, who was religious, gradually began to accept his misfortune, and to count his blessings. His sons found wives and his younger daughter married Vladimir, which, believe me, was no blessing, for he did not get on with the brothers. And the mother was a ghost. She hardly ate, she hardly slept. She hardly talked, and if it hadn't been for the war she would have ended up beside her daughter in the clinic. She was in tears almost all the time, and so was I, for I became fond of her even though she was always short-tempered with me, and I couldn't wait till the summer was over so we could get back to Dvinsk. But then – this must have been a year or two before the war – I became friendly with a man working in the clinic, a nurse. I asked him if he ever saw Esther. "She's tall and graceful and slender," I said, "like a queen." And he said there was a patient called Marcovitch in the place, but she was big and fat. I couldn't imagine it, and a few months later he swore me to secrecy and told me that she had had a child. It had been delivered by the doctor himself. I don't know why I'm telling you all this, because I've never told a soul before. I was married to Jacob for thirty years, and we never discussed it once, though I suppose he must have known. It was a boy, healthy and normal, but I never set eyes on him, for the war came and that was the end of everything.'

She then went on to describe the events of the war years. When the Russians came they began arresting and deporting people, including the two Marcovitch brothers, but not Vladimir:

'They say Vladimir was a Communist informer and that he betrayed Avner and Jacob to the police. I don't think he was that bad, but he was somebody important and could have saved them, but he didn't. In the end it was all to the good because if the brothers hadn't been deported the Nazis would have killed them, which is why Jacob would never say anything bad about him, or at least nothing very bad. I was also sent away to work in a factory in Riga, and didn't know what happened to the family until after the war. When I came back everyone was dead, the mother, the daughters, the daughter-in-law, the children. The Germans killed the Jews, and not only the Germans. The Latvians also joined in and some of them were even worse than the Germans. And when the Russians came back they began shooting Latvians right and left. I couldn't find a single living soul from my own family, except for my youngest sister, and she went mad. I heard Vladimir was alive; he would be – the devil looks after his own. In Dvinsk they told me that he had left for Moscow before the Germans came in. He left his wife and child with his mother-in-law, and they were all there together in two small rooms, the old woman, her daughter, two daughters-in-law and four children, without anyone to look after them. Their house had been taken over and so had their *datcha*. I don't know how they managed to stay alive. Dr Rhiner may have helped them, and when the Germans came he sheltered them in the woods, but I only heard all that after the war, because, as I said, I was taken away. I was in Riga at first and then, after the Germans came, we were all moved to Stettin. When the war was over I made my way back on foot, first to Riga, and then to Dvinsk, looking for relatives, friends, a familiar face. Jacob told me about his adventures, but he at least was a man, a big man, and could look after himself. I was a woman, and also learned to look after myself, but I'd be ashamed to tell you what I went through. The Russians were as bad as the Germans. Then in Resznitz I found Jacob searching among the ashes. He had nobody, I had nobody, so we married each other. It wasn't what you'd call love at first sight, but it worked, thank God. We were very happy together. We'd have been happier still if my legs didn't keep swelling up. He was a good man, Jacob, a good son to his father, a good husband to me.'

She then went on to describe their life together in Latvia, the hardships they suffered, and the harassment.

'What I didn't know was that two of my brothers had served in a Latvian unit with the German army. How could I have known? They were small boys when I left home and they could not have been all that old when they were in the army, eighteen at most. They were both killed, I don't know how or when, but because of them they thought I could be some sort of Fascist sympathizer. Believe me, I didn't even know what the word meant. They didn't drag me away or anything like that, but they had ways of making things difficult and they did. And if they had it in for me because of my brothers, they had it in for poor Jacob because he was a Jew. So it was difficult for us to get food, accommodation, jobs, and when I became ill it was difficult to get treatment. Not that it was easy for anyone else, but it was even more difficult for us, but God is good, and we survived.'

Circumstances eased a little as the years went on. They found jobs, and instead of living in one tiny room they finally managed to obtain a flat. They moved on to Riga, where there was a sizeable Jewish community.

'Jacob became something of a Jew again. There was no Rabbi where we lived, so he acted as the Rabbi, and conducted services, and said prayers for the dead. I'm not Jewish myself, as you know, but living first with the Marcovitch family and then with Jacob, I became a bit Jewish in my way, and even learned to read Hebrew, and I learned to say *kaddish*, you know what I mean, the prayer for the dead, even though it's only men who are supposed to say it, and not women, but that's what brought people together, the prayer for the dead, that and Israel. We spoke about Israel to cheer ourselves up, but in the same way as people used to talk about paradise, never dreaming that we would ever get there. We thought we were lucky to get to Riga. Then, suddenly, about ten years ago, twelve years ago, they began to let people go, whole families. We also applied to go. I didn't believe we would ever get a permit, when we got it I didn't believe we had it, and even now that I'm here I still sometimes can't believe it. So there you are, that's my story, our story. I don't suppose it sounds cheerful but, thank God, at least it's got a happy ending.'

'I don't know if you've seen Brecht's *Mother Courage*,' said Sue, 'but that's her, indomitable.'

'I know, I've met her.'

'Meeting her is nothing. She's a huge, bloated mess, a coarse-faced peasant woman. It's when you start talking to her, if only through an interpreter, that you get the measure of her stature, but she's also rather prim, with a strong sense of her own dignity. I wanted to know more about Esther, and she obviously found the whole subject not only sad, but indelicate, as if it smacked of low gossip, and when I asked her who she thought the father could be, it almost brought an end to our special relationship. I put the question as tactfully as I could, but I don't know how it came over in translation, for she has a sweet smile which suddenly vanished, and she said quite sharply: "How could I know who the father was? I heard all sorts of rumours about this doctor and that doctor, but I paid no attention to any of them." '

'What Russian word did she use?'

'I don't know. It sounded like doctor to me, but that's how it came over in translation.'

'This doctor or that doctor? How many doctors could there have been around the place?'

'Exactly. Never more than two from what I've been able to find out, and if it was, indeed, a doctor this or a doctor that, it could have been either your grandfather – '

'Which is inconceivable.'

'An unfortunate word, given the context, but let's say it's unlikely.'

'Which leaves Apteker.'

'I asked her about him, of course, but she seemed a little guarded. He was only in Resznitz a short time, she said, not even a year, but she remembered him from Dvinsk, because he too was friendly with Esther, but he wasn't in the least religious so the family didn't like having him around.'

'Was Vladimir religious?'

'No, but he was prepared to play the part – to the point even of growing a beard. She almost spat every time she mentioned his name. And finally, I asked her about Rhiner and the child. She only saw the child once, but remembered it clearly, for it had huge blue eyes, but she presumed, as everyone else did, that it was a grandchild. Moshe told me it could have been his wife's.'

'When he spoke to me he seemed equally certain that it wasn't.'

'I'm not sure how reliable he is. His sister-in-law said he was a spendthrift, a wastrel and a liar to boot, and I found him an odious little snob. "I couldn't understand how my brother could have married a peasant-woman," he kept saying, "he was a Marcovitch." To which I felt like saying, so are you, but you managed to live that down. He's found himself a very grand and, I suspect, a very rich wife and is obviously anxious to distance himself from his past – '

'He spoke to me openly and with candour.'

'But you met at the funeral, and I suppose while he was still feeling emotional he was off-guard; but when I saw him he was very much on guard and, for the first ten minutes or so, he kept questioning me. It was only when I mentioned that you were a banker that he opened up. If it wasn't for the fact that he'd married money, I think he might have claimed you as a son. As it is, he may have been at pains to disown any suggestions that his first wife may have had a child, in case anyone should claim him as a father. Either way, I wouldn't attach too much weight to anything he told you.'

'Did he say anything about Esther?'

'Never directly. He let slip the fact that he had two sisters, and when I asked what happened to them he said, "How should I know? I wasn't there. They're dead. What more can I tell you?" – and when I asked if they were married, he said: "Look, I left Latvia when I was hardly more than a kid. I'm an old man now and anything I did remember, I've forgotten." He obviously didn't want to be drawn.'

'So you're not, in fact, certain exactly when she had the child.'

'I presume it was sometime in 1938.'

'You're presuming that because it fits in with Apteker's movements, but you're working backwards from your conclusion.'

'You're forgetting the sequence of the woman's narrative. She met the male nurse just before the war – '

'It could have been in 1939.'

'It wasn't. Their last summer in Resznitz was in 1938. The following year armies were moving, frontiers were closing, everybody was standing by for war, and they stayed put in Dvinsk. It could only have happened in 1938 and, if so, Apteker was the father.'

243

'And you're presuming I am the child?'

'Well, it all fits, doesn't it? Rhiner has this child on his hands while, about the same time, his daughter dies in a fire in Chicago, and he therefore makes a pretence of going to America and coming back with her child, though the infant is in fact Esther's.'

'Unless he in fact did go to America and come back with a child.'

'Oh, God, we're going round in circles. But we agreed that he didn't, and couldn't have done, because there was no child to come back with.'

'Moshe said there could have been.'

'But he also – as you yourself told me – said there couldn't. So forget Moshe.'

'What about Carla? She distinctly recalled meeting her brother when he came back with the child.'

'That's possible, but there's no certainty that it wasn't Esther's child.'

'The whole ruse is too elaborate. The old man wasn't a trickster.'

'We can all be tricksters if we have to be. He had to hide his own negligence and his colleague's culpability, otherwise his clinic could have been closed down. You're unwilling to face up to an obvious fact. Do you prefer a mother who died in a brothel to one who died in a mental home? Don't we both agree that heredity is bunk? Or are you merely unable to reconcile yourself to the thought that not only are your wife and children Jewish, but you may be a Jew yourself?'

'No, but I've been trained to respect facts and to weigh evidence, and the case you're trying to make out is not proven. Have you tried to get hold of Apteker at least? The earth couldn't have swallowed him up.'

'As a matter of fact it has. He's dead.'

Her news came as a blow. I don't know why it should have done, for the man was hardly more than a name to me, and the very strength of my reaction almost confirmed Sue's belief that he may have been my father; but, as she had said, one should not put too much trust in one's instincts.

'Where? How? When?' The questions poured out of me in a torrent. 'I had a chap on his trail for years who discovered nothing. You're quite sure?'

'As sure as one can be of anything.'

'How did you find out?'

'Quite by chance. There was a reunion of Holocaust survivors in Jerusalem while I was there, and in a hall right next to the Hilton an entire wall was covered with notices from people looking for relatives, friends, *lantsleit*. I put up a notice asking anyone who knew, or knew of, Dr Apteker, to contact me at my hotel. I got six calls, two from men who knew him as students but hadn't heard of him since, two from people who thought they may have known him but had mistaken him for another Apteker, one from a menopausal woman who had been his patient in New York and was still obviously in need of treatment, and one from a psychiatrist who had actually worked with him in America and who had kept in contact with him since. It was he who told me that he was dead. But he also told me that there was a Mrs Apteker alive and well in the South of France.'

It was now three in the morning. She waited till about ten before trying to phone her and got an instant, emphatic rebuff: 'I am sorry, I have no wish to speak about my husband to anyone. Good day.'

Sue blinked at that: 'Do you think she might have something to hide?'

'There's one thing that media people don't seem to understand. There are individuals – millions of them – who have a strong sense of privacy and who do not care to speak about themselves or their loved ones to complete strangers.'

Sue was never one to take no for an answer and sent her a copy of her book on my grandfather with a covering letter. A week or so later there came a reply:

'Thank you for sending me your book, which I read with interest, but I'm afraid I cannot help you. My husband kept no papers and was even in the habit of losing important documents. I must also add that, although he did refer frequently to his past, his memory was erratic and unreliable. He did speak warmly of Dr Rhiner, and mentioned more than once that he had saved his life, which can hardly be news to you, but if you should still wish to come and see me, do so by all means.'

We were there the next day.

She lived in a small but elegant *pension* in Nice, in the old part of town, and she was a small but elegant woman, although rather more austere-looking than I expected, with white hair done up in a bun at the back. At first glance, one could have taken her for the headmistress of a rather exclusive finishing school.

'I am sorry if I was curt on the phone, but you didn't explain who you were. I have, of course, read your book. It is beautifully written. I am only sorry that my husband did not survive to read it.'

Sue lost no time in getting to the point.

'Did he ever talk about the Marcovitch family?'

'A great deal, especially towards the end of his life, when distant events were more vivid and possibly more significant than near ones. He was not all that old, as a matter of fact, but he had been through a lot in his life and was in a sorry state physically and mentally by the time he died. As you know, he had to flee for his life from the Germans. That he took in his stride, but he also fled from East Germany. You see, he was deported from the United States because of his Communist affiliations, and he was given a very senior post in East Germany; but although he may have been a Marxist in theory, his habits and tastes did not go with Marxism in practice. He defected after a few years, and moved from place to place like a hunted criminal. I don't know if anyone was actually after him, but he thought there was and he went in fear of his life. I managed to calm him down, but he was a dying and broken man by then, full of regrets. I suppose, given his many gifts, his life amounted to a tragedy.'

'Did he have any children?' asked Sue.

She paused for a moment, then said:

'I have the feeling you know the answer.'

At which my heart gave a leap.

'Do you?'

'One hears all sorts of stories,' said Sue.

'No doubt. Are we talking about the Marcovitch girl? Yes, he fathered her child. I must add that I wasn't around at the time, of course – he was very much older than me – but he spoke about it, and claimed to have acted in the name of science. He was even preparing a paper about it when he died. He was preparing papers all the time, without ever finishing or submitting them. You see, he was an exponent of something he called natal therapy. Childbirth is a shock to the entire nervous system and much as it can cause depression in a stable woman, he believed that it could cure an unstable one – I'm putting it all very roughly – and he collected statistics on women who had conceived while in care, so that his affair with the Marcovitch girl was something in the nature of an experiment. He had a genius for rationalizing every outrage he perpetrated. I don't know if he convinced anyone else, but he certainly convinced himself, until his last moment, when he finally saw himself for what he was. He was racked with guilt and remorse.'

'What happened to the girl?'

'I understand she was swept up in the German euthanasia programme.'

'And the child?'

'It was stillborn.'

'Stillborn?' Sue echoed.

The woman stopped and looked at her with something like impatience.

'Have you any information to the contrary?'

Sue hesitated.

'I did hear that the child survived.'

'I should be asking you questions rather than the other way about, for you seem to be infinitely better informed. Rhiner said it was stillborn, and even showed my husband an autopsy to that effect. Could he have been lying?'

'I wouldn't know.'

'If you don't, who does? Your book suggests that you knew all there was to know about him.'

'I never actually met him,' said Sue defensively. 'All my information was second-hand, and sometimes not even that. Did your husband have any reason to believe he was lying?'

'Hardly. As you know, he owed his life to him. When the Germans invaded Latvia he was working in a hospital in Riga and was hidden by one of the nurses and then smuggled out to Resznitz, where he found refuge in the clinic. But he wasn't safe even there, and Rhiner eventually got him papers which enabled him to escape to Sweden. But he was in Resznitz for some weeks, and walking in the courtyard one evening he came across a child playing on his own, and he said it was like being confronted with his younger self, the same lankiness, the same blue eyes, the same forlorn look. He asked Rhiner who the boy was, and he said it was his grandson.'

Sue and I exchanged looks but we did not interrupt her.

'He met Rhiner again in Germany after the war and asked him about the boy, but he seemed reluctant to talk about him at all, as if something unfortunate had happened. I can only hope that if the child did survive he only inherited his father's looks and not his character.'

Sue later asked me, and indeed I asked myself, why I did not interject at that point to say that I was the child. In fact, I drew breath to do so but I was checked by my distaste for drama, and especially melodrama. 'Madam, I am your stepson' would have sounded like a very bad line from a very bad play. I also had a curious feeling of detachment, as if what she was saying couldn't really have anything to do with me, rather like my reaction to grandfather's letter, for I couldn't associate myself with the sort of tragedy he described. Moreover, she obviously had more to say and I was impatient to hear her say it.

'He was an utter scoundrel,' she went on, 'devious, deceitful, corrupt, but only if you knew him well. In the short-term he was charming, full of good stories and wit, and, of course, he was very good-looking, and if people spoke highly of him it was because he was always on the move. He could do many a passing kindness but caused lasting grief. He lived for himself. Even his Communism, which made him look like a martyr for a time, was fraudulent. He believed in it not through any knowledge of its principles – the word principle in any form did not enter his thinking – but because he thought it would sweep everything before it. He believed in being on the winning side, and when it became clear that it wasn't winning and couldn't win, he switched. I'm surprised Rhiner was prepared to take him under his wing, for he must have known him well, and I can only assume that he fell in love with him. Men did as often as women, you know, which is why he got away with murder. As a matter of interest, was Rhiner homosexual? You had very little to say about his private life in your book – I mean his very private life.'

'He was married and had a child, as you know,' said Sue.

'That's neither here nor there, is it? Oscar Wilde was also a family man.'

'Do you think your husband was homosexual?'

'He was, as one of his colleagues said, omnisexual. He would go for anything that moved, and perhaps even for things that didn't, though to do him justice, more often than not they came to him. We only married in the last year of his life, but we had lived together for the previous twenty. I left a husband and young children to be with him, and it has been one long, sorry story of heartache and betrayal. I left him a dozen times, but always came crawling back – one acquires an addiction to pain which it is difficult to shake off. No doubt he made many women and perhaps even a few men happy, but never for long. When you phoned me last week I thought you were yet another one who wanted to come here and talk over his life and weep over his grave, that's why I was so rude. The only thing I can say in mitigation is that he suffered from diminished responsibility. And, yes, there was his remorse, but by then he had outlived his appetites.'

I had, throughout the interview, hardly uttered a word and felt a little like an intruder upon a confidential private exchange. She addressed all her remarks to Sue, as if only another woman could appreciate the sort of situation and heartache she was describing. There were moments when I almost felt bound to interject: 'But madam, you are talking about my father,' except that I still had doubts on the matter; but as she continued they became less pronounced, and I concluded that if Rhiner had not told me the whole truth, he had told me part of it, that I was a child of a Marcovitch daughter, and almost certainly the Jew he wanted me to be.

But did it all matter? I kept thinking of the lines from Matthew Arnold:

> We cannot kindle when we will
> The fire which in the heart resides,
> The spirit bloweth and is still,
> In mystery our soul abides.

I was, as a child, naturally curious about my origins, but as I grew older I was, in a way, happy with the mystery which surrounded them and, but for Sue, I would have been inclined to continue with the tentative identity I had been accorded at birth.

Sue had ascribed various motives to my reluctance to look back: the fear of what I might discover, the confirmation that I might indeed be Jewish, but it was nothing like that. My motives, if any, were mixed and, in some ways, contradictory. First, there was something to be said for mystery for its own sake, the retention of unexplored areas where the imagination could play. Secondly, I was content simply to be a member of the human race, with all its faults and virtues, and felt no compulsion to be classified with this or that group. And finally, I had an instinctive aversion to the dominant passwords of the age: roots, identity, heritage, and the dominant pastime: the search for self, or, as Mrs Eissenmacher called it, 'doing a Forsythe'.

Unfortunately, fate abhors a mystery. I had not tried to kill the truth, I was merely unwilling to strive officiously to expose it, but it came out all the same, though, as with most truths, in a tentative form.

About a week after Sue's book on the Marcovitch family appeared, and nearly two years after we thought we had laid the matter of my identity to rest, a young man phoned us. He was writing a thesis on the history of the Latvian Communist Party, and he was particularly interested in the career of Vladimir Bergmann. Was it, he asked, true that Bergmann's son had survived the Holocaust and could still be alive . . . ?